TRANSFORMED THINKING

ENDORSEMENTS

"In the years I've taught high school seniors, Tom Wheeler's *Transformed Thinking* has proved to be truly effective in establishing and strengthening Biblical thinking in a world full of opposing views. For our church and school, the approach Tom takes fits the practical, real-life objectives we are striving for in order to equip our younger brothers and sisters in Christ to engage the world effectively with the gospel. And even more basic, to understand their world and where they fit in it according to God's plan. We serve others to see God transform their lives and the lives of those around them. This textbook serves well our pursuing that mission."

—Dr. Drew Conley, Ph.D.

Pastor for Preaching and Teaching/Hampton Park Baptist Church, Greenville, SC

"Dr. Wheeler has dedicated many years to the careful development of the material in this work. It is a veritable encyclopedia of knowledge that provides foundational aspects in developing a Christian worldview. He cultivates his resources from some of the finest scholarship available today and synthesizes the critical matters in an approachable form. As a pastor, parent, and Christian, I commend his work wholeheartedly and enthusiastically with eager anticipation that future works will follow this one."

—Dr. Brian Fairchild

D.Min./Pastor, Colonial Bible Church, Midland, Texas

"Dr. Wheeler has given us a call to action. This book is a must read for every Christian layperson and leader in the Church. The Church must strive by the grace of God to set forth the Christian worldview as set forth in the Scriptures. All believers need a thoroughly biblical worldview to think and act pleasing to God. The rising generation in the Church is especially in desperate need of the teaching in this book. Our children are too precious for us to allow them to fall prey to competing worldviews. I highly recommend this book."

—Dr. Sidney Dyer, Ph.D.

Professor of Greek and New Testament/Greenville Presbyterian Theological Seminary

TRANSFORMED THINKING

- A Defense of the Christian Worldview -

ENGLISH STANDARD VERSION

DR. TOM WHEELER

Transformed Thinking

A Defense of the Christian Worldview, English Standard Version

Hardcover ISBN: 978-1-64960-250-3
Paperback ISBN: 978-1-62020-728-4
eISBN: 978-1-62020-747-5

Cover Design and Page Layout by Hannah Nichols
eBook Conversion by Anna Riebe Raats

Scripture quotations in this edition are from theologically conservative modern English translations that used translators committed to the inerrancy of Scripture.

Chapters 1-5, title page and introduction, Scripture quotations are from the English Standard Version. Chapters 6-7, Scripture quotations are from the New King James Version.

Emphasis is the author's where there is underlining of a word in a Scripture quote.

AMBASSADOR INTERNATIONAL
Emerald House
411 University Ridge, Suite B14
Greenville, SC 29601, USA
www.ambassador-international.com

AMBASSADOR BOOKS
The Mount
2 Woodstock Link
Belfast, BT6 8DD, Northern Ireland, UK
www.ambassadormedia.co.uk

The colophon is a trademark of Ambassador, a Christian publishing company.

This book is dedicated to Ken Ham of Answers in Genesis, Jonathan Sarfati with Creation Ministries International, and John Morris of The Institute for Creation Research in appreciation for their faithful defense of:

- *The full inspiration and inerrancy of Scripture;*
- *The literal historicity of Genesis;*
- *Biblical creation against evolution;*
- *Recent creation against the concept of billions of years for the Earth and universe;*
- *The harmony of the Bible with true science;*
- *The Biblical view of marriage, sex, and life against the sexual revolution and abortion;*
- *Foundational Christian doctrines in their ministry doctrinal statements.*

The author also expresses his appreciation to Ambassador International for publishing this book.

"Do not be conformed to this world, but be transformed by the renewal of your mind" (Rom. 12:2).

"We destroy arguments and every lofty opinion raised against the knowledge of God and take every thought captive to obey Christ" (2 Cor. 10:5).

"Christ, in whom are hidden all the treasures of wisdom and knowledge. . . . Therefore, as you received Christ Jesus the Lord, so walk in him, rooted and built up in him and established in the faith, just as you were taught, abounding in thanksgiving. See to it that no one takes you captive by philosophy and empty deceit . . . " (Colossians 2:2-3, 6-8).

CONTENTS

INTRODUCTION

A HELP FOR CHRISTIANS

This is a book that seeks to biblically defend the Christian worldview against its two leading opponents in the world today, the Humanist worldview and the Islamic worldview. This study explains that the Christian worldview appeals to the Bible as God's inspired Word and our ultimate authority for what we believe and how we live (2 Tim. 3:15-17). The goal of this study is to help us align our thinking about life with the viewpoint of God's Word, the Bible.

Ken Ham of Answers in Genesis teamed up with researcher Britt Beemer to write a book, *Already Gone,* about young adults and defection from the Christian worldview.[1] Britt Beemer's research group surveyed one-thousand young adults in their twenties who had attended theologically conservative churches as teens, but who no longer attended church. Concerning the beliefs of these who dropped out of church, his survey found the following results:

- Does the Bible contain errors? Forty percent said yes and thirty percent did not know.[2]
- Do you believe other holy books like the Qur'an are inspired by God? About fifteen percent said yes and twenty-nine percent did not know.[3]
- Has secular science dating the earth as billions of years caused you to doubt the Bible? Forty-six percent said yes and eleven percent did not know.[4]
- Do you believe humans evolved from an ape-like ancestor? Thirty percent said yes and fifteen percent did not know.[5]
- Is premarital sex okay? About fifty-two percent said yes and about five percent did not know.[6]

This survey shows the impact of a Humanist worldview on many young adults in our culture with a Christian background. Answers in Genesis noted another survey in 2017 that shows only ten percent of Americans hold a consistent Biblical worldview:

> "The American Culture and Faith Institute (ACFI) recently conducted nationwide surveys of over 6,000 people to determine how many Americans have a biblical worldview. . . . Participants were asked a series of 40 questions, 20 relating to belief and 20 relating to behavior. . . . The questions included: 'The Bible is totally accurate in all of the life principles it teaches.' . . . A person who is generally good, or does enough good things for others, will earn a place in Heaven.' 'When He lived

> on earth, Jesus Christ was fully human and therefore committed sins, like other people.' . . . 'Satan does not exist; he is just a symbol of evil.' . . . 'The Holy Spirit is not a living entity but is a symbol of God's presence or purity.' . . . According to this study . . . only ten percent of Americans think and act according to the most basic biblical principles."[7]

Also, our culture is pressuring people with a Christian background to view Islam as equally acceptable as Christianity, as a religion that worships the same God and as another way to God and Heaven. Christians need to guard their thinking and be discerning and guide their thinking by the Bible as their God-given authority, so that they are not shaken in their thinking by unbiblical worldviews (2 Thess. 2:2).

Believers need to learn to defend the Christian worldview. The Bible exhorts Christians to "always be prepared to make a defense to anyone who asks you for a reason for the hope that is in you" (1 Pet. 3:15). Believers need to be able to instruct people they know who have unbiblical thinking so they may come to a knowledge of God's truth (2 Tim. 2:24–25).

The material in this book can help Christians answer questions, better understand the Christian faith, strengthen their personal faith and defend their faith to others. It can also be useful for a class in a Bible-believing Christian college or seminary or for group studies in Bible-believing Christian churches. It can be useful for Christians for individual study.

The Humanist worldview and the Islamic worldview have been attacking foundational beliefs of the Christian worldview about God, the Bible, man, Creation, marriage, sex, the church and the Earth. The goal of this book is to strengthen faith of Christians in the Biblical foundations of the Christian worldview. Scripture declares, "If the foundations are destroyed, what can the righteous do?" (Psalm 11:3).

This study can help Christians identify flaws in the Humanist and Islamic worldviews. Also, this material can help Christians be a witness to people they know who are taken captive by these worldviews. Christians should lovingly speak God's truth (Eph. 4:15) to such individuals and graciously and wisely share the truth of God's Word with them (Col. 4:5-6) and pray for their conversion (1 Tim. 2:1-4).

As an explanatory note, this book will refer to Humanism in a broad sense. We will use the term *Humanism* to describe the thinking of people who hold to evolution as a foundational belief, who reject the Bible as the fully inspired and infallible Word of God, who do not accept the teaching of the Bible about the Trinity and the Deity of Christ, and who look to the thinking of man as their ultimate authority about belief and conduct, rather than any religious books.

A person might or might not personally identify as a Humanist. A person might be an atheist, an agnostic, a pantheist, or they might even believe in some form of God. But a person who holds the beliefs just described has a Humanist worldview. The Islamic worldview, like Humanism, rejects the Bible as the fully inspired and infallible Word of God and the biblical teaching about the Trinity and the Deity of Christ. However, unlike Humanism, Islam holds to the Qur'an as the inspired Word of God and as its ultimate authority.

Also, this book will refer to the Christian worldview in a specific sense. We do not use the term to refer to the thinking of all professing Christians. Rather, we use the term to refer to a way of thinking that begins with the Triune God revealed in the Bible and looks to the Bible as the fully inspired, inerrant Word of God and the ultimate authority for belief and conduct.

INTRODUCTION ENDNOTES

1 Ken Ham and Britt Beemer, with Todd Hilliard, *Already Gone: Why Your Kids Will Quit Church and What You Can Do To Stop It* (Green Forest, AR: Master Books, 2009).

2 Ibid, p. 170.

3 Ibid, p. 173.

4 Ibid, p. 174.

5 Ibid, p. 175.

6 Ibid, p. 179.

7 Avery Foley, "Study Shows Only 10% of Americans Have a Biblical Worldview," Answers in Genesis, https://answersingenesis.org/culture/study-shows-only-10-percent-americans-have-biblical-worldview (May 2, 2017).

CHAPTER 1

INTRODUCTION TO WORLDVIEWS

INTRODUCTION TO THE CHRISTIAN WORLDVIEW

God is concerned about how we think. His Word addresses every area of life and He calls us to think biblically about all of it. God exhorts believers to "take every thought captive to obey Christ" (2 Cor. 10:5). The most important commandment God gave in the Bible includes loving God with our whole heart and mind. Jesus said, "You shall love the Lord your God with all your heart and with all your soul, and with all your <u>mind</u>. This is the great and first commandment" (Matt. 22:37–38).

However, people by nature have a sinful mind that is in rebellion toward God in its thinking, and they need a new mind: "For to set the mind on the flesh is death, but to set the mind on the Spirit is life and peace. For the <u>mind</u> that is set on the flesh is hostile to God" (Rom. 8:6-7). Scripture warns us to "no longer walk as the Gentiles do in the futility of their <u>mind</u>. They are darkened in their understanding" (Eph. 4:17-18). Because of this warning, Scripture calls us to "be renewed in the spirit of your <u>mind</u>" (Eph. 4:23).

We need to examine our thinking by the Word of God because God's Word is "a discerner of the <u>thoughts and intentions of the heart</u>" (Heb. 4:12). The spiritual heart of man is where thinking occurs, and thinking leads people to how they live their lives. That is why Scripture says it is important for people to guard their heart from wrong thinking and influences (Prov. 4:23).

Scripture warns us about people who promote "philosophy . . . according to the elemental spirits of the world and not according to Christ" (Col. 2:8). God's Word says, "Do not be conformed to this world, but be transformed by the <u>renewal of your mind</u> . . . " (Rom. 12:2). A Christian worldview writer states: "It is in the arena of worldviews that one of the greatest battles of our time is now being waged."[1]

Two major worldviews especially oppose the Christian worldview. Both have millions of followers in the world today and both claim to be a total worldview. These opposing worldviews are Humanism and Islam.

The worldview battle in our world today involves a clash between the Christian worldview, the Humanist worldview, and the Islamic worldview. The clash is between what God has said in the Bible (Biblical Christianity) versus what Muhammad claimed God said (Islam) versus what man decides is true (Humanism). **The Christian worldview appeals to the Bible as the ultimate authority. Islam appeals to the Qur'an as its ultimate authority. Humanism appeals to the thinking of man as its ultimate authority**.

Dr. Del Tackett, in his worldview DVD series, points out that **the clash between the Christian worldview and opposing worldviews is a battle for truth.**[2] Truth addresses the mind. Jesus emphasized the importance of truth. Concerning truth, Jesus said, "For this purpose I have come into the world, to bear witness to the truth" (John 18:37). Jesus declared that God's Word is absolutely true (John 17:17). Jesus said His great opponent, the devil, is a liar and that only His truth will make us free from the devil's lies (John 8:32, 8:44).

From the beginning, Satan has tempted man to doubt God's Word (Gen. 3:1–5). People who reject the Christian worldview exchange God's revealed truth for Satan's substitute lies (Rom. 1:18–25). We need to communicate the truth of the Christian worldview in a manner that involves "correcting opponents with gentleness," so that people may come "to a knowledge of the truth" and "escape from the snare of the devil" (2 Tim. 2:25).

To understand the Christian worldview or opposing worldviews, we must first understand what the term "worldview" means. Consider these helpful definitions of the term by some Christian worldview writers:

> A worldview is the comprehensive framework of one's basic beliefs about things.[3]
>
> A worldview comprises one's collection of presuppositions, convictions, and values from which a person tries to understand and make sense out of the world and life.[4]
>
> The term worldview . . . refers to any set of ideas, beliefs, convictions, or values that provides a framework or map to help you understand God, the world, and your relationship to God and the world.[5]
>
> A worldview is the way each of us looks at and evaluates everything that is seen, experienced, or thought about.[6]

Some sociologists and worldview writers have used the term "metanarrative" to describe a worldview. An online information site gives this definition of a metanarrative:

> "A metanarrative is an overarching story or storyline that gives context, meaning, and purpose to all of life. . . . The concept of a metanarrative is similar to a worldview. "[7]

In other words, we can describe a metanarrative as an overarching story that seeks to give a unified sense to all of life. God's written Word, the Bible, is a metanarrative. It is a unified and comprehensive account about all of life.

A worldview includes basic presuppositions or assumptions about life. To think, people must presuppose certain things, which include a starting point in their thinking and an ultimate standard they use to evaluate things. To presuppose something, according to a dictionary, is to "assume beforehand . . . to require an antecedent condition."[8] Note what some Christian worldview writers state about the meaning of presuppositions:

> Every worldview starts with presuppositions—i.e., beliefs that one presumes to be true without supporting evidence from other sources or systems.[9]

> A presupposition is a belief over which no other takes precedence.[10]

> A worldview is a set of presuppositions (assumptions which may be true, partially true, or entirely false) which we hold (consciously or subconsciously, consistently or inconsistently)about the basic makeup of our world.[11]

> Presuppositions are the deciding factor in determining how facts are interpreted and combined to give particular content to a worldview. . . . A presupposition is not proved by anything else more ultimate.[12]

A simple way to summarize the idea of a worldview is to use an acrostic, CALL. A worldview is a person's Controlling Assumptions about Life and Living. Let's analyze that definition. A worldview starts with basic presuppositions. These are the assumptions that control how a person thinks about the world in which they live. A worldview provides a metanarrative, a unified story about the meaning of life and the world. A worldview seeks to explain life's origin and purpose. It deals with core beliefs and values that influence how a person lives.

Whether you realize it or not, you already have a worldview. Everyone does. You have basic assumptions about the world in which you live. You have certain beliefs and values that influence choices you make about how to live your life.

In fact, you cannot reason unless you have a starting assumption in your thinking. And you could not come to a conclusion without an authority to which you appeal. Note what these Christian worldview writers have observed about worldviews:

> "Most people would not have an answer if they were asked what their worldview is. Yet their basic beliefs emerge quickly enough when they are faced with practical emergencies, current political issues, or convictions that clash with their own."[13]

> "Each of us carries a model of the universe inside our heads that tells us what the world is like and how we should live in it. . . . Even ordinary people have a set of convictions about how reality functions and how they should live."[14]

Your worldview influences how you look at every area of life. It is like glasses through which you look at life. A Christian worldview writer, James Anderson, makes this observation:

> "A worldview is an all-encompassing perspective on everything that exists and matters to us. Your worldview represents your most fundamental beliefs and assumptions about the universe you inhabit. It reflects how you would answer all the . . . fundamental questions we ask about life, the universe and everything. . . . Your worldview shapes and informs your experiences of the world around you. Like a pair of spectacles with colored lenses, it affects what you see and how you see it."[15]

Dr. Greg Bahnsen was a Christian expert in apologetics. He noted that presuppositions as a starting point for thinking and an authority for conclusions are essential to man's thinking:

> "Every system must have some unproven assumptions, a starting point not antecedently established, with which reasoning begins and according to which it proceeds to conclusions. Therefore, all argumentation over ultimate issues of truth and reality will come down to an appeal to authorities."[16]

Worldviews deal with basic questions of life: Where did I come from? Where did my world come from? What is the basic problem with me and my world? What is the solution to problems in my world? How do we know what is true? How should I live? Such questions ultimately find answers in God's Word, the Bible and are ultimately religious in nature.

Roy Clouser, a Christian philosopher, did lengthy research about presuppositions and disagreements in beliefs. He concludes that every person has some type of ultimate religious belief as a presupposition. He makes the following observations based on his research:

> "As a result of investigating religious belief and its influence for over thirty years, I have become convinced that religious belief is the most influential of all beliefs. . . . So extensive is this religious influence that virtually all the major disagreements between competing theories in science and in philosophy can ultimately be traced back to differences in their religious presuppositions. . . . Religious beliefs all have in common that they believe in something or other as the non-dependent divinity on which all else depends. . . . A person who believes matter/energy to be self-existent, would, indeed, be regarding it to be divine and would have a materialist religious belief."[17]

We established that every person has a worldview and every worldview has presuppositions. Christian apologetic writers, Gary DeMar and Dr. Greg Bahnsen observe:

> "Presuppositions are necessary to reasoning. Every system of thought has some starting point, some standard of authority by which truth and error are evaluated."[18]

In order to think, every person must have a starting assumption in their thinking and an authoritative standard for drawing conclusions.

The two beginning presuppositions of the Christian worldview are:

(1) The Triune Creator God revealed in the Bible is real.

(2) The Bible is God's infallible revelation to man.

The God of the Bible is the ultimate reality and the beginning point for Christian thinking. And His infallible revelation in the Bible is the ultimate authority for Christian thought.

To truly understand life, a person must begin their thinking with the God of the Bible, with the presupposition of His existence. Proverbs 1:7 says, "The fear of the Lord is the beginning of knowledge." And Hebrews 11:6 declares, "Whoever would draw near to God must believe that He exists." The God revealed in the Bible is one God in three Persons—Father, Son, and Holy Spirit (Matt. 28:19) and His existence is foundational for understanding the world around us.

God has revealed His plan, precepts, and purposes in Scripture, which is His inspired Word (2 Tim. 3:16). Christians must look to God's Word as the ultimate authority for their conclusions. No greater authority than God's Word exists for judging conclusions. Jesus taught that Scripture as God's Word is absolutely true (John 17:17). John MacArthur and Alan Cairns, respected theological writers, emphasize these presuppositions for a Christian worldview.

> "Two major presuppositions underlie the chapters that follow—the eternal existence of the personal, transcendent, triune Creator God, and the God of Scripture has revealed His character, purposes, and will in the infallible and inerrant pages of His special revelation, the Bible, which is superior to any other source of revelation or human reason."[19]

> "To presuppose God is not to make an unverifiable assumption. . . . The Bible presupposes God (Gen. 1:1; Heb. 11:6). The God of the Bible is the absolute, eternal, ontological Trinity, who has revealed Himself in His Word, the Bible. . . . The God of the Bible is necessary to the existence of all the facts of the universe."[20]

Simply put, we believe God exists and has revealed Himself in the Bible. Presupposing God and His Word are not blind, arbitrary assumptions. There are good reasons for beginning our thinking with God and judging conclusions by the Bible, God's Word. Chapters two and three will develop and defend the Christian worldview presuppositions of God's Word and God's Person.

The message of the Bible is a metanarrative that explains life in man's world. God used over forty human authors, writing over a period of fifteen-hundred years, to tell a unified, true story of real events and real people. The unified story of the Bible points to one ultimate author, God.

A story normally has a central character and central theme. Christ is the central person in the Bible and His redeeming work and glorious kingdom is the central theme of the Bible. A story develops its plot and unified theme with several key ideas. The biblical account is like a great drama with three major acts, Creation, Fall, and Redemption.

The beginning chapters of the Bible tell of God's creation of the world and man and then continue the storyline with the Fall of man (Gen. 1-3). Then the rest of the Old Testament tells of the promise of the Redeemer and the New Testament tells of the fulfillment of that promise in Jesus (1 Pet. 1:10-11). Consider what Jesus said about the message of redemption in Scripture:

> "Was it not necessary that the Christ should suffer these things and enter into his glory? And beginning with Moses and all the prophets, He interpreted to them in all the Scriptures the things concerning himself. . . . Everything written about me in the Law of Moses and the Prophets and the Psalms must be fulfilled. . . . Thus it is written, that the Christ should suffer and on the third day rise from the dead and that repentance and forgiveness of sins should be proclaimed in His name to all nations . . . " (Luke 24:26–27, 44, 46, 47).

The Bible's message of Creation, Fall, and Redemption encompasses all of reality. God created everything (John 1:3). Man's fall into sin affects all people and the whole created universe (Rom. 5:12 and 8:20–22). God sends His message of redemption to the whole world (Luke 24:47). Several Christian worldview writers point out that Creation, Fall, and Redemption summarize the story of the Bible and give the basis for a total worldview:

> "The narrative of Creation, Fall and Redemption includes the whole Bible. . . . After Creation and Fall, the story is about redemption, and thus about Jesus."[21]

> "This book approaches the topic of worldview by . . . crafting a biblically based worldview in any field using the structural elements of Creation, Fall, and Redemption. . . . Creation, Fall, and Redemption are cosmic in scope, describing the great events that shape the nature of all created reality."[22]

> "Scripture speaks centrally to everything in our life and world. . . . Such matters are approached in terms of a worldview based squarely on such central scriptural categories as creation, sin, and redemption."[23]

The Bible's message of Creation, Fall, and Redemption gives God's answers to basic worldview questions. One Christian worldview writer has observed the following:

"Every philosophy or ideology has to answer the same fundamental questions.

1. Creation: How did it all begin? Where did we come from?

2. Fall: What went wrong? What is the source of evil and suffering?

3. Redemption: What can we do about it? How can the world be set right again?"[24]

For further development of Creation, Fall, and Redemption in relation to our worldview, see the Christian high school textbook, *Biblical Worldview: Creation, Fall, Redemption.*[25]

Ken Ham develops this metanarrative further with **"Seven C's of Bible History"**:[26]

Creation—The beginning of history (Genesis 1).

Corruption—Man's fall into sin (Genesis 3).

Catastrophe—God's judgment of the whole world in the Flood (Genesis 6–8).

Confusion—God confused man's languages at the tower of Babel (Genesis 11).

Christ—Christ comes as God in the flesh (John 1:14).

Cross—Christ's death and Resurrection to redeem man (1 Corinthians 15:1–4).

Consummation—The new heavens and new earth (Revelation 21–22).

This book defends the Christian worldview with an understanding of Scripture that is consistent with standard conservative Protestant theology. The term "Protestant" refers to Bible-believing churches that are distinct from the Roman Catholic Church. This book deals with the canon and authority of the Bible and the way of salvation from a conservative Protestant understanding of Scripture, which differs from the Roman Catholic view of the canon of Scripture and way of salvation.

The term "conservative" distinguishes Bible-believing churches that conserve historic orthodox Bible doctrines, as opposed to liberal Protestant views in the World Council of churches and the Unitarian-Universalist church. The Humanist worldview has influenced these religious groups to exalt the thinking of man over the Bible and to reject the full inspiration and infallibility of the Bible. Conservative Protestants also reject the unbiblical teaching of unorthodox sects such as Mormonism and Jehovah's Witnesses.

For centuries, Bible-believing Protestants have affirmed the sixty-six books of the canon of Scripture as the complete, infallible and inspired Word of God and our authority for what we believe and how we live. They have confessed God as Creator and a Trinity, one God in three Persons. They have affirmed that salvation comes through faith in Christ alone. They have affirmed marriage as only for one man and one woman committed to each other for life and all sexual activity as only for biblical marriage.

This book especially defends the biblical account of creation by God against the Humanist belief in evolution. There are a number of Christian Creationist ministries that defend the biblical account of Creation against evolution who have helpful websites. These websites include: Answers in Genesis (AIG; www.answersingenesis.org), The Institute of Creation Research (ICR; www.icr.org), The Biblical Science Institute (www.biblicalscienceinstitute.com), Creation Astronomy (www.creationastronomy.com), and Creation Ministries International (CMI; www.creation.com).

Answers in Genesis and The Institute for Creation Research have very helpful statements of faith. This book is written in harmony with their doctrinal statements, which are quoted here:

ANSWERS IN GENESIS STATEMENT OF FAITH

> "The 66 books of the Bible are the written Word of God. The Bible is divinely inspired and inerrant throughout. Its assertions are factually true in all the original autographs. It is the supreme authority in everything it teaches. Its authority is not limited to spiritual, religious, or redemptive themes but includes its assertions in such fields as history and science. The final guide to the interpretation of Scripture is Scripture itself.
>
> The account of origins presented in Genesis is a simple but factual presentation of actual events and therefore provides a reliable framework for scientific research into the question of the origin and history of life, mankind, the earth, and the universe. The various original life forms (kinds), including mankind, were made by direct creative acts of God. The living descendants of any of the original kinds (apart from man) may represent more than one species today, reflecting the genetic potential within the original kind. Only limited biological changes (including mutational deterioration) have occurred naturally within each kind since creation.
>
> The great Flood of Genesis was an actual historic event, worldwide (global) in its extent and effect. The special creation of Adam (the first man) and Eve (the first woman), and their subsequent fall into sin, is the basis for the necessity of salvation for mankind. Death (both physical and spiritual) and bloodshed entered into this world subsequent to and as a direct consequence of man's sin.
>
> The Godhead is triune: one God, three Persons—God the Father, God the Son, and God the Holy Spirit.
>
> All mankind are sinners, inherently from Adam and individually (by choice), and are therefore subject to God's wrath and condemnation.
>
> Freedom from the penalty and power of sin is available to man only through the sacrificial death and shed blood of Jesus Christ and His complete and bodily resurrection from the dead. The Holy Spirit enables the sinner to repent and

believe in Jesus Christ. The Holy Spirit lives and works in each believer to produce the fruits of righteousness. Salvation is a gift received by faith alone in Christ alone and expressed in the individual's repentance, recognition of the death of Christ as full payment for sin, and acceptance of the risen Christ as Savior, Lord, and God. All things necessary for our salvation are expressly set down in Scripture.

Jesus Christ was conceived by the Holy Spirit and born of the virgin Mary. Jesus Christ rose bodily from the dead, ascended to heaven, and is currently seated at the right hand of God the Father and shall return in person to this earth as Judge of the living and the dead. Satan is the personal spiritual adversary of both God and mankind. Those who do not believe in Christ are subject to everlasting conscious punishment, but believers enjoy eternal life with God.

The only legitimate marriage sanctioned by God is the joining of one man and one woman in a single, exclusive union, as delineated in Scripture. God intends sexual intimacy to only occur between a man and a woman who are married to each other, and has commanded that no intimate sexual activity be engaged in outside of a marriage between a man and a woman. Any form of sexual immorality, such as adultery, fornication, homosexuality, lesbianism, bisexual conduct, bestiality, incest, pornography, or any attempt to change one's gender or disagreement with one's biological gender, is sinful and offensive to God.

It is the duty of Christians to attend a local Bible believing church, as portrayed in the New Testament.

All human life is sacred and begins at conception (defined as the moment of fertilization). The unborn child is a living human being, created in the image of God, and must be respected and protected both before and after birth. The abortion of an unborn child or the active taking of human life through euthanasia constitutes a violation of the sanctity of human life and is a crime against God and man.

The following are held by members of the Board of Answers in Genesis to be either consistent with Scripture or implied by Scripture: Scripture teaches a recent origin for man and the whole creation, spanning approximately 4,000 years from creation to Christ. The days in Genesis do not correspond to geologic ages, but are six consecutive twenty-four hour days of creation. The Noachian Flood was a significant geological event and much (but not all) fossiliferous sediment originated at that time. The gap theory has no basis in Scripture. The view commonly used to evade the implications or the authority of biblical teaching, that knowledge and/or truth may be divided into secular and religious, is rejected. By definition, no apparent, perceived or claimed evidence in any field, including history and chronology, can be valid if it contradicts the scriptural record. Of primary importance is the fact that evidence is always subject to interpretation by fallible people who do not possess all information."[27]

THE INSTITUTE OF CREATION RESEARCH STATEMENT OF FAITH

"The Creator of the universe is a triune God: Father, Son, and Holy Spirit. There is only one eternal and transcendent God, the source of all being and meaning, and He exists in three Persons, each of whom participated in the work of creation.

• The Bible, consisting of the thirty-nine canonical books of the Old Testament and the twenty-seven canonical books of the New Testament, is the divinely-inspired revelation of the Creator to man. Its unique, plenary, verbal inspiration guarantees that these writings, as originally and miraculously given, are infallible and completely authoritative on all matters with which they deal, free from error of any sort, scientific and historical as well as moral and theological.

• All things in the universe were created and made by God in the six literal days of the Creation Week described in Genesis 1:1-2:3, and confirmed in Exodus 20:8-11. The creation record is factual, historical, and perspicuous; thus all theories of origins or development that involve evolution in any form are false. All things that now exist are sustained and ordered by God's providential care. However, a part of the spiritual creation, Satan and his angels, rebelled against God after the creation and are attempting to thwart His divine purposes in creation.

• The first human beings, Adam and Eve, were specially created by God, and all other men and women are their descendants. In Adam, mankind was instructed to exercise "dominion" over all other created organisms, and over the earth itself (an implicit commission for true science, technology, commerce, fine art, and education), but the temptation by Satan and the entrance of sin brought God's curse on that dominion and on mankind, culminating in death and separation from God as the natural and proper consequence.

• The biblical record of primeval earth history in Genesis 1-11 is fully historical and perspicuous, including the creation and Fall of man, the Curse on the Creation and its subjection to the bondage of decay, the promised Redeemer, the worldwide cataclysmic deluge in the days of Noah, the post-diluvian renewal of man's commission to subdue the earth (now augmented by the institution of human government), and the origin of nations and languages at the tower of Babel.

• The alienation of man from his Creator because of sin can only be remedied by the Creator Himself, who became man in the person of the Lord Jesus Christ, through miraculous conception and virgin birth. In Christ were indissolubly united perfect sinless humanity and full deity, so that His substitutionary death is the only necessary and sufficient price of man's redemption. That the redemption was completely efficacious is assured by His bodily resurrection from the dead and ascension into heaven; the resurrection of Christ is thus the focal point of history, assuring the consummation of God's purposes in creation.

- The final restoration of creation's perfection is yet future, but individuals can immediately be restored to fellowship with their Creator on the basis of His redemptive work on their behalf, receiving forgiveness and eternal life solely through personal trust in the Lord Jesus Christ, accepting Him not only as estranged Creator, but also as reconciling Redeemer and coming King. Those who reject Him, however, or who neglect to believe on Him, thereby continue in their state of rebellion and must ultimately be consigned to the everlasting fire prepared for the devil and his angels.

- The eventual accomplishment of God's eternal purposes in creation, with the removal of His curse and the restoration of all things to divine perfection, will take place at the personal bodily return to earth of Jesus Christ to judge and purge sin and to establish His eternal kingdom.

- Each believer should participate in the "ministry of reconciliation" by seeking both to bring individuals back to God in Christ (the "Great Commission") and to "subdue the earth" for God's glory (the Edenic-Noahic Commission). The three institutions established by the Creator for the implementation of His purposes in this world (home, government, church) should be honored and supported as such."[28]

INTRODUCTION TO THE HUMANIST WORLDVIEW

The type of philosophy that Humanism holds began with Satan's original temptation of man to reject God's Word and to determine right and wrong apart from God. Satan tempted Eve, saying, "Did God actually say, 'You shall not eat of any tree in the garden?' . . . You will not surely die. . . . You will be like God, knowing good and evil" (Gen. 3:1, 4, 5). Similarly, Humanism today exalts man's thinking over the authority of God's Word.

In regards to the development of their philosophy, Humanists state, "Humanism traces its roots from Ancient China, classical Greece and Rome, through the Renaissance and Enlightenment, to the scientific revolution of the modern world."[29] Dr. Cairns, in his *Dictionary of Theological Terms,* describes "The Enlightenment" as:

> "The title given to the development of thought in Europe and America in the 17th and 18th centuries. Essentially, the Enlightenment was the expression of modern man's attempt to break free from the rule of dogma based on divine revelation and to exercise his own reason and complete autonomy. Hence, the Enlightenment has been called the "Age of Reason."[30]

The Humanist worldview begins with the material world and rejects the idea of a personal, all-powerful God who directly created all things. **Humanists do not accept the Bible as God's Word or the reality of the God revealed in the Bible.** They look to human logic, observation, experience, and study to guide their thinking. They look to the conclusions of human "experts" in various fields as their ultimate authority for drawing their own conclusions. Humanist leaders claim, "As non-theists, we begin with humans, not God, nature not deity."[31]

Humanism has also influenced liberal religious thinkers. Humanist writers note,

> "Many kinds of Humanism exist in the contemporary world. . . . 'Religious' and 'Marxist' Humanism, free thought, atheism, agnosticism, skepticism, deism, rationalism, ethical culture and liberal religion all claim to be heirs of the Humanist tradition."[32]

Liberal religious Humanists reject the inspiration of Scripture and the deity of Christ, while holding to theistic evolution.

Dr. David Noebel, in his book, *Understanding the Times*, notes **four varieties of Humanism. These include Secular Humanism, Marxist Humanism, Postmodern Humanism, and New Age Humanism.** Dr. Noebel states:

> "Marxism, Postmodernism, and Secular Humanism have a number of similarities. . . . Marxism and Postmodernism are the daughters of Humanism. . . . Commonly referred to as the New Age movement, this worldview is more accurately known by its real name, Cosmic Humanism."[33]

SECULAR HUMANISM

Secular Humanism developed in Western culture through the movement known as the "Enlightenment." A Christian worldview writer said:

> "Enlightenment thinkers rejected the idea that religion can be a source of truth and believed instead that the application of reason to the evidences of the senses is the sole source of the truth."[34]

Humanism makes man's reason the ultimate authority, as they have stated: "Secular Humanism places trust in human intelligence rather than in divine guidance.[35] Humanism looks to man's thinking as the ultimate source for determining truth, rather than the Bible. Secular Humanists also reject any claim by other religions to have revelation from God.

Some who identify with Secular Humanism might claim a religious belief in some kind of "higher power." However, most who identify as Secular Humanists are either atheists or agnostics. All Secular Humanists would reject the Bible as God's Word, reject the God revealed in the Bible, and emphasize a secular approach to life. Humanist leaders state:

> "We find that traditional views of the existence of God either are meaningless or have not yet been demonstrated to be true. . . . We reject the divinity of Jesus. . . . We do not accept as true the literal interpretation of the Old and New Testaments."[36]

Secular Humanists also reject religious moral absolutes. They do not accept the idea of universal standards of right and wrong coming from divine revelation to man. They state:

> "We affirm that moral values derive their source from human experience. Ethics is autonomous and situational, needing no theological or ideological sanction. . . . The many varieties of sexual exploration should not in themselves be considered evil."[37]

MARXIST HUMANISM

Karl Marx was a nineteenth century German philosopher. As an atheist and a materialist, Marx believed that matter is all there is. He promoted total government control of the economy and property in his key book, *The Communist Manifesto.* Marx collaborated with the English atheist, Friedrich Engels, to promote socialism. Marx and Engels viewed Communism as a form of Humanism, saying, "Communism, as fully developed naturalism, equals Humanism."[38]

Marxist ideas led to twentieth century Communism, a movement dedicated to the abolition of private property and total control of the economy by the civil government.[39] In the twentieth century, communists violently seized power in the Soviet Union and Eastern Europe. Communists later fell from power there, but still continue to exert an influence. However, Marxists still dominate the civil government in China, North Korea, Vietnam, Cuba, and Zimbabwe. Many Marxists teach in colleges in Western nations.

Vladimir Lenin, a follower of Marx, who led the Communist Revolution in Russia in 1917, summarized the atheistic basis of Marxism and Communism. He stated:

> "The philosophical basis of Marxism, as Marx and Engels repeatedly declared, is . . . a materialism which is absolutely atheistic and positively hostile to all religion."[40]

> "In what sense do we deny ethics, morals? In the sense in which they are preached by the bourgeoisie, which deduces these morals from God's commandments. Of course, We say that we do not believe in God."[41]

Marxists see all of history as an evolutionary, economic class struggle. They divide people into categories of property owners (bourgeoisie) and working class people (proletariat), and they see the two parties as in constant conflict. Marx and Engels emphasized this idea:

> "The history of all hitherto existing society is the history of class struggles. The state, then, is . . . simply a product of society at a certain stage of evolution."[42]

But Marxist ideas bring dire consequences. Adding societal evolution to biological evolution, Marx advocated violent revolution to overthrow existing governments in order to establish communist governments. Marx stated, "There is but one way of . . . concentrating the death agony of the old order . . . Revolutionary Terror.[43] Marxist commitment to violent revolution and rejection of moral absolutes has led to mass murders within communist countries. Dr. Noebel points out documentation for this fact:

> "The death toll of this 'scientific socialism' experiment has exceeded the 100 million mark, according to University of Hawaii professor, R.J. Rummel, author of *Death by Government.*"[44]

POSTMODERN HUMANISM

Postmodernism is a Humanist movement that reacts against elements within Secular Humanism, or "Modernism," and against elements of Marxism. Dr. Cairns notes:

> "Modernity is the term employed by social scientists to describe the world of the Enlightenment with its reliance on science and technology as the keys to understanding life and defining progress."[45]

Postmodernists do not have faith in God's Word, but they also do not share the same degree of faith in science and technology and reason as Secular Humanists do. Dr. Noebel states:

> "Though Postmodernism comes in many forms, there are three unifying values: (1) a commitment to relativism; (2) an opposition to rationalism; and (3) the promotion of culturally created realities."[46]

Many Postmodernist leaders have an atheistic and Marxist background.[47] Many Postmodernists are troubled by the extreme past violence in Marxism. However, with the influence of their Marxist background, they emphasize class struggle. They often set females against males and homosexuals against heterosexuals. A worldview writer observes:

> "While Marxists focus on the proletariat rising against the bourgeoisie, Postmodernists focus on one gender, race, or socially identifiable group in a struggle for dominion over another."[48]

Postmodernists use the term "metanarrative." A worldview writer observes:

> "A metanarrative is a single overarching objective interpretation or narration of reality. . . Postmodernists deny the existence of all metanarratives."[49]

The Christian worldview looks to the Creation, Fall, Redemption metanarrative of the Bible and "The Seven Cs of Biblical History" to explain all of reality. Postmodernists reject the Biblical metanarrative, including biblical Creation, and they accept evolution. But they do not believe that human reason and science can provide a single unifying narrative that explains all of reality.

> "Postmodernists reject universal moral absolutes. A postmodern psychiatrist said: Universal moral principles must be eradicated and reverence for individual and cultural uniqueness inculcated. . . . No group or society can know what's best for another group or society."[50]

Postmodernists also reject universal absolute truth. Postmodernists emphasize what is true for one's particular cultural group. A worldview writer notes:

> "Postmodernists insist there is no eternal truth that is true around the world. Truth for some Postmodernists is what their community allows each member to say is true."[51]

One postmodern writer states:

> "We . . . (should) give up the correspondence theory of truth and start treating moral and scientific beliefs as tools for achieving greater human happiness, rather than as representations of the intrinsic nature of reality."[52]

Some Postmodernists reject the correspondence of reality with words. They engage in literary "deconstructionism," a term that means "(1) words do not represent reality, and (2) that concepts expressed in sentences in any language are arbitrary.[53] For instance, in the study of literature, they allow students and teachers to interpret a writer's words however they wish. However, most Humanists in general would not advocate literary "deconstructionism."

One researcher observes that in spite of the Postmodern reaction against modernism and rationalism, "Postmodernism has not fully displaced modernism or naturalism."[54] This is especially true in the field of science.

NEW AGE HUMANISM

Douglas Groothuis is a Christian researcher who has written about the New Age Movement. He describes the New Age movement as a Humanist movement:

> "The New Age and Secular Humanism are branches of the same tree. They both look to humanity for hope and salvation. They both reject the Christian God in favor of their own autonomous agenda. But the New Age's appeal lies in its mystical dimension. . . . It appeals to human subjectivity—the divine within—as its prime source of truth."[55]

Groothuis describes the New Age Movement as a blend of western science with elements of pantheistic Eastern religions. He notes the following distinctive New Age beliefs:[56]

1. New Age Humanism believes in Monism, that all is one.
2. They believe in Pantheism, that all is god.
3. They believe humanity is god.
4. They believe in a change in consciousness.
5. They believe all religions are one.
6. They believe in cosmic evolution.

By a "change in consciousness," New Age leaders refer to people achieving an altered state of consciousness in which they discover their godhood:

"We have forgotten our true identity. . . . This metaphysical amnesia can be reversed by techniques designed to alter ordinary consciousness. . . . This change in consciousness . . . leads to an awareness of oneness and spiritual power. . . . They may use self-hypnotism, internal visualization, biofeedback, or even the sexual act."[57]

To illustrate New Age philosophy, Groothuis quotes a leading New Age thinker and writer, Barbara Hubbard. She embraces evolution and human goodness and teaches that people can evolve into Messianic godhood:

"We must embrace . . . 'evolutionary futurism.' . . . In her book, *The Evolutionary Journey,* Hubbard explains . . . 'Each person is called upon to recognize that the Messiah is within."[58]

New Age leaders also stress sexual amorality and human goodness. New Age advocate Kevin Ryerson states, "An individual's sexual preference should be viewed as neither good nor evil. . . . Mankind and all life are basically good.[59]

Also, many people within the New Age movement believe in reincarnation, the idea that after death a person's soul comes back in another body or as another form (either human or animal). However, the Bible plainly says that, "It is appointed for man to die once, and after that comes judgment" (Heb. 9:27). According to Scripture, at death the soul of a saved person enters Heaven and the soul of an unsaved person enters Hell (Luke 16:19-31).

HUMANISM AND EVOLUTION

These varieties of Humanism have differences among themselves. However, they all reject the Bible as God's infallible Word and God as revealed in the Bible. **All varieties of Humanism hold to evolution as a foundational belief:**

Secular Humanism: "Science affirms that the human species is an emergence from natural evolutionary forces."[60]

Marxism: "What Marxian philosophy derived from Hegel was that the way to understand the world was not to see it as a collection of things but as an evolving process."[61]

Postmodernism: "Temporal divine creation is abandoned in favor of eternal process."[62]

New Age: "The New Age world view emphasizes . . . change and evolution."[63]

INTRODUCTION TO THE ISLAMIC WORLDVIEW

BASIC FACTS ABOUT ISLAM

The religious movement known as Islam began with their prophet Muhammad, who lived in Arabia from AD 570–632.[64] He claimed to have revelations from God, which his followers compiled in a book known as the Qur'an. Muhammad conquered Arabia in the name of his religion. His followers spread Islam, and now there are over one billion Muslims in the world.[65]

Three key beliefs are foundational for Islam:

1. Allah is the one true God.
2. The Qur'an is God's verbally inspired word.
3. Muhammad is God's final and greatest prophet.

The Qur'an makes these claims:

- "We sent by inspiration to thee an Arabic Qur'an" (Surah 42:7).
- "There is Allah, the One and Only" (Surah 112).
- "Muhammad is the Messenger of Allah" (Surah 48:29).
- "Believe, therefore, in Allah and His Messenger" (Surah 64:8).[66]

Followers of Islam collected reports of sayings (hadith) and actions (sunnah) of Muhammad. The volumes of the Hadith were written to preserve this tradition of Muhammad's life and sayings. An early Muslim, Al-Bukhari, made a collection of this tradition about Muhammad that Muslims widely respect and accept. In the twentieth century, Muhammad Khan translated Al-Bukhari's collection of the Hadith into English.[67] A Muslim writer explains:

> "The Hadith is not a Holy Book (revelation) as the Qur'an and the previous Scriptures. However, to the Muslims, the importance of the Hadith ranks only second to the Holy Qur'an. The Hadith is complementary to the Qur'an. It helps to explain and clarify the Holy Qur'an and to present the Qur'an in a more practical form."[68]

Ergun and Emir Caner are brothers who grew up as Muslims but later became Christians and wrote a book about Islam. They summarize the "five pillars" of Islam:

> "The five pillars of Islam . . . are non-negotiable. . . . 1. The Creed (Shahada): 'There is no God but Allah. Muhammad is the messenger of Allah.' . . . 2. Prayer (Salat) . . . If prayers were not repeated five times daily, believers would soon forget about Allah. . . . 3. Almsgiving (Zakat). . . . 4. Ramadan: Fast (Sawm). . . . 5. Pilgrimage (Hajj)."[69]

The Caners also explain the difference between the two great divisions in Islam, Sunni Muslims and Shiite Muslims, who differ over leadership among Muslims:

> "Following the death of Muhammad, caliphs led the quickly growing Islamic community.
>
> . . . Abu Bakr officially became the first caliph, but his claim was not undisputed. Ali, Muhammad's cousin and the husband of his daughter, Fatima, was fourth caliph until he was assassinated and replaced by the Umayyad dynasty in 661. A

> faction had believed Ali was the true first caliph. Most Muslims supported the "mainstream" line of caliphs and came to be known as Sunnis. . . . The dissenters became known as the Shia (faction) of Ali. . . . This split . . . eventually defined the first division in Islam—that between the Sunnis and the Shiites."[70]

The Caners document several other variations within Islam. Sufism emphasizes mysticism, a personal experience with Allah, and pantheistic views. The Nation of Islam is a movement within the African American community in the United States. Wahhabism is a radical movement within Sunni Islam that emphasizes warfare against non-Muslims. Shiites look for the coming of the Mahdi, a messianic figure, at the end of time.[71]

Islam seeks to be a total worldview. Its teachings encompass God and worship, marriage and family life, government, crime and warfare, diet, clothing, charity, the afterlife, etc. The Muslims' goal is to see the entire world come under Islam. A majority of Muslims do not advocate or practice violence to spread their religion. However, there are a significant number of Muslims who appeal to Muhammad's practice and verses in the Qur'an to justify Islamic violence. **All of the divisions of Islam are contrary to the Biblical worldview at key points:**

1. The God of the Bible is different from the description of Allah in the Qur'an.
2. Jesus in the Bible is different in character from Muhammad.
3. The message of the Bible is different from the message of the Qur'an.

THE GOD OF THE BIBLE VERSUS ALLAH

Muslim scripture, the Qur'an, claims that Allah in the Qur'an and the God of the Bible are the same God:

> "And dispute ye not with the People of the Book . . . But say, 'We believe in the Revelation which has come down to us and in that which came down to you; our God and your God is one; and it is to Him we bow" (Surah 29:46).[72]

However, biblical Christianity has a Trinitarian view of God. Scripture refers to the Holy Spirit, Jesus as the Son of God, and God the Father as the one true God (1 John 5:6, 5:20). The Bible clearly teaches that there is one true God who exists simultaneously in three Persons—Father, Son, and Holy Spirit (Matt. 28:19).

Also, in the Christian worldview, God is knowable, and man can have a personal relationship with Him (John 17:3). Scripture reveals that God has unchanging character attributes and would not act contrary to these attributes (Mal. 3:6). And God has revealed His name to us in Scripture as well: "Yahweh," the "LORD," the "I AM" (Exo. 3:4, 13–15).

In contrast, Islamic scripture specifically rejects the biblical teaching of the Trinity. The Qur'an states:

"O People of the Book! Commit no excesses in your religion. . . . Christ Jesus the son of Mary was a Messenger of Allah. . . . Believe in Allah and His Messengers. Say not 'Trinity;' desist" (Surah 4:171).[73]

Also, Islam teaches that the name of God is "Allah," rather than "Jehovah" or "Yahweh." Muslim theologians do not understand the Qur'an to teach that man can know Allah in a personal, saving relationship. A Muslim theologian confirms this, saying, "It is absolutely impossible for them to know Him.[74]

Dr. Robert Morey is a Christian scholar who has done detailed study of Islam and the Qur'an. He concludes from his research that the God of the Bible and Allah as revealed in the Qur'an are not the same. He documents that Islam teaches that there is only one person in their godhead and his name is Allah, Allah is not a person who is knowable, and Allah is not bound by fixed character attributes in his actions:

"When we compare the attributes of God as found in the Bible and the attributes of Allah found in the Qur'an, it is rather obvious that these two are not the same God. . . . According to the Bible, God is knowable. . . . But in Islam, Allah is unknowable . . . . The God of the Bible is spoken of as a personal being. . . .Allah is not to be understood as a person. . . . The God of the Bible is one God in three Persons. When we turn to the Qur'an, we find that it explicitly denies the Trinity. . . . The God of the Bible is limited by His own righteous nature. . . . He is completely consistent and trustworthy. . . . Allah in the Qur'an . . . is not bound by his nature or his word."[75]

JESUS VERSUS MUHAMMAD

The Bible clearly teaches that Jesus Christ is God manifest in the flesh:

"In the beginning was the Word, and the Word was with God, and the Word was God. . . . And the Word became flesh . . . and we have seen His glory, glory as of the only Son from the Father" (John 1:1, 1:14).

Jesus Christ also demonstrated His deity by rising from the dead (Rom. 1:4). In contrast, the Qur'an nowhere claims that Muhammad rose from the dead. Also, Muhammad, in the Qur'an, rejects the deity of Christ: "The Christians call Christ the Son of God. . . . Allah's curse be on them; how they are deluded away from the Truth! (Surah 9:30).[76]

Jesus also demonstrated His deity by working miracles (John 20:30–31) and empowering His apostles to work miracles (Heb. 2:3–4). The New Testament writers provided eyewitness testimony of the miracles of Jesus (Acts 2:22). The Qur'an does not claim that Muhammad worked miracles, but it does admit that Jesus worked miracles (Surah 5:110).[77]

Realizing this difference, later Muslim apologists tried to make miraculous claims for Muhammad in the Hadith. However, these claims come from later tradition and not from the Qur'an or from eyewitness testimony. Dr. Norman Geisler and Abdul Saleeb have done detailed research on Islam from a biblical perspective. They note:

> "Alleged miracles in the Hadith . . . none of them are recorded in the Qur'an. . . . They do not come from contemporary eyewitnesses of the events. . . . Even among Muslims there is no generally agreed upon list of miracles from the Hadith. . . . The collections of the Hadith that are generally accepted by most Muslims are far removed from the original events by several generations."[78]

The Bible presents Jesus as living a sinless life. Jesus "was in all points tempted as we are, yet without sin" (Heb. 4:15). In contrast, the Qur'an does not say Muhammad was sinless. The Muslim writings about Muhammad, the Hadith, quote Muhammad as saying, "O Allah! Wash off my sins."[79]

Jesus taught that marriage was to be between one man and one woman and He taught against divorce and remarriage, except in cases of fornication (Matt. 19:3–9). In contrast, Muhammad gave men much more latitude for divorce than Jesus did (Surah 2:229, 230).[80] Muhammad took multiple wives for himself and claimed divine revelation for his actions:

> "O Prophet! We have made lawful to thee thy wives to whom thou hast paid their dowers, and those whom thy right hand possesses out of the prisoners of war whom Allah has assigned to thee (Surah 33.50)."[81]

Also, Jesus taught that His kingdom is not a worldly kingdom advanced by force. "My kingdom is not of this world. If my kingdom were of this world, my servants would fight." (John 18:36). Jesus taught His followers to peacefully advance His kingdom through the spread of the Gospel and the teaching of His Word (Matt. 28:19–20; Luke 24:47).

Robert Spencer has done extensive historical research on Islam. He concludes, "The early spread of Islam and that of Christianity sharply contrast in that Islam spread by force and Christianity didn't."[82] He documents Muhammad's teaching:

> "In one key Hadith, Muhammad delineates three choices that Muslims are to offer to non-Muslims: ". . . When you meet your enemies . . . Invite them to accept Islam; if they respond to you, accept it from them and desist from fighting against them. . . . If they refuse to accept Islam, demand from them the Jizyah (a tax on non-Muslims). If they agree to pay, accept it from them and hold off your hands. If they refuse to pay the tax, seek Allah's help and fight against them."[83]

THE BIBLE VERSUS THE QUR'AN

The Bible claims to be the inspired Word of God (2 Tim. 3:16), and the Qur'an claims to be the inspired word of Allah (Surah 42:7).[84] Islam claims it accepts God's earlier revelation in the

Bible: "People of the Book . . . We believe in the Revelation which has come down to us and in that which came down to you" (Surah 29:46).[85]

However, God in the Bible clearly warns against adding to Scripture (Rev. 22:18). But Islam adds the Qur'an to the Bible. And God also warns against taking away from Scripture (Rev. 22:19). Islam rejects the New Testament Scriptures and claims that later Christians corrupted the original gospel of Jesus. Ali, the Muslim translator of the Qur'an into English, makes this claim:

> "The Injil (Gospel) spoken of by the Qur'an is not the New Testament. It is the single Gospel which Islam teaches was revealed to Jesus and which he taught. Fragments of it survive in the received canonical Gospels."[86]

However, we have New Testament manuscripts from before the time of Muhammad. No other book from ancient history has anywhere near the number of surviving manuscripts as the Bible. This fact attests to its Divine authenticity.[87] Also, the Bible demonstrates the reality of its claim to be the inspired Word of God by giving many long range prophecies about nations and about Christ that have already been fulfilled (Isa. 46:9–10).

The Qur'an, however, does not have fulfilled prophecies. The best Muslim apologists can offer as fulfilled prophecy in the Qur'an is a claim of Roman victory over the Persians in a few years (Surah 30:2–4). This is a reference to a victory by the Eastern Roman Empire over the Persian armies after an initial defeat in the A.D. 600s. Dr. Geisler points out, "The prophecy is less than spectacular since it is neither long range nor unusual. One would have expected the defeated Romans to bounce back in victory."[88]

The nature of Muhammad's alleged revelations are different from the experiences of the writers of the Old and New Testament books. The human authors of Scripture do not describe going through seizures under divine inspiration. They also never expressed doubt about whether God or Satan was the source of their revelation. Contrast that with Muhammad's experiences:

> "Muhammad had seizures, during which he sweat vigorously during revelations, according to his wife Aishah. Bells rang in his ears. He became upset and his face changed. Umar ibnu'l Khattab tells that Muhammad shivered, his mouth foamed and he roared like a camel. . . . According to 'Amr ibn Sharhabil, Muhammad himself told his wife Khadija that he feared he was possessed by demons. . . . Sahih al-Bukhari, a Muslim scholar of the ninth and tenth centuries, wrote that when Muhammad fell into one of his unpredictable trances, his revelations were written on whatever was handy. Leg or thigh bones of dead animals were used, as well as palm leaves, skins, mats, stones and bark. When nothing was available, his disciples attempted to memorize the revelations."[89]

Also, throughout the Bible we find a unified central message of Creation, Fall, and Redemption. But the message of the Qur'an contradicts the teaching of the Bible in the areas of Creation, Fall, and Redemption. Obviously, both books cannot be correct.

Consider the area of Creation. Like the Bible, the Qur'an teaches that there is one Creator of all things. However, there are conflicting and confusing statements in the Qur'an about creation of the earth and man. Some Muslims try to mix creation and evolution. It is interesting that Ali, the Muslim scholar who translated the Qur'an into English, claims the six days of creation are "metaphorical" for "six epochs of evolution" on the earth.[90]

The Qur'an speaks of Allah creating everything in six days (Surah 7:54); however, elsewhere the Qur'an described eight days for creation—two days for making the Earth, plus four days for all things on the Earth, plus two days for the "seven firmaments" (Surah 41:9–12).[91] And the Qur'an says Allah created man from dust (Surah 3:59), but elsewhere it says Allah made man out of nothing (Surah 19:67) and all living things out of water (Surah 21:30).[92]

Concerning the Fall, Muslims would agree that people are capable of doing sinful acts. However, Muslims do not understand the Qur'an to teach that Adam and Eve passed down a sinful nature to their descendants or that people are born sinners, which directly contradicts the teaching of the Bible (Rom. 5:12). A modern Muslim writer, Yahiya Emerick, says, "Yes, Adam and Eve sinned, the Qur'an says, but . . . no sin was passed on to their descendants."[93]

Concerning Redemption, the Qur'an denies that Jesus died on the cross as a substitutionary atonement for sin. Ali, the Muslim translator of the Qur'an into English, says:

> "The theological doctrine of blood sacrifice and vicarious atonement for sins is rejected by Islam. . . . The Quranic teaching is that Christ was not crucified nor killed by the Jews.
>
> . . . That Jesus did not die the usual human death, but still lives in the body in heaven, is the generally accepted Muslim view."[94]

The Bible teaches that a person receives salvation and eternal life by God's grace through faith in Christ and specifically rejects salvation by man's works (Gal. 2:16; Eph. 2:8–9; Tit. 3:5; Rom. 3:28). However, the Qur'an describes those whose good deeds outweigh their bad deeds going to Paradise, and those with more bad deeds going to Hell (Surah 101).[95] The Qur'an teaches that a person enters heaven by faith in Islam plus their good works:

> "Verily Allah will admit those who believe and do righteous deeds to Gardens beneath which rivers flow. . . . For those who believe and do righteous deeds will be Gardens, beneath which Rivers flow: That is the great salvation (Surah 47:12, 85:11)."[96]

The Qur'an contradicts the Bible in the area of marriage as well. The Bible clearly teaches that marriage is to be between one man and one woman (Gen. 2:24; Mark 10:6–8; 1 Tim. 3:2, 3:12). It is true that some Old Testament men of faith had more than one wife, but Scripture does not praise them for this or advocate polygamy. In contrast, the Qur'an specifically allows polygamy: "Marry women of your choice, two, or three or four" (Surah 4:3).[97]

The Qur'an also allows a husband to beat his wife: "As to those women on whose part ye fear disloyalty and ill-conduct, admonish them, refuse to share their beds, beat them (Surah 4:34).[98] Robert Spencer documents studies that show that many Muslim women have suffered physical beatings by their husband.[99] But the Bible teaches a man to treat his wife with gentleness (1 Pet. 3:7) and nowhere allows a man to beat his wife.

The Qur'an permits Muslims to sexually possess certain women in warfare:

> "Prohibited to you are . . . women already married, except those whom your right hands possess. . . . (i.e., captives in a jihad)" (Surah 4:1, 24).[100]

A Palestinian Muslim who converted to Christianity confirms this, saying he was taught that Muslims could sexually possess women of people they defeated in combat, based on this passage in the Qur'an.[101]

Additionally, there are a number of errors about plain biblical teaching in the Qur'an. For instance, the Qur'an wrongly says that one of Noah's sons did not enter the Ark (Surah 11:42–43), that Haman (found in the book of Esther) built a great tower to heaven for Pharaoh in Egypt during Moses' time (Surah 28:38, 29:39) and that Mary, the mother of Jesus, was daughter of Imram (Surah 66:12).[102]

CHAPTER 1 STUDY GUIDE
INTRODUCTION TO WORLDVIEWS

KEY SCRIPTURE VERSES TO READ:

Genesis 3:1-5; Proverbs 4:23; Matthew 22:37-38; John 1:1-3, 14; 20:28-31; John 8:32; 17:17; 18:37; Romans 12:2; 2 Corinthians 10:4-5; Ephesians 4:17-18, 21-24; Colossians 2:6-10; 2 Timothy 2:24-26; 2 Timothy 3:15-17; Hebrews 4:12; 1 Peter 3:15

KEY POINTS TO NOTE (NOTE BOLD TYPE IN CHAPTER):

What three worldviews are the center of the major worldview clash in our day?

____

____

What is the ultimate authority for each of these worldviews?

____

____

What is the clash between the Christian worldview and opposing worldviews?

(Note Dr. Tackett; Jesus in John 18:37)

____

____

What can we C.A.L.L. a worldview?

____

____

What are the two basic beginning presuppositions of the Christian worldview?

____

____

What are the seven C's of Biblical history?

____

____

____

What do Humanists especially not accept?

____

____

What are the four varieties of Humanism?

____

____

What do all four varieties of Humanism hold as a foundational belief?

____

____

What are three key foundational beliefs for Islam?

____

____

____

What are three key points in which the Islamic and Christian worldviews differ?

____

____

____

CRITICAL THINKING:

What does every worldview have?

Can a person reason without presuppositions?

Is the Christian worldview unnecessarily biased in having presuppositions?

Do the Humanist and Islamic worldviews have presuppositions?

CHAPTER 1 ENDNOTES

1 David Noebel, *Understanding the Times,* revised 2nd ed. (Manitou Springs, CO: Summit Press, 2006), p. 2.

2 *The Truth Project,* session 1, "Veritology: What is Truth?" featuring Del Tackett (Colorado Springs, CO: Focus on the Family, 2006, DVD).

3 Albert Wolters, *Creation Regained: Biblical Basis for a Reformational Worldview, 2nd ed.* (Grand Rapids: Eerdmans Publishing Company, 2005), p. 2.

4 *Thinking Biblically: Recovering a Christian Worldview,* John MacArthur, ed. (Wheaton, IL: Crossway Books, 2003), p. 13.

5 Noebel, p. 16.

6 Gary DeMar, *Thinking Straight in a Crooked World* (Powder Springs, GA: American Vision, 2001), p. 41.

7 "What is a Metanarrative?" Got Questions, https://www.gotquestions.org/metanarrative.html. (Accessed 3/16/2019).

8 *Webster's College Dictionary,* "presuppose" (New York: Random House, 1992), p. 1069.

9 MacArthur, p. 13.

10 John Frame, *The Doctrine of the Knowledge of God* (Phillipsburg, NJ: Presbyterian and Reformed, 1987), p. 125.

11 James Sire, *The Universe Next Door—A Basic Worldview Catalog,* 3rd edition (Downers Grove, IL: InterVarsity Press, 1997), pp. 17–18.

12 DeMar, *Thinking Straight in a Crooked World,* p. 109.

13 Wolters, *Creation Regained,* p. 4.

14 Nancy Pearcey, *Total Truth* (Wheaton, IL: Crossway Books, 2004), p. 23.

15 James Anderson, *What's Your Worldview?—An Interactive Approach to Life's Big Questions* (Wheaton, IL: Crossway, 2014), pp. 12–13.

16 Greg Bahnsen, *Presuppositional Apologetics Stated and Defended* (Powder Springs, GA: American Vision, 2008), p. 87.

17 Roy Clouser, *The Myth of Religious Neutrality* (South Bend, IN: Notre Dame University Press, 1991), pp. 1, 3, 19, 20.

18 Gary DeMar, ed., *Pushing the Antithesis—The Apologetic Methodology of Greg Bahnsen* (Powder Springs, GA: American Vision, 2007), p. 121.

19 MacArthur, p. 14.

20 Alan Cairns, "Presuppositionalism" in *Dictionary of Theological Terms,* Expanded 3rd Edition, (Greenville, SC: Ambassador International, 2002), p. 339.

21 John Frame, *The Doctrine of the Christian Life* (Phillipsburg, NJ: P&R Publishing, 2008), pp. 272, 273.

22 Pearcey, pp. 25, 95.

23 Wolters, pp. 8–9, 12.

24 Pearcey, p. 25.

25 *Biblical Worldview: Creation, Fall, Redemption,* Mark Ward, ed. (Greenville, SC: Bob Jones University Press, 2017).

26 Ken Ham, "Seven C's of History" (*Answers in Genesis,* May 20, 2004; https://answersingenesis.org/bible-history/seven-cs-of-history).

27 "Statement of Faith," *Answers in Genesis,* updated August 10, 2015, www.answersingenesis.org/about/faith. (Accessed 3/16/2019).

28 "Principles of Biblical Creationism," *The Institute of Creation Research,* http://www.icr.org/tenets. (Accessed 3/16/2019).

29 Paul Kurtz, ed., *Humanist Manifestos I and II* (Buffalo, NY: Prometheus Books, 1981), p. 15.

30 Cairns, "Enlightenment," p. 146.

31 Kurtz, *Humanist Manifesto,* p. 16.

32 Ibid, p. 15.

33 Noebel, pp. 28, 25.

34 Herbert Kohl, *From Archetype to Zeitgeist: Powerful Ideas for Powerful Thinking* (Boston: Little, Brown and Company, 1992), p. 65. Quoted by Gary DeMar in his article, "The Left Wing and Right Wing Enlightenments" (https://americanvision.org/1662/left-wing-right-wing-enlightenments/January 4, 2010). (Accessed 3/16/2019).

35 Paul Kurtz, ed., *A Secular Humanist Declaration* (Buffalo, NY: Prometheus Books, 1980), p. 24.

36 Kurtz, *A Secular Humanist Declaration,* p. 18.

37 Kurtz, *The Humanist Manifesto,* pp. 17, 18.

38 Noebel, p. 28, quoting Marx and Engels.

39 Cleon Skousen, *The Naked Communist* (Salt Lake City, UT: The Reviewer, 1961), Chapter 4, "The Communist Approach."

40 Noebel, p. 67, quoting Vladimir Lenin.

41 Skousen, p. 51, quoting Vladimir Lenin.

42 Skousen, pp. 46, 47, 49, quoting Marx and Engels.

43 Skousen, p. 56.

44 Noebel, p. 341.

45 Cairns, p. 334.

46 Noebel, p. 26.

47 Noebel, pp. 26, 27, 425.

48 Noebel, p. 425.

49 Noebel, p. 9.

50 Noebel, pp. 155, 158, quoting from *The Weekly Standard,* 2005.

51 Noebel, p. 9.

52 Noebel, p. 119, quoting a postmodernist, Richard Rorty.

53 Noebel, p. 26.

54 David Dockery, ed., *The Challenge of Postmodernism* (Wheaton, IL: Victor Books, 1995), p. 40.

55 Douglas Groothuis, *Unmasking the New Age* (Downers Grove, IL: Intervarsity Press, 1986), pp. 161, 163.

56 Ibid, pp. 18-30.

57 Ibid, pp. 22, 25.

58 Ibid, p. 30, quoting Barbara Hubbard.

59 Noebel, pp. 272, 310, quoting Kevin Ryerson.

60 Kurtz, *The Humanist Manifesto,* p. 17.

61 Thomas Sowell, *Marxism* (New York: William Morrow, 1985), p. 17.

62 D.A. Carson, *The Gagging of God: Christianity Confronts Pluralism* (Grand Rapids, MI: Zondervan, 1996), p. 78.

63 Groothuis, p. 18.

64 Robert Spencer, *The Politically Incorrect Guide to Islam and the Crusades* (Washington, D.C.: Regnery Publishing, 2005), p. 4.

65 Norman Geisler and Abdul Saleeb, *Answering Islam,* revised edition (Grand Rapids: Baker Book House, 2002), p. 11.

66 *The Holy Qur'an,* English Translation and Commentary by Allama Abdullah Yusuf Ali (Muhammad Ashraf Publishers, Lahore, Pakistan, 1979 edition), pp. 1247, 1713, 1336, 1478.

67 Robert Morey, *The Islamic Invasion* (Las Vegas, NV: Christian Scholars Press, 1992), p. 178.

68 Geisler and Saleeb, p. 83, quoting Badru Kateregga.

69 Ergun Caner and Emir Caner, *Unveiling Islam* (Grand Rapids: Kregel, 2009), pp. 122-128.

70 Ibid, pp. 161-164.

71 Ibid, pp. 164-167.

72 *Qur'an*, pp. 998, 999.

73 *Qur'an*, p. 239.

74 Geisler and Saleeb, p. 141.

75 Morey, pp. 58, 59, 60.

76 *Qur'an*, p. 446.

77 *Qur'an*, p. 283.

78 Geisler and Saleeb, *Answering Islam,* p. 169.

79 Morey, p. 187, quoting The Hadith.

80 *Qur'an*, pp. 92, 93.

81 *Qur'an*, pp. 1071, 1072.

82 Spencer, p. 107.

83 Spencer, pp. 35, 36.

84 *Qur'an*, p. 1247.

85 *Qur'an*, pp. 998, 999.

86 *Qur'an*, p. 292, comments by Ali, the translator.

87 Norman Geisler and William Nix, *A General Introduction to the Bible*, revised edition (Chicago: Moody Press, 1986), chapters 20-22.

88 Geisler and Saleeb, p. 201.

89 Caner and Caner, pp. 83, 84, 85.

90 *Qur'an*, p. 359, comments on Surah 7:54.

91 *Qur'an*, pp. 359 and pp. 1231-1233.

92 *Qur'an*, pp. 142, 758, 801.

93 Gene Gurganus, *The Peril of Islam* (Taylors, SC: Truth Publishers, 2004), p. 50.

94 *Qur'an*, p. 236.

95 *Qur'an*, pp. 1687, 1688.

96 *Qur'an*, pp. 1317, 1628.

97 *Qur'an*, p. 184.

98 *Qur'an*, p. 195.

99 Spencer, pp. 69, 70.

100 *Qur'an*, p. 192.

101 Susan Crimp and Joel Richardson, eds., *Why We Left Islam* (Los Angeles: WorldNetDaily Books, 2008), p. 24.

102 *Qur'an*, pp. 521, 971, 972, 996, 1495.

CHAPTER 2

GOD'S WORD—THE AUTHORITY FOR OUR WORLDVIEW

THE INSPIRATION OF SCRIPTURE

EXPLANATION OF THE INSPIRATION OF SCRIPTURE

We established in the first chapter that the basic presuppositions of the Christian worldview are that the God revealed in the Bible is real and that the Bible is the fully inspired and infallible Word of God. In order to think, every person must have a beginning assumption. Our beginning assumption is God as revealed in the Bible. To come to conclusions, a person must appeal to an ultimate authority. Our ultimate authority is the Bible, God's Word.

In contrast, the Humanist worldview, in *A Secular Humanist Declaration,* declares:

> Secularists deny that morality needs to be deduced from religious belief. . . . Secular Humanists . . . reject the idea that God has intervened miraculously in history. . . We do not accept as true the literal interpretation of the Old and New Testaments."[1]

In other words, Humanists specifically reject the Bible as the inspired Word of God and the authority for what we believe and how we live.

Also, the Islamic worldview appeals to the Qur'an as the word of Allah and their ultimate authority. The Qur'an claims to be the word of Allah and Muslims claim the Qur'an is his supreme revelation to man.[2] Islam does not accept all of the Bible as the inspired Word of God.

In contrast, the Bible repeatedly identifies itself as God's message to man:

> **Moses**: "And the Lord said to Moses . . . you shall speak all that I command you" (Exo. 7:1–2). **David**: "The Spirit of the Lord speaks by me; His Word is on my tongue" (2 Sam. 23:2). **Isaiah**: "Hear the word of the Lord" (Isa. 1:10). **Paul**: "You received the word of God which you heard from us" (1 Thess. 2:13).

When writing to Timothy, the apostle Paul wrote that God uses Scripture not only to bring the message of the way of salvation through faith in Christ, but also to tell us what we should believe and how we should live—"doctrine" and "instruction in righteousness."

> "And how from childhood you have been acquainted with the sacred writings, which are able to make you wise for salvation through faith in Christ Jesus. All Scripture is breathed out by God and is profitable for teaching, for reproof, for correction and for training in righteousness, that the man of God may be complete, equipped for every good work" (2 Tim. 3:15–17).

This passage is a key statement that sets forth the Bible's claim to be the fully inspired Word of God. This passage asserts that all of the Scripture is "breathed out by God" or "given by inspiration of God."[3] God inspired "all Scripture," not just part (2 Tim. 3:16).

The Bible calls the writings of the Old Testament and New Testament "Scripture" (2 Pet. 1:16–21, 3:15–16). God inspired the writing of all sixty-six books of the Old and New Testaments. God used men and their personalities to write the books of Scripture. However, He guided the men He chose to write the very words He wanted written. For example, the apostle Paul speaks of the apostles communicating "in words . . . taught by the Spirit" (1 Cor. 2:13).

Because the Bible is God's Word, it is an infallible authority for what we believe and how we live. It is without error as originally written. God guarded the writers of Scripture from error as they wrote. Jesus declared, "Scripture cannot be broken" (John 10:35) and "Your word is truth" (John 17:17). The psalmist declares, "The sum of your word is truth and every one of your righteous rules endures forever" (Psalm 119:160).

The Bible teaches that God does not lie (Tit. 1:2) and that the Bible is God's Word and truth (John 17:17). Therefore, the Bible claims to be without any mistake in what it teaches in any area. That would include doctrine, personal morals, church practice, history, science, etc.[4] What the Bible says about these matters is true because it is God's Word and is, therefore, trustworthy.

God inspired the writing of the original manuscripts of every book of Scripture in both the Old and New Testaments. God builds His Church upon the foundation of His Word that He revealed through apostles and prophets whom He chose to communicate His Word (Eph. 2:19–21). He chose men from the nation of Israel to write the original manuscripts of the books of the Old Testament in Hebrew (and a few passages in Aramaic).

The apostle Peter referred to the Old Testament prophets, calling what they wrote "the word" and "Scripture," and he taught that the prophets of the Old Testament "spoke from God as they were carried along by the Holy Spirit" (2 Pet. 1:21). Jesus also exhorted His disciples to believe everything written by the prophets, which includes all of the Old Testament Scriptures (Luke 24:25–27, 24:44).

God also chose apostles and those who labored with those apostles to write the original manuscripts of the books of the New Testament in Greek. Jesus promised the inspiration of the Holy Spirit to His apostles, who either wrote or helped to inform the writing of the books of the New Testament:

> "The Holy Spirit . . . will teach you all things and bring to your remembrance all that I have said to you" (John 14:26). "The Spirit of truth . . . will guide you into all truth . . . . He will declare to you the things that are to come" (John 16:13).

A Christian theological writer, Dr. Alan Cairns, gives a good definition of biblical inspiration in his theological dictionary:

> Inspiration is the work of God, by His Holy Spirit, communicating His word to the writers of the Bible and enabling them to write that word without error, addition, or deletion. . . . These writings are in the strictest sense God's word, and are therefore authoritative, the final rule of faith and practice . . . a book inspired and infallible in all its parts. It extends to all the expressions of Scripture, even the words.[5]

Over many centuries, Jewish scribes carefully and faithfully copied the Hebrew manuscripts of the Old Testament books and early Christians carefully and faithfully copied the Greek manuscripts of the New Testament books. Now we have more of these biblical manuscripts than any other ancient document. From these Greek and Hebrew manuscripts, scholars have translated the Bible into many languages, allowing people to have the privilege of reading the Word of God in their own language around the world.

In these Hebrew and Greek manuscripts of Scripture, God has preserved His Word.

Jesus declared, "Until heaven and earth pass away, not an iota, not a dot, will pass from the Law until all is accomplished. . . . My words will not pass away" (Matt. 5:18; 24:35). Theological writers, Norman Geisler and William Nix, make this observation:

> "There are not only countless manuscripts to support the integrity of the Bible . . . but a study of the procedures of preparation and preservation of the biblical manuscript copies reveals the fidelity of the transmission process itself. In fact, it may be concluded that no major document from antiquity comes into the modern world with such evidence of its integrity as does the Bible."[6]

CONFESSIONS OF THE INSPIRATION OF SCRIPTURE

Bible-believing Christians from a variety of church backgrounds agree that the Bible is the fully-inspired, inerrant Word of God. Dr. Stewart Custer did extensive study of the Bible's claims and historic church beliefs about the inspiration of Scripture. He concludes:

> The inerrancy of Scripture—the Scripture itself teaches it. . . .The verbal inerrancy of Scripture has been the historic faith of the church in all ages.[7]

A number of conservative Protestant churches work together to support Christian education and Christian schools. Two of the largest Christian school associations are the American Association of Christian Schools (AACS) and the Association of Christian Schools International (ACSI). Here are their statements of faith, affirming faith in the Bible as the fully inspired and infallible Word of God:

> AACS: "We believe that the Bible, both the Old and New Testaments, was verbally inspired of God, and is inerrant and is our only rule in matters of faith and practice.[8]

> ACSI: "We believe the Bible to be the inspired, the only infallible, authoritative, inerrant Word of God."[9]

One Christian homeschool group that involves Christian parents from a variety of Bible-believing churches is called "Teach Them Diligently." Their statement of faith says,

> "The Bible is God's verbally inspired Word. It is inerrant and the standard for faith and practice (2 Tim. 3:16)."[10]

Baptist church groups have historically affirmed the Divine inspiration and inerrancy of Scripture. Many Baptist groups follow the 1833 Baptist Confession, which says,

> "We believe that the Holy Bible was written by men divinely inspired and is a perfect treasure of heavenly instruction; that it has God for its author, salvation for its end and truth without any mixture of error for its matter."[11]

Bible-believing Presbyterian groups commonly use the Westminster Confession of Faith, which says about the Bible:

> "Under the name of holy Scripture, or the Word of God written, are now contained all the Books of the Old and New Testament . . . All of which are given by inspiration of God.

> . . . The Old Testament in Hebrew . . . and the New Testament in Greek . . . being immediately inspired by God and by His singular care and providence kept pure in all ages are therefore authentic; so as in all controversies of religion the Church is finally to appeal to them. . . . They are to be translated into the . . . language of every nation."[12]

The Lutheran Church Missouri Synod is a conservative Protestant denomination. Their statement of belief and practice says this about the inspiration of Scripture:

> "The Bible is God's inerrant and infallible Word, in which He reveals His Law and His Gospel of salvation in Jesus Christ. It is the sole rule and norm for Christian doctrine."[13]

The American Council of Christian Churches is a fellowship of Bible-believing conservative Protestant churches from various church backgrounds. Concerning the Bible, their statement of faith affirms:

> "We believe in the plenary divine inspiration of Scriptures in the original languages, their consequent inerrancy and infallibility, and as the Word of God the supreme and final authority in faith and life."[14]

As you can see through these examples, though they have denominational differences, conservative Protestant churches have statements of faith that confess the full inspiration and inerrancy of the Bible as the Word of God. The Bible clearly teaches its inspiration by God and Christian churches of the past and present have confessed that truth.

THE INTERPRETATION OF GOD'S INSPIRED WORD

The Bible is an inspired revelation of God to man. God intends for man to understand the revelation in His Word. The most foundational teachings in God's Word are understandable. Note what God's Word says about how clear, useful and important it is:

> "And how from childhood you have been acquainted with the sacred writings, which are able to make you wise for salvation . . . All Scripture is breathed out by God and profitable" (2 Tim. 3:15-16).

> "This commandment that I command you today is not too hard for you" (Deut. 30:11).

> "The unfolding of your words gives light; it imparts understanding to the simple" (Psalm 119:30).

> "Like newborn infants, long for the pure spiritual milk, that by it you may grow up into salvation" (1 Pet. 2:2).

> "For we did not follow cleverly devised myths. . . . And we have the prophetic word more fully confirmed, to which you do well to pay attention as to a lamp shining in a dark place" (2 Pet. 1:16, 19).

However, some matters in Scripture are more difficult than others and require more diligent study and more careful principles of interpretation. Scripture distinguishes milk level teaching for spiritual babes and solid food for believers that are more spiritually mature:

> "For everyone who lives on milk is unskilled in the word of righteousness, since he is a child. But solid food is for the mature, for those who have their powers of discernment trained by constant practice to distinguish good from evil" (Heb. 5:13, 14).

Scripture warns about some people who twist the meaning of some harder to understand portions of Scripture and harm themselves and others spiritually:

> "There are some things in them that are hard to understand, which the ignorant and unstable people twist to their own destruction, as they do the other Scriptures" (2 Pet. 3:16).

As believers study the inspired Word of God, they need to use proper principles of interpretation of Scripture, which theologians call "hermeneutics—the science of Bible interpretation."[15] A textbook on the subject makes these statements about foundational principles of sound interpretation of Scripture:

> "The divine inspiration of the Bible is the foundation of Protestant hermeneutics."[16]
>
> "Interpretations of specific passages must not contradict the total teaching of Scripture."[17]
>
> "It is the interpreter's responsibility to guard the use of Holy Scripture by the hedge of literal exegesis."[18]
>
> "Grammatical interpretation involves consideration of the context."[19]

In other words, we can say basic principles of sound interpretation of the Bible include:

1. We must approach the Bible as the inspired Word of God (2 Tim. 3:16).
2. We must interpret Scripture in harmony with other Scripture—God's Word does not contradict itself.
3. We must interpret Scripture in context, in its grammatical and historical setting.

Sound principles of interpretation of the Bible involve a literal, grammatical, and historical approach to Scripture. By literal, we mean that we should interpret words in their normal sense, unless the context dictates otherwise. By grammatical, we mean that we should interpret words in light of their contextual and grammatical usage. By historical, we mean that we should interpret a passage in light of its historical background. We will find these principles especially important in later chapters in dealing with various issues.

THE AUTHORITY OF SCRIPTURE

THE CANON OF SCRIPTURE

All of written Scripture is God's Word (2 Tim. 3:16) and as such it is useful for instruction in doctrine—what we believe—and for righteousness—how we live. All of Scripture is authoritative for our faith and practice. All of Scripture is true in what it says, even in regards to science and history. The Bible as God's Word is our ultimate authority.

The sixty-six books of Scripture constitute the authority for our worldview. The thirty-nine books of the Old Testament and the twenty-seven books of the New Testament form the complete written revelation from God. In the last chapter of the book of Revelation, God's Word warns against adding to Scripture (Rev. 22:18). The apostles in the first century have given us the Christian faith "once for all" (Jude 3).

Christian theologians commonly speak of the "canon of Scripture." Dr. Cairns, in his theological dictionary, points out that the word "canon" means "rule" and theologically refers to "the entire body of inspired Scripture, as distinct from spurious or non-inspired writings . . . to be received as authoritative in all matters of doctrine and practice."[20] The sixty-six books of the Bible are our complete, divinely inspired authority for what we believe and how we live.

Creation Ministries International, a Bible-believing ministry, has an excellent statement of faith. Concerning the Divine authority and canon of Scripture, their statement of faith says:

> "The 66 books of the Bible are the written Word of God. The Bible is divinely inspired and inerrant throughout. Its assertions are factually true in all the original autographs. It is the supreme authority, not only in all matters of faith and conduct, but in everything it teaches. Its authority is not limited to spiritual, religious or redemptive themes, but includes its assertions in such fields as history and science. The final guide to the interpretation of Scripture is Scripture itself."[21]

The Bible is the ultimate authority for our worldview. We cannot make anything else equal to or greater in authority than Scripture. That would include other religious writings, church tradition, human philosophy, man-made scientific theories, opinions of historians or opinions of secular psychotherapists. God's written Word is our ultimate authority.

How do we know which writings belong in the Bible? The key is authorship. According to Christian scholar, Dr. Laird Harris, who did extensive study on the inspiration and canonicity of Scripture, "The canonicity of a book of the Bible depends upon its authorship."[22] He notes that **the Jews viewed the Old Testament books as written by God-called prophets. And the early Christian church accepted the New Testament books because they were written by God-called apostles or prophets who labored with the apostles.**[23]

The Bible itself teaches that the church is "built on the foundation of the apostles and prophets" (Eph. 2:20). Jesus affirmed the divine authority of every word of the Old Testament, as He exhorted His followers to believe in everything spoken by the prophets (Matt. 5:17–18; Luke 24:25), equating Moses and the Prophets, as well as the Psalms, with Scripture (Luke 24:27, 24:44).

The Jews believed God gave prophetic revelation in Israel from the time of Moses through the prophet Malachi—over a period of one-thousand years.[24] Scripture teaches that the Holy Spirit inspired the message of the Old Testament prophets (2 Pet. 1:21). The Bible says that God spoke to man through His chosen prophets (Heb. 1:1).

God declared that He revealed His message to His prophets (Amos 3:7). And although we may not be certain about who wrote a few of the Old Testament books, the Jews in Bible times recognized all of the books of the Old Testament as being written by God-inspired prophets.

God entrusted the Jews with the Scriptures, and they knew which books belonged. God's Word says, "The Jews were entrusted with the oracles of God" (Rom. 3:2).

Josephus, the first century, Jewish historian, summed up the ancient Jewish view of the Old Testament canon. He referred to twenty-two books as inspired by God and accepted as Scripture. These twenty-two books equal the exact same thirty-nine books of the Old Testament which we have in our Bible today. (The Jews had combined certain books together which have been separated in our modern translations.) Josephus stated:

> We have . . . 22 books which contain the records of all the past times, which are justly believed to be divine. . . . Of these, five belong to Moses. . . .From the death of Moses to the reign of Artaxerxes . . . the prophets who were after Moses wrote what was done in their times in thirteen books. The remaining four books contain hymns to God and precepts for the conduct of human life. . . . No one has been so bold to add anything to them or take anything from them or to make any change in them, but it is become natural to all Jews . . . to esteem these books to contain divine doctrines.[25]

Moses wrote the first five books of the Old Testament (Neh. 10:29). God called Moses as a prophet and confirmed him as God's prophet by miraculous signs (Exo. 4:1–9; Deut. 34:10-11). Then after the time of Moses, God's prophets spoke in harmony with the Law God had given through Moses: "Yet the Lord warned Israel and Judah . . . 'Keep My commandments . . . in accordance with all the Law that I commanded" (2 Kings 17:13).

God called a succession of prophets in Israel from Moses through Malachi to reveal His Word (Heb. 1:1). But after Malachi, the Jews recognized that God had stopped sending prophetic revelation.[26] During the time between Malachi and Jesus, some religious books, known as the apocryphal books, were written. However, these books were not recognized by the Jews as inspired or part of Scripture, and these books do not claim to be inspired by God.[27]

God gave us the books of the Bible through Old Testament prophets and New Testament apostles and their associates. Jesus confirmed the Old Testament canon of the books of the Law and the Prophets that the Jews historically accepted (Matt. 5:17–18; Luke 24:25–27, 24:44). Jesus also guaranteed the inspiration of the writers of the New Testament:

> "The Holy Spirit . . . will teach you all things, and bring to your remembrance all that have I said to you. . . . He will guide you into all the truth" (John 14:26, 16:13).

God used the Apostles Matthew, Peter, and John to write eight of the New Testament books: the Gospel of Matthew, 1 and 2 Peter, John's Gospel, 1, 2, and 3 John, and Revelation. Also, the early church recognized the Apostle Peter as the key source for Mark's Gospel.[28]

Jesus later called Paul as an apostle (Acts 26:16–18; 1 Cor. 9:1) and revealed God's Word through him (1 Thess. 2:13; Gal. 1:11–12). Paul wrote half the books of the New Testament—the 13 epistles, Romans–Philemon. According to an early church tradition, either the Apostle Paul, or a prophetic associate of the apostles wrote Hebrews.[29]

Luke, a companion of the Apostle Paul, wrote the book of Acts. Luke wrote his Gospel account based on the eyewitness testimony of the apostles who followed Christ during His earthly ministry: "Just as those who from the beginning were eyewitnesses and ministers of the word delivered them to us . . . it seemed good . . . to write to you an orderly account" (Luke 1:2–3).

James[30] and Jude,[31] who each wrote a New Testament epistle, were the half-brothers of Jesus. Along with the apostles, they were witnesses of the risen Christ (1 Cor. 15:7). And they labored with the apostles as the church was established (Acts 1:13–14). Jesus called them to be his servants and prophets to communicate His Word (Jude 1:1; James 1:1).

God enabled those first century apostles to work miracles in confirmation of their message (2 Cor. 12:12; Heb. 2:3–4). It is a mark of knowing God to accept the teachings of these true first century apostles of Christ (1 John 4:6). The Scripture did not say there would be new apostles to follow them. So with the passing away of the first century apostles and their prophetic associates, the biblical canon closed.

Scripture warned us about people who make false apostolic claims ("false apostles"—2 Cor. 11:13). Christ specifically called and miraculously gifted twelve men to be apostles (Mark 3:14-15; Rev. 21:14), plus the apostle Paul (apostle to the Gentiles—Gal. 2:8), in the first century. In the first few centuries after the apostles, the early church rejected certain later books because they falsely claimed to be from the apostles. These books, called the Pseudepigrapha, or false writings, were not accepted as part of the biblical canon.[32]

Christian scholars, Dr. Norman Geisler and William Nix, wrote a lengthy study on the Bible. They stress the importance of authorship by the prophets and apostles for the canon:

> "If a book was written after the prophetic period, it was not considered canonical. . . . Canonical writings were by the Jews considered to be those sacred and authoritative writings from Moses to Malachi . . . The Hebrew canon was that collection of writings which, because they possessed divine inspiration and authority, were the norm or rule for the believer's faith and conduct . . . . Christ is the key to the inspiration and canonization of the Scriptures. It was He who confirmed the inspiration of the Hebrew canon of the Old Testament, and it was He who promised that the Holy Spirit would direct the apostles into all truth. The fulfillment of that promise resulted in the writing and collection of the New Testament . . . . It was necessary to have prophetic gifts in order to write canonical Scripture (Hebrews 1:1) . . . . The

> church is built upon the foundation of the apostles and prophets (Eph. 2:20) . . . It was the apostles who were given special signs (miracles) to confirm their message (Heb. 2:3–4; 2 Cor. 12:12) . . . Every New Testament book was written by an apostle or prophet. Thus each book has either apostolic authorship or apostolic teaching. And in either case it possesses apostolic authority. . . . There is good evidence that all twenty-seven books of the New Testament come from the apostles and their associates. . . . The canon is closed. . . . God used to speak through the prophets of the Old Testament, but in the "last days" He spoke through Christ (Heb. 1:1) and the apostles whom He empowered with special "signs" (miracles). But because the apostolic age ended with the death of the apostles (Acts 1:22) and because no one since apostolic times has had the "signs of a true apostle" (2 Cor. 12:12) whereby they could raise the dead (Acts 20:10–12) . . . it may be concluded that God's last day revelation is complete. . . . Athanasius (A.D. 367) . . . clearly and emphatically listed all twenty-seven New Testament books as canonical."[33]

The thirty-nine books of the Old Testament and the twenty-seven books of the New Testament constitute the completed inspired canon of Scripture. At the end of the Bible, Scripture warns against adding to Scripture (Rev. 22:18–19). The Holy Spirit indwelling Christians has led Christians through the centuries to affirm these books as inspired by the Spirit of God (1 John 2:20).

In contrast, the Humanist worldview states, "We do not accept as true the literal interpretation of the Old and New Testaments or the Koran."[34] In relation to the canon of Scripture, the Islamic worldview adds the Qur'an to the Bible and rejects the full authority of the New Testament Scriptures. Islamic scholars claim, "The Gospel spoken of by the Qur'an is not the New Testament. . . . Fragments of it survive in the canonical Gospels."[35]

Various other religious church groups also wrongly add to or take from the Biblical canon of Scripture. For example, the Mormon Church adds the Book of Mormon.[36] The Roman Catholic Church adds the apocryphal books and makes church tradition equal in authority to Scripture.[37]

The Unitarian-Universalist Church is a religious Humanist organization and rejects the inspiration and authority of the Bible in favor of human reason. A Unitarian writer states, "With us reason holds the place that is ordinarily accorded to revelation in orthodox religions. . . . In our way of life there are no infallible guides."[38]

The Humanist worldview has influenced Liberal Protestant leaders in the World Council of Churches to exalt man's thinking over Scripture and to reject the Divine inspiration and absolute authority of the canon of Scripture. The World Council of Churches published a book about the Bible which reflects the liberal theological views of their leaders. It states:

> "The authority of the Bible is not a fixed quality belonging to the Bible per se. . . . The dividing line between canonical and non-canonical writings is not a hard and fast one. . . . No text is directly applicable to any present-day dogmatic or ethical question. . . . Attention is increasingly drawn to the diversity amongst or even the contradiction between biblical writers. . . . We are not to regard the Bible primarily as a standard to which we must conform in all the questions arising in our life."[39]

This liberal approach to the canon of Scripture comes from the Humanist worldview of the Enlightenment and puts the thinking of man over the authority of the canonical Word of God. With this mindset, liberal theologians developed the historical-critical method of approaching the canon of the Bible. Bible-believing scholar, Harold Lindsell, observes:

> "It behooves us to inquire about the presuppositions of those who employ the historical-critical methodology. This methodology is not neutral. It starts with a negative assumption. It says that nothing can be accepted as the Word of God in Scripture unless it can be proven to be so. . . . I might phrase it this way: Does the Bible sit in judgment upon men or do men sit in judgment upon the Bible? . . . . If I reject a historical datum contained in the Bible, it can only mean that something outside the Bible is considered more definitive and more authoritative than the Bible."[40]

In summary, the Westminster Confession of Faith, and the London Baptist Confession which follows it, both give this statement about the canon of Scripture:

> "Under the name of holy Scripture, or the Word of God written, are now contained all the Books of the Old and New Testament, which are: (then lists the 39 books of the Old Testament and the 27 books of the New Testament) . . . All of which are given by inspiration of God, to be the rule of faith and life. The books commonly called the Apocrypha, not being of divine inspiration, are no part of the Canon of the Scripture and therefore are of no authority in the Church. . . . The authority of the holy Scripture . . . is to be received because it is the Word of God. . . . The whole counsel of God concerning all things necessary for His own glory, man's salvation, faith and life is . . . set down in Scripture . . . unto which nothing at any time is to be added, whether by new revelations of the Spirit or traditions of men."[41]

THE MORAL AUTHORITY OF SCRIPTURE

The Bible is our absolute authority for how we should live. The Bible teaches that all of Scripture is inspired by God and thus is useful for correction of how we live and instruction in right living (2 Tim. 3:16). The Bible refers to these instructions for righteousness as God's Law (Exo. 18:16; Rom. 7:7, 7:22).

God's law in the Bible contains ceremonial laws and moral laws. There are ceremonial laws in the Old Testament that the New Testament sets aside and no longer requires Christians to practice. These include matters such as circumcision (Gal. 6:15), the priesthood (Heb. 7:12), animal sacrifices (Heb. 10:11–12), Jewish feast days (Gal. 4:10–11), dietary laws (Acts 10:12–15), and cleansing rituals (Heb. 9:10, 9:14).

However, there are moral laws written in the Scripture that stem from God's nature. God declares in Scripture that He does not change (Mal. 3:6). Because God's character does not change, neither do His absolute standards of right and wrong in His moral law change. The Bible reveals these moral absolutes that are true and binding for all people, in all places, at all times. And the Christian worldview believes in these moral absolutes from God.

In contrast, the Islamic worldview appeals to the Qur'an, rather than the Bible, to determine right and wrong. And the Humanist worldview rejects God and His moral absolutes. Humanists believe that man determines right and wrong for himself—apart from God, stating:

> "We begin with humans, not God, nature not deity. . . . Moral values derive their source from human experience."[42]

God has placed these moral laws found in the Bible in the conscience of all people. "They show that the work of the law is written in their hearts, while their conscience also bears witness" (Rom. 2:15). God uses these moral laws to show all people that they are sinners: "Now we know that whatever the Law says it speaks . . . so that the whole world may be held accountable to God. . . . Through the law comes knowledge of sin" (Rom. 3:19–20).

No person can gain redemption from sin and eternal life with God by keeping God's Law. Scripture teaches that we cannot earn God's favor by keeping His law (Rom. 3:20). God's Law shows man his sin and his need of Christ as Savior (Gal. 3:24).

When God brings salvation to someone, He forgives violations of His Law and gives a heart love for His Law on the basis of Christ's redeeming work: "I will put my laws on their hearts. . . . I will remember their sins and their lawless deeds no more" (Heb. 10:16–17). As a result, believers can say with the psalmist, "Oh how I love Your law! . . . I will keep Your statutes" (Psalm 119:97, 119:145).

Jesus Christ affirmed the authority of God's moral law in the New Testament:

> "Do not think that I have come to abolish the Law or the Prophets . . . . Therefore whoever relaxes one of the least of these commandments and teaches others to do the same will be called least in the kingdom of heaven; but whoever does them and teaches them, he shall be called great in the kingdom of heaven" (Matt. 5:17, 19).

Jesus summarized God's moral laws in two commandments, to love God with our entire being (Deut. 6:5) and to love our neighbors as ourselves (Lev. 19:18):

> "You shall love the Lord your God with all your heart and with all your soul, and with all your mind. This is the great and first commandment. And a second is like it: 'You shall love your neighbor as yourself.' On these two commandments depend all the Law and the Prophets" (Matt. 22:37–40).

Jesus says these two commandments are the greatest commands in the Bible and the chief priorities of a Christian worldview. Every instruction for living in Scripture relates to them. The Ten Commandments in the Bible give a basic summary of God's moral law. The Ten Commandments all relate to the two great commandments summarized by Jesus. The first four commandments express how to love God with your whole heart (Exo. 20:3–11; Deut. 6:5) and the last six commandments tell how to love your neighbor as yourself (Exo. 20:12–17; Lev. 19:18). Here is a summary of the Ten Commandments:

1. You shall have no other gods before Me.
2. You shall not make for yourself a carved image. You shall not bow down to them nor serve them.
3. You shall not take the name of the Lord your God in vain.
4. Remember the Sabbath day to keep it holy. Six days you shall labor and do all your work, but the seventh day is the Sabbath of the Lord your God.
5. Honor your father and your mother.
6. You shall not murder.
7. You shall not commit adultery.
8. You shall not steal.
9. You shall not bear false witness against your neighbor.
10. You shall not covet anything that is your neighbor's.

Bible-believing Christians share common moral values that are rooted in the Bible. Bible-believing church groups recognize the absolute authority of God's moral law, while at the same time rejecting the idea of salvation through keeping the Law. Note these confessions of faith:

BAPTIST CONFESSION OF 1833

We believe that the Law of God is the eternal and unchangeable rule of His moral government; that it is holy, just and good; and that the inability which the Scripture ascribes to fallen men to fulfill its precepts arises entirely from their sinful nature; to deliver them from which and to restore them through a Mediator to unfeigned obedience to the holy Law is one great end of the Gospel.[43]

REFORMED EPISCOPAL ARTICLES

Although the law given from God by Moses as touching ceremonies and rites does not bind Christian men . . . yet notwithstanding, as a rule of right living, no Christian man whatsoever is free from the obedience of the Commandments which are called moral . . . . We are justified by faith only.[44]

LUTHERAN FORMULA OF CONCORD

Although they who truly believe in Christ, and are sincerely converted to God, are through Christ set free from the curse and constraint of the Law, they are not, nevertheless, on that account without Law, inasmuch as the Son of God redeemed them for the very reason that they might meditate on the Law of God day and night.[45]

METHODIST ARTICLES OF RELIGION

No Christian whatsoever is free from the obedience of the commandments which are called moral . . . We are accounted righteous before God only for the merit of our Lord and Savior Jesus Christ by faith and not for our own works.[46]

PRESBYTERIAN WESTMINSTER CONFESSION

Although true believers be not under the law as a covenant of works, to be thereby justified or condemned; yet it is of great use to them, as well as to others; in that, as a rule of life, informing them of the will of God and their duty, it directs and binds them to walk accordingly, discovering also the sinful pollution of their nature.[47]

EVIDENCE FOR THE INSPIRATION OF SCRIPTURE

THE DIVINE CHARACTER OF SCRIPTURE

How do we know that the Bible is God's Word? As an illustration, think about how you would recognize that a written note, email, or text message came from a family member or a friend. You would expect them to say the message is from him or her. You would expect the message to communicate things that they would know. And you would recognize reflections of their character and personality in the message.

The Bible—a collection of sixty-six separate books—is like that. These books, written by over forty different men over a period of 1,500 years, make up God's message to man. He signs His name, so to speak, by repeatedly claiming that what is written is the Word of God. As we saw in the preceding chapter, the Bible claims to be the Word of God. "All Scripture is breathed out by God" (2 Tim. 3:16).

The Bible contains within itself evidences of its supernatural Divine character that man can recognize. As creatures made in God's image (Gen. 1:26-27), people should recognize the voice of their Creator in the Bible. The Holy Spirit illumines the mind of believers to recognize the Bible as God's inspired Word and true (1 John 2:26-27). The Westminster and London Confessions of Faith appeal to the character of the Bible as evidence for its divine inspiration:

> "The heavenliness of the matter, the efficacy of the doctrine, the majesty of the style, the consent of all the parts, the scope of the whole (which is to give all glory to God), the full discovery it makes of the only way of man's salvation, the many other incomparable excellencies and the entire perfection thereof are arguments whereby it does abundantly evidence itself to be the Word of God."[48]

One way these confessions point to the Divine character of Scripture is by pointing to its godly content. As noted above, the confessions speak of "the heavenliness of the matter . . . the majesty of the style . . . the scope of the whole (which is to give all glory to God) . . . evidence itself to be the Word of God." The Bible's message reflects the holy character of God.

The authors communicate certain matters that they could learn only from God. Only by accepting the Bible as God's Word can we truly know with certainty man's past and future and understand man's present condition. Consistent with God as the Author, the human authors seek to bring glory to God, not men, in their writing. The style of Scripture is serious and weighty, not superficial, consistent with its Divine authorship.

Another way these confessions point to the Divine character of Scripture is by pointing to its supernatural power. As noted above, the confessions speak of "the efficacy of the doctrine . . . the full discovery it makes of the only way of man's salvation . . . whereby it does abundantly evidence itself to be the Word of God." The Gospel message of redemption is powerful in saving people and changing lives (1 Thess. 2:13).

For example, the Bible records the conversion to Christ of one of its greatest enemies, Saul of Tarsus, to Paul the apostle (Acts 9; Acts 26). God's Word sets forth Paul as an illustration of God's saving power (1 Tim. 1:16). Paul also points to the changed lives of converts as proof of the power of the Gospel (1 Cor. 6:9–11; 2 Cor. 3:2).

These confessions also appeal to "the consent of all the parts . . . and the entire perfection thereof . . . whereby it does abundantly evidence itself to the Word of God." The amazing unity and consistency of the Bible demonstrates its supernatural character as the inspired Word of God. Bible scholars have been able to show the consistency of the Bible when critics have alleged errors in the Bible. And fulfilled prophecies in the Bible demonstrate the perfection of the Bible as the inspired Word of God. We will further consider these lines of evidence.

FULFILLED PROPHECIES OF SCRIPTURE

Another important biblical evidence for the Bible's claim to be the Word of God is fulfilled prophecy. In the multivolume work defending the inspiration of the Bible, *The Fundamentals,* one of the writers declared, "The fulfilled predictions of the Bible give the clearest and most conclusive evidence that the Bible is the revelation of God."[49]

God is unique in having the ability to declare in advance what He will do in the future and to bring it to pass. God said through the prophet Isaiah:

> "I am God, and there is none like Me, declaring the end from the beginning and from ancient times things not yet done, saying, 'My counsel shall stand, and I will accomplish all my purpose" (Isa. 46:9–10).

For example, through Isaiah, God told of the future destruction of Judah by Babylon, even though Isaiah lived long before Babylon destroyed Jerusalem (Isa. 1:1). And long before King Cyrus was even born, Isaiah spoke of him by name. He prophesied that Cyrus would destroy Babylon (Isa. 45:1) and permit the rebuilding of the Temple in Jerusalem (Isa. 44:28). Historical records document the fulfillment of each of these prophecies.[50]

History records detailed fulfillments of Daniel's prophecies as well.[51] Daniel prophesied during the Babylonian and Persian empires and told about the rise of the Greek and Roman Empires centuries before their fulfillment (Dan. 7–11). History records fulfillment of his prophesies of the desecration of the Jewish Temple in the second century B.C.[52]

Though Bible-believing scholars differ in how they explain it, they make a scholarly case for the historical fulfillment of Daniel's prophecy of sixty-nine sevens of years (483 years), ending with the earthly ministry of Christ (Dan. 9:24–27). Daniel's prophecy of the 483 years gives the time for the rebuilding of Jerusalem and the Temple and the appearance of the Messiah after a decree to rebuild Jerusalem. Scripture records the rebuilding of the Temple and the city in the books of Ezra and Nehemiah and the coming of Christ in Mark chapter one within this time frame.

Philip Mauro[53] and Gleason Archer[54] make a case for a decree given to rebuild Jerusalem in 457 B.C. They note seven sevens or forty-nine years would cover the time of the rebuilding of Jerusalem and the Temple. Then 434 more years (sixty-two sevens of years) would come to around A.D. 26 or 27 during Christ's public ministry. Historical researchers have found evidence pointing to the year of Christ's birth as possibly 4–5 B.C. and the beginning of His public ministry in A.D. 26–27.[55]

John Walvoord[56] and Josh McDowell[57] argue for the decree to rebuild Jerusalem several years later in 445 B.C. They appeal to the arguments of Robert Anderson for 360-day years, evidence for the traditional year for Christ's birth with the crucifixion of Christ around A.D. 33, and the ending of sixty-nine sevens around A.D. 33 before Christ's crucifixion.

In the New Testament, Jesus Himself spoke to His disciples about how He fulfilled all of the Messianic prophecies in the Old Testament Scripture. Jesus said, "All things must be fulfilled which were written in the Law of Moses and the Prophets and the Psalms concerning Me" (Luke 24:44–45). The Bible attests to its own inspiration through fulfilled prophecies.

Professor Peter Stoner, who studied mathematical laws of probability, also studied the fulfillment of Messianic prophecies in Jesus. He concluded that the odds of one person fulfilling just eight of these prophecies are incredible. Only Jesus could have fulfilled these prophecies.

Josh McDowell, in his book *More Than a Carpenter,* notes Professor Stoner's conclusion:

> "Stoner says that by applying the science of probability to eight prophecies, 'we find that the chance that any man might have lived down to the present time and fulfilled all eight prophecies is 1 in 10 to the 17th power.'"[58]

In light of Professor Stoner's note about the incredible odds of one person fulfilling eight Messianic prophecies, consider just eight Old Testament Messianic prophecies that are documented in the New Testament as fulfilled by Jesus. No other religious book has fulfilled prophecies like the Bible. Here are texts of eight Old Testament Messianic prophecies and the New Testament texts that identify their fulfillment in Jesus.

1. The place of Christ's birth: The prophet Micah prophesied that the Messiah would be born in Bethlehem. "Bethlehem Ephrathah . . . from you shall come forth for Me one who is to be ruler in Israel" (Mic. 5:2). Jesus was born in Bethlehem (Matt. 2:1–6).
2. Christ's descent from David: The Old Testament prophesied that the Messianic King would descend from King David of Judah. "I will set up your offspring after you . . . and I will establish the throne of his kingdom forever" (2 Sam. 7:12–13). The biblical historian Luke gives the genealogical descent of Jesus from David (Luke 1:31–33, 3:23–31).

3. Timing of Christ's appearance: The Old Testament prophesied that the Messiah would come within 483 years of the decree to rebuild Jerusalem (Daniel 9:24-25). At the end of this time period, Jesus appeared and said, "The time is fulfilled" (Mark 1:14). See the prior discussion about Daniel's prophecy.
4. Christ's entry into Jerusalem: The Old Testament prophesied that the Messiah would enter Jerusalem as King, riding on a donkey. "O daughter of Jerusalem! Behold, your King is coming to you; righteous and having salvation is He, humble and mounted on a donkey" (Zech. 9:9). The New Testament documents that Jesus entered Jerusalem riding a donkey in fulfillment of this prophecy, and the people hailed Him as the promised King (Matt. 21:4–5, 9).
5. Christ's cleansing of the Temple: The Old Testament prophesied that Christ would appear at the Temple in Jerusalem and purify it. "And the Lord whom you seek will suddenly come to His temple . . . He will purify the sons of Levi" (Mal. 3:1, 3). Matthew records that Jesus cleansed the Temple (Matt. 21:12).
6. Christ's wounds, stripes, and death: The Old Testament prophesied that the Messiah would receive wounds and be killed for the sins of His people. "He was pierced for our transgressions . . . and with his wounds we are healed. . . . He was . . . stricken for the transgression of my people" (Isa. 53:5, 8). The New Testament documents that Jesus was scourged and crucified (Mark 15:15) and applies Isaiah 53 to the atoning death of Jesus (1 Pet. 2:24).
7. Christ pierced in Jerusalem: The Old Testament prophesied that the Jews would pierce the Messiah in Jerusalem. It's interesting to note that this prophecy was made long before the practice of crucifixion was brought into the land. "The inhabitants of Jerusalem . . . look on me, on him whom they have pierced" (Zech. 12:10). The New Testament applies this prophecy to the crucifixion of Jesus in Jerusalem (John 19:17–18, 19:37).
8. Christ's burial: The Old Testament prophesied that the Messiah would be buried with the rich. "And they made His grave with the wicked and with a rich man in his death" (Isa. 53:9). The New Testament documents that Jesus Christ was buried in a rich man's tomb (Matt. 27:57–60).

The apostles in the New Testament repeatedly recognized Jesus as the fulfillment of Old Testament Messianic prophecy (Matt. 1-2; John 20:31; Acts 2:22-36; 13:32-39; 28:23; Rom. 1:1-3). Jesus, as the unique Son of God and the promised Christ, recognized that He fulfilled the Old Testament Scriptures about the coming Messiah. In the New Testament Scripture we read that Jesus explained to His disciples how He fulfilled the Messianic prophecies in the Old Testament Scriptures (Luke 24:27).

THE UNITY AND CONSISTENCY OF SCRIPTURE

A key evidence for the Bible's claim to be Word of God is its amazing consistency. The Bible shows this consistency by having a unified message throughout all of its sixty-six books. That is an amazing fact, considering that many different human authors, over a period of centuries, contributed to its composition. Yet they agree in their writings about Jesus Christ as Redeemer and about His kingdom (Luke 24:25–27, 24:44–47; 1 Pet. 1:10–11).

In the early part of the twentieth century, Christian scholars, from various denominations, came together to defend the inspiration of the Bible and its essential doctrines under attack. They wrote a defense of the Bible called *The Fundamentals*. One chapter, "The Testimony of the Organic Unity of the Bible to Its Inspiration," appeals to the unity and consistency of the Bible as confirming evidence for its divine inspiration:

> "Here are some sixty or more separate documents, written by some forty different persons, scattered over wide intervals of space and time, strangers to each other. These documents are written in three different languages, in different lands . . . with marked diversities of literary style . . . and yet they all constitute one volume. All are entirely at agreement. . . . All the criticism of more than 3000 years has failed to point out one . . . irreconcilable contradiction. . . . How can this be accounted for? There is no answer which can be given unless you admit . . . God actually superintended the production of this book."[59]

The Bible presents itself as real history with eyewitness testimony (Luke 1:1–4). The events in the Bible involve careful record keeping (Gen. 5:1–32; Matt. 1:1–17), recorded under inspiration by God (2 Tim. 3:16). The writers of the Bible emphasize that they do not set forth "myths," but that they speak as "eyewitnesses" (2 Pet. 1:16). And the Bible records events in real places in Israel and surrounding nations, places that we can verify today as real.

Some people think archaeology has proved that the history of the Bible is wrong. However, Josh McDowell, a Christian apologetics writer, quotes from famous archeologists that many archaeological discoveries have supported the historical record of the Bible, and no archaeological find has disproved any statement in the Bible:

> William F. Albright: "Discovery after discovery has established the accuracy of innumerable details and has brought increased recognition to the value of the Bible as a source of history." Jewish scholar, Nelson Glueck: "It is worth emphasizing that in all this work no archaeological discovery has ever controverted a single,

properly understood biblical statement." William Ramsay: "Luke's history is unsurpassed in respect of its trustworthiness."[60]

For further defense of the historical accuracy of the Bible in relation to archaeology, note *The Archaeology Book* by David Down.[61]

Some critics try to argue that Egyptian chronology contradicts the Bible and therefore, the Bible is not historically accurate. However, fallible men, centuries later, put together what historians now refer to as Egyptian chronology. In contrast, Bible authors carefully recorded historical records from original eyewitnesses and wrote under divine inspiration. The Bible has much more manuscript evidence than other ancient documents. Scholars observe,

> The accuracy of the Old Testament text is largely the result of the meticulous care taken by rabbinical scholars in the transmission process . . . . The New Testament rests on a multitude of manuscript evidence . . . . By way of contrast, most other books from the ancient world survive in only a few and late manuscript copies.[62]

The *New Answers Book 2,* part of the Answers in Genesis "Answers Book" series, documents problems with Egyptian chronology and defends the historical accuracy of the Bible. In one chapter, Dr. Elizabeth Mitchell makes this observation from her research:

> "Traditional Egyptian chronology bases its outlines of Egyptian dynasties on Manetho's history. However, Manetho's writings are unsuitable for establishing a reliable Egyptian chronology because Manetho's history was never intended to be a chronological account of Egyptian history and is inconsistent with contemporary Egyptian sources. . . . Professor J. H. Breasted, author of a *History of Egypt,* calls Manetho's history 'a late, careless and uncritical compilation, which can be proven wrong from the contemporary monuments in the vast majority of cases where such documents have survived."[63]

The Bible is also internally consistent. It does not truly contradict itself. From his research, Josh McDowell gives advice in responding to people who claim that the Bible has contradictions:

> "When facing possible contradictions, it is important to remember that two statements can differ from one another without being contradictory. . . . Take, for example, the case of the blind men at Jericho. Matthew relates how two blind men met Jesus, while both Mark and Luke mention only one. However, neither of these statements denies the other. Rather they are complementary. . . . Sometimes two passages appear contradictory because the translation is not as accurate as it could be. A knowledge of the original languages of the Bible can immediately solve these difficulties. . . . Some difficulties in Scripture result from our inadequate knowledge about the circumstances."[64]

Believers should recognize that there are valid responses to these alleged contradictions in the Bible. We need to keep in mind that differing accounts may contain supplementary, not contradictory, information; a more accurate understanding of the original Greek and Hebrew may clear up the difficulty in some passages; and a better understanding of the historical background of the passages in question may clear up a difficulty as well.

Understanding the original language can help us clear up some alleged discrepancies in the Bible. For example, in describing Paul's encounter with Christ, some critics allege a discrepancy between Acts 9:7 and Acts 22:9 about hearing Christ's voice. The original Greek has a case system for nouns. In these two verses the Greek has different cases for the noun after the verb, which gives a different meaning. Dr. Gleason Archer explains this passage:

> In the original Greek, however, there is no real contradiction between these two statements. Greek makes a distinction between hearing a sound as a noise (in which case the verb takes the genitive case) and hearing a voice as a thought-conveying message (in which case it takes the accusative). Therefore, as we put the two statements together, we find that Paul's companions heard the Voice as a sound . . . but they did not (like Paul) hear the message that it articulated.[65]

Another alleged contradiction is in the King James Version translation of 2 Kings 8:26 and 2 Chronicles 22:2. Second Kings 8:26 says Ahaziah was twenty-two when he began to reign and 2 Chronicles 22:2 says Ahaziah was forty-two. However, there is a way to resolve this difficulty.

Dr. Gleason Archer, in his work on Bible difficulties, points out that the correct age is twenty-two. Ahaziah could not be forty-two, since 2 Kings 8:17 shows his father was forty at that time. A scribe could have easily copied the number incorrectly in later Hebrew manuscripts.[66] The book *Demolishing Supposed Bible Contradictions* documents that there are ancient texts of 2 Chronicles 22:2 that have the number 22.[67] The English Standard Version, a modern English translation, has twenty-two in 2 Chronicles 22:2.

Some critics allege contradictions involving the reigns of kings in Israel and Judah.

Dr. Edwin Thiele has written a book, *The Mysterious Numbers of the Hebrew Kings,* which shows how the dates for these reigns actually harmonize with each other and with known dates of ancient Near Eastern history.[68] He found that sometimes record keepers calculated the beginning of a king's reign when a son began co-reigning with his father and others calculated when a king started reigning by himself. Understanding this, one can harmonize the accounts.

Some people claim the Bible has a contradiction between the teachings of the apostle Paul and James about justification. Paul teaches that a person is "justified by faith apart from works" (Rom. 3:28). James writes about being "justified by works" (James 2:21, 24-25). However, when we understand the context and purpose of their statements and interpret in light of other Scripture, we will see that there is no contradiction.

It is important to note that Paul and James met in Jerusalem and Paul explained to James the Gospel message that he preached (see Gal. 1:18-19; 2:1-2, 7-9; Acts 15:1-35). James clearly agreed with the Gospel message Paul preached about salvation through faith in Christ (Acts 15:1-2, 12-29; Gal. 2:1, 7-9). It is also important to note that Paul, like James, emphasized the importance of good works as a fruit of genuine saving faith in Christ (Eph. 2:8-10; Gal. 5:19-24; Acts 26:19-24; Rom. 2:5-8 and 6:6, 17-18, 22).

When Paul teaches about being "justified by faith apart from works" (Rom. 3:28) and James speaks about being "justified by works" (James 2:21, 24-25), they are dealing with different issues. Paul is dealing with the issue of how a person initially comes into a right relationship with God and receives eternal life. Paul is defending the Gospel message against false teachers who said a person must do good works in order to receive eternal life (Romans and Galatians).

James, on the other hand, is dealing with the issue of people who give mental assent to believing in God and Christ, but who do not show fruit of good works following their profession of faith (James 2:14, 19). James emphasizes, "I will show you my faith by my works" (James 2:18). James teaches that a professed faith in Christ that does not lead to good works is dead and is not saving faith (James 2:14, 17, 26). Paul teaches we are saved through faith in Christ, not works, but also that a believer is "created in Christ Jesus for good works" (Eph. 2:10).

Both Paul and James use Abraham in the Scripture to illustrate their point, but they appeal to different times in Abraham's life. Paul appeals to Abraham's faith in God's promise in Genesis 15 and declares that Abraham was justified by faith apart from works (Rom. 4). James appeals to Abraham's obedience to God many years later as an illustration of "justification by works" (James 2:21) and he teaches that Abraham's obedience proved he was truly justified by faith in Genesis 15 (James 2:23). Hebrews 11:17 says Abraham obeyed by faith.

The word "justify" means to "declare righteous."[69] When a person puts faith in Christ for salvation from sin and eternal life with God, God justifies them, declares them righteous and gives them eternal life as a gift, not by works. After that, a person who has truly put faith in Christ for salvation will do good works that show they truly have saving faith in Christ. They are "justified by works," not in the sense of meriting eternal life, but in the sense that their good works declare that they have become righteous through faith in Christ (James 2:18, 22-23).

The Bible clearly teaches its own Divine inspiration and inerrancy and Christians have historically held to the inerrancy of Scripture. In 1978, many Christian scholars gathered together and set forth a detailed confession on the inerrancy of Scripture, called the Chicago

Statement on Biblical Inerrancy. There is a helpful website that documents this confession and that defends the inerrancy of Scripture from attack and gives answers to alleged contradictions.[70]

THE SUPERIORITY OF BIBLICAL PRESUPPOSITIONS

In the opening chapters we have set forth two foundational presuppositions of the Christian worldview: belief in the God of the Bible as the starting point for thinking, and belief in God's Word as the ultimate authority for conclusions. People who oppose the Christian worldview state an objection, saying that we are merely assuming what we need to prove first—God and His Word. However, it is not arbitrary or irrational for the Christian worldview to have these presuppositions. These presuppositions enable us to understand reality.

As we have already pointed out, every worldview has starting assumptions and an authority to which it appeals to draw conclusions. It is impossible to think without a starting point for thinking. It is impossible to draw conclusions without an authority to appeal to for our conclusions. Christian apologetic writers, Gary DeMar and Dr. Greg Bahnsen observed:

> "Presuppositions are necessary to reasoning. Every system of thought has some starting point, some standard of authority by which truth and error are evaluated."[71]

In response to the Humanist worldview, we would say that they, too, have assumptions that control their thinking. Why do they begin thinking with man and nature? Why do they appeal to man's limited thinking and experience as the ultimate authority as opposed to the Bible? What proof and what authority do they have for these assumptions?

Then in response to the Islamic worldview, we could say that they also have assumptions that control their thinking. Why do they begin thinking with Allah rather than the Triune God of the Bible? Why do they make the Qur'an their ultimate authority rather than the sixty-six books of the Bible? What proof do they have that the Qur'an is a superior revelation to the Bible?

We would say in response to both the Humanist and Islamic worldviews that starting our thinking with the God of the Bible and drawing our conclusions by the authority of God's Word gives us a firm basis for how we think and how we draw conclusions. Those assumptions enable us to make sense of the world, and they give us answers to life's most basic questions.

The Humanist worldview and Islamic worldview challenge the Christian worldview to prove that the Bible is the infallible Word of God and is superior to man's thinking and the Qur'an. There is no greater authority to which we could appeal to prove the Bible. The

Bible itself claims to be truth from God (John 17:17) and it gives evidence of its supernatural character as God's Word (1 Thess. 2:13).

We recognize the Bible to be the Word of God by its claims and its supernatural character. The Bible identifies itself as the Word of God (2 Tim. 3:16). As we have just shown, the Bible demonstrates the reality of its claim to be the Word of God by its amazing consistency and its fulfilled prophecies (Luke 24:25–27, 24:44–47; Isa. 46:9–11).

In response to the Islamic worldview, the Christian worldview argues that the Bible is superior to the Qur'an. The Qur'an does not have fulfilled prophecies like the Bible does. Also, Moses in the Old Testament and the apostles in the New Testament worked miracles by God's power that were witnessed by many people, showing that God sent them to reveal His Word (Exo. 4; Heb. 1:1–2, 2:3–4). The Qur'an records no miracles by Muhammad.

In response to the Humanist worldview, the Christian worldview would argue that the Bible as God's Word is superior to the thinking of man. The Christian worldview agrees with Humanism that man should use logic and observation. However, by using logic and observation of people, we observe that the thinking of man is finite, fallible, and capable of falsehood. Humanists have to admit from observation that this is true about how man thinks.

For example, we observe that people are finite and do not know everything. Humanists know that secular scientists have revised books or ideas because of new information they did not know before. Humanists know they are limited in knowledge. They are limited in the knowledge they have in interpreting evidence. All evidence is interpreted evidence.

We can easily see, too, that people are fallible and make mistakes. Humanists know, for instance, that people sometimes make errors in mathematical calculations. So, Humanists have to admit that they could make mistakes in interpreting evidence about the past. Also, we observe that people are capable of falsehood. Even Humanists know that people have sometimes made fraudulent claims, including some evolutionists, as we will document later.

In contrast to this, Scripture presents itself as the true and perfect Word of an all wise and true God (John 17:17; Col. 2:2–3). For something to be true, it must be internally consistent and match reality. People have claimed that there are contradictions in the Bible, but no one has proven any real contradictions. There are good answers that refute these claims. See the two volumes by Answers in Genesis, *Demolishing Supposed Bible Contradictions.*

The message of the Bible is internally consistent and the teaching of the Bible matches reality. Man and the world are just like what the Bible says. This fact gives confirmation of the truthfulness of the Bible as the Word of God. Consider what Scripture says about itself as the true Word of God:

- It is true: "Your Word is truth" (John 17:17).
- It is, in its entirety, the Word of God: "All Scripture is breathed out by God" (2 Tim. 3:16).
- God does not lie: "God never lies" (Tit. 1:2).
- God has all knowledge: "In whom are hidden all the treasures of wisdom and knowledge" (Col. 2:3).

The Bible is a superior authority as the true Word of a perfect, all knowing God, in contrast to the finite, fallible, and sometimes fraudulent ideas of man.

The Christian worldview, rooted in God's Word, provides the basis for true knowledge.

Humanists claim to know things only through the collective thinking of finite, fallible men. The Christian worldview recognizes we can know things through logic and observation and, with more certainty, through God's revelation in the Bible. Christian apologetics writers state:

> "Worldviews involve three fundamental issues: (1) metaphysics (which deals with the nature of reality), (2) epistemology (which deals with the nature of knowledge, and (3) ethics (which deals with the nature of morality). . . . Only on the basis of your Christian worldview can anyone make sense of reality, logic, and morality."[72]

The worldview revealed in the Bible provides a solid foundation for a theory of reality and ethics. The revelation of God's Word about Creation shows us that we are observing a real world, not an illusion. The revelation of God's moral law in the Bible enables us to know right and wrong with certainty, as opposed to the conflicting thinking of sinful man about right and wrong. The Humanist worldview cannot provide an objective, indisputable standard for right and wrong for all people.

Man uses logic and observation to know and understand things. The worldview revealed in the Bible provides the only sound basis for the ability of man to think logically. The Bible presents God as the source of all knowledge (Col. 2:3). He made man in His image (Gen. 1:27). And God is absolutely true, without contradiction (Tit. 1:2). All of these biblical truths together provide the basis for true and logical thinking. The Humanist worldview, rooted in evolution, cannot provide a basis for immaterial laws of logic.

CHICAGO STATEMENTS ON BIBLICAL INERRANCY AND BIBLICAL HERMENEUTICS

In 1978, around 300 conservative Protestant Bible scholars gathered in Chicago and produced the "Chicago Statement on Biblical Inerrancy." In 1982, a followup conference produced the "Chicago Statement on Biblical Hermeneutics." These statements give an outstanding articulation of historic Christian belief concerning the full inspiration and inerrancy of Scripture and proper interpretation of the Bible as the written Word of God. For further background and elaboration, see the website, http://www.defendinginerrancy.com/chicago-statements.

STATEMENT ON BIBLICAL INERRANCY

Article I. WE AFFIRM that the Holy Scriptures are to be received as the authoritative Word of God.

WE DENY that the Scriptures receive their authority from the Church, tradition, or any other human source.

Article II. WE AFFIRM that the Scriptures are the supreme written norm by which God binds the conscience, and that the authority of the Church is subordinate to that of Scripture.

WE DENY that Church creeds, councils, or declarations have authority greater than or equal to the authority of the Bible.

Article III. WE AFFIRM that the written Word in its entirety is revelation given by God.

WE DENY that the Bible is merely a witness to revelation, or only becomes revelation in encounter, or depends on the responses of men for its validity.

Article IV. WE AFFIRM that God who made mankind in His image has used language as a means of revelation.

WE DENY that human language is so limited by our creatureliness that it is rendered inadequate as a vehicle for divine revelation. We further deny that the corruption of human culture and language through sin has thwarted God's work of inspiration.

Article V. WE AFFIRM that God's revelation within the Holy Scriptures was progressive.

WE DENY that later revelation, which may fulfill earlier revelation, ever corrects or contradicts it. We further deny that any normative revelation has been given since the completion of the New Testament writings.

Article VI. WE AFFIRM that the whole of Scripture and all its parts, down to the very words of the original, were given by divine inspiration.

WE DENY that the inspiration of Scripture can rightly be affirmed of the whole without the parts, or of some parts but not the whole.

Article VII. WE AFFIRM that inspiration was the work in which God by His Spirit, through human writers, gave us His Word. The origin of Scripture is divine. The mode of divine inspiration remains largely a mystery to us.

WE DENY that inspiration can be reduced to human insight, or to heightened states of consciousness of any kind.

Article VIII. WE AFFIRM that God in His work of inspiration utilized the distinctive personalities and literary styles of the writers whom He had chosen and prepared.

WE DENY that God, in causing these writers to use the very words that He chose, overrode their personalities.

Article IX. WE AFFIRM that inspiration, though not conferring omniscience, guaranteed true and trustworthy utterance on all matters of which the Biblical authors were moved to speak and write.

WE DENY that the finitude or fallenness of these writers, by necessity or otherwise, introduced distortion or falsehood into God's Word.

Article X. WE AFFIRM that inspiration, strictly speaking, applies only to the autographic text of Scripture, which in the providence of God can be ascertained from available manuscripts with great accuracy. We further affirm that copies and translations of Scripture are the Word of God to the extent that they faithfully represent the original.

WE DENY that any essential element of the Christian faith is affected by the absence of the autographs. We further deny that this absence renders the assertion of Biblical inerrancy invalid or irrelevant.

Article XI. WE AFFIRM that Scripture, having been given by divine inspiration, is infallible, so that, far from misleading us, it is true and reliable in all the matters it addresses.

WE DENY that it is possible for the Bible to be at the same time infallible and errant in its assertions. Infallibility and inerrancy may be distinguished, but not separated.

Article XII. WE AFFIRM that Scripture in its entirety is inerrant, being free from all falsehood, fraud, or deceit.

WE DENY that Biblical infallibility and inerrancy are limited to spiritual, religious, or redemptive themes, exclusive of assertions in the fields of history and science. We further deny that scientific hypotheses about earth history may properly be used to overturn the teaching of Scripture on creation and the flood.

Article XIII. WE AFFIRM the propriety of using inerrancy as a theological term with reference to the complete truthfulness of Scripture.

WE DENY that it is proper to evaluate Scripture according to standards of truth and error that are alien to its usage or purpose. We further deny that inerrancy is negated by Biblical phenomena such as a lack of modern technical precision, irregularities of grammar or spelling, observational descriptions of nature, the reporting of falsehoods, the use of hyperbole and round numbers, the topical arrangement of material, variant selections of material in parallel accounts, or the use of free citations.

Article XIV. WE AFFIRM the unity and internal consistency of Scripture.

WE DENY that alleged errors and discrepancies that have not yet been resolved vitiate the truth claims of the Bible.

Article XV. WE AFFIRM that the doctrine of inerrancy is grounded in the teaching of the Bible about inspiration.

WE DENY that Jesus' teaching about Scripture may be dismissed by appeals to accommodation or to any natural limitation of His humanity.

Article XVI. WE AFFIRM that the doctrine of inerrancy has been integral to the Church's faith throughout its history.

WE DENY that inerrancy is a doctrine invented by scholastic Protestantism, or is a reactionary position postulated in response to negative higher criticism.

Article XVII. WE AFFIRM that the Holy Spirit bears witness to the Scriptures, assuring believers of the truthfulness of God's written Word.

WE DENY that this witness of the Holy Spirit operates in isolation from or against Scripture.

Article XVIII. WE AFFIRM that the text of Scripture is to be interpreted by grammatico-historical exegesis, taking account of its literary forms and devices, and that Scripture is to interpret Scripture.

WE DENY the legitimacy of any treatment of the text or quest for sources lying behind it that leads to relativizing, dehistoricizing, or discounting its teaching, or rejecting its claims to authorship.

Article XIX. WE AFFIRM that a confession of the full authority, infallibility, and inerrancy of Scripture is vital to a sound understanding of the whole of the Christian faith. We further affirm that such confession should lead to increasing conformity to the image of Christ.

WE DENY that such confession is necessary for salvation. However, we further deny that inerrancy can be rejected without grave consequences, both to the individual and to the Church.

STATEMENT ON BIBLICAL HERMENEUTICS

Article I. WE AFFIRM that the normative authority of Holy Scripture is the authority of God Himself, and is attested by Jesus Christ, the Lord of the Church.

WE DENY the legitimacy of separating the authority of Christ from the authority of Scripture, or of opposing the one to the other.

Article II. WE AFFIRM that as Christ is God and Man in one Person, so Scripture is, indivisibly, God's Word in human language.

WE DENY that the humble, human form of Scripture entails errancy any more than the humanity of Christ, even in His humiliation, entails sin.

Article III. WE AFFIRM that the Person and work of Jesus Christ are the central focus of the entire Bible.

WE DENY that any method of interpretation which rejects or obscures the Christ-centeredness of Scripture is correct.

Article IV. WE AFFIRM that the Holy Spirit who inspired Scripture acts through it today to work faith in its message.

WE DENY that the Holy Spirit ever teaches to anyone anything which is contrary to the teaching of Scripture.

Article V. WE AFFIRM that the Holy Spirit enables believers to appropriate and apply Scripture to their lives.

WE DENY that the natural man is able to discern spiritually the biblical message apart from the Holy Spirit.

Article VI. WE AFFIRM that the Bible expresses God's truth in propositional statements, and we declare that biblical truth is both objective and absolute. We further affirm that a statement is true if it represents matters as they actually are, but is an error if it misrepresents the facts.

WE DENY that, while Scripture is able to make us wise unto salvation, biblical truth should be defined in terms of this function. We further deny that error should be defined as that which willfully deceives.

Article VII. WE AFFIRM that the meaning expressed in each biblical text is single, definite and fixed.

WE DENY that the recognition of this single meaning eliminates the variety of its application.

Article VIII. WE AFFIRM that the Bible contains teachings and mandates which apply to all cultural and situational contexts and other mandates which the Bible itself shows apply only to particular situations.

WE DENY that the distinction between the universal and particular mandates of Scripture can be determined by cultural and situational factors. We further deny that universal mandates may ever be treated as culturally or situationally relative.

Article IX. WE AFFIRM that the term hermeneutics, which historically signified the rules of exegesis, may properly be extended to cover all that is involved in the process of perceiving what the biblical revelation means and how it bears on our lives.

WE DENY that the message of Scripture derives from, or is dictated by, the interpreter's understanding. Thus we deny that the "horizons" of the biblical writer and the interpreter may rightly "fuse" in such a way that what the text communicates to the interpreter is not ultimately controlled by the expressed meaning of the Scripture.

Article X. WE AFFIRM that Scripture communicates God's truth to us verbally through a wide variety of literary forms.

WE DENY that any of the limits of human language render Scripture inadequate to convey God's message.

Article XI. WE AFFIRM that translations of the text of Scripture can communicate knowledge of God across all temporal and cultural boundaries.

WE DENY that the meaning of biblical texts is so tied to the culture out of which they came that understanding of the same meaning in other cultures is impossible.

Article XII. WE AFFIRM that in the task of translating the Bible and teaching it in the context of each culture, only those functional equivalents which are faithful to the content of biblical teaching should be employed.

WE DENY the legitimacy of methods which either are insensitive to the demands of cross-cultural communication or 'distort biblical meaning in the process.

Article XIII. WE AFFIRM that awareness of the literary categories, formal and stylistic, of the various parts of Scripture is essential for proper exegesis, and hence we value genre criticism as one of the many disciplines of biblical study.

WE DENY that generic categories which negate historicity may rightly be imposed on biblical narratives which present themselves as factual.

Article XIV. WE AFFIRM that the biblical record of events, discourses and sayings, though presented in a variety of appropriate literary forms, corresponds to historical fact.

WE DENY that any event, discourse or saying reported in Scripture was invented by the biblical writers or by the traditions they incorporated.

Article XV. WE AFFIRM the necessity of interpreting the Bible according to its literal, or normal, sense. The literal sense is the grammatical-historical sense, that is, the meaning which the writer expressed. Interpretation according to the literal sense will take account of all figures of speech and literary forms found in the text.

WE DENY the legitimacy of any approach to Scripture that attributes to it meaning which the literal sense does not support.

Article XVI. WE AFFIRM that legitimate critical techniques should be used in determining the canonical text and its meaning.

WE DENY the legitimacy of allowing any method of biblical criticism to question the truth or integrity of the writer's expressed meaning, or of any other scriptural teaching.

Article XVII. WE AFFIRM the unity, harmony and consistency of Scripture and declare that it is its own best interpreter.

WE DENY that Scripture may be interpreted in such a way as to suggest that one passage corrects or militates against another. WE DENY that later writers of Scripture misinterpreted earlier passages of Scripture when quoting from or referring to them.

Article XVIII. WE AFFIRM that the Bible's own interpretation of itself is always correct, never deviating from, but rather elucidating, the single meaning of the inspired text. The single meaning of a prophet's words includes, but is not restricted to, the understanding of those words by the prophet and necessarily involves the intention of God evidenced in the fulfillment of those words.

WE DENY that the writers of Scripture always understood the full implications of their own words.

Article XIX. WE AFFIRM that any preunderstandings which the interpreter brings to Scripture should be in harmony with scriptural teaching and subject to correction by it.

WE DENY that Scripture should be required to fit alien preunderstandings, inconsistent with itself; such as naturalism, evolutionism, scientism, secular humanism, and relativism.

Article XX. WE AFFIRM that since God is the author of all truth, all truths, biblical and extrabiblical, are consistent and cohere, and that the Bible speaks truth when it touches on matters pertaining to nature, history, or anything else. We further affirm that in some cases extrabiblical data have value for clarifying what Scripture teaches, and for prompting correction of faulty interpretations.

WE DENY that extrabiblical views ever disprove the teaching of Scripture or hold priority over it.

Article XXI. WE AFFIRM the harmony of special with general revelation and therefore of biblical teaching with the facts of nature.

WE DENY that any genuine scientific facts are inconsistent with the true meaning of any passage of Scripture.

Article XXII. WE AFFIRM that Genesis 1-11 is factual, as is the rest of the book.

WE DENY that the teachings of Genesis 1-11 are mythical and that scientific hypotheses about earth history or the origin of humanity may be invoked to overthrow what Scripture teaches about creation.

Article XXIII. WE AFFIRM the clarity of Scripture and specifically of its message about salvation from sin.

WE DENY that all passages of Scripture are equally clear or have equal bearing on the message of redemption.

Article XXIV. WE AFFIRM that a person is not dependent for understanding of Scripture on the expertise of biblical scholars.

WE DENY that a person should ignore the fruits of the technical study of Scripture by biblical scholars.

Article XXV. WE AFFIRM that the only type of preaching which sufficiently conveys the divine revelation and its proper application to life is that which faithfully expounds the text of Scripture as the Word of God.

WE DENY that the preacher has any message from God apart from the text of Scripture.

CHAPTER 2 STUDY GUIDE
GOD'S WORD—THE AUTHORITY FOR OUR WORLDVIEW

KEY SCRIPTURE PASSAGES TO READ:

2 Timothy 3:15-17; Exodus 7:1-2; 2 Samuel 23:2; Isaiah 1:10; 1 Thessalonians 2:13; Psalm 19:7-11; Psalm 119:11, 97-98, 105, 127-130, 160; Isaiah 46:9-10; Matthew 4:4; Matthew 5:17-19; Matthew 24:35; Luke 24:25-27 and 44; John 10:35; John 14:26; John 16:13; John 17:17; Ephesians 2:19-21; Hebrews 1:1-2 and 4:12; James 1:21; 1 Peter 1:10-12; 2 Peter 1:16-21; Revelation 22:18-19

KEY POINTS TO NOTE (NOTE BOLD TYPE):

What is a key passage in the Bible teaching that all of the Bible is the inspired Word of God?

____

How do we know what books belong in the Bible?

____

____

Who qualified to write the books of Scripture?

____

How many books make up the canon of Scripture?

____

What are 4 key lines of evidence for the Divine inspiration of Scripture?

____

____

____

____

CRITICAL THINKING:

What are the differing positions of the Christian worldview, the Humanist worldview and the Islamic worldview concerning the inspiration and authority of the Bible and the inspiration and authority of the Qur'an?

How would you answer a skeptic who says that he or she do not believe the Bible and who asks you why you believe the Bible is the fully inspired Word of God?

What is the Christian worldview position concerning moral absolutes? What does the Bible teach about the Law in relation to salvation and in relation to moral authority for how man should live?

How is the Christian presupposition of the authority of the Bible as God's Word superior to the presuppositions of the Humanist and Islamic worldviews?

CHAPTER 2 ENDNOTES

1 Paul Kurtz, ed., *A Secular Humanist Declaration* (Buffalo, NY: Prometheus Books, 1980), pp. 15, 18.

2 *The Holy Qur'an: Arabic Text,* English Translation and Commentary (Translation and commentary by Allama Abdullah Yusuf Ali; Muhammad Ashraf Publishers, Lahore, Pakistan, 1979 edition), pp. 1247.

3 Homer Kent, Jr., *The Pastoral Epistles* (Chicago: Moody Press, 1958), p. 290.

4 Edward Young, *Thy Word is Truth* (Grand Rapids: Eerdmans Publishing Company, 1957).

5 Alan Cairns, "Inspiration," in *Dictionary of Theological Terms,* expanded 3rd edition (Greenville, SC: Ambassador International, 2002), p. 237.

6 Norman Geisler and William Nix, *A General Introduction to the Bible,* revised and expanded edition (Chicago: Moody Press, 1986), p. 355.

7 Stewart Custer, *Does Inspiration Demand Inerrancy?* (Nutley, NJ: Craig Press, 1968), pp. 86, 63.

8 Statement of faith, American Association of Christian Schools and American Association of Christian Colleges and Seminaries, http://www.aacs.org/about-us/membership/statement-of-faith. (Accessed 3/16/2019).

9 Statement of faith, Association of Christian Schools International, (https://www.acsi.org/membership/acsi-overview/statement-of-faith-and-history). (Accessed 3/16/2019).

10 Statement of faith, Teach Them Diligently, http://teachthemdiligently.net/about/statement-of-faith). (Accessed 3/16/2019).

11 Philip Schaff, ed., Article I, "Of the Holy Scriptures," in The New Hampshire Baptist Confession of 1833, *Creeds of Christendom,* vol. 3, Evangelical Protestant Creeds (Grand Rapids: Baker Book House, 1985 reprint), p. 742.

12 Philip Schaff, ed., "Westminster Confession of Faith," *Creeds of Christendom,* vol. 3, Evangelical Protestant Creeds (Grand Rapids: Baker Book House, 1985 reprint), pp. 604, 605.

13 Lutheran Church Missouri Synod, Statement of faith about Scripture, http://www.lcms.org/belief-and-practice. (Accessed 3/16/2019).

14 "Doctrinal Statement," the American Council of Christian Churches, https://accc4truth.org/about-2/doctrinal-statement/ (Accessed 3/16/2019).

15 Cairns, "Hermeneutics," p. 207.

16 Bernard Ramm, *Protestant Biblical Interpretation,* 3rd revised edition (Grand Rapids, MI: Baker Book House, 1970), p. 93.

17 Ibid, p. 107.

18 Ibid, p. 125.

19 Ibid, p. 138.

20 Cairns, "Canon," p. 76.

21 "What We Believe," Creation Ministries International, https://creation.com/about-us#what_we_believe. (Accessed 3/16/2019).

22 R. Laird Harris, *Inspiration and Canonicity of the Scriptures* (Grand Rapids: Zondervan Publishing House, 1995), p. 285.

23 Ibid, chapters 7–15.

24 Dr. James White, "Has God Said—Is the Apocrypha Scripture?" (Phoenix, AZ: Alpha & Omega Ministries, 2009 DVD).

25 Harris, p. 134.

26 Harris, p. 166.

27 Harris, chapter 9.

28 Harris, p. 251.

29 Homer Kent, Jr., *The Epistle to the Hebrews* (Grand Rapids: Baker Book House, 1972), pp. 17–22.

30 John MacArthur, *James* (Chicago: Moody Press, 1998), pp. 3–5.

31 John MacArthur, *2 Peter/Jude* (Chicago: Moody Press, 2005), pp. 141–142.

32 Geisler and Nix, *A General Introduction to the Bible,* chapter 17, "The New Testament Apocrypha and Pseudepigrapha."

33 Geisler and Nix, pp. 206, 207, 212, 213, 217, 293.

34 Kurtz, ed., *A Secular Humanist Declaration,* p. 18.

35 *Qur'an,* p. 292.

36 John Gerstner, *The Theology of the Major Sects* (Grand Rapids: Baker Book House, 1960), p. 51.

37 Philip Schaff, ed., "The Canons and Decrees of the Council of Trent," *The Creeds of Christendom,* vol. 2, (Grand Rapids: Baker Book House, 1985 reprint), pp. 79–82.

38 Jack Mendelson, *Why I Am a Unitarian-Universalist* (New York: Thomas Nelson and Sons, 1965), p. 37.

39 Ellen Flesseman-van Leer, *The Bible: Its Authority and Interpretation in the Ecumenical Movement* (Geneva: The World Council of Churches, 1980), pp. 6–7, 11, 40, 56.

40 Harold Lindsell, *The Bible in The Balance* (Grand Rapids: Zondervan, 1979), pp. 283-284.

41 Schaff, "The Westminster Confession of Faith," *Creeds of Christendom*, vol. 3, pp. 601-603.

42 Paul Kurtz, ed., *Humanist Manifestos I and II* (Buffalo, NY: Prometheus Books, 1973), pp. 16-17.

43 Schaff, *Creeds of Christendom*, vol. 3, p. 746.

44 Schaff, *Creeds of Christendom*, vol. 3, pp. 816, 818.

45 Schaff, *Creeds of Christendom*, vol. 3, p. 131.

46 Schaff, *Creeds of Christendom*, vol. 3, pp. 808-809.

47 Schaff, *Creeds of Christendom*, vol. 3, pp. 641, 642.

48 Schaff, *Creeds of Christendom*, vol. 3, p. 603.

49 R. A. Torrey and A. C. Dixon, editors, "Fulfilled Prophecy a Potent Argument for the Bible," *The Fundamentals*, volume 2 (Grand Rapids: Baker Book House, 1980 reprint), p. 113.

50 Bill Wilson, *The Best of Josh McDowell: A Ready Defense* (Nashville, TN: Thomas Nelson Publishers, 1993), pp. 56-57.

51 Gleason Archer, *A Survey of Old Testament Introduction*, revised edition (Chicago: Moody Press, 1994), chapters 28 and 29.

52 John Walvoord, Daniel: *The Key to Prophetic Revelation* (Chicago: Moody Press, 1971), pp. 184–190.

53 Philip Mauro, *The Seventy Weeks and the Great Tribulation*, revised edition (Sterling, VA, Grace Abounding Ministries), chapters 1–5.

54 Gleason Archer, *Encyclopedia of Bible Difficulties* (Grand Rapids, MI: Zondervan, 1982), pp. 289–292.

55 Philip Volmer, *The Modern Student's Life of Christ* (Old Tappan, NJ: Fleming H. Revell Company, 1912), pp. 45-49.

56 Walvoord, Daniel: *The Key to Prophetic Revelation*, pp. 223–231.

57 Josh McDowell and Bill Wilson, *The Best of Josh McDowell: A Ready Defense* (Nashville, TN: Thomas Nelson Publishers, 1992), pp. 57-59.

58 Josh McDowell, *More than a Carpenter* (Tyndale House Publishers, 2009), pp. 148-149.

59 R. A. Torrey and A. C. Dixon, editors, *The Fundamentals,* volume 2 (Grand Rapids, MI: Baker Book House, 1980 reprint), pp. 97-98.

60 McDowell, *The Best of Josh McDowell,* pp. 92-93, 109.

61 David Down, *The Archaeology Book* (Green Forest, AR: Master Books, 2010).

62 Geisler and Nix, p. 385.

63 Dr. Elizabeth Mitchell, "Doesn't Egyptian Chronology Prove that the Bible is Unreliable?" Chapter 24 in *The New Answers Book 2,* (Green Forest, AZ: Master Books, 2008).

64 *The Best of Josh McDowell,* pp. 127-128.

65 Archer, *Encyclopedia of Bible Difficulties,* p. 382.

66 Archer, *Encyclopedia of Bible Difficulties,* pp. 206-207.

67 *Answers in Genesis, Demolishing Supposed Bible Contradictions, Volume 1* (Master Books, 2010), pp. 69-74.

68 Edwin Thiele, *The Mysterious Numbers of the Hebrew Kings,* new revised edition (Grand Rapids: Kregel Publications, 1994).

69 Cairns, "Justification," p. 244.

70 Chicago Statement on Inerrancy, http://defendinginerrancy.com/chicago-statements, 1978. (Accessed 3/16/2019).

71 Gary DeMar, ed., *Pushing the Antithesis: The Apologetic Methodology of Greg Bahnsen* (Powder Springs, GA: American Vision, 2007), p. 121.

72 DeMar, *Pushing the Antithesis,* pp. 111, 104.

CHAPTER 3

GOD'S PERSON—THE STARTING POINT FOR WORLDVIEW THINKING

THE CASE FOR GOD AS CREATOR

GOD AS THE BEGINNING OF KNOWLEDGE

Greg Bahnsen, a Christian apologetics writer, notes,

> "Every system must have some unproven assumptions, a starting point not antecedently established, with which reasoning begins and according to which it proceeds to conclusions. Therefore, all argumentation over ultimate issues of truth and reality will come down to authorities, which in the nature of the case are ultimate authorities."[1]

God's Word teaches us to begin our thinking with God. Scripture says, "The fear of the Lord is the beginning of knowledge" (Prov. 1:7). A right attitude (fear) towards the God revealed in the Bible (the Lord) is the starting point (beginning) of understanding life and the world (knowledge). A commentator on Proverbs makes this observation:

> This [Proverbs 1:7] is the motto of the Wisdom writings in general. . . . "The beginning," i.e. the first and controlling principle . . . is . . . a worshipping submission (fear) to the God of the covenant, who has revealed Himself by name (the Lord, i.e. Yahweh, Exodus 3:13–15).[2]

The Christian worldview begins its thinking with God. In contrast, the Humanist worldview rejects the God revealed in the Bible and begins its thinking with man. Humanists state, "As non-theists we begin with humans, not God.[3] Also, the Islamic worldview does not describe the nature of God in the same way as the Bible.

But it is not just the concept of God that is the foundation for knowledge. The God of the Bible, the Lord Himself, is the beginning of knowledge (Prov. 1:7). "Lord" is the special name of the God described in the Bible (Exo. 3:13–15). Scripture clearly teaches that there is only one true God, the Lord, the God revealed to us in the Bible: "I am the Lord, and there is no other; besides Me there is no God" (Isa. 45:5).

Historically, non-Christian religions have held to polytheistic or pantheistic views of God. Polytheism is the idea that there are many gods.[4] Pantheism identifies "god" with nature and makes everything part of "god."[5] New Age Humanism embraces pantheism, while other varieties of Humanism tend to be atheistic or agnostic. The Humanist Manifesto says,

> "As non-theists, we begin with . . . nature not deity. No deity will save us, we must save ourselves."[6]

In contrast to pantheism, the Bible presents God as a real and personal God, distinct from creation. In contrast to polytheism, Scripture sets forth the God of the Bible as the one and only true God. God specifically distinguishes Himself in His Word uniquely as our Creator and our Redeemer, the only true God:

> "Before me no god was formed, nor shall there be any after me. I, I am the Lord, and besides me there is no savior" (Isa. 43:10-11).

> "Thus says the Lord, your Redeemer, who formed you from the womb, 'I am the Lord who made all things" (Isa. 44:24).

> "For thus says the Lord, who created the heavens (he is God!), who formed the earth and made it. . . I am the Lord, and there is no other. . . . And there is no other god besides me, a righteous God and a Savior; there is none besides me" (Isa. 45:18, 21).

The Christian worldview begins thinking with the God revealed in the Bible. The Bible does not set out to formally prove the existence of God. Scripture presupposes the existence of God as Creator from its very first verse (Gen. 1:1). God's existence as Creator is foundational to the rest of the Bible and foundational to our understanding of the world and life.

Humanists would say that the Christian worldview makes an arbitrary faith assumption by presupposing God as Creator. They would argue that no one observed God creating everything and that we do not see or hear God in our world. It is true that faith in God as Creator is a faith assumption:

> "By faith we understand that the universe was created by the word of God, so that what is seen was not made out of things that are visible" (Heb. 11:3).

Because we do not see or hear God, we must approach Him in faith, which God requires:

> "Now faith is the assurance of things hoped for, the conviction of things not seen . . . And without faith it is impossible to please him, for whoever would draw near to God must believe that He exists and that He rewards those who seek Him" (Heb. 11:1, 6).

However, presupposing God is not an arbitrary or irrational presupposition. God's Word explains that we do not see God because God is a Spirit (John 4:24) and no one is able to physically see Him as a Spirit (1 Tim. 6:16). But beginning our thinking with God enables us to have true knowledge and is the foundation of knowledge. Dr. Cairns gives some helpful comments in his theological dictionary about this foundational presupposition of the Christian worldview. About presupposing God's existence, he states:

> "Man cannot think of anything aright apart from God His Creator. All unbelief proceeds, therefore, on the willful and sinful suppression of man's innate knowledge of God (Rom. 1:19–20). To presuppose God is not to make an unverifiable assumption. Nor is it to accept His existence as a working hypothesis. Rather it is to recognize that our creaturehood demands that we recognize our Creator . . . The God of the Bible is the absolute, eternal, ontological Trinity, who has revealed Himself in His Word, the Bible. . . . The God of the Bible is necessary to the existence of all the facts of the universe."[7]

Also, Dr. Jason Lisle, a scientist and defender of biblical creation, has written a book on Christian apologetics. In his book, he emphasizes that the truth of God as Creator and the worldview God reveals in His Word, the Bible, gives the foundation for knowledge. Dr. Lisle makes this important observation:

> "A consistent Christian believes that the Bible is true, God exists, there are laws of logic, there is uniformity in nature, there is an absolute and binding moral code, and our sense and memory are basically reliable. . . . The Christian's presuppositions form a rational consistent worldview in which knowledge is possible."[8]

Humanists have their own faith assumptions. Humanists assume the heavens, earth, animals and man originated through a long process of evolution. However, no man observed the origin of the heavens, earth, animals or man and no man has observed evolution taking place. Humanists begin their thinking with man and nature, not God. But what authority do they have for their assumption of beginning thinking with man and nature and leaving God out?

Faith in God as Creator is not a blind assumption without any evidence. The Christian worldview asserts that God has revealed Himself to man. God has revealed Himself to man through His Word, the Bible (2 Tim. 3:16). God has also revealed Himself to man through His work of Creation (Romans 1:18-20). Consider the evidence of God's revelation to man through His Word and through His creative work.

THE CASE FOR GOD AS CREATOR FROM SPECIAL REVELATION

Two basic presuppositions of the Christian worldview are that God exists and that God has revealed Himself to man. These two basic presuppositions enable us to have true knowledge about man, his life and his world. Man knows of the existence of God as Creator through God's revelation to man. God has revealed Himself to man through what theologians call

"general revelation" and "special revelation." In his theological dictionary, Dr. Cairns gives a helpful explanation of these theological terms:

> "The study of revelation must include 'general' or 'natural' revelation and 'special revelation.' . . . God has revealed Himself in His works of creation, hence the term 'natural' revelation. This revelation of God in nature is accessible to all mankind without distinction, hence the term 'general' revelation. The Scriptures speak of this revelation (Acts 14:17; Romans 1:20; Psalm 19:1). . . . Since general revelation has no reference to redemption, special revelation is necessary if God is to convey any message of grace to fallen men. Special revelation is the revelation by God of His redemptive purpose. . . . It is inspired and infallible, comprising all the Scriptures of the Old and New Testaments (2 Timothy 3:16; 2 Peter 1:20, 21). God's special revelation is identified with the Bible as His written word."[9]

In summary, God has revealed Himself to man through the general revelation of Creation and through His special revelation, the Bible as the Word of God. Man can know the reality of God as Creator through the testimony of what God has made in Creation and through God's testimony of His Person and works in His Word. We will consider first the case for God as Creator from the testimony of the Bible, God's special revelation.

Humanists assume that man only knows things through what he sees and hears and logically reflects upon. However, how do Humanists know man can only know things through human learning and observation? How do they know that God has not revealed Himself through His written Word, the Bible? By rejecting God's revelation in the Bible, Humanists must make huge faith conjectures about the origins of man and his world, because no man was present to observe. How can man know that his finite and fallible conjectures about origins are correct?

God has not chosen to reveal Himself directly to the sight and hearing of each person. Rather than visibly appearing and audibly speaking to every person, **God has chosen to reveal Himself to man through His completed written word (2 Tim. 3:16).** Also, according to the Bible, God has chosen to reveal Himself through amazing design in Creation (Rom. 1:19-21). Through God's revelation in the Bible, man can find answers to worldview questions and find the truth about human origins.

However, according to the Bible, God has revealed Himself in the past to the sight and hearing of the first man and woman, Adam and Eve, and God recorded this testimony in His written Word, the Bible (Gen. 1-3). Biblical theologians believe this was an appearance of the pre-incarnate Jesus, Son of God, who is described in the Bible as Creator (John 1:3). The Bible also says that God revealed Himself to the sight and hearing of people in Israel long ago through the incarnation and life of Jesus Christ, recorded in the Bible:

"In the beginning was the Word and the Word was with God and the Word was God. . . . All things were made through him. . . . He was in the world and the world was made through Him. . . . And the Word became flesh and dwelt among us and we have seen his glory, glory as of the only Son of the Father, full of grace and truth" (John 1:1, 3, 10, 14).

Humanists believe in the existence of many people whom they have never seen with their eyes or heard with their ears. They believe in the existence of those people because of recorded historical testimony of people who observed those individuals. The Bible gives recorded testimony of eyewitnesses to the revelation of God to man. Note the eyewitness testimony of Christ's apostle, John, to Jesus as God in the flesh:

"Now Jesus did many other signs in the presence of the disciples which are not written in this book, but these are written that you may believe that Jesus is the Christ, the Son of God" (John 20:30, 31). "That which was from the beginning, which we have heard, which we have seen with our eyes, which we looked upon and have touched with our hands concerning the word of life" (1 John 1:1).

The Bible traces each generation of the human race from Jesus, the God-Man, back to the first man, Adam (Luke 3:23-38). The first man and woman, Adam and Eve, were eyewitnesses to the revelation of God the Creator (Gen. 1-3). God talked to them. The beginning presuppositions of the first man and woman were that God the Creator exists and has revealed Himself to man. Those facts were as real to them as their own existence. God gave revelation to Adam about God's creation of man, the world and the universe (Gen. 1-2).

Dr. Henry Morris, a biblical creationist and a scientist, wrote a commentary on Genesis. He sets forth a very plausible conclusion that Adam and his descendants wrote down the account that God revealed about His work of creation and the first generations of man. Then Moses, under inspiration by God, compiled these patriarchal records and added information given by God into the book of Genesis. Dr. Morris states:

"It is suggested in this commentary, therefore, that Moses compiled and edited earlier written records that had been handed down from father to son via the line of the patriarchs listed in Genesis. That is, Adam, Noah, Shem, Terah, and others each wrote down an individual account of events which had occurred in his own lifetime, or concerning which he in some way had direct knowledge. These records were kept, possibly on tablets of stone, in such a way that they would be preserved until they finally came into Moses' possession. He then selected those that were relevant to his own purpose (as guided by the Holy Spirit), added his own explanatory editorial comments and transitional sections and finally compiled them into the form now known as the Book of Genesis. It is probable that these original documents can still be recognized by the key phrase, 'these are

> the generations of.' The word 'generation' is a translation of the Hebrew toledoth and it means essentially 'origins,' or, by extension, 'records of the origins.' There are eleven of these divisions marked off in Genesis."[10]

No man was present to observe the creation of the universe and the world and the first man. God the Creator was present and He has revealed to man about His work of Creation. God gave revelation about creation to the first man, Adam. Moses testified that God the Creator revealed Himself to him (Exo. 3) and God enabled Moses to work miraculous signs as confirmation of God's revelation through him (Deut. 34:10-12). God used Moses to give us the divinely inspired book of Genesis (Luke 24:27, 44), with its revelation of God as Creator.

In chapter 2, we set forth the case that the Bible is the inspired and infallible Word of God. In that chapter we established that the Bible identifies itself as the Word of God and demonstrates itself to be the Word of God. The Bible claims to be the fully inspired Word of God (2 Tim. 3:16). The Bible demonstrates itself to be the Word of God by fulfilled prophecy (Isa. 46:9-11) and by its amazing unity and consistency (Luke 24:25-27, 44; John 17:17). The Bible is our ultimate authority for drawing conclusions.

In the matter of Creation, origins and God's existence as Creator, are we going to trust the thinking of finite, fallible people who were not present to observe the origins of man and his world? Or, are we going to trust the revelation of God in His Word about His existence and His work of Creation, Who testifies He was there and knows what He did? The Bible clearly testifies to God as real and as capable Creator of all things and the Bible as God's Word.

God has revealed Himself to man in the Bible. He declares His Word is true (John 17:17). There are good answers to critics about alleged contradictions in the Bible. The Bible is reliable. It has eyewitness testimony, recorded under Divine inspiration. It is the most trustworthy authority to which we can appeal for conclusions. There is no higher authority to which we can turn. We know from observation that the thinking of man is finite, fallible, and capable of falsehood.

The Bible clearly testifies to the revelation and reality of God as the Creator of all things. God specifically and directly spoke in Scripture about being the Creator of man and the universe.

We are encountering the very Word of our Creator when we read what Scripture says about God's own testimony about Creation. Note what God said in various Old Testament Scripture passages about His work of Creation:

> "In the beginning, God created the heavens and the earth. . . . And God said, 'Let there be lights in the expanse of the heavens . . . to give light on the earth. . . . So God created . . .every living creature that moves with which the waters swarm, according to their kind, and every winged bird according to its kind. . . . And God made the

> beasts of the earth according to their kinds and the livestock according to their kinds and creeping thing according to its kind and everything that creeps on the earth according to its kind. . . . Then God said, 'Let us make man in image' . . . Male and female he created them. And God blessed them. And God said to them, 'Be fruitful and multiply and fill the earth and subdue it, and have dominion over the fish of the sea and over the birds of the heavens and over living thing that moves on the earth.' . . . Then God saw everything that He had made, and indeed it was very good" (Gen. 1:1, 14, 15, 21-28, 31).

> "And God spoke all these words saying . . . 'For in six days the Lord made heaven and earth, the sea, and all that is in them, and rested on the seventh day" (Exo. 20:1, 11).

> "Then the Lord answered Job . . . 'Where were you when I laid the foundation of the earth?' (Job 38:1, 4) "Then Lord answered Job. . . 'Behold Behemoth, which I made as I made you" (Job 40:6, 15).

> "Thus says the Lord . . . 'I made the earth and created man on it. It was my hands that stretched out the heavens. . . . I am God and there is no other" (Isa. 45:11-12, 22).

Also, God inspired Old Testament prophets (Jon. 1:9) and New Testament apostles (Rev. 4:11) to testify to God as Creator of all things. For example, the Old Testament prophet, Nehemiah, testified to God as Creator and preserver of everything:

> "You are the Lord, you alone. You have made heaven, the heaven of heavens with all their host, the earth and all that is on it, the seas and all that is in them, and you preserve all of them" (Neh. 9:6).

The New Testament apostle, Paul, testified of God as Creator in Scripture. He declared that God is the Creator of the heavens, the earth, and all people:

> "You should turn from these vain things to a living God, Who made the heaven and the earth and the sea and all that is in them" (Acts 14:15).

THE CASE FOR GOD AS CREATOR FROM GENERAL REVELATION

In addition to the special revelation of God in the Bible, God has revealed Himself to man through the general revelation of Creation. In the Bible, the Apostle Paul emphasized the clear evidence of God's power and Person through His design in creation:

> "For the wrath of God is revealed from heaven against all ungodliness and unrighteousness of men, who by their unrighteousness suppress the truth in. For what can be known about God is plain to them, because God has shown it to them. For his invisible attributes, namely, his eternal power and divine nature, have been clearly perceived, ever since the creation of the world, in the things that have been made. So they are without excuse" (Rom. 1:18–20).

Man can observe the complexity, order, and design in the world around him. And all of that reveals God as Creator and man knows of God's existence by creation.

As an intelligent being made in God's image (Gen. 1:27), man recognizes the logic of causation. For every effect there has to be a cause. God appeals to creation and causation as a revelation of His Person in Rom. 1:18–20. The tremendous size, complexity, order and design in the universe demands an infinitely powerful and wise God as Creator. Wilbur Smith, a Christian apologetics writer in the previous century, quotes a secular philosopher who says:

> "If we did not believe in the truth of causation, namely everything which has a beginning has a cause and that in the same circumstances the same things invariably happen, all the sciences would at once crumble to dust."[11]

Man can look at the created heavenly bodies, for example, and see testimony to God's creative design and power:

> "The heavens declare the glory of God; and the firmament shows His handiwork. Day unto day utters speech, and night unto night reveals knowledge. There is no speech nor language where their voice is not heard" (**Psalm 19:1–3**).

Stars point to a common Designer. God made the sun, moon, and stars for man's benefit on earth (Gen. 1:14–18). People in every place in the world throughout time can see design in the orderly arrangement and vastness of the stars in the sky. Astronomers estimate that there are trillions of stars.[12]

Also, **God uniquely and perfectly designed the earth for human life.** "The earth He has given to the children of man" (**Psalm 115:16**). God created it with an oxygen atmosphere and liquid water to sustain human life. The earth is not so close to the sun that people would burn to death or so far from the sun that people would freeze to death. That points to detailed design, not random chance. As one scientist observes, "It is almost certain that no other planet in our solar system now supports the phenomenon of life."[13]

Some skeptics falsely claim that the Bible describes a flat earth on pillars. However, the Bible describes the earth as circular (Isa. 40:22). Scripture also describes God as suspending the earth in space, not supported by any other physical object (Job 26:7). The descriptions in the Bible of the earth match scientific observations of the earth.

The Bible describes God's amazing design of man, who was made in God's own image. The psalmist says, "I praise you, for I am fearfully and wonderfully made" (Psalm 139:14). Dr. Jonathan Sarfati wrote a book about design in Creation pointing to God as Creator and he gives the illustration of the many complex components in the eye pointing to design by God.[14] Another example is the many processes involved for blood clotting to work. Such a system shows amazing design and could not have gradually evolved over time.[15]

Think about it this way: a person who observes a computer or an airplane would, of course, recognize that it had an intelligent designer. But man's inventions cannot reproduce or repair themselves. Man's body can reproduce and repair itself. Man is so much more complex than any machine he can make. How could man's body and mind come about by chance?

Animals also show amazing design. God Himself, when speaking to Job, appealed to His creative power and design in the animals He made (Job 39-41). For example, Dr. Gary Parker explains how the woodpecker has to have a particular beak, skull, tongue, etc. to do what it does.[16] The woodpecker could not survive and function if these features just gradually evolved.

The atheistic evolutionist Richard Dawkins states, "Biology is the study of complicated things that give the appearance of having been designed for a purpose."[17] Dawkins does not believe in intelligent design. However, he has to concede that there are things that give the appearance of purposeful design. Another secular scientist makes this observation:

> "A telescope, a telephone, or a typewriter is a complex mechanism serving a particular function. Obviously, its manufacturer had a purpose in mind, and the machine was designed and built in order to serve that purpose. An eye, an ear, or a hand is also a complex mechanism serving a particular function. It too, looks as if it had been made for a purpose. This appearance of purposefulness is pervading in nature."[18]

Molecular biologists point out that even a single-celled organism is "irreducibly complex" and could not come about by gradual processes. Each of its existing components is necessary for it to function at all.[19] This points to an infinitely wise and powerful Creator. Molecular biologist Dr. Michael Behe said this about structures within the simple cell:

> "As biochemists have begun to examine apparently simple structures like cilia and flagella, they have discovered staggering complexity, with dozens or even hundreds of precisely tailored parts. The Darwinian theory has given no explanation for the cilium or flagellum."[20]

How could the complex machinery that makes up a cell come about by random processes? The odds of such happening are statistically impossible according to mathematical formulations of probability. Even a scientist who is not a biblical creationist observes: "Imagine 10 to the 50th blind persons each with a scrambled Rubik cube and try to conceive of the chance of them all simultaneously arriving at the solved form. You then have the chance of arriving by random shuffling of just one of the many biopolymers on which life depends."[21]

Dr. Werner Gitt, an information scientist, observes that DNA and information science point to God as Creator:

> "With my finger I write sentences in the sand. . . . I erase the information by smoothing out the sand. . . . The mass of the sand did not alter at any time. . . . The information itself is thus massless. . . . Because information is a non-material entity, its origin is likewise not explainable by material processes. . . . There can be no information without a code . . . utilizing a symbol set. . . . Information always has a sender. . . . Because all forms of life contain a code (DNA/RNA) . . . we are within the definite domain of information. We can therefore conclude that there must be an intelligent sender. . . . In DNA molecules we find the highest density of information known to us. . . . We can conclude that there must be one sender who . . . must be all-knowing . . . and eternal. . . . He must be immensely powerful. . . . There has never been a process in the material world, demonstrable through observation or experiment, in which information has arisen by itself. . . . By consulting the Bible, the sender reveals Himself as the Almighty Creator."[22]

THE ISSUE OF GOD AND EVIL

UNDERSTANDING THE PROBLEM IN LIGHT OF GOD'S ATTRIBUTES

The Christian worldview emphasizes God's revelation of Himself as Creator through His written Word and through design in Creation. However, many atheists, agnostics, and Deists claim that one of the major reasons that they do not believe in the existence of the God revealed in the Bible is the issue of God and evil. A major issue in defending the Christian faith is explaining the problem of God and evil.

Skeptics ask Christians, if God is all powerful as Bible-believing Christians claim, why does He not stop evil from happening? If God is absolutely good, why does evil exist in the world at all? If God exists, why do bad things happen to "good people"? Why do tsunamis, earthquakes, wind storms, wars, diseases, and animal attacks harm so many people?

Some people think if God exists, He must be powerless to stop evil, or He would do so. Some people end up denying or doubting the existence of a good and loving God because of the existence of evil in the world. Some people believe that God exists and that He is good. But because they see evil in the world, they conclude that God must not be all powerful or in full control of history.[23] They try to preserve their belief in God's goodness by denying His power.

Other people think that the God revealed in the Bible could not be good because He claims to be all powerful and yet does not prevent what they consider to be evil things from happening to people in the world. A number of skeptics attack the character of God and view the God of the Bible as evil in their eyes. For example, consider how an atheist and evolutionist, Richard Dawkins, views the God of the Bible and the problem of evil. He claims:

> "The God of the Old Testament is arguably the most unpleasant character in all fiction: jealous and proud of it; a petty, unjust, unforgiving control-freak; a vindictive, bloodthirsty ethnic cleanser; a misogynistic, homophobic, racist, infanticidal, genocidal, filicidal, pestilential, megalomaniacal, sadomasochistic, capriciously malevolent bully."[24]

Of course, these words blaspheme and distort the God of the Bible. Dawkins is just a man—finite, fallible, and fallen according to Romans 1:21 and 8:7. Who is he to set himself up above our Creator? As God's Word says, "But who are you, O man, to answer back to God?" (Rom. 9:20). God and His Word give the only solid basis for morality. So where did this man get his morality to make judgments about the God of the Bible when his belief in random evolution provides no sound basis for moral judgment?

To understand God in relation to the problem of evil, we need to understand what the Bible says about the attributes of God and what the Bible says about the way in which God relates to evil. When we understand what the Bible reveals about God and evil, we will see that the Christian worldview has superior answers to worldly philosophy about the problem of evil in the world.

God reveals in His Word that He is at the same time absolutely great in power and absolutely good in character:

> "They shall speak of the might of your awesome deeds, and I will declare your greatness. They shall pour forth the fame of your abundant goodness" (Psalm 145:6–7).

God's Word reveals God as great, what theologians call "omnipotent" or all powerful: "He does according to his will among . . . the inhabitants of the earth and none can stay His hand" (Daniel 4:35). God's Word also reveals God as perfectly good: "You are good and do good" (Psalm 119:68). God never does wrong, and He shows undeserved goodness to sinful man.

God shows His greatness in creating everything and in sustaining what He made. He did not just create and then leave His creation alone. As we saw earlier in Nehemiah 9:6, Scripture declares that God created the heavens, the earth and all people and He preserves what He created.

Because God is, continues to be, and always will be, everything in His creation is, and continues to be, according to His will. The immensity, order, and design in creation reveals God's infinite power (Rom. 1:20). God sustains His creation by His powerful word (Heb. 1:3). God is all powerful in ruling over man's world (Dan. 4:34–37).

God is eternal (Rom. 1:20). No one made God. And because God is eternal, as Creator of the world, He preceded His creation and is distinct from His creation: "From everlasting to everlasting you are God" (Psalm 90:2).

As perfectly good, God has the attribute of perfect righteousness, or holiness, without sin. God says in His Word: "You shall be holy for I am holy" (1 Pet. 1:16). God has put His righteous Law and awareness of right and wrong within the conscience of man whom He made (Rom. 2:14–16). Man has rebelled against His Creator, and so all people are sinners (Rom. 3:10, 3:23). The prophet Isaiah wrote that all people have turned to their own sinful way (Isa. 53:6).

Perfect knowledge is another attribute of God. He has "all the treasures of wisdom and knowledge" (Col. 2:3). He sees and knows the actions of people all over the world (Psalm 66:7). Because God is perfectly holy, totally wise, and sees everything, He will righteously and accurately judge man for his sins (Acts 17:31). And people who do not repent of their sin will face eternal punishment by their Creator (Rom. 2:5; Rev. 21:8).

However, the God revealed in the Bible is also a gracious, loving Redeemer to sinful man. God is holy and must punish sin. However, He does not delight in judgment: "For I have no pleasure in the death of anyone, declares the Lord God; so turn and live" (Ezek. 18:32). Rather, God delights in showing mercy to those who repent (Luke 15:10). God's Word says: "Who is a God like you, pardoning iniquity? . . . He delights in steadfast love" (Mic. 7:18).

God showed His great love to sinful man by sending His Son, Jesus Christ, as Redeemer to die and pay the penalty for man's sin: "In this is love, not that we have loved God, but that He loved us and sent His Son to be the propitiation for our sins" (1 John 4:10). God reveals His undeserved goodness to sinful man in the world as Creator and Redeemer. Note these Scriptures:

> "The Lord is gracious and merciful, slow to anger and abounding in steadfast love. The Lord is good to all, and His mercy is over all that he has made" (Psalm 145:8–9).
>
> "For he makes his sun rise on the evil and the good" (Matt. 5:45b).
>
> "Yet he did not leave Himself without witness, for he did good by giving you rain from heaven and fruitful seasons, satisfying your hearts with food and gladness" (Acts 14:17).

In spite of all of the evil in the world that man sees, God shows many acts of goodness to sinful man. Man needs to think about these acts of God's goodness and kindness and repent of sin toward His Creator: "Or do you presume on the riches of His kindness and forbearance and patience, not knowing that God's kindness is meant to lead you to repentance?" (Rom. 2:4).

BIBLE TEACHING ABOUT HOW GOD RELATES TO EVIL

So how does God relate to evil? First, understand what evil is. Evil can be sinful things that people do. Evil can also be calamities and suffering that people experience. God never does evil in the sense of doing something sinful. However, God does not always stop sinful people from doing evil things. God also permits evil, in the sense of calamity or suffering, to occur in mans' fallen world for His own purposes.

The evil in this world does not come from the character of God. God has no sin or evil in His nature (1 John 1:5). God does not make people do evil things or tempt people to do evil. That is contrary to His character. People choose to do evil things because of their own sinful desires and passions:

> "Let no one say when he is tempted, 'I am being tempted by God;' for God cannot be tempted with evil and he himself tempts no one. But each person is tempted when he is lured and enticed by his own desire" (James 1:13-14).

God permits evil for His ultimate good purposes, because He is essentially good: "For the Lord is good; His mercy is everlasting" (Psalm 100:5). When God permits evil as a judgment, God does not delight in judgment. God says in His Word that He does not take pleasure in the death of sinners (Ezek. 18:32). His judgments of man's sins are just and good:

> "Are My ways not just? Is it not your ways that are not just? . . . I will judge . . . every one according to his ways,' declares the Lord God. 'Repent, and turn from all your transgressions, lest iniquity be your ruin" (Ezek. 18:29–30).

Because God is all powerful, He exercises control over the evil things that people do. God sometimes restrains people from doing evil acts. For example, God's Word reveals He stopped a king from committing adultery with Abraham's wife: "God said . . . 'It was I who kept you from sinning against me" (Gen. 20:6). In many cases, God permits people to do evil, but then **God uses evil choices of people to accomplish a good purpose He has** (Rom. 8:28).

For example, consider the illustration of Joseph in the Bible. Joseph's brothers chose to do an evil act against Joseph when they sold him into slavery in Egypt. However, God exalted Joseph to power in Egypt and used him to save his family, God's chosen people, from starvation.

> "You meant evil against me, but God meant it for good, in order to bring it about that many people should be kept alive" **(Gen. 50:20).**

Look at God's power and goodness in the case of Job. God allowed Satan to act with evil intent against Job. Satan afflicted Job, who then lost all of his sons and daughters, possessions, and health (Job 1–2). God was not punishing Job for any specific sin; rather He was testing Job's faith. In the end, God blessed Job with new sons and daughters, new possessions, and restored health (Job 42).

The biblical account of Job teaches us that God may allow evil things to happen to His people in order to test their faith and strengthen their dependence on Him. In Job

38–41, God did not explain to Job why he suffered. Instead, God gave many illustrations of His superior power and wisdom in creation and showed Job his own lack of knowledge. Man does not know enough to challenge God's wisdom in allowing human suffering.

Not every calamity is the direct result of a particular sin. In John 9 for instance, the Son of God brought glory to Himself by healing a man born blind and saving his soul. The man was not blind due to any specific sin he committed, but so God would be glorified **(John 9:3). God can glorify Himself by giving grace to people to cope with their suffering and by redeeming them from sin.**

Another reason for the suffering we see is that God does not want man to be comfortable with a sinful world that is in rebellion against Him. The evil and suffering God allows in this world should lead us to desire a better world and reconciliation with our Creator **(2 Pet. 3:7).** God promises His people a perfect new heaven and earth in the future where there will be no more death or sorrow or pain **(Rev. 21:1, 4).**

In the midst of a world filled with evil and suffering, people need to think about the revelation of God's goodness and power in Scripture, as well as in their own, personal experience. Our food, our life, our every breath, every good human relationship and material possession are good gifts from God (Acts 14:17, 17:25; James 1:17). No one comes anywhere close to giving us as many good things as God does.

Looking at the problem of evil in the world in light of the Biblical message of Creation, Fall, and Redemption can help us better understand the problem of God and evil in the world. As we look at God and evil in light of the Biblical story of Creation, we see that God originally made everything very good (Genesis 1:31). God originally created everything with a good purpose, not with death and suffering in it.

Now look at God and evil in light of the biblical story of the Fall. Death and suffering entered the world because of man's original sin (Rom. 5:12). Since the Fall, all people have a sinful nature (Romans 3:10). With a sinful nature, all people choose to sin (Rom. 3:23). All people justly die because they are sinful (Rom. 6:23). There is so much evil in the world because all people are evil, having a sinful nature.

God allows man to live in an evil world with all of its problems as a consequence of sin. God created man and the world originally good. Man chose to sin and brought God's curse upon himself and his world. Mankind is a fallen, sinful race. But God still gives good things to evil people in this world. God still blesses evil people with rain and sunshine (Matt. 5:45).

Now look at God and evil in light of the Biblical story of Redemption. People committed the most unjust act in history when they crucified Jesus, the sinless Son of God. **Jesus was**

the most innocent victim of evil in the history of the world. Yet, God used this ultimate evil act to accomplish His good plan of redemption of man from sin (Acts 2:23). God loved sinful man so much He sent His Son to die for their sins and satisfy His righteous wrath against sin (1 John 4:10; Romans 5:8-9).

Another important point to note is that God endures suffering with the evil in the world. People suffer grief when they have broken relationships during their few years on the earth. People complain of all the evil in the world from people harming other people and from people all over the world having broken relationships with other people.

However, no one comes anywhere close to experiencing the amount of grief God has experienced from broken relationships. God loves the world of sinful mankind (John 3:16) that He has created and shows longsuffering and mercy (Psalm 145:9). God experiences grief in His heart over the sinful rebellion of people against Him all over the world.

> "The Lord saw that the wickedness of man was great in the earth . . . and it grieved him to his heart" (Gen. 6:5-6).

God has experienced grief from the sin against Him of all of the billions of people that He has made who have ever lived on earth. God feels pity for people who suffer through tragic circumstances and broken relationships. Yet in spite of evil in the world and the grief He has from it, God finds joy in redeeming sinful people (Luke 15:10) and bringing them into eternal joyful fellowship with Himself (Psalm 16:11).

God the Son came to earth and experienced what life is like in an evil world. Scripture tells us that He came to earth "because of the suffering of death, so that . . . he might taste death for everyone" (Heb. 2:9). The Bible teaches that Jesus experienced sorrow and grief (Isa. 53:3). We read in Scripture that Jesus wept over the death of a close friend (John 11:32-36). God's Word also tells us that Christ can help us in our suffering and trials and temptations because of what He went through:

> "Since then we have a great high priest who has passed through the heavens, Jesus, the Son of God, let us hold fast our confession. For we do not have a high priest who is unable to sympathize with our weaknesses, but one who in every respect has been tempted as we are, yet without sin. Let us then with confidence draw near to the throne of grace that we may receive mercy and find grace to help in time of need" (Heb. 4:14-16).

Jesus endured more excruciating suffering than any person ever experiences in this life. He suffered the agonizing pain of crucifixion, rejection by His own nation, separation from God the Father on the cross and the wrath of God against man's sin on the cross. Yet He endured this suffering because of the joy He would experience through redeeming people from sin (Heb. 12:2). Therefore, believers should consider how Jesus endured suffering as an encouragement not to grow weary or discouraged in the trials of life (Heb. 12:3).

It is also important to consider that Scripture reveals that God is infinite in wisdom (Col. 2:3) and is perfectly just (Psalm 89:14). God's Word tells us that God has an appointed time in the future when He will righteously judge the world (Acts 17:31). With God's final just judgment, evil will be finally dealt with. God will ultimately banish evil from the earth and there will be a new eternal earth where there is no more sin, evil, or suffering (2 Pet. 3:13; Rev. 22:4).

THE SUPERIOR ANSWERS OF THE CHRISTIAN WORLDVIEW

The Bible has superior answers to the issue of God and evil. The Humanist worldview has no answers as to why there is evil, death, and suffering in the world. The Humanist worldview also has no objective standard to determine what is good and what is evil. The Humanist worldview also cannot offer any certain hope of resolution of evil in the future.

If evolution and survival of the fittest is true, as they claim, why should evil bother them? Death and suffering is just part of the inevitable process of evolution and evil behavior is just part of man's evolving nature. If man is just a highly evolved animal, why condemn the evil of man's violence towards man and not condemn animals for violence against each other?

Christian author, Randy Alcorn, has written a detailed study of the problem of God and evil in the world (*If God is Good: Faith in the Midst of Suffering and Evil*). He writes:

> "In contrast to non-theistic worldviews, the Biblical worldview offers a foundation for determining both good and evil. . . . The Christian worldview affirms that God's character provides the objective standard that determines good and evil (Leviticus 19:2). . . . That God has planted in all His image bearers an ability to recognize good and evil in their consciences (Romans 2:15) accounts for why people who do not believe Scripture can nonetheless feel guilty when they do wrong and feel good when they do right. Even those who reject the claims of the Christian worldview should acknowledge that it does in fact offer a moral foundation upon which to discern good and evil. And they should ask themselves whether, without realizing it, they sometimes borrow from the Christian worldview because their own worldview cannot provide a foundation on which to judge good and evil."[25]

In contrast, the Christian worldview, based on the Bible does have answers to the problem of evil. **The Bible tells us why there is evil, death, and suffering in the world. The Bible gives us an objective standard to determine what is good and what is evil. The Bible also sets forth God's promise of eliminating evil from the world in the eternal state.**

In a world filled with evil, all people, Christian and non-Christian, face trouble in life.

> "But man is born unto trouble as the sparks fly upward. . . . Man who is born of woman is few of days and full of trouble" (Job 5:7; 14:1).

The Christian worldview is superior to the Islamic and Humanist worldviews because it truly offers help to people to deal with trouble in an evil world. The Islamic worldview holds that man cannot know God in a personal saving relationship in this life. The Humanist worldview denies that there is a real personal God to help man in trouble.

A Christian believer can recognize that no matter how evil the circumstances he or she may endure in this life, God is able to "work all things together for good to those who love God" (Rom. 8:28). Because God is great and all powerful, He is able to make evil things work together for the ultimate good of His people. Because God is perfectly good, He has a good ultimate purpose for troubles He allows His people to endure.

The Bible reveals that God does not change (Mal. 3:6), so we can count on the God of the Bible to always be great and all-powerful and to always be perfectly good. In a world filled with evil, God's Word assures His people of His faithfulness and grace:

> "God is faithful, and he will not let you be tempted beyond your ability" (1 Cor. 10:13).

> "My grace is sufficient for you, for my power is made perfect in weakness" (2 Cor. 12:9).

The key to finding help for trouble in the world is to know God in a personal relationship and thinking biblically about God in relation to troubles in the world. Consider how the psalmist in the Bible found hope in trouble by thinking from a biblical perspective about God:

> "God is our refuge and strength, a very present help in trouble. Therefore we will not fear" (Psalm 46:1–2).

> "I will say to the Lord, my refuge and my fortress, my God, in whom I trust. . . . When he calls to me, I will answer him; I will be with him in trouble" (Psalm 91:2, 15).

A good source to help Christians think biblically about their troubles in this life is the book by Jerry Bridges, *Trusting God Even When Life Hurts.* He gives this helpful observation:

> "In the area of adversity, the Scriptures teach us three essential truths about God—truths we must believe if we are to trust Him in adversity. They are: God is completely sovereign. God is infinite in wisdom. God is perfect in love."[26]

Jim Berg is a Christian teacher and writer who has produced a study for Christians dealing with trouble in life. He produced a DVD series called *Quieting a Noisy Soul.*[27] In this study he emphasizes the importance of personally knowing God and thinking biblically about God in relation to troubles. After years of biblical study and counseling, he concludes that failure to believe and apply the promises of God in His Word is at the root of our lack of peace:

> "Unbelief is the primary cause of the noise in your soul. You do not yet see that God Himself is more than enough for you. . . . Unbelief is a disorder because it accepts the reasoning of fallen man over the revelation of God."[28]

A DEFENSE OF THE TRINITY

The Christian worldview begins thinking with God and emphasizes what the Bible clearly teaches about God. The Bible clearly teaches that the true God is a Trinity and that Jesus Christ is God. Humanism and Islam both reject these Biblical truths.

The biblical doctrine of the Trinity is that there is one true God Who exists as three Persons. **The Bible teaches that there is only one true God:**

> **"I am the Lord, and there is no other; besides me there is no God" (Isa. 45:5).**
>
> "The Lord our God, the Lord is one" (Mark 12:29).

And the Bible also teaches that the one true God exists in three Persons—the Father, the Son, and the Holy Spirit (Matt. 28:19). These are not 3 separate Gods, but 3 Persons in the one true God.

Other religions such as Judaism and Islam agree that there is only one God, but they teach that there is only one Person in the Godhead.[29] Jehovah's Witnesses also teach there is only one person in the Godhead.[30] The Islamic worldview emphasizes only one person in the Godhead and specifically rejects the biblical teaching of the Trinity:

> "O People of the Book! Commit no excesses in your religion . . . . Say not 'Trinity;' desist (Surah 4:171). . . . They do blaspheme who say: 'Allah is one of three in a Trinity'. . . . Christ, the son of Mary, was no more than a messenger" (Surah 5:73, 74, 75).[31]

In contrast, **faith in the Triune God is so foundational in Scripture that Christ teaches every disciple of His to confess faith in one God in three Persons—Father, Son, and Holy Spirit—in Christian baptism.** Jesus commanded, "Go therefore and make disciples of all the nations, baptizing them in the name of the Father and of the Son and of the Holy Spirit (Matt. 28:19). A Christian commentator makes this statement about Matthew 28:19:

> "It is a commitment to (in the name is . . . implying entrance into an allegiance) the Father, Son and the Holy Spirit (all three of whom, interestingly, were involved in the event of Jesus' own baptism—Matt. 3:16–17). Jesus thus takes his place along with his Father and the Spirit as the object of worship and of the disciple's commitment. The experience of God in these three Persons is the essential basis of discipleship. At the same time the singular noun 'name' (not names) underlines the unity of the three Persons."[32]

The Bible refers to the Father as God (Eph. 4:6). The Bible also calls Jesus, the Son, God (John 1:1, 1:14). The Bible views the Holy Spirit as God, stating that lying to the Holy Spirit was the same as lying to God (Acts 5:3–4). Father, Son, and Spirit each are God, yet they are one God.

The three Persons of the Trinity, as one God, share the same Divine essence and attributes. They exist at the same time and commune with one another, yet they are three separate Persons. When Jesus was baptized on earth, God the Father spoke from heaven and called Jesus His Son, while at the same time, the Spirit came upon Him (Matt. 3:16–17). The Persons of the Triune God also communed with one another during the time of creation saying,

> "Let us make man in our image, after our likeness" (Gen. 1:26).

The Triune God is actively involved in the world He made. For example, God the Father sustains the physical world (Neh. 9:6). God the Son has ultimate authority over the world (Matt. 28:18). God the Holy Spirit convicts people all over the world of sin and the need of Christ for salvation (John 16:8–9, 14).

So, the Father is God, the Son is God, and the Spirit is God, yet they are all together one God (Mark 12:29). In John 14, Jesus teaches that He is so much one God with the Father and one God with the Spirit, that to see God the Son is to see God the Father. In the same passage, Jesus teaches that where the Holy Spirit indwells a believer, Jesus also indwells and the Father indwells (John 14:9-24).

The apostle John wrote in the Bible under inspiration by God about each of the three Persons of the Trinity in connection with truth. He describes the Father as true (Revelation 6:10). He quotes the Son as declaring that He is the Truth (John 14:6). He describes the Holy Spirit as the Spirit of truth (John 14:17). Father, Son, and Spirit are perfect in truth.

The God revealed in the Bible is the Father, His Son Jesus Christ, and the Spirit (1 John 5:6, 20). And the Bible refers to Father, Son, and Spirit as the true God (1 John 5:20). The Bible, as God's Word, is the ultimate authority for drawing conclusions in a Christian worldview (2 Tim. 3:16). All three Persons of the Trinity were involved in the Divine work of communicating the Bible as the Word of God:

> The Bible is the Word of the Father: "Your Word is truth" (John 17:17).
>
> The Bible is the Word of Christ: "Let the word of Christ dwell in you richly" (Col. 3:16).
>
> The Bible is the Word of the Spirit: "But men spoke from God as they were carried along by the Holy Spirit" (2 Pet. 1:21).

We have seen that the Bible contains a basic unified message of Creation, Fall, and Redemption. The biblical message of Creation is foundational to the Christian worldview.

Only someone with infinite power like the God of the Bible could have created man and his world and the universe. The Bible reveals that each of the three Persons in the Trinity participated in the supernatural work of Creation, showing the Divine power of each of the three Persons:

> "In the beginning God created the heavens and the earth . . . And the Spirit of God was hovering over the face of the waters . . . . God said, "Let Us make man in our image" (Gen. 1:1, 2, 26).
>
> "In the beginning was the Word. . . . All things were made through him" (John 1:1, 3).
>
> "The Spirit of God has made me" (Job 33:4).

Another foundational truth of the Christian worldview is the biblical message of Redemption, which involves all three Persons of the Trinity. God the Father planned redemption (John 3:16). God the Son purchased man's redemption by His atoning death on the Cross (Eph. 1:7). God the Spirit applies redemption by giving new life to believers (John 3:5–8). Titus 3:4–7 mentions all three Persons of the Trinity in connection with man's salvation.

There is no exact analogy to fully illustrate the Trinity because God is unique and distinct from His creation. We can see reflections of oneness and threeness in what God has made. God made time and water (Gen. 1:1-2). We can speak of time as a single entity and see that time has three aspects: past, present, and future. We can speak of water as a single entity and recognize it can exist in three states: solid ice, liquid, and vapor. However, these do not exactly illustrate the Trinity, because God is one God and three Persons at the same time and always.

In his theological dictionary, Dr. Cairns summarizes this biblical teaching:

> "Since there is one God and since the Father is God, the Son is God and the Holy Spirit is God and since these three are clearly distinguished in Scripture, we are left with the glorious truth of the Trinity—one God eternally existing as Father, Son and Holy Spirit."[33]

The doctrine of the Trinity is clearly taught in Scripture and is important for a right view of God. For centuries, Bible-believing Christians have recognized this teaching in Scripture. The Christian church debated and settled that the Bible clearly teaches that God is a Trinity, one God in three Persons. Throughout church history confessions of faith assert this biblical truth.

The Athanasian Creed is an ancient Christian creed. Bible-believing Christians from a variety of church backgrounds have accepted this statement of faith as an accurate summary of Biblical truth for centuries. It clearly states the biblical Christian belief about the Trinity:

> "We worship one God in Trinity. . . . There is one Person of the Father; another of the Son; and another of the Holy Spirit. But the Godhead of the Father, of the Son, and of the Holy Spirit is all one . . . . The Father is God; the Son is God; and the Holy Spirit is God. And yet they are not three Gods, but one God. . . . The whole three Persons are coeternal and coequal."[34]

The Association of Christian Schools International represents Christian schools from a variety of church backgrounds with denominational differences, but they confess agreement about the biblical doctrine of the Trinity. Their statement of faith on the Trinity says, "We believe there is one God, eternally existent in three persons—Father, Son, and Holy Spirit."[35]

Bible-believing Protestant church groups confess the biblical doctrine of the Trinity in their confessions of faith. They have denominational differences, but they confess faith in the same Triune God and Creator on the basis of the Bible. Note the following Protestant confessions of faith regarding the Trinity:

BAPTIST CONFESSION OF 1833

Of the true God: We believe that there is one and only one, living and true God, an infinite, intelligent Spirit, whose name is Jehovah, the Maker and Supreme Ruler of heaven and earth; inexpressibly glorious in holiness and worthy of all possible honor, confidence and love; that in the unity of the Godhead there are three Persons, the Father, the Son and the Holy Ghost; equal in every divine perfection, and executing distinct and harmonious offices in the great work of redemption.[36]

LUTHERAN AUGSBURG CONFESSION

There is one divine essence which is called and is God, eternal . . . the Creator and Preserver of all things . . . and that yet there are three persons of the same essence and power, who are also coeternal, the Father, the Son, and the Holy Ghost.[37]

METHODIST ARTICLES OF RELIGION

Of Faith in the Holy Trinity: There is but one living and true God, everlasting, without body or parts, of infinite power, wisdom and goodness; the Maker and Preserver of all things, visible and invisible. And in the unity of this Godhead there are three Persons, of one substance, power, and eternity, the Father, the Son, and the Holy Ghost.[38]

PRESBYTERIAN WESTMINSTER CONFESSION

There is but one only living and true God, who is infinite in being and perfection, a most pure spirit . . . eternal . . . almighty, most wise, most holy . . . most loving . . . In the unity of the Godhead there be three persons, of one substance, power and eternity: God the Father, God the Son, and God the Holy Ghost. . . . It pleased God the Father, Son, and Holy Ghost . . . in the beginning to create . . . all things.[39]

REFORMED EPISCOPAL ARTICLES OF RELIGION

There is but one living and true God . . . the Maker and Preserver of all things . . . and in the unity of this Godhead there be three persons of one substance, power and eternity: the Father, the Son and the Holy Ghost.[40]

An important Biblical truth about the Trinity is that the Triune God seeks to establish a personal relationship with man by His unmerited grace. This truth gives hope to man. This Christian hope, based on the Bible, is something that the Humanist and Islamic worldviews cannot offer. The Bible reveals that the Triune God has an eternal personal relationship with His people through faith in Christ for salvation. God the Father, God the Son, and God the Holy Spirit are all involved in this saving relationship.

Jesus describes God the Father, God the Son, and God the Spirit providing eternal life to people who believe on Jesus Christ for salvation. Jesus describes the essence of eternal life as a personal knowledge and relationship with God the Father and God the Son (John 17:3). God the Father promises eternal life to those who believe on God the Son and trust Him for salvation (John 6:40). Jesus teaches that a person must be born again by God the Holy Spirit to be part of God's eternal kingdom (John 3:5).

When a person has eternal life that is described and offered in the Bible, that person has a personal relationship with God the Father and God the Son that lasts forever (John 17:3). God the Holy Spirit brings a person into that eternal relationship (John 3:6, 16; 15:26). As result of this relationship that is established through salvation, Jesus teaches that the three Persons of the Trinity are present in the life of the believer:

> "I will ask the Father and He will give you another Helper, to be with you forever, even the Spirit of truth. . . . He dwells with you and will be in you. . . . I will come to you. . . . If anyone loves me . . . My Father will love him, and we will come to him and make our home with him" (John 14:16-18, 23).

And in this relationship, all three Persons of the Trinity personally care for God's people throughout their lives. The Bible speaks of peace coming from God the Father and God being a God of comfort (2 Cor. 1:2–3). God the Son promised to give peace to His followers (John 14:27). And God the Holy Spirit produces the fruit of the Spirit in the life of a believer, which includes peace (Gal. 5:22–23).

As part of this personal relationship, God calls His people to come to Him in prayer and find His help for trials and needs (Heb. 4:16). Believers pray to God the Father (Matt. 6:9), in the name of God the Son (John 14:13), through the help of God the Spirit (Rom. 8:26–27). In His Word, God the Father promises to give peace to His people through prayer and to guard the heart of His people from anxiety through God the Son (Phili. 4:6–7). God the Father and God the Son promise to provide for the needs of believers (Matt. 6:25-34).

The Humanist worldview cannot offer this hope. They do not believe in the resurrection of the dead, eternal life, or the idea of praying to God. The Humanist Manifesto states,

> "Humanists still believe that . . . faith in the prayer-hearing God, assumed to love and care for persons, to hear and understand their prayers and to be able to do something about them, is an unproved and outmoded faith."[41]

The Islamic worldview cannot offer the same hope as the Biblical worldview either. To a Muslim, having a personal relationship with God is simply not possible. As one Muslim theologian has said, "It is absolutely impossible for them to know Him."[42] According to Islam, Jesus and Mohammad are just prophets, and neither one is believed to be a savior who can bring sinful people into a personal relationship with God by grace. However, the Bible teaches that we are saved by God's grace through faith in Christ and not by works (Eph. 2:8-9).

A DEFENSE OF THE DEITY OF CHRIST

The Biblical teaching about the Trinity includes the doctrine of the Deity of Christ. One of most important worldview questions for which a person needs an answer is, "Who is Jesus?"

The Bible clearly teaches the Deity of Jesus Christ, that Jesus is God the Son, God in the flesh. The Humanist worldview and the Islamic worldview and various other religious groups reject this critically important assertion of the Christian worldview from the Bible.

To be redeemed from sin, a person must seek redemption through the Jesus revealed in the Bible. Many unbiblical views of Jesus have abounded throughout history. Scripture warns us about believing in any false Jesus who is different from what the apostles taught about Him in Scripture. The apostle Paul expressed deep concern about this matter:

> "But I am afraid that as the serpent deceived Eve by his cunning, your thoughts will be led astray from a sincere and pure devotion to Christ. For if someone comes

> and proclaims another Jesus than the one we proclaimed . . . or a different gospel from the one you accepted, you put up with it readily enough!" (2 Cor. 11:3–4).

Redemption is based upon what the Bible says about the Person and work of Christ.

Scripture teaches that we must believe that Jesus is the Christ come in the flesh (John 1:14; 1 John 4:2–3). Jesus had to take on a human body so He could die to redeem man from sin. The Bible says:

> "Since therefore the children share in flesh and blood, he himself likewise partook of the same things, that through death He might destroy the one who has the power of death, that is, the devil" (Heb. 2:14).

But the Bible says that Jesus is more than a man. The Bible presents Jesus as God, Savior, and Lord. Scripture refers to Jesus as God and Savior (2 Pet. 1:1; Tit. 2:13). He eternally pre-existed as God (Mic. 5:2; John 1:1–2, 8:58). In his book, *More Than a Carpenter,* Christian apologetics writer Josh McDowell notes,

> "Many people want to regard Jesus not as God, but as a good moral man or as an exceptionally wise prophet. . . . Jesus claimed to be God. . . . If when Jesus made his claims, he knew that he was not God, then he was lying. . . . How could he be a great moral teacher and mislead people? . . . Someone who lived as Jesus lived, taught as Jesus taught and died as Jesus died could not have been a liar."[43]

The Bible describes Jesus as fully God and fully man, supernaturally born of a virgin in fulfillment of prophecy and God in the flesh (Isa. 7:14; Matt. 1:18–25).

> **The Word was with God, and the Word was God. . . . All things were made through him. . . . And the Word became flesh"** (John 1:1, 3, 14).

> "Behold, the virgin shall conceive and bear a son, and they shall call His name Immanuel (which means God with us)" (Matt. 1:23).

Jesus identified Himself as God in the flesh when He said,

> "I and the Father are one" (John 10:30).

> "Before Abraham was, I AM" (John 8:58).

> "Unless you believe that I am He, you will die in your sins" (John 8:24).

The words "I AM" refer to the special name of God found in Exodus 3:13–14. The Jews who heard Jesus recognized Jesus was claiming to be God (John 10:30–33 and 8:58–59). And in John 8:24, Jesus states very clearly that if a person do not believe Jesus is God, equal with God the Father, that person will die condemned as a sinner.

Belief in the deity of Christ is essential for salvation. The Bible connects saving faith and believing in the Deity of Christ. Note the confession of Christ's Deity by the apostle Thomas:

> "Thomas answered Him, 'My Lord and my God!' Jesus said to him, 'Have you believed because you have seen Me? Blessed are those who have not seen and yet have believed'" (John 20:28-29).

Note that Jesus called Thomas' confession of Jesus as Lord and God as believing. Jesus calls other people blessed who also believe on Him as Lord and God, but who have not seen Jesus risen from the dead with their own eyes like Thomas did.

The Bible also describes Jesus as the Savior from sin:

> "For unto you is born this day in the city of David a Savior, who is Christ the Lord" (Luke 2:11).

> "You shall call his name Jesus, for he will save His people from their sins" (Matt. 1:21).

As Savior, Jesus Christ is the Redeemer from sin. He died to redeem sinful man from sin's penalty, so sinful people could receive forgiveness from God and deliverance from God's wrath in Hell (Eph. 1:7; Rom. 5:8-9). Christ also died to redeem sinful man from sin's power (Tit. 2:13-14; Rom. 6). The section on redemption in chapter 4 will further explain the meaning of Christ's redemptive work and Christ delivering sinners from sin's penalty and power.

In order to save man from sin, Jesus must be truly God and truly man. The penalty for man's sin is death according to Romans 6:23. But if Jesus had not become a man, He would not have had a body with which to die for man's sin (Heb. 10:5–14). If Jesus were not God, He would not have the power to save man from sin. Only God can save man from sin:

> "A righteous God and a Savior; there is none besides me. Turn to me, and be saved, all the ends of the earth! For I am God, and there is no other" (Isa. 45:21–22).

The Bible describes Jesus as the sinless Savior:

> "For our sake he made him to be sin who knew no sin, that in him we might become the righteousness of God" (2 Cor. 5:21).

Jesus had to be sinless in order to save us; otherwise, someone else would have to die for His sins (Heb. 4:15, 7:26–27). Unfortunately, according to worldview surveys, the majority of people have an unbiblical worldview because they do not recognize the sinlessness of Jesus.[44]

Jesus is the sinless, substitutionary sacrifice for our sins. He did not die as a martyr or just as an example. As sinners we deserve to die eternally for our sins. But Jesus died in sinful man's place and satisfied God's wrath toward sin:

> "But God shows His love for us in that while we were still sinners, Christ died for us. Since therefore we have now been justified by his blood, much more shall we be saved by him from the wrath of God" (Rom. 5:8–9).

The Bible also describes Jesus as the risen Lord. By rising from the dead, Jesus conquered death so He could give us eternal life (1 Cor. 15:17–20). A person must believe in Jesus as the risen Lord to be saved (Rom. 10:9). As risen Lord, Jesus will return and raise the dead (1 Cor. 15:51–52; 1 Thess. 4:16).

Jesus is Lord and King. God calls all people to confess Jesus as Lord (Phil. 2:9–11). Jesus has all authority in heaven and earth (Matt. 28:18). His redemptive work brings people into His kingdom (Col. 1:13–14). Jesus is "King of kings" (Rev. 19:16).

This Biblical view of Jesus as God, Savior, and Lord is the historic view of Bible-believing Christians. Consider the ancient Nicene Creed, historically accepted by Christians as accurately stating biblical truth:

> "I believe . . . in one Lord Jesus Christ, the only-begotten Son of God . . . very God of very God . . . by whom all things were made; who, for us men and for our salvation, came down from heaven, and was incarnate by the Holy Spirit of the Virgin Mary, and was made man; and was crucified also for us under Pontius Pilate; He suffered and was buried; and the third day He rose again, according to the Scriptures; and ascended into heaven, and sits on the right hand of the Father; and He shall come again, with glory, to judge both the quick (living) and the dead; whose kingdom shall have no end."[45]

In contrast, among people with a Humanist worldview, some extreme skeptics view Jesus merely as a myth. Other Humanists view Jesus as a real man who was a religious teacher of love for one's neighbor. However, all Humanists agree in not viewing Jesus as God in the flesh. Humanists state in their writings, "Humanists reject the divinity of Jesus."[46]

The Islamic worldview holds that Jesus was a prophet sent from God. However, Islamic teaching emphasizes that Jesus was only a man and definitely not God in the flesh. For example, the Qur'an states:

> "They do blaspheme who say: 'Allah is Christ the son of Mary.' . . . Christ, the son of Mary, was no more than a messenger. . . . The Christians call Christ the Son of God. . . . Allah's curse be on them; how they are deluded away from the Truth!" (Surah 5:72, 5:75, 9:30).[47]

Many religious groups are in error because they do not believe Jesus is uniquely God in the flesh. Judaism rejects the claim of Jesus to be the Christ, the Son of God, and Savior.[48] Mormonism teaches that Jesus and Lucifer were brothers, physically begotten by God the Father. They believe Jesus became a god, and man can also become a god.[49] Jehovah's Witnesses reject the deity of Jesus and identify Him with Michael the Archangel.[50] Unitarians and liberal Protestant theologians also reject the Deity of Christ.[51]

For example, a Jehovah's Witness leader wrote,

> "We may be sure that he was not raised from the dead with a human body. . . . Some have earnestly believed that Jesus was God himself. But such a conclusion is not warranted by the Scriptures."[52]

As another example, a Unitarian writer states about his church group:

> "The Nicene formula declared . . . Jesus was of the same essential substance as God. It is characteristic of Unitarian-Universalists to doubt the validity of this decision."[53]

If someone asked you what your personal view of Jesus is and why you believe as you do, what would you say? The Bible calls believers to "honor Christ as holy, always being prepared to make a defense to anyone who asks you for a reason for the hope that is in you" (1 Pet. 3:15). The Bible gives evidence for the deity of Christ. **Believers can defend their faith in Jesus as Savior, God, and Lord by appealing to the biblical evidences of Christ's miracles and resurrection.**

Jesus claimed to be God in the flesh and He demonstrated the reality of His divine claims by working miracles before many witnesses (John 5:17–18, 20:30–31). Then He ultimately proved His claim to be the Son of God, God in the flesh, by rising from the dead as He said He would (Rom. 1:3–4). And God inspired the writers of Scripture to record these miracles and eyewitness testimonies as part of His written Word to us (John 14:26). The biblical narratives about Christ's miracles and resurrection are real history and clearly stated.

The miracles that Jesus performed demonstrated that He is truly God in the flesh:

> "The very works that I am doing bear witness about me that the Father has sent me" (John 5:36).

> "Now Jesus did many other signs in the presence of the disciples, which are not written in this book; but these are written so that you may believe that Jesus is the Christ, the Son of God . . . " (John 20:30–31).

Courts of law recognize eyewitness testimony as especially valuable in drawing conclusions. We know about Christ's miracles through historical records that come from eyewitness testimonies. The Bible records the eyewitness testimonies of the apostles to the miracles of Christ. Luke introduces his Gospel account of Christ by stating, "Those who from the beginning were eyewitnesses and ministers of the word delivered them to us" (Luke 1:2).

The apostles of Jesus knew they were not teaching myths when they talked about Christ's miracles and Divine power. For example, the apostle Peter declared:

> "For we did not follow cleverly devised fables when we made known to you the power and coming of our Lord Jesus Christ, but we were eyewitnesses of his majesty" (2 Pet. 1:16).

> "Jesus of Nazareth, a Man attested to you by God with mighty works and wonders and signs that God did through him in your midst, as you yourselves know" (Acts 2:22).

The miracles of Jesus involved exercising power over creation. Many people witnessed Jesus change water into wine at a wedding feast (John 2:1–11). The apostles witnessed Christ calming a storm at sea (Mark 4:37–41). And multitudes of people observed Jesus multiplying a few loaves and fishes to feed over five thousand people at one time (John 6:2–14).

Jesus also performed many witnessed miracles of extraordinary healing during His earthly ministry, which showed that He was the promised Messiah (Matt. 4:23–25). When John the Baptist needed reassurance that Jesus was indeed the Promised One, Jesus responded,

> "The blind receive their sight and the lame walk; lepers are cleansed and the deaf hear and the dead are raised up" (Matt. 11:5).

Jesus exercised power over diseases and disabilities. He instantly healed a nobleman's son of a deadly disease, cleansed a man from leprosy, and caused a man with paralyzed legs to stand up and walk (John 4:46–54; Matt. 8:1–3, 9:1–7). He even restored sight to a man who had been blind from birth—such a miracle had never been heard of before (John 9:1–41)! And many people glorified God when they saw all these things (Matt. 9:8).

Jesus showed His power over demons and even over death! He cast demons out of many people, including a multitude of demons out of a man whom no one could control (Mark 3:10–11; Luke 8:26–39). Jesus also raised his friend Lazarus from the dead after he had been in the tomb for four days! Many Jews saw this miracle and believed (John 11:1–45).

Jesus also demonstrated that He is God in the flesh by His resurrection from the dead (Rom. 1:3-4). The resurrection of Christ is foundational to the Christian faith (1 Cor. 15):

> "I would remind you brothers of the gospel I preached to you, which you received, in which you stand, and by which you are being saved . . . that Christ died for our sins in accordance with the Scriptures, that he was buried, that he was raised on the third day in accordance with the Scriptures, and that he appeared to Cephas, then to the twelve. Then he appeared to more than five hundred brothers at one time. . . . Then he appeared to James. . . . He appeared also to me. . . . And if Christ has not been raised, your faith is futile and you are still in your sins. . . . But in fact Christ has been raised from the dead" (1 Cor. 15:1-8, 17, 20).

The New Testament testimony to Christ's resurrection is based on the eyewitness testimony of the apostles recorded under divine inspiration (Luke 24:39–48; John 14:26). Scripture says that after He had died on the cross, Jesus presented Himself alive to His apostles with many proofs (Acts 1:3). Christ's apostles saw and touched the risen Christ (Luke 24:36-43; 1 Cor. 15:4-8; 1 John 1:1).

The apostles were godly men. None of the people who knew the apostles testified that they were given to lying. And the apostles specifically stated that they were not making up myths or giving deceitful testimony (2 Pet. 1:16; 1 Thess. 2:3). What's more, they ended up dying martyrs' deaths for their testimony about Christ. And it isn't likely that someone would risk death to proclaim something that they knew to be false.

Simon Greenleaf, a law professor and expert on evidence, studied the biblical evidence of the Resurrection of Jesus. A Christian apologetics book records his testimony:

> "Simon Greenleaf . . . Professor Law at Harvard University . . . [wrote] 'A Treatise on the Law of Evidence' . . . Greenleaf wrote . . . "An Examination of the Testimony of the Four Evangelists by the Rules of Evidence Administered in Courts of Justice." The author devotes a number of pages to the consideration of the value of the testimony of the Apostles to the Resurrection of Christ: 'The great truths which the apostles declared were that Christ had risen from the dead, and that only through repentance from sin and faith in Him could men hope for salvation. This doctrine they asserted with one voice . . . in the face of the most appalling terrors. . . . One after another was put to a miserable death. . . . They had every possible motive to review carefully the grounds of their faith and the evidences of the great facts and truths which they asserted. . . . It was therefore impossible that they could have persisted in affirming the truths they have narrated, had not Jesus actually risen from the dead, and had they not known this fact as certainly as they knew any other fact."[54]

Humanism and Islam both reject the bodily resurrection of Jesus from the dead. With a Humanist skeptical perspective, a number of critics have tried to explain away the accounts in the Bible about the resurrection of Jesus. They have tried to come up with other explanations.

Some skeptics have claimed that Christ merely fainted on the Cross, revived in the tomb, escaped, and then claimed to rise from the dead. However, Pilate would not have released Christ's body for burial unless the centurion certified that Jesus was dead (Mark 15:42–46). Moreover, it would be humanly impossible for a person to survive crucifixion, roll away a giant stone, and overcome the Roman guard (Matt. 27:35, 27:64–66).

Some people have said that the women went to the wrong tomb and spread the story of an empty tomb. However, the Bible says the women carefully observed where Jesus was buried (Luke 23:55, 24:12). Besides, hostile leaders in Jerusalem would have taken people to the right tomb to reveal the body and disprove the Resurrection claim—if they could.

Some people have said the apostles just dreamed they saw a vision of Christ. However, the Bible documents that they touched the risen Christ (Luke 24:39–40; 1 John 1:1) and saw Him repeatedly over a forty-day period after His resurrection (Acts 1:3). Over five hundred people saw the risen Jesus at once (1 Cor. 15:6). It is not believable that they were all just dreaming.

The Bible documents that Jewish authorities actually paid the Roman soldiers to say that the disciples stole the body while they slept (Matt. 28:11–15). But how did they know what happened if they were sleeping? And what were the guards doing sleeping anyway? Besides, the disciples did not have sufficient numbers, arms, or courage to overcome the Roman guard. Scripture testifies that after the crucifixion of Jesus they hid themselves out of fear (John 20:19).

Bible-believing Christians unite in confessing Christ as God, Savior, and risen Lord.

Since the 1600s, many Presbyterians and Baptists have used the Presbyterian Westminster Confession of Faith and the London Baptist Confession of Faith. These historic confessions give this same confession about Christ based upon the Bible:

> "The Son of God, the second person in the Trinity, being very and eternal God . . . equal with the Father, did . . . take upon him man's nature . . . yet without sin; being conceived by the power of the Holy Ghost in the womb of the virgin Mary. . . . Which person is very God and very man. . . .The Lord Jesus . . . was crucified and died. . . . On the third day he arose from the dead . . . He ascended into heaven and there sits at the right hand of the Father making intercession, and shall return to judge men and angels at the end of the world."[55]

The Methodist Articles of Religion from 1784 and the Reformed Episcopal Articles of Religion from 1875 give a similar confession about Jesus Christ:

> "The Son . . . very and eternal God, of one substance with the Father, took man's nature in the womb of the blessed virgin . . . so that . . . the Godhead and manhood were joined together in one person. . . Christ . . . was crucified . . . to be a sacrifice . . . for the actual sins of men. . . . Christ did truly rise again from the dead. . . . He ascended into heaven. . . . He will return to judge the world."[56]

In addition to these older confessions, more modern confessions by Bible-believing groups similarly confess the Deity of Christ. For example, The American Association of Christian Schools (AACS) and the Association of Christian Schools International (ACSI), representing Christian schools affiliated with various churches, confess the Deity of Christ:

> "We believe in the Incarnation, the Virgin Birth, and the Deity of our Lord and Savior, Jesus Christ. We believe in the vicarious and substitutionary atonement for the sins of mankind by the shedding of His blood on the cross. We believe in the resurrection of His body from the tomb, His ascension to Heaven, and that He is now our Advocate. We believe that He is personally coming again" (AACS).[57]

> "We believe in the deity of Christ (John 10:33), His virgin birth (Isa. 7:14, Matt. 1:23, Luke 1:35), His sinless life (Heb. 4: 15, 7:26), His miracles (John 2:11), His vicarious and atoning death (1 Cor. 15:3, Eph. 1:7, Heb. 2:9), His resurrection (John 11:25, 1 Cor.

> 15:4), His ascension to the right hand of God (Mark 16:19), His personal return in power and glory (Acts 1:11, Rev. 19:11) (ACSI).[58]

The Baptist Faith and Message doctrinal statement of Southern Baptists states:

> "Christ is the eternal Son of God. In His incarnation as Jesus Christ He was conceived of the Holy Spirit and born of the virgin Mary. Jesus perfectly revealed and did the will of God, taking upon Himself human nature with its demands and necessities and identifying Himself completely with mankind yet without sin. He honored the divine law by His personal obedience, and in His substitutionary death on the cross He made provision for the redemption of men from sin. He was raised from the dead with a glorified body and appeared to His disciples as the person who was with them before His crucifixion. He ascended into heaven and is now exalted at the right hand of God where He is the One Mediator, fully God, fully man, in whose Person is effected the reconciliation between God and man. He will return in power and glory to judge the world and to consummate His redemptive mission. He now dwells in all believers as the living and ever present Lord."[59]

CHAPTER 3 STUDY GUIDE
GOD'S PERSON—THE STARTING POINT FOR WORLDVIEW THINKING

KEY SCRIPTURE PASSAGES TO READ:

Genesis 1:1, 21, 25-28, 31; Genesis 50:20; Deuteronomy 6:4; Nehemiah 9:6; Job 38:4; Psalm 19:1-3, 90:2, 115:16, 119:68, 139:13-14; Isaiah 44:24, 45:12, 18; Ezekiel 18:32; Micah 7:18; Daniel 4:35; Matthew 5:45, 28:19; John 1:1, 3, 14, 10:30, 14:16-17, 23; 20:26-31; Acts 5:3-4, 14:17, 17:24; Romans 1:3-4, 18-21, 2:4-5, 8:28; Colossians 1:16, 2:9; Titus 2:13; Hebrews 4:14-15, 11:3, 6; James 1:13, 17; 1 Peter 1:16, 2:21-24; Revelation 4:11

KEY POINTS TO NOTE (NOTE BOLD TYPE IN CHAPTER):

What does the Bible say is the proper starting point for man's thinking? (Prov. 1:7)

____

____

Through what two means has God revealed Himself to Man? (2 Tim. 3:16; Rom. 1:18-21)

____

____

What are three areas of general revelation in which God has revealed Himself as Creator? (Psalm 19:1-3; Psalm 115:16; Psalm 139:14)

____

____

____

What are four reasons that God permits evil and suffering? (Note Joseph, Job, the man born blind, and 2 Pet. 3:7 and Rev. 21:1-4.)

____

____

____

____

What is a key Bible verse that teaches that there is only one true God?

What is a key Bible verse that teaches that the one true God exists in three Persons?

What is a key Bible passage that teaches that Jesus is fully God and fully man?

To what can believers appeal to defend their faith in Jesus Christ as God?

CRITICAL THINKING:

Summarize in your own words what is true about the attributes of God in relation to evil and suffering in the world, how God relates to evil and suffering, and how what the Bible says about evil and suffering is superior to the Humanist worldview.

Why is the doctrine of the Trinity and the Deity of Christ important?

CHAPTER 3 ENDNOTES

1 Greg Bahnsen, *Presuppositional Apologetics Stated and Defended* (Powder Springs, GA: American Vision, 2008), p. 87.

2 Derek Kidner, *Tyndale Old Testament Commentaries: Proverbs (*Downers Grove, IL: InterVarsity Press, 1964), p. 59.

3 Paul Kurtz, ed., *Humanist Manifestos I and II* (Buffalo, NY: Prometheus Books, 1973), p. 16.

4 *Webster's College Dictionary* (New York: Random House, 1990), p. 1048.

5 *Webster's College Dictionary* (New York: Random House, 1990), p. 978.

6 Kurtz, *Humanist Manifestos I and II,* p. 16.

7 Alan Cairns, *Dictionary of Theological Terms* (Greenville, SC: Ambassador International, 2002), p. 339.

8 Jason Lisle, *The Ultimate Proof of Creation* (Green Forest, AR: Master Books, 2009), pp. 68-69.

9 Cairns, "Revelation," *Dictionary of Theological Terms,* pp. 383-384.

10 Henry Morris, *The Genesis Record* (Grand Rapids: Baker Book House, 1976), pp. 26-27.

11 Wilbur Smith, *Therefore Stand: Christian Apologetics* (Grand Rapids: Baker Book House, 1974 reprint), p. 284.

12 Henry Morris, *The Biblical Basis for Modern Science* (Grand Rapids: Baker Book House, 1984), p. 156.

13 Morris, *The Biblical Basis for Modern Science,* p. 244, quoting William Pollard.

14 Jonathan Sarfati, *By Design: Evidence for Nature's Intelligent Designer—the God of the Bible* (Australia: Creation Book Publishers, 2008), p. 39.

15 Dr. Del Tackett, "The Truth Project" DVD, #5: "Science" (Colorado Springs, CO: Focus on the Family, 2006).

16 Gary Parker, "From Evolution to Creation" DVD (Answers in Genesis, 2007).

17 Richard Dawkins, *The Blind Watchmaker* (New York: Norton, 1986), p. 1.

18 Nancy Pearcey, *Total Truth* (Wheaton, IL: Crossway Books, 2005), p. 184, quoting George Gaylord Simpson.

19 Michael Behe, *Darwin's Black Box* (New York: The Free Press, 1996), p. 39.

20 Ibid, pp. 52, 73.

21 Wendell Bird, *The Origin of Species Revisited,* volume 1 (New York: Philosophical Library, 1991), p. 304, quoting Fred Hoyle.

22 Werner Gitt, "Design by Information," in Ashton, John and Michael Westcott, eds., *The Big Argument: Does God Exist?* (Green Forest, AR: Master Books, 2006)," pp. 51-71.

23 Harold Kushner, *When Bad Things Happen to Good People* (New York: Random House, 1981).

24 Douglas Wilson, *The Deluded Atheist* (Powder Springs, GA: American Vision, 2008).

25 Randy Alcorn, *If God is Good: Faith in the Midst of Suffering and Evil* (Colorado Springs, Colorado: Multnomah Books, 2009), p. 117.

26 Jerry Bridges, *Trusting God—Even When Life Hurts* (Colorado Springs, CO: NavPress, 2008), pp. 16-17.

27 Jim Berg, *Quieting a Noisy Soul—Overcoming Guilt, Anxiety, Anger and Despair,* DVD series (Greenville, SC: Bob Jones University Press, 2005).

28 Jim Berg, *Taking Time to Quiet Your Soul: Overcoming Guilt, Anxiety, Anger and Despair* (Greenville, SC: Bob Jones University Press, 2005), pp. 5, 9.

29 Josh McDowell and Don Stewart, *Handbook of Today's Religions* (Nashville: Thomas Nelson Publishers, 1983), Part III, chapters 8 and 9 on Judaism and Islam.

30 McDowell and Stewart, Part I, chapter 5 on Jehovah's Witnesses.

31 *The Holy Qur'an: Arabic Text, English Translation and Commentary* (Translation and commentary by Allama Abdullah Yusuf Ali) (Lahore, Pakistan: Muhammad Ashraf Publishers, 1979 edition), pp. 239, 271–272.

32 R. T. France, *Tyndale New Testament Commentaries: Matthew* (Grand Rapids: Eerdmans Publishing Company, 1985), pp. 414–415.

33 Cairns, "Trinity," p. 496.

34 Philip Schaff, *The Creeds of Christendom,* vol. 2, (Grand Rapids: Baker Book House, 1985 reprint), pp. 66-68.

35 Association of Christian Schools International, "ACSI Statement of Faith," http://www.acsiglobal.org/about-acsi/statement-of-faith. (Accessed 3/16/2019).

36 Schaff, *The Creeds of Christendom,* vol. 3, The New Hampshire Baptist Confession, p. 742.

37 Schaff, *The Creeds of Christendom,* vol. 3, The Augsburg Confession, p. 7.

38 Schaff, *The Creeds of Christendom,* vol. 3, Methodist Articles of Religion, p. 807.

39 Schaff, *The Creeds of Christendom,* vol. 3, The Westminster Confession, pp. 606-608. 611.

40 Schaff, *The Creeds of Christendom,* vol. 3, Reformed Episcopal Articles of Religion, p. 814.

41 Kurtz, *Humanist Manifestos I and II,* p. 13.

42 Norman Geisler and Abdul Saleeb, *Answering Islam* (Grand Rapids, MI: Baker Book House, 2002), p. 141.

43 Josh McDowell, *More Than a Carpenter* (Carol Stream, IL: Tyndale House Publishers, 2009 edition), pp. 27, 30, 33.

44 https://www.barna.com/research/barna-survey-examines-changes-in-worldview-among-christians-over-the-past-13-years (March 9, 2009). (Accessed 3/16/2019).

45 Schaff, *Creeds of Christendom,* vol. 2, pp. 58–59.

46 Paul Kurtz, ed., *A Secular Humanist Declaration* (Buffalo, NY: Prometheus Books, 1980), p. 18.

47 *Qur'an,* pp. 271, 272, 446.

48 McDowell and Stewart, chapter 8 on Judaism.

49 McDowell and Stewart, chapter 6 on Mormonism.

50 McDowell and Stewart, chapter 5 on Jehovah's Witnesses.

51 John Gerstner, *The Theology of the Major Sects,* (Grand Rapids: Baker Book House, 1960), chapter 5 on Liberalism.

52 Joseph Rutherford, *The Harp of God* (Brooklyn, NY: Watchtower Bible and Tract Society, 1921), pp. 171, 200.

53 Jack Mendelson, *Why I Am a Unitarian-Universalist* (New York: Thomas Nelson and Sons, 1965), p. 43.

54 Smith, *Therefore Stand,* pp. 423–424.

55 Schaff, *Creeds of Christendom,* vol. 3, pp. 619-621.

56 Schaff, *Creeds of Christendom,* volume 3, pp. 807, 814.

57 American Association of Christian Schools, Statement of Faith, AACS.org, http://www.aacs.org/about-us/membership/statement-of-faith. (Accessed 3/16/2019).

58 Association of Christian Schools International, Statement of Faith, ACSI.org, http://www.acsiglobal.org/about-acsi/statement-of-faith. (accessed 3/16/2019).

59 Baptist Faith & Message, http://www.sbc.net/bfm2000/bfm2000.asp. (Accessed 3/16/2019).

CHAPTER 4

MAN'S PERSON—CREATED, FALLEN, OBJECT OF REDEMPTION

Scripture describes itself as a light to see how to walk through life (Psalm 119:105). The Bible also describes itself as a mirror by which we can see ourselves and life clearly (James 1:23). So, God's Word is useful for seeing ourselves and life in the proper way.

We have seen that the Bible is God's message to man of Creation, Fall, and Redemption. The biblical account of Creation, Fall, and Redemption gives us God's lens to look through so we can see man in the right way, from God's viewpoint.

Look at man through the biblical lens of Creation. The Bible says that God created man in God's image (Gen. 1:27; Psalm 139:13), with God-given purpose (Gen. 1:26-28). Viewing man as created in God's image, with purpose, gives dignity to man. Neither the Humanist nor Islamic worldviews see man as created in God's image.

The Bible appeals to the image of God in man in connection with respect for people. For instance, we must put to death murderers, because they kill people made in God's image (Gen. 9:6). We must not curse people, because God made them in His image (James 3:9).

Look at man through the lens of the Fall. According to the Bible, man has a fallen, sinful nature (Rom. 8:7; Psalm 51:5). Viewing man as fallen in sin helps man avoid pride and see his greatest need—redemption from sin against God. Neither the Humanist nor the Islamic worldviews see man as having a fallen, sinful nature.

Look at man through the lens of Redemption. God freely offers redemption from sin to man by His grace through faith in Christ (Isa. 45:22; Rev. 22:17; John 3:16). Viewing man as the object of God's redeeming love gives hope to man. Neither the Humanist nor the Islamic worldviews believe in God's redeeming grace to man through Christ.

The Christian worldview answers the basic worldview questions, "Who am I? What is my biggest problem? What is the solution to my biggest problem?" According to the Bible, man is created by God, fallen in sin, and the object of redemption by God. We should view ourselves and every other person in the world as created, fallen, and the object of redemption. The Christian worldview gives a superior way to look at and understand man.

MAN AS CREATED BY GOD

The Humanist worldview sees man as evolved from animals. The Islamic worldview sees God as so unlike man that man could not be made in God's image. The Christian worldview, based on Scripture, sees man as made in the image of God. God's Word declares:

"God created man in His own image" (Gen. 1:27).

But what does "the image of God" mean? It cannot mean that God made man into a god. Thinking he could be a god was part of man's fall into sin (Gen. 3:5). Also, the image of God cannot apply to animals. Genesis 1 applies the image of God to only man, not animals.

Comparing Genesis 1:26–27 with Colossians 3:10 and Ephesians 4:24 helps us form an idea of at least a minimum of what is involved in the image of God in man. Colossians 3:10 states, "[You] have put on the new self, which is being renewed in knowledge after the image of its Creator." Ephesians 4:24 states, "Put on the new self, created after the likeness of God in true righteousness and holiness."

The image of God in man includes aspects of knowledge and righteousness. Biblically we can say that God created man in His likeness with knowledge and righteousness. Man's fall into sin impaired man's knowledge of God and man's righteous character. Redemption through Christ renews man to be like God in true knowledge and righteousness.

Based on Colossians 3:10 and Ephesians 4:24, Bible-believing Protestant theologians have seen in Scripture at least these two key aspects to the image of God in man, knowledge, and righteousness. The Westminster catechism states: "God created man . . . after his own image in knowledge, righteousness and holiness."[1] Knowledge points to a rational and relational aspect in the image of God in man. Righteousness points to a moral aspect in the image of God in man.

Consider what two respected theological writers say about the matter:

> "The image of God is true righteousness, holiness, and a true knowledge of God . . . . Ephesians 4:21–24 . . . Colossians 3:10 . . . The allusion in these verses to Genesis 1:26–27 is inescapable, and the renewal through Christ is described in terms of true righteousness and holiness in the former verse and in terms of knowledge in the latter verse."[2]

> "Col. 3:10 and Eph. 4:24 indicate that knowledge, righteousness, and holiness characterized the state in which man was originally created. Gen. 1:27 teaches that he was created in the image of God, and so we can conclude that his creation in knowledge, righteousness, and holiness constitutes, at least in part, the image of God in man."[3]

Consider the aspect of knowledge. Although man does not have infinite knowledge like God, he can know and understand things in a finite way and has a basic knowledge of God (Rom. 1:18-21). According to Romans 8:7, man's fall into sin affects his thinking and desires. More specifically, part of the image of God that has been marred is the aspect of knowledge. The apostle Paul says that a believer, though, is a new man who is renewed in God's image in knowledge (Col. 3:10). Redemption repairs man's knowledge of God.

There is a relational aspect to knowledge. In the Bible, knowledge includes knowing God in a personal relationship (John 17:3). Man's fall into sin destroyed man's original perfect relationship with God (Gen. 3). Only redemption through Christ restores believers to a right relationship with God (2 Cor. 5:19).

There is a rational aspect of knowledge, also. Unlike animals, but like God, man was created as a rational being. God reasons, and He created man in His image also with the ability to reason (Isa. 1:18). Using God-given intelligence, man can reflect the image of God in how he functions. God is a king and a worker (Psalm 44:4; John 5:17). Man in God's likeness is to engage in ruling and working on the earth (Gen. 1:28).

Ephesians 4:24 connects the image of God in man to righteousness. After creating man, "God saw everything that He had made, and behold, it was very good" (Gen. 1:31). God's Word reveals that God is holy (1 Pet. 1:15) and perfect (Matt. 5:48). Scripture says, "God man upright" (Ecc. 7:29). God created man originally without sin, like Himself.

However, when man sinned he became unrighteous. Since the Fall, no person is righteous (Rom. 3:10). God gives sinful people a new righteous nature when they repent and put faith in Christ for salvation (1 John 2:29; 2 Pet. 1:3-4). God the Father has determined to conform His redeemed people to the sinless image of His Son, Jesus Christ (Rom. 8:29).

Also, the Bible teaches that God created man as one race, the human race, not many races. God created every person from every nation in His image (Gen. 1:27) and all people of every skin color and ethnic background descend from the original pair of people that God created (Genesis 3:20). Note the book by Charles Ware and Ken Ham, *One Race/One Blood.*[4] God's Word says: "And he made from one man every nation of mankind to live on all the face of the earth . . . that they should seek God" (Acts 17:26-27).

The Bible also teaches that God created man with purpose. The Christian worldview gives people hope and meaning to life as revealed in God's Word, the Bible. The Bible answers the worldview question, "Why am I here?" The beginning of the answer to that question is found in Genesis 1:26–28, which presents God's Creation Mandate to man:

> "Then God said, 'Let us make man in our image, after our likeness. And let them have dominion over the fish of the sea and over the birds of the heavens and over the livestock and over all the earth and over every creeping thing that creeps on the earth.' So God created man in his own image; in the image of God he created him; male and female he created them.' And God blessed them. And God said to them, 'Be fruitful and multiply and fill the earth and subdue it, and have dominion over the fish of the sea and over the birds of the heavens and over every living thing that moves on the earth."

Let's consider the elements of the Creation Mandate.

The text speaks of God's image in man before speaking of God's command to man. As a creature made in God's image, man is capable of communication with God. God created man to fellowship with Him and serve Him. God talked and had fellowship with man in the Garden of Eden (Gen. 1–3). And God gave man commands about how to serve Him.

God commanded man to rule the animals on the earth. God tells man to "have dominion" over the earth. This dominion in Genesis 1:28 involves ruling over animals. Man is distinct from and superior to animals. And he has been given the responsibility to govern animals in the water, in the air, and on land.

God commands man to subdue the earth (Gen. 1:28). God instructs man to work the earth that God created and take charge of it. God put man to work on the earth the same day He created Him (Gen. 2:15). Man must study the earth and use its resources for God's glory—"Do all to the glory of God" (1 Cor. 10:31)—and for man's good—"Through love serve one another" (Gal. 5:13).

God commands man to fill the earth (Gen. 1:28; 9:1). The human race began with two people and repopulated with eight people after the Flood. God made man as male and female (Gen. 1:27). God ordained that marriage should be between one man and one woman for reproduction and companionship (Gen. 1:28, 2:18).

These 4 elements of the Creation Mandate of Genesis 1:26–28 describe God's original purpose for man:

1. **Fellowship with and serve God as a person in God's image.**
2. **Govern animals on the earth for God.**
3. **Study the earth and use its resources for God's glory and man's good.**
4. **Fill the earth with people through marriage.**

God repeated this Creation Mandate to Noah and his sons after the Flood:

> "Be fruitful and multiply and fill the earth . . . . The fear of you . . . shall be upon every beast of the earth and upon every bird of the heavens, upon everything that

creeps on the ground and all the fish of the sea. Into your hand they are delivered" (Gen. 9:1–2).

Centuries later God's Word mentions this Creation Mandate of God to man again in the book of Psalms (Psalm 8:6-8).

Man should follow the two great commandments, to love God and love his neighbor (Matt. 22:36–40), as he follows the Creation Mandate. The Bible nowhere repeals the Creation Mandate. The fall of man in Genesis 3 made the Creation Mandate more difficult for man to fulfill, but the Fall did not abolish the Creation Mandate.

A theologian, Dr. John Frame, gives comments on the Creation Mandate of Genesis 1:28:

> "Man is to subdue the earth and have dominion over all other creatures. Here, Adam and Eve are to image the power of God's lordship, taking control over the world to God's glory. . . . It is right and good for us to explore and inhabit the earth and to use its resources for the glory of God and the betterment of human life."[5]

In his commentary on Genesis, Dr. Henry Morris, a Bible-believing creationist scientist, also recognizes the Creation Mandate in Genesis 1:26–28 as still applying to man on earth today:

> "Here is the primeval commission to man authorizing both science and technology as man's basic enterprises relative to the earth. 'Science' is man's disciplined study and understanding of the phenomena of his world. 'Technology' is the implementation of this knowledge in the effective ordering and development of the earth and its resources, for the greater good of all earth's inhabitants (including such fields of human service as engineering, agriculture, medicine, and a host of other practical technologies). This two-fold commission to subdue and have dominion, to conquer and rule, embraces all productive human activities . . . . This command established man as God's steward over the created world. . . . This primeval commission has never been abrogated. Man is still under its obligations. The scientific and technological enterprises still comprise God's mandate to man relative to the earth and its inhabitants. Man would find himself immeasurably more productive and effective in such pursuits if he would only approach them in the reverent and believing attitude of an honest and good servant of his Maker."[6]

God's Creation Mandate involves subduing the earth. That involves science and technology. Science involves studying what God has created. Technology involves using what God has created.

Christian worldview assumptions rooted in the biblical account of Creation give the foundation for the pursuit of science. God created a real world and made man in His image with the mental ability to study the world. God sustains creation by His power and has designed a basic uniformity in nature (Heb. 1:3; Gen. 8:22).

The Christian worldview is foundational for man's use of technology. John Dyer, a Christian with both seminary and computer training, has written a helpful book on technology from a Christian worldview perspective, *From the Garden to the City: The Redeeming and Corrupting Power of Technology.*[7] He gives a helpful definition of technology: "The human activity of using tools to transform God's creation for practical purposes."[8]

Man's advances in technology have benefited people all over the earth. Home appliances, medical advances, printers and computers, motorized transportation and communication devices have helped human life on the earth. Technology has also given Christians greater opportunities to spread God's Word to the world and to communicate with one another.

However, Humanism takes faith in human technology to an extreme. John Dyer, in his Christian book on technology, notes some Humanists have written about human directed evolution through technology, or possibly overcoming death through technology or solving all human problems through technology.[9] *The Humanist Manifesto* states:

> "Using technology wisely, we can control our environment, conquer poverty, markedly reduce disease, extend our life span, significantly modify our behavior, alter the course of human evolution and cultural development, unlock vast new powers and provide humankind with unparalleled opportunity for achieving an abundant and meaningful life. . . . No deity will save us; we must save ourselves"[10]

God's Creation Mandate also involves governing animals. At the beginning, God had Adam name the animals (Gen. 2:19). God's Word instructs man to give proper care for animals (Deut. 5:14, 22:6-7, 25:4). God gave livestock for man to tend for his use (Gen. 4:20; Prov. 27:23, 27:26–27). God appeals to animals as a testimony to His creative design, wisdom, and power (Job 39-40). God uses animals as lessons for man (Prov. 6:6).

Radical environmentalism clashes with the Christian worldview about animals and man.

Radical environmentalists are evolutionists and believe that man evolved from animals, rather than being directly created by God in God's image. Therefore, many of them view animals as equal in value and rights to man.

Thus, many environmentalists attack the practice of people using animal skin and fur in clothing. Of course, it is not right to torture animals. However, God Himself killed an animal to make clothes for man (Gen. 3:21). Thus, man may take fur and skin from dead animals for clothes.

A number of environmentalists attack the practice of eating animal meat. It is true that God originally gave plants to man for food (Gen. 1:29), which people should still eat today for a balanced diet. But God in His Word clearly tells man he can eat animal meat in addition to plants (Gen. 9:1–3; Acts 10:9–15; 1 Tim. 4:1–5). And there are nutritional benefits for man from animal protein.

Jesus ate animal meat (John 21:5-12). It is wrong to forbid people to eat animals for food, "foods that God created to be received with thanksgiving . . . for everything created by God is good" (1 Tim. 4:3, 4). God also tells man to kill animals that kill or attack people (Gen. 9:5).

God views people as of more value than animals. Man is superior to animals, being made in God's image and with a God-given purpose to govern animals (Gen. 1:26-28). Jesus said of people in comparison to animals, "Are you not of more value than they?" (Matt. 6:26). We should not sacrifice the good of people for animals.

One illustration of environmentalists favoring animals over people is the matter of DDT, insects and malaria among people. Environmentalist writings and lobbying led to a ban on DDT because they feared that it killed birds.[11] However, DDT had helped millions of people by killing insect populations that spread malaria. It did not destroy the bird population where it was used. But after it was banned, malaria and human deaths greatly increased in the poor and undeveloped areas where DDT was previously effective.

Dr. J. Y. Jones is a Bible-believing Christian who is a long-time student of Scripture, a physician, and a hunter. He has written a helpful book that refutes extreme environmental views about animals, *Worship Not the Creature: Animal Rights and the Bible.*[12] Dr. Jones writes as one who believes in biblical creation and rejects evolution.[13]

He documents from the overall teaching of Scripture that God gives man the right to kill animals for food and clothing.[14] He points out scientific evidence that a totally meatless lifestyle can lead to health problems and that meat provides important vitamins.[15] He also documents the fact that animal rights extremists have engaged in hundreds of terrorist attacks on law-abiding animal operations.[16] Dr. Jones gives this quote from an animal rights leader about the worldview clash of animal rights with Christianity and the Bible:

> "Dr. Peter Singer, a noted author and the father of the modern animal rights movement . . . states, 'Christianity is our foe. If animal rights is to succeed, we must destroy the Judeo-Christian religious tradition.'"[17]

God's Creation Mandate also involves filling the earth with people (Gen. 1:28 and 9:1). God's Word views children as a blessing from the Lord (Psalm 127:3–5). However, Humanist environmental groups advocate abortion to limit human population.[18] Many Humanist environmentalists express alarm about the growth of human population and want government action to curb population growth. One radical environmentalist even stated:

> "Until such time as 'Homo Sapiens' should decide to rejoin nature, some of us can only hope for the right virus to come along."[19]

Calvin Beisner is a Christian economist and theologian. He has written a very helpful book on this issue, *Prospects for Growth: A Biblical View of Population, Resources and the Future.*[20] He shows in his book that our current population in the Earth is not a problem for crowding or food production.

As people look at themselves, they can see evidence of God's creative design. Man is as the Bible says. David, under Divine inspiration, wrote:

> "For you formed my inward parts; you knitted me together in my mother's womb. I praise you, for I am fearfully and wonderfully made. Wonderful are your works; my soul knows it very well" (Psalm 139:13-14).

God's Word teaches that God created man to reproduce people (Gen. 1:26-28), while at the same time God created different kinds of animals to reproduce after their own kind (Gen. 1:21-25). Man has never observed animals evolve into a different kind of animal or animals evolve into people. Man is not an evolved animal. It is biologically impossible for animal DNA to produce humans. The information in man's DNA gives a powerful testimony to God's creation of man. Dr. Jason Lisle, a scientist and Biblical creationist, observes:

> "DNA qualifies under the definition of information: it contains an encoded message (the base pair triplets represent amino acids) and has an expected action (the formation of proteins) and an intended purpose (life). . . . No one reading this book would conclude that it was generated by a sequence of typos that gradually accumulated over time. . . . The information in DNA cannot have come about by mutations and natural selection because the laws of information science tell us that all information comes from a mind. But the information in DNA makes sense in light of biblical creation."[21]

The Bible says God made man in His image (Gen. 1:26-28). We have seen that creation in God's image includes the aspects of knowledge and righteousness. People can look at themselves and see aspects of rational and relational knowledge and a sense of right and wrong. Such aspects of rational and relational knowledge and a sense of right and wrong could not have come about by random evolution.

People recognize that there are immaterial laws of logic, such as the law of non-contradiction. Something and its opposite cannot be true in the same way and at the same time. Evolution in a universe that is only material cannot produce immaterial laws of logic.

Also, people can observe that man has a sense of right and wrong. That comes from the aspect of righteousness in the image of God in man. God put that awareness of right and wrong in the inner nature of people. Throughout time, people all over the world have had that sense of right and wrong human behavior even without the Bible. How can evolution, based on death and the survival of the fittest, produce an inner sense of right and wrong? God's Word says:

> "For when Gentiles, who do not have the law, by nature do what the law requires . . . they show that the work of the law is written on their hearts, while their conscience also bears witness" (Rom. 2:14-15).

Finally, God's Creation Mandate involves a command for man to work. In Genesis 1:28 God commands man to subdue the earth and govern animals, which involves work. God put man to work immediately after his creation, tending a garden and naming the animals (Gen. 2:15, 19). Then in the rest of Scripture God gives further instruction to man about work.

God's Word teaches that work is necessary for man to provide his basic needs. God told man, "By the sweat of your face you shall eat bread" (Gen. 3:19). Scripture commands man to work in order to eat: "If anyone is not willing to work, let him not eat" (2 Thess. 3:10). The apostle Paul who gave this Scriptural command set an example. He said, "These hands ministered to my necessities and to those who were with me" (Acts 20:34).

The Bible teaches us to be diligent in our work in order to avoid poverty and gain wealth. Proverbs warns people about laziness and poverty. "The soul of the sluggard craves and gets nothing, while the soul of the diligent is richly supplied" (Prov. 13:4). "In all toil there is profit, but mere talk tends only to poverty" (Prov. 14:23). The New Testament urges people to be diligent in work. "Whatever you do, work heartily, as for the Lord and not for men" (Col. 3:23).

God wants man to be sincere and honest in work. A person should work hard, even if an employer is not watching. "Obey your earthly masters . . . with a sincere heart, as you would Christ, not by the way of eye-service, but as bondservants of Christ, doing the will of God from the heart, rendering service with a good will as to the Lord and not to man" (Eph. 6:5-7).

God teaches us to do honest work to provide for our family and to have something to give to people in need. "But if anyone does not provide for . . . members of his household, he has denied the faith and is worse than an unbeliever" (1 Tim. 5:8). "Let the thief no longer steal, but rather let him labor, doing honest work with his own hands, so that he may have something to share with anyone in need" (Eph. 4:28).

God wants to bless people with the enjoyment of the fruit of their labor. God's Word declares, "There is nothing better for a person than that he should eat and drink and find enjoyment in his toil. This also I saw is from the hand of God" (Ecc. 2:24). We may use a portion of what we earn from our work for our personal enjoyment. We should thank God for these material blessings that we earn through work.

The Bible teaches that God gifts man in different kinds of work according to His will. The Holy Spirit gives various abilities to people (1 Cor. 12:4-6, 11). The story of Bezalel who worked on the tabernacle shows us that God gives us our work abilities:

> "See, I have called by name Bezalel . . . and I have filled him with the Spirit of God, with ability and intelligence, with knowledge and all craftsmanship, to devise artistic designs, to work in gold, silver and bronze, in cutting stones for setting and in carving wood, to work in every craft. . . . And I have given to all able men ability, that they may make all that I have commanded you" (Exo. 31:2-6).

Finally, God's Word urges us to work with the right motivation. We should seek to glorify God through our work. "Whatever you do, do all to the glory of God" (1 Cor. 10:31). We should serve other people out of love through our work. "Through love serve one another" (Gal. 5:13). We should do our work as a service to the Lord, to please Him. "Rendering service with a good will as to the Lord and not to man, knowing that whatever good anyone does, this he will receive back from the Lord" (Eph. 6:7-8).

MAN AS FALLEN IN SIN

Is man basically good? Or, is man basically sinful? Where does evil behavior come from? Why is death a universal human experience? The Bible answers these questions.

How we view man's nature and his condition is an important part of a worldview.

The old Blue-Backed Speller, which American colonists used for early education, used the Bible to teach the alphabet. For example, a Bible-based rhyme for the letter "A" stated, "In Adam's fall, we sinned all."[22] This simple rhyme summed up the truth of Romans 5:12:

> "Therefore just as sin came into the world through one man, and death through sin, and so death spread to all men because all sinned."

The Bible gives the account of man's fall into sin (Gen. 3). God created Adam and Eve in a state of moral goodness (Gen. 1:31). God commanded them not to eat of the tree of the knowledge of good and evil lest they die (Gen. 2:17). Satan tempted Eve to eat of the forbidden tree by raising doubts about God's Word (Gen. 3:1). He then denied God's Word when he said that man would not die (Gen. 3:4).

Satan used three lines of temptation with Eve (Gen. 3:5–6; 1 John 2:15-16):

1. The lust of the flesh (unlawful physical pleasures)—"The woman saw that the tree was good for food" (Gen. 3:6);

2. The lust of the eyes (unlawful desire for things)—"It was a delight to the eyes" (Gen. 3:6).
3. The pride of life (exalting self)—"You will be like God, knowing good and evil" (Gen. 3:5) Satan tempted Eve to determine right and wrong for herself apart from God. Satan deceived Eve, and she ate the forbidden fruit (Gen. 3:6). But when she gave the fruit to Adam, he ate in knowing, undeceived disobedience (1 Tim. 2:14). In their guilt, Adam and Eve hid from God, and God cursed them for their sin (Gen. 3:7–11, 3:14–21).

This was the beginning of sin in the world (Rom. 5:12). The sin of Adam and Eve was the first sin in man's history on earth. The Bible teaches that Adam's sin plunged the whole human race into sin (Rom. 5:19). But what does it mean that "all sinned" in connection with Adam's sin (Rom. 5:12)?

Consider man's connection to Adam. Adam and Eve were the first two humans—the parents of the whole human race—and all the people of the world are their descendants (Gen. 3:20). All people inherit a sinful nature from Adam because of his sin (Eph. 2:3). And because of that sinful nature, all people choose to sin, as Scripture says "all have sinned" (Rom. 3:23).

Scripture describes Christ as a second Adam (1 Cor. 15:21–22, 45–49). Adam is the representative head of the human race, so Adam's disobedience brought death to all mankind. But Christ's obedience brought salvation to mankind (Rom. 5:12–21). Theologians use the term "imputation" to describe what Paul teaches in Romans 5. A theological dictionary gives this definition for imputation:

> "The reckoning or placing to a person's account the merit or guilt that belongs to him on the basis of his personal performance or of that of his federal head."[23]

God charged Adam's sin to the whole human race that he represented. But God also imputes Christ's righteousness to His believing people. Adam's sin involves the biblical doctrine of "original sin." Original sin is the sin nature every person inherits from Adam. A theological dictionary explains original sin as:

> "Fallen man's natural sinfulness, the hereditary depravity and corruption of human nature because of Adam's fall. Though it inheres in human nature and is propagated by natural generation, it does not arise from anything in man's original natural constitution."[24]

Romans 5:12 teaches that all mankind experience death as a result of Adam's fall into sin. **Because of sin, all people die physically.** Also because of sin, **all people experience spiritual death**, as all people are born with a sinful nature, separated from God because of sin:

> "It is appointed for man to die once" (Heb. 9:27).
>
> "You were dead in trespasses and sins . . . and were by nature children of wrath" (Eph. 2:1, 3).

A commentary on Romans 5:12 notes, "Paul may simply have in mind this death in both its physical and spiritual aspects. . . . So most commentators."[25]

In Genesis 2:17 God warned Adam that death would be the penalty for disobedience. The Hebrew phrase for *die* can be translated as, "dying you shall die." When Adam and Eve sinned, God told them they would die physically because of their sin (Gen. 3:19), and the process of physical death began in their bodies until they died many years later (Gen. 5:5). When Adam and Eve sinned, they also experienced spiritual death. They were immediately alienated from God, hiding themselves from Him in their guilt and shame (Gen. 3:7–13).

Also, Genesis 3 reveals that God cursed man's world as a result of man's sin, relating to God's Creation Mandate to man (Gen. 1:26-28). Man was to rule animals and animals began to experience death (Gen. 3:14-15, 3:21, 4:4). Male and female were to reproduce and God brought pain to childbirth (Gen. 3:16). Man was to subdue the earth and God brought thorns to the ground and difficulty in working on the earth (Gen. 3:17-19).

The Bible tells us that the just penalty of sin is death (Rom. 6:23). Scripture speaks of two deaths for sinful man. The first death involves death for all people as a result of Adam's sin (Rom. 5:12). This involves spiritual death, being born with a sinful nature and separated from God (Eph. 2:1-3), and physical death (Heb. 9:27). The second death is eternal separation from God in Hell for people's punishment for their own sin, who die without repentance and faith (Ezek. 18:4; Luke 13:3; John 3:36; Rom. 6:20–23; Rev. 20:11–15, 21:8).

The state of spiritual death, in which people are born with a sinful nature, involves what theologians call "total depravity." This term does not mean that man acts as totally sinful as possible. It means that depravity extends to the totality of man's being (Jer. 17:9) and that man is totally unable to save himself (Rom. 3:10, 19-20). A theological dictionary states:

> "Total depravity means that corruption has extended to all aspects of man's nature, to his entire being, and total depravity means that because of corruption there is nothing man can do to merit saving favor with God."[26]

Because of this total depravity of man's nature, every person has sinful thinking. Every person has sinful desires. Every person chooses to do sinful things:

> "The mind that is set on the flesh is hostile to God" (Rom. 8:7).
>
> "Out of the heart of man come evil thoughts . . . coveting" (Mark 7:22).
>
> "For all have sinned and fall short of the glory of God" (Rom. 3:23).

Neither the Humanist worldview nor the Islamic worldview accepts this biblical teaching of man's sinful, depraved nature. For example, a Muslim writer states:

> "The Christian witness that the rebellion by our first parents has tragically distorted man and that sinfulness pervades us individually and collectively is very much contrary to Islamic witness. . . . Man is not born a sinner and the doctrine of the sinfulness of man has no basis in Islam."[27]

A leading Humanist psychologist, Abraham Maslow, stated, "As far as I know, we just don't have any intrinsic instincts for evil."[28]

In contrast, Bible-believing Christians, even from different church backgrounds, agree that man is not basically good and has a fallen, sinful nature. Note that the following Protestant confessions all express a basic agreement about man's fall into sin and sinful nature:

BAPTIST CONFESSION OF 1833

"Man was created in holiness, under the law of his Maker; but by voluntary transgression fell from that holy and happy state; in consequence of which all mankind are now sinners, not by constraint but choice; being by nature utterly void of that holiness required by the law of God, positively inclined to evil."[29]

LUTHERAN FORMULA OF CONCORD

"Original sin is so profound a corruption of human nature as to leave nothing sound, nothing uncorrupt in the body or soul of man, or in his mental or bodily powers. . . . Original sin is innate in us by reason of the corrupted seed from which we spring and is moreover a fountain of all other actual sins."[30]

METHODIST ARTICLES OF RELIGION

"Original sin is the corruption of the offspring of Adam, whereby man is very far gone from original righteousness, and of his own nature inclined to evil, and that continually. . . . The condition of man after the fall of Adam is such that . . . we have no power to do good works, pleasant and acceptable to God, without the grace of God."[31]

PRESBYTERIAN WESTMINSTER CONFESSION

"Our first parents . . . fell from their original righteousness . . . and became dead in sin and wholly defiled in all the faculties and parts of soul and body. . . . They being the root of all mankind, the guilt of this sin was imputed and the same death in sin and corrupted nature conveyed to all their posterity."[32]

REFORMED EPISCOPAL ARTICLES OF RELIGION

"Original sin . . . is the fault and corruption of the nature of every man, that is naturally engendered of the offspring of Adam; whereby man is very far gone from original righteousness and is of his own nature inclined to evil."[33]

Consider an illustration from literature. J. F. Baldwin is a Bible-believing Christian worldview writer. He points out that how you understand man's nature will affect your worldview. He used two books, *Frankenstein* and *Dr. Jekyll and Mr. Hyde,* to illustrate differing worldviews about the nature of man. He observes,

> "People believe that either the story of Frankenstein or the story of Jekyll is the story of themselves, and of Everyman. They either believe that the monster of Frankenstein speaks for them when he says, "I was benevolent and good; misery made me a fiend. Make me happy, and I shall be again virtuous." Or, they believe Jekyll speaks for them when he says, "It was the curse of mankind that these incongruous personalities (the good and the bad) were thus bound together—that in the agonized womb of consciousness, these polar twins should be continuously struggling." Either Mary Shelley wrote the story of Everyman in Frankenstein, or Robert Louis Stevenson wrote it in Dr. Jekyll and Mr. Hyde. What kind of monster are you? The way you answer this question forms the foundation for your beliefs about all of reality—your religion, your worldview."[34]

The story of Frankenstein communicates the idea that man is basically good and only man's bad environment corrupts him. The story of Dr. Jekyll and Mr. Hyde communicates the idea that man has a sinful nature with which he struggles. Clearly, the story of Jekyll and Hyde better illustrates the Christian worldview about man's nature.

In this world we can easily observe what we read in the Bible about man's sinful nature. Every person has a sinful nature, and as a result people sin in their actions, words, thoughts, and in their failure to do good things (Rom. 3:23; James 3:2; Rom. 8:7; James 4:17). People all over the world and throughout time have observed the universal reality of death (Rom. 5:12). We can observe and objectively define sin by the standard of God's moral law in the Bible.

God's Word says that "through the law comes the knowledge of sin" (Rom. 3:20). God's law is summarized in the two great commandments—to love God and love your neighbor (Matthew 22:35–40), as well as the Ten Commandments (Exo. 20:3–17). Jesus says these commands include our thoughts and desires. "Out of the heart proceed evil thoughts, murders, adulteries, fornications, thefts, false witness, blasphemies (Matt. 15:18).

Consider the Ten Commandments as a summary of God's moral law. The first commandment forbids worshipping any other god. It demands that man honor and serve the one true God. The second commandment forbids using images to represent God or worshipping any image. The third commandment forbids any profane use of God's name, including false or casual swearing or using God's name in anger.

The fourth commandment demands that man work for six days and rest one day and worship God. Most Christians see the requirement to observe the seventh day of the week (Saturday) as having been set aside (Col. 2:16–17). But it is still good for man to rest from usual labor one day each week (Mark 2:27–28; Deut. 5:13–14). The New Testament points to Christians gathering for worship on Sunday, the first day of the week (Acts 20:7).

In commandments five through ten, two of these commandments emphasize respect for the family. The fifth commandment requires children to obey parents (Eph. 6:1–2) and adults to respect and care for aged parents (Matt. 15:4–6). The seventh commandment forbids all sexual activity outside of monogamous, heterosexual marriage (1 Thess. 4:3). It also forbids sexual lust and divorce and remarriage on unbiblical grounds (Matt. 5:27–32).

Two commandments refer to respect for our neighbor's person. The sixth commandment forbids intentionally taking innocent human life. It also forbids heart hatred as a form of murder (Matt. 5:21–22). The ninth commandment forbids false witness against our neighbor by lying about or to another person.

Two commandments speak of respect for our neighbor's property. The eighth commandment forbids taking property from our neighbor that doesn't belong to us. The tenth commandment condemns covetousness and forbids even desiring to take anything that rightly belongs to our neighbor (Eph. 5:5). Sinful man violates these commandments of God.

Do you observe yourself ever having hateful, lustful, dishonest, or covetous thoughts or thoughts that are disrespectful to God? Such inward, evil thoughts confirm the Christian worldview about man's nature. Have you always loved God with your entire being? Or have you sometimes loved other people more than God or valued things more than God? Have you ever used the name of God or Christ in an angry or frustrated way? Maybe you've intentionally missed church or gone through a day without praying or giving thanks to God for what you have.

Have you disobeyed or spoken disrespectfully to a parent or a lawful authority? Perhaps you've murdered someone by hating them in your heart (Matt. 5:21–22). Have you engaged in sexual acts outside of marriage or had sexual lust in your thoughts (Matt. 5:27–30)? Have you ever taken something that did not belong to you or wanted to? Have you failed to help people in need? Have you told a lie or held false views? Have you envied other people's possessions? Do you see that what the Bible says is true about our sinful nature?

The Christian worldview and the Humanist worldview clash about the idea of sin. Humanists do not see man as having a sinful nature. They see man as basically good. They do not see bad behavior as a sin against God. They think of wrong behavior as just hurting other people or abusing animals or harming the environment. They define wrong behavior by man's thinking, not the Bible. They view bad behavior as due either to social institutions or to vestiges of evolution or to a mental illness or disease.

Secular psychology and secular psychiatry reflect the Humanist view. Dr. Paul Vitz has written a critique of secular psychotherapy and psychiatry. He has a Ph.D. in psychology and many years of experience in that field. He was a former skeptic, but he converted to Christianity. He wrote a book called *Psychology as Religion: The Cult of Self-Worship.*[35] In his book, Dr. Vitz documented the view of a leading secular psychologist, Eric Fromm, about man's nature:

> "Fromm described human nature as intrinsically and naturally good and attributed anything bad—evil—to society, especially when society causes the self to deny its own potential for growth and expression."[36]

Dr. Vitz also quotes the observation of a former president of the American Psychological Association about psychology, evolution, and man's nature:

> "There is in psychology today a general background assumption that the human impulses provided by biological evolution are right and optimal."[37]

However, this same former APA president went on to say, "This assumption may now be regarded as scientifically wrong."[38] Some secular psychiatrists or psychologists may recognize bad or violent inner desires in people, but with their belief in evolution they would attribute such desires or tendencies to man's evolution from animals and not to a sin nature.

Another illustration of worldview conflict about sin is the problem of alcoholism. Secular psychiatry views alcoholism as a disease or mental illness, rather than as a sin. However, the Bible clearly teaches that drunkenness is a sin (Prov. 23:29-35; 1 Cor. 6:9-11; Gal. 5:19-21; Eph. 5:18-19). For a good discussion of alcoholism as a sin rather than a disease from a Christian worldview perspective, see the chapter on "Alcoholism" by Christian counselor, Dr. Edward Welch, in his book, *Blame it on the Brain?*[39]

The Christian worldview sees man's greatest problem as sin against God. Christian worldview writers note that the various manifestations of the Humanist worldview define man's problem—and the solution—contrary to God's Word.[40] How you define the problem determines the solution. Humanists reject the idea of man's greatest problem being an inward sin nature and personal sin against God, but they vary in what they identify as man's greatest problem.

Some see man's greatest problem as lack of education and lack of counseling with man's wisdom and lack of sufficient technology (Secular Humanism). Some see man's greatest problem as lack of possessions and unfair economic institutions (Marxism). Some see man's greatest problem as human technology harming the physical environment (Environmentalism). Some see man's greatest problem as outward restraints on sexual freedom that inhibit fulfillment of personal desires (Sexual Revolution). All see man's problems as outside of himself, rather than within.

According to the Bible, man's greatest problem is not outside of himself—his physical or social environment—but is within himself, in a sinful nature that leads to sinful deeds (Matt. 15:19). A Christian worldview writer aptly says:

> "Only Christianity provides true redemption—a restoration to our created state and the hope of eternal peace with God. No other worldview identifies the real problem—the stain of sin in our souls."[41]

BASIC BIBLE TEACHING ABOUT REDEMPTION

According to the Bible, the solution to the problem of sin is to receive the redemption from sin offered by Jesus Christ. Jesus came to save people from sins (Matt. 1:21). Sin enslaves man, according to the teaching of Jesus (John 8:34). When Jesus died on the Cross, He paid the ransom for sin, delivering men from sin's captivity. Sinful man is redeemed through the precious blood of Christ (1 Pet. 1:18–19).

The Bible words related to redemption are translated from Greek words that people used in everyday language. These words for redemption describe payment to deliver a slave or prisoner from captivity. A Bible dictionary explains the terms for redemption:

> "Redemption means deliverance from some evil by payment of a price. . . . Thus prisoners of war might be released on payment of a price, which was called a "ransom" (Greek lutron). . . . Christ's death may be regarded as "a ransom for many" (Mark 10:45). Again, slaves might be released by a process of ransom. . . . Paul reminds the Romans that in earlier days they had been "slaves of sin" (Romans 6:17). From another point of view men were under sentence of death on account of their sin (Romans 6:23). . . . The cross of Christ is seen against this background. It is the price paid to release the slaves, to let the condemned go free."[42]

Scripture describes the nature of the redemption that man needs. Because man has a sinful heart (Jer. 17:9), he commits sinful deeds (Rom. 3:23) and is a slave to sin (John 8:34). Because of sin, man faces God's judgment, eternal separation from God in a terrible place called Hell (Rev. 20:12–15). Man needs to be given a new heart that loves God and His Law and he also needs to be forgiven of his sins against God. This redemption from sin comes only through Christ's atoning death and bodily resurrection:

> "By means of his own blood, thus securing eternal redemption" (Heb. 9:12).
>
> "This is the covenant that I will make . . . I will put my laws into their hearts. . . . I will remember their sins and their lawless deeds no more" (Heb. 10:16–17).
>
> "The Gospel . . . by which you are being saved . . . that Christ died for our sins in accordance with the Scriptures . . . that he was raised on the third day in accordance with the Scriptures" (1 Cor. 15:1–4).

The Bible calls Christ's redemptive death a "propitiation" (1 John 2:2; 4:10), which satisfies God's wrath against sin. Christ's redemptive work brings salvation from the penalty of sin and the power of sin.

> "In him we have redemption through His blood, the forgiveness of our trespasses" (Eph. 1:7).
>
> "Our great God and Savior Jesus Christ who gave himself for us to redeem us from all lawlessness and to purify for himself a people for His own possession, who are zealous for good works" (Tit. 2:13b–14).

Let's summarize these basic Christian worldview teachings from the Bible on personal redemption:

1. **Man's basic problem is sin.**
2. **Sin imprisons and enslaves people.**
3. **The solution is personal redemption through Christ.**
4. **Redemption is deliverance through payment of a price.**
5. **Only Christ's redemptive work delivers man from sin's penalty and power.**

Two key blessings of salvation that are associated with redemption are what the Bible calls justification (Rom. 5:1) and regeneration (Tit. 3:5). In justification, God declares the redeemed believer righteous in Christ. In regeneration, God gives the believer a new right nature.

Redemption through Jesus delivers believers from sin's penalty. Ephesians 1:7 says believers in Christ have "redemption through his blood, the forgiveness of our trespasses." When a person receives forgiveness of sins through Christ's redemptive work, Scripture says that person receives deliverance from condemnation in Hell and receives eternal life with God.

> "But God shows His love for us, in that while we were still sinners, Christ died for us. Since therefore we have now been justified by His blood, we shall be saved from the wrath of God" (Rom. 5:8-9). "The free gift of God is eternal life in Christ Jesus our Lord" (Rom. 6:23).

Through faith in Jesus Christ, a believer is justified, which means declared righteous in God's sight. The book of Romans especially speaks of justification:

> "For all have sinned and fall short of the glory of God and are justified by His grace as a gift, through the redemption that is in Christ Jesus" (Rom. 3:23–24).

> "Therefore since we have been justified by faith, we have peace with God through our Lord Jesus Christ" (Rom. 5:1).

Concerning this justification, a theological dictionary states,

> "The imputed righteousness of Christ gives the believer 'the adoption of children' (Galatians 4:5) and . . . eternal life. . . . 'Justify' means 'to declare righteous' (Romans 5:9). . . . The righteousness of Christ's obedience in life and death is imputed as the ground of justification. . . . It is received by faith, without works" (Romans 3:20–22).[43]

In the matter of justification, God put the believer's sin on Christ at the Cross and gives the believer Christ's perfect righteousness:

> "For our sake he made him to be sin who knew no sin, so that in him we might become the righteousness of God" (2 Cor. 5:21).

Christ's redeeming work also delivers the believer from the power of sin (Tit. 2:14). When a person puts his or her faith in Christ for salvation, he or she is adopted as a child of God and the Holy Spirit comes to dwell in that person's life (Rom. 8:9–16; Gal. 3:14; 4:6). The Holy Spirit gives new life to the believer, the salvation blessing that the Bible calls "regeneration" or being "born again" (Eph. 2:1–5; John 3:8–9; Tit. 3:5).

We have seen that redemption through Christ gives the believer a new heart (Heb. 10:16). Regeneration, or being born again, gives the believer a new righteous nature that is essential for living with God in heaven. Jesus said, "Unless one is born again, he cannot see the kingdom of God" (John 3:3b).

Being born again also brings forth fruits of new life now in the believer. One important evidence that a person is truly born again is a love for God and Christian brethren (1 John 3:14-15 and 4:7-8). Another important fruit of being born again is that a person will seek to be righteous like Christ (1 John 2:3, 29; 3:2-10):

> The Islamic and Humanist worldviews do not believe in these redemptive blessings. In contrast to the Bible, the Qur'an does not teach that a person can personally

> know God as Heavenly Father and have eternal life with God through faith in Christ. In fact, Islamic writers say it is impossible to personally know Allah.[44] And Humanist writings state that Humanists "reject the idea that God . . . can save or redeem sinners."[45]

Man's redemption would not be complete without dealing with death. God's Word promises resurrection from the dead and eternal life in a new world for His people. Humanists reject the idea of the resurrection of the dead. Islam believes in the resurrection of the dead, but it bases eternal life on man's works, unlike the Bible, which presents eternal life as a gift (Rom. 6:23). Scripture describes the future redemption of man's body and world:

> "The creation itself also will be set free from its bondage to corruption and obtain the freedom of the glory of the children of God. . . . We ourselves . . . groan inwardly as we wait eagerly for . . . the redemption of our bodies" (Rom. 8:21, 23).

In the Gospel of Luke, Jesus referred to a future age and a resurrection when he spoke of those who "attain to that age and to the resurrection from the dead" (Luke 20:35), and when He used the phrase "in the age to come, eternal life" (Luke 18:30). Jesus promises resurrection and eternal life to those who believe on Him:

> "For this is the will of my Father, that everyone who looks on the Son and believes in Him should have eternal life, and I will raise Him up on the last day" (John 6:40).

At His return, Christ will raise His people from the dead and transform the bodies of His people who are alive at that time (1 Cor. 15:22–26, 50–55). However, the death of a believer before this resurrection does not leave the believer without hope. Before Christ's return, the spirit of a saved person goes at death to be with the Lord in heaven. The apostle Paul speaks of the believer being "away from the body and at home with the Lord" (2 Cor. 5:8).

The Bible also speaks of the coming of a new heaven and new earth:

> "Then I saw a new heaven and a new earth, for the first heaven and the first earth had passed away" (Rev. 21:1). "But according to his promise, we are waiting for new heavens and a new earth" (2 Pet. 3:13).

At the same time though, the Bible says He has established the earth forever (Psalm 78:69). This can be rather confusing. However, Randy Alcorn, in his detailed biblical study of heaven and the new earth, agrees with John Piper that:

> "To say that the present earth and heavens will 'pass away' does not have to mean they go out of existence, but . . . there will be such a change in them that their present condition passes away."[46]

The new earth is described as a place of righteousness (2 Pet. 3:13) and where the curse, death, and suffering are removed:

> "No longer will there be anything accursed" (Rev. 22:3). "Death shall be no more, neither shall there be mourning, nor crying, nor pain anymore, for the former things have passed away" (Rev. 21:4).

Christ will rule forever over this new world and believers will serve and worship God there (Dan. 7:14; Rev. 4–5, 22:3). God's people will have eternal joy in fellowship with God:

> "He will dwell with them, and they will be His people and God Himself will be with them as their God" (Rev. 21:3). "In your presence there is fullness of joy; at your right hand are pleasures forevermore" (Psalm 16:11).

The eighteenth century English hymn writer, Isaac Watts, captured the thought of redemption of man's world in his well-known, hymn, "Joy to the World":

Joy to the world! The Lord is come. Let earth receive her King.

Let every heart prepare Him room, and heaven and nature sing.

No more let sins and sorrows grow, nor thorns infest the ground.

He comes to make His blessings flow far as the curse is found.[47]

To receive the benefits of redemption, deliverance from the penalty and power of sin and eternal life, a person must repent toward God and put faith in Christ for salvation (Acts 20:21). In Scripture, Christ and His apostles emphasized the necessity of repentance:

> Christ: "Unless you repent you will all likewise perish" (Luke 13:3). "Repentance and forgiveness of sins should be proclaimed in His name to all nations" (Luke 24:47).
>
> Christ's apostles: "Repent therefore . . . that your sins may be blotted out. . . . God, having raised up his servant Jesus, sent him to bless you by turning every one of you from your wickedness" (Acts 3:19, 26). "God . . . commands all people everywhere to repent" (Acts 17:30).

Repentance is a change of mind toward God. A Greek lexicon says the word for "repent" means "change one's mind . . . be converted."[48] A person must realize their sin against God is wrong and want to be saved from sin and be right with God. A theological dictionary gives this explanation about repentance:

> "Repentance is necessary for sinners to be saved. It does not merit pardon. . . . It involves a basic change in attitude toward sin. . . . It is a change of mind. It includes a realization of sin. . . . It includes a definite purpose to forsake sin and obey God."[49]

Along with repentance, God's Word teaches the necessity of faith in Christ for salvation.

The Bible repeatedly stresses receiving salvation from sin and eternal life with God through faith in Jesus Christ. For example, note these statements from the apostle John:

"But to all who did receive him, who believed in his name, he gave the right to become children of God" (John 1:12). "For God so loved the world that he gave his only Son, that whoever believes in him should not perish but have eternal life" (John 3:16). "Everyone who looks on the Son and believes in him should have eternal life" (John 6:40). "But these are written so that you may believe that Jesus is the Christ, the Son of God, and that by believing you may have life in His name" (John 20:31). "God gave us eternal life, and this life is in His Son. Whoever has the Son has life; whoever does not have the Son does not have life" (1 John 5:11–12).

The Christian worldview rejects the idea that there are many ways to God. The Bible says a person receives salvation from sin and eternal life with God only through faith in Christ:

"Jesus said to him, 'I am the way and the truth and the life. No one comes to the Father except through me' (John 14:6). "And there is salvation in no one else, for there is no other name under heaven given among men by which we must be saved" (Acts 4:12).

A person must trust Jesus Christ alone, not good works, to save from sin and give eternal life. Note the emphasis that the Apostle Paul gives in Scripture to the truth that man's works cannot bring salvation from sin and eternal life, only faith in Christ:

"For we hold that one is justified by faith apart from works of the law" (Rom. 3:28).

"We know that a person is not justified by works of the law but through faith in Jesus Christ, so we also have believed in Christ Jesus, in order to be justified by faith in Christ and not by the works of the law, because by the works of the law no one will be justified" (Gal. 2:16). "For by grace you have been saved through faith. And this is not your own doing; it is the gift of God, not a result of works, so that no one may boast" (Eph. 2:8–9). "He saved us, not because of works done by us in righteousness, but according to his own mercy, by the washing of regeneration and renewal of the Holy Spirit, whom he poured out on us richly through Jesus Christ our Savior" (Tit. 3:5–6).

Saving faith in Christ involves assenting to the Gospel truths about Christ's Person and work (John 20:31; 1 Cor. 15:1–4) and trusting Christ alone for salvation from sin and eternal life (Gal. 2:16). One theologian explains it this way:

"The type of faith necessary for salvation involves both believing that and believing in, or assenting to facts and trusting in a Person."[50]

Scripture uses the phrase "believe that" in describing saving faith. A person must assent that what the Bible says about Christ's Person is true, that He is Lord and God (John 20:28-31).

Also, a person must believe the biblical truths of the Gospel that Christ died for our sins and rose again in order to be saved (1 Cor. 15:1-4).

However, saving faith involves more than just mentally assenting that what the Bible says about Christ's Person and work is true and that God and eternal life in heaven are real. The Bible says that demons believe that one true God exists (James 2:19) and that Jesus is the Son of God (Matt. 8:29). Demons, however, are not saved (Matt. 25:41).

The Bible also describes saving faith as "believing in" or "believing on Christ." That includes the idea of trusting Christ, not works, for salvation from sin and eternal life. When a person believes on Christ for eternal life, that person comes into union with Christ in a personal, life-changing relationship (John 17:3; John 15:1-8; 2 Cor. 5:17). The following Protestant doctrinal statement gives a good statement on the meaning of repentance and faith:

> "The repentance required by Scripture is a change of mind toward God and is the effect of the conviction of sin wrought by the Holy Ghost. . . . We are pardoned and accounted righteous before God only for the merit of our Lord and Savior Jesus Christ, by faith, and not for our own works or deserving. . . . Christ is himself the righteousness of all them that truly do believe in him. He for them paid their ransom by his death. He for them fulfilled the law in his life.[51]

In contrast, the Humanist worldview denies redemption from sin and eternal life:

> "Humanists . . . reject the idea that God . . . can save or redeem sinners. . . . Men and women are responsible for their own destinies and they cannot look toward some transcendent Being for salvation. . . . We have found no convincing evidence that there is a separable 'soul' that . . . survives death. . . . The ethical life can be lived without the illusions of immortality."[52]

The Unitarian-Universalist church, a religious Humanist group, similarly states, "Salvation no longer suggests to most Universalists an event in the afterlife, but a process of self-fulfillment and social transformation."[53]

On the other hand, religious groups such as Islam, Jehovah's Witnesses, Mormonism, and Roman Catholicism believe in eternal life, but unlike the Bible, they teach a works salvation:

> Islam: "Verily Allah will admit those who believe and do righteous deeds to Gardens beneath which rivers flow. . . . For those who believe and do righteous deeds will be Gardens, beneath which Rivers flow: That is the great salvation (Surah 47:12, 85:11).[54]

> Jehovah's Witnesses: "Those who thankfully accept redemption as God's gift may continue to live everlastingly on the original condition of obedience. Perfect obedience will be required.[55]

> Mormonism: "We believe that through the atonement of Christ, all mankind may be saved by obedience to the laws and ordinances of the Gospel."[56]

Catholicism: "The Church communicates Christ's mercy to sinners through the Mass and the sacraments and all the prayers and good works of the faithful."[57]

REDEMPTION AND THE BELIEVER'S PRESENT LIFE

Redemption by Christ impacts the life of the believer in this present world:

> **"For the grace of God has appeared, bringing salvation for all people, training us to renounce ungodliness and worldly passions** and to live self-controlled, upright and godly lives in the present age, waiting for our blessed hope, the appearing of the glory of our great God and Savior Jesus Christ, who gave himself for us to redeem us from all lawlessness and to purify for himself a people for His own possession, zealous for good works" (Tit. 2:11–14; emphasis mine).

When a person repents and puts faith in Jesus for salvation, that person enters a new relationship with Christ—a spiritual union with the Savior. The Bible says believers are "in Christ" and states: "Therefore, if anyone is in Christ, he is a new creation" (2 Cor. 5:17).

God's Word uses several different word pictures to help us understand this unique relationship of union with Christ. For example, Christ is the Shepherd, and believers are His sheep who follow Him (John 10:11, 10:27); Jesus is the Vine, and believers are branches who draw life from Him to bear fruit (John 15:5); and Christ is the Head and believers are His spiritual body who should submit to His authority (Eph. 5:23–24).

This relationship with Jesus Christ is foundational to God's goal in the life of the believer. **According to God's Word, God's plan for the life of every believer is to become like Jesus Christ** (Rom. 8:29). Believers will have perfect bodies and pure spirits like Jesus Christ when He returns. And having this hope of becoming like Christ in eternity should motivate the believer to start becoming like Him now:

> "We know that when he appears we shall be like him. . . . Everyone who thus hopes in him purifies himself as he is pure" (1 John 3:2–3).

People who truly have faith in Christ for salvation will bring forth fruit of that relationship in a changed life. That fruit of salvation will include a love for God and fellow believers in Christ and seeking to live a righteous life like Christ:

> Fruit of Love: "Beloved, let us love one another, for love is from God and whoever loves has been born of God and knows God. Anyone who does not love does not know God, because God is love. . . . By this we know that we love the children of God, when we love God and obey his commandments" (1 John 4:7, 8; 5:2).

> Fruit of Righteousness: "And by this we know that we have come to know Him, if we keep His commandments. . . . If you know that he is righteous, you may be sure that everyone who practices righteousness has been born of him" (1 John 2:3, 29).

Christians will not be perfectly loving and righteous in this present life. But thankfully, when believers sin, they can confess it to God and find His forgiveness and restored fellowship:

> "If we say we have no sin, we deceive ourselves. . . . If we confess our sins, He is faithful and just to forgive us our sins" (1 John 1:8–9).

Then believers need to seek God's enabling grace to know Christ better and add Christ-like character traits to their faith, as the apostle Peter described:

> "May grace and peace be multiplied to you in the knowledge of God and of Jesus our Lord. His divine power has granted to us all things that pertain to life and godliness, through the knowledge of Him. . . . Make every effort to supplement your faith with virtue . . . knowledge . . . self-control . . . steadfastness . . . godliness . . . brotherly affection . . . love. For if these qualities are yours and are increasing, they keep you from being . . . unfruitful in the knowledge of our Lord Jesus Christ" (2 Pet. 1:2–3, 1:5–8).

The Bible calls this process of becoming like Christ "sanctification:" "This is the will of God, your sanctification" (1 Thess. 4:3). For further study on sanctification, note the helpful book by Jim Berg, *Changed Into His Image.*[58] Sanctification has the idea of being set apart from sin unto God, or to be holy (1 Pet. 1:15–16). In his theological dictionary, Dr. Cairns defines biblical sanctification:

> "The verb 'to sanctify' may mean . . . to set apart for a sacred purpose . . . to purify or make holy. . . . Sanctification is a work of grace that is gradual and progressive. It relates to the conflict with and the victory over indwelling sin. There is a dying more and more unto sin and living more and more unto righteousness."[59]

Two key means of the believer's sanctification are the Word of God and prayer:

> "In all circumstances take up the shield of faith, with which you can extinguish all the flaming darts of the evil one. And take the helmet of salvation, and the sword of the Spirit, which is the word of God, praying at all times in the Spirit, with all prayer and supplication" (Eph. 6:16–18a).

Meditating on God's Word helps a believer cleanse his or her life from past sin and avoid sin in the future (Psalm 119:9–11). Believers need to meditate on God's Word every day and listen to regular preaching of God's Word (Psalm 1:2; 2 Tim. 3:16–4:2). Jesus knew Scripture is vitally important for the believer's sanctification. He prayed for believers saying,

> "Sanctify them in the truth; Your word is truth" (John 17:17).

Prayer is also of vital importance for the believer's sanctification. Believers need to pray for God's enabling grace to overcome sin in their life as they mature spiritually (Heb. 4:14–16). Jesus taught His disciples to pray for forgiveness of sins in order to restore fellowship with the Father and to pray for God's protection against sin in the future: "Father. . . forgive us our sins. . . . Lead us not into temptation" (Luke 11:2, 4).

Ephesians 6:17–18 says that the Word of God is "the sword of the Spirit" and that believers pray "in the Spirit" in their battle against sin. In Ephesians 5:18, when the apostle Paul gave instructions about living in the relationships of life, he began with the command to be filled with the Holy Spirit: "And do not get drunk with wine, for that is debauchery, but be filled with the Spirit" (Eph. 5:18).

Paul emphasizes that believers find enablement for right living in life's relationships through having one's mind controlled, or filled, by the Holy Spirit, in contrast to a mind controlled by alcohol. Getting high on drugs would have the same effect as being under the control of alcohol (see Gal. 5:19-21). Being filled by the Spirit and free from addiction to substances is an important issue for life in this world. We must be controlled by the Holy Spirit rather than controlled by harmful substances.

Many people in the world often turn to intoxication by alcohol or drugs to find satisfaction in life or to enable them to cope with life, rather than trusting Christ's power and seeking satisfaction in the Lord. Scripture warns about the spiritual danger of drunkenness and drug abuse. It is a battle for the mind. God wants us to love Him with all of our heart and mind (Matt. 22:37-38). God's Word exhorts believers to have a sober mind (Tit. 2:2-6).

Proverbs warns us about how drunkenness leads to poverty, contention, or lustful thoughts (Prov. 20:1; 23:20-21, 29-35). Jesus and His apostles also taught in Scripture that drunkenness leads to God's judgment and exclusion from God's kingdom (Matt. 24:48–51; 1 Cor. 6:9–11; Gal. 5:19–21). Scripture exhorts believers to avoid drinking parties (1 Pet. 4:3). God's Word instructs the church to discipline members who do not repent of drunkenness (1 Cor. 5:11).

Also, Galatians 5:19–21 and Revelation 9:21 condemn "sorcery" as a sinful work that God judges. "Sorcery" translates a Greek word from which we get the word "pharmacy" or "mixer of drugs."[60] In Bible times, some people wrongly used drugs for altered consciousness or occult practices. Today, people often abuse drugs for non-medicinal purposes like mental escape from life's problems, altered consciousness, or getting high and they suffer harm to their brain and body in the process.[61]

A parallel passage to being "filled with the Spirit" in Ephesians 5:18-19 is Colossians 3:16–17. Colossians 3:16 speaks about being filled with the Word of God: "Let the Word of Christ dwell in you richly in all wisdom" (Col. 3:16). The Holy Spirit inspired the Word of God (2 Pet. 1:19–21). To be filled or controlled by the Holy Spirit, the believer must fill his mind with Scripture, the

Spirit-inspired Word of God, which leads to cleansing from sin and gives instruction for life (Psalm 119:9–11, 105; Eph. 6:16-18).

In the Christian worldview, becoming like Christ is the goal of life for Christians. In contrast, the Humanist worldview sees the goal of living as learning to fit into society and to function in it according to man's wisdom, while fulfilling one's personal desires. A person with a Christian worldview looks to God's Word for wisdom and prays to God for enablement for living. The Humanist worldview, however, rejects the God of the Bible and looks to man's wisdom and technology to deal with man's personal problems. The Humanist Manifesto states:

> "Humanists still believe that . . . faith in the prayer-hearing God . . . is an unproven and outmoded faith. . . . Using technology wisely, we can . . . significantly modify our behavior. . . . We affirm a set of common principles that . . . are a design for a secular society on a planetary scale. . . . Humans are responsible for what we are or will become. No deity will save us, we must save ourselves. . . . Modern science discredits . . . the separable soul. . . . Ethics is autonomous and situational. . . . Reason and intelligence are the most effective instruments that humankind possesses."[62]

Humanism looks to secular psychotherapy and psychiatry to deal with life's personal problems. Secular psychologists and psychiatrists believe in dealing with personal problems through man's reasoning and experience, secular counseling techniques, and psychiatric drugs—without Christ or God's Word, the Bible. However, to produce the fruit of right living (John 15:1-8), Jesus said, "Apart from me, you can do nothing" (John 15:5).

As mentioned earlier, Dr. Paul Vitz, a trained Christian psychologist, has written a critique of secular psychotherapy and psychiatry. In his book, *Psychology as Religion: The Cult of Self-Worship,* he sets forth evidence to show the non-Christian religious nature of psychology. Dr. Vitz concludes, "Psychology as religion exists, and it exists in strength throughout the United States. . . . Psychology as religion is deeply anti-Christian."[63]

Dr. Vitz points out that key leaders in the development of modern secular psychotherapy, such as Carl Jung, Carl Rogers, Abraham Maslow, Eric Fromm, and Rollo May rejected biblical Christianity. They emphasized the ego and cultivating self-expression. They replaced Scripture with man's wisdom, while dealing with human problems that pastors previously dealt with.

For example, Dr. Vitz quotes Carl Jung as saying, "We psychotherapists must occupy ourselves with problems which strictly speaking belong to the theologian."[64] Additionally, a follower of Jung claimed, "Psychotherapy . . . has the means to lead the individual to his 'salvation."[65] Dr. Vitz documents that secular psychotherapy makes the goal of life "self-realization" or "self-actualization," with the emphasis on self, rather than God and others.[66]

Dr. Vitz explains how secular psychotherapists developed the concept of "values clarification" that many public schools use with children. Rather than teaching biblical values, they teach children to express their own feelings and ideas and develop their own values. They stress the self. Dr. Vitz notes,

> "Values clarification theorists explicitly support the position that . . . morality is relative to each individual. . . . It explicitly rejects all absolute or non-relativist interpretations of the moral life. . . . It represents an attack on traditional religious morality."[67]

Scripture clearly teaches that all people have a fallen nature and that the human heart is deceitful and wicked (Rom. 3:10, 5:12; Jer. 17:9). Fallen people have a sinful nature that causes them to live according to wrong thinking (Eph. 4:17). Jesus taught that the impulses of the human heart are toward sinful behavior, and He calls on people to deny themselves and follow Him, instead of seeking to satisfy sinful, selfish impulses (Matt. 15:19, 16:24).

Sometimes reason and experience may lead secular psychotherapists to give counsel that is similar to biblical principles. Other times, it may be contrary to God's Word. Secular counselors may have patients look within themselves or outside of themselves to experts to solve problems. Sometimes they help patients to outwardly cope with personal problems, but many other patients continue to struggle.

However, all secular counseling fails to address the root problems of sinful desires and thinking that are contrary to God's Word. God's Word is the best source of wisdom for solving life's problems (Rom. 15:4, 13-14; Col. 2-3; 2 Tim. 3:15–17). For a helpful book on biblical counseling for life's problems, see Jay Adams', *The Christian Counselor's Manual.*[68] John MacArthur has written about how secular psychotherapy conflicts with the Christian worldview. He made this observation:

> "When we reach down inside ourselves to get answers, we get lies" (Jer. 17:9–10).
>
> ". . . Scripture does what psychoanalysis can't do—it pierces the heart" (Heb. 4:12–13).[69]

Dr. MacArthur points out that in the time of the New Testament, the gnostic heresy attacked the early church, and the writers of the New Testament epistles refuted this heresy. One gnostic belief was that they had special hidden knowledge not found in the teaching of Christ and the apostles, which the average believer in Christ did not have. Dr. MacArthur explains:

> "Nothing epitomizes neo-gnosticism more than the church's fascination with humanistic psychology. . . . The neo-gnostics would have us believe that sharing Scripture and praying with someone who is deeply hurting emotionally is too

> superficial. Only those who are trained in psychology—those with the secret knowledge—are qualified to help people with serious spiritual and emotional problems. The acceptance of that attitude is misleading millions and crippling church ministry. The word 'psychology' is a good one. Literally it means 'the study of the soul.' . . . Outside the Word and the Spirit there are no solutions to any of the problems of the human soul. Only God knows the soul and only God can change it. Yet the widely accepted ideas of modern psychology are theories originally developed by atheists on the assumption that there is no God and the individual alone has the power to change himself into a better person through certain techniques."[70]

People who believe in Christ for salvation have resources for living life in this world that the Humanist worldview cannot offer. Believers in Christ have the Word of God, union with Christ, the indwelling Spirit of God, and fellowship with fellow believers in the Christian church. These resources are adequate for living life in this world, overcoming sin, and solving spiritual problems, without secular psychotherapy. Note what God's Word says:

> The Word of God: "All Scripture is breathed out by God and profitable for teaching, for reproof, for correction, and for training in righteousness, that the man of God may be complete, equipped for every good work" (2 Tim. 3:16-17).
>
> Union with Christ: "All of us who have been baptized into Christ Jesus were baptized into His death. . . . Just as Christ was raised from the dead by the glory of the Father, we too might walk in newness of life. . . . We know that our old self was crucified with Him in order that the body of sin might be brought to nothing, so that we would no longer be enslaved to sin. . . . Consider yourselves dead to sin and alive to God in Christ Jesus" (Rom. 6:3, 6, 11).
>
> The Indwelling Spirit: "Walk by the Spirit and you will not gratify the desires of the flesh. . . . The fruit of the Spirit is love, joy, peace, patience, kindness, goodness, faithfulness, gentleness, self-control" (Gal. 5:16, 22, 23).
>
> Help of Fellow Believers: "I myself am satisfied about you, my brothers, that you yourselves are full of goodness, filled with all knowledge and able to instruct one another" (Rom. 15:14).

These spiritual resources enable a believer to effectively deal with life problems such as guilt about the past, discouragement about the present, anxiety about the future, and addiction to alcohol or drugs. Christian counseling ministries are available to help believers in these areas:[71]

> Guilt about the past: "If we walk in the light as he is in the light, we have fellowship with one another, and the blood of Jesus his Son cleanses us from all sin. . . . If we confess our sins, He is faithful and just to forgive us our sins and to cleanse us from all unrighteousness" (1 John 1:7, 9).

> Discouragement in the present: "Let us then with confidence draw near to the throne of grace, that we may receive mercy and find grace to help in time of need. . . . Let us run with endurance the race that is set before us, looking to Jesus, the founder and perfecter of our faith. . . . Consider him who endured from sinners such hostility against himself, so that you may not grow weary or fainthearted" (Heb. 4:16; 12:2-3).
>
> Anxiety about the future: "Do not be anxious about anything, but in everything by prayer and supplication with thanksgiving let your requests be made known to God. And the peace of God, which surpasses all understanding, will guard your hearts and your minds in Christ Jesus" (Phili. 4:6-7).
>
> Overcoming addiction to alcohol or drugs: "Do you not know that the unrighteous will not inherit the kingdom of God? Do not be deceived, neither the sexually immoral . . . nor drunkards . . . will inherit the kingdom of God. And such were some of you. But you were washed, you were sanctified, you were justified in the name of the Lord Jesus Christ and by the Spirit of our God" (1 Cor. 6:9-11; emphasis mine).

A Christian may have physical issues associated with matters such as anxiety, depression, and trauma. It is proper for a believer to seek help from a qualified physician to deal with physical problems associated with these matters. However, issues such as guilt, anxiety, discouragement, and problems with alcohol or drugs typically involve either wrong thoughts, wrong beliefs, sinful desires, or sinful choices. Those are spiritual matters that a believer needs to seek help about through Christian counsel from God's Word, prayer, and reliance on Christ.

For helpful instruction in a biblical view of counseling, see "Bob Jones University's Philosophy of Biblical Counseling."[72] For a good explanation of how application of the believer's union with Christ is vital for our sanctification, see Dr. Mike Barrett's, *Complete in Him.*[73] Dr. Barrett observes, "Right thinking about the Gospel produces right living in the Gospel."[74]

CHAPTER 4 STUDY GUIDE
MAN'S PERSON—CREATED, FALLEN, OBJECT OF REDEMPTION

KEY SCRIPTURES TO READ:

Man as created by God: Genesis 1:26-28; Psalm 139:13-4; Ephesians 4:24; Colossians 3:10

Man as fallen in sin: Romans 3:10, 19-20, 23; Romans 5:12; Ephesians 2:1; Jeremiah 17:9

Man as object of redemption: Ephesians 1:7; 2:8-10; Titus 2:11-14; Titus 3:3-7; John 3:16; John 14:6; John 20:26-31; Romans 3:24-28; Romans 6:3-4, 6, 11, 22-23; 1 Corinthians 6:9-11; Galatians 2:16; Galatians 5:16, 19-24; 2 Peter 1:2-11; 1 John 1:7-9; 1 John 2:3, 29; 1 John 4:7, 10; 1 John 5:1-5, 11-13

KEY POINTS TO NOTE (NOTE BOLD TYPE IN CHAPTER):

According to the Bible, the image of God in man includes what two key aspects?

____

____

What are four key areas of God's Creation Mandate to man in Genesis 1:26-28?

____

____

____

____

____

According to Romans 5:12, because of Adam's sin, what do all people experience?

____

____

What are five key points that summarize basic Bible teaching about redemption?

____

____

____

____

____

Saving faith in Christ involves what two key aspects?

___

___

___

According to God's Word, what is God's plan for the life of every believer?

___

___

___

What are two key means God uses for the believer's sanctification?

___

___

___

CRITICAL THINKING:

What evidence can man see for his creation by God?

How does viewing man as having a fallen sinful nature, rather than being basically good, affect:

How you counsel people about their personal desires and problems?

What you see as man's deepest and most basic problem?

How does the Christian worldview differ from the Humanist worldview and the Islamic worldview about redemption of man from sin and receiving eternal life?

CHAPTER 4 ENDNOTES

MAN AS CREATED BY GOD

1 Alan Cairns, "Image of God," *A Dictionary of Theological Terms,* (Greenville, SC: Ambassador International, 2002), p. 222.

2 Robert Reymond, *A New Systematic Theology of the Christian Faith* (Nashville, TN: Thomas Nelson Publishers,1998), pp. 428–429.

3 Cairns, p. 222.

4 Charles Ware and Ken Ham, *One Race/One Blood* (Master Books, 2010).

5 John Frame, *The Doctrine of the Christian Life* (Phillipsburg, NJ: Presbyterian and Reformed, 2008), pp. 308, 310.

6 Henry Morris, *The Genesis Record* (Grand Rapids, MI: Baker Book House, 1976), p. 77.

7 John Dyer, *From the Garden to the City: The Redeeming and Corrupting Power of Technology* (Grand Rapids: Kregel Publications, 2011).

8 Ibid, p. 65.

9 Ibid, chapter 10 on Technicism.

10 Paul Kurtz, ed., *Humanist Manifestos 1 and 2* (Buffalo, NY: Prometheus Books, 1973), pp. 14, 16.

11 Michael Sanera and Jane Shaw, *Facts Not Fear* (Washington, D.C.: Regnery Publishing, 1996), pp. 26-27.

12 J. Y. Jones, *Worship Not the Creature: Animal Rights and the Bible* (Ventura, CA: Nordskog Publishing, 2009).

13 Ibid, chapters 1-3.

14 Ibid, chapters 4-9.

15 Ibid, chapter 10.

16 Ibid, pp. 107-108, 113.

17 Ibid, p. 162.

18 Chris Horner, *The Politically Incorrect Guide to Global Warming and Environmentalism* (Washington, D.C.: Regnery Publishing, 2007), p. 10.

19 Sanera and Shaw, p. 36.

20 Calvin Beisner, *Prospects for Growth: A Biblical View of Population, Resources and the Future* (Westchester, IL: Crossway Books, 1990).

21 Jason Lisle, *The Ultimate Proof of Creation* (Green Forest, AR: Master Books, 2009), pp. 18-19.

MAN AS FALLEN IN SIN

22 Gary DeMar, *America's Christian History: The Untold Story* (Powder Springs, GA: American Vision, second edition, 1995), pp. 99–100.

23 Cairns, "Imputation," p. 225.

24 Cairns, "Original Sin," pp. 317–319.

25 Douglas Moo, *The Epistle to the Romans* (Grand Rapids: Eerdmans Publishing Company, 1996), p. 320.

26 Walter Elwell, ed., *The Evangelical Dictionary of Theology* (Grand Rapids: Baker Book House, 1984), p. 312.

27 Norman Geisler and Abdul Saleeb, *Answering Islam* (Grand Rapids: Baker Book House, 2002), p. 44., quoting Badru Kateregga.

28 David Noebel, *Understanding the Times* (Manitou Springs, CO: Summit Ministries, 2006), p. 226, quoting "Humanist Psychology."

29 Philip Schaff, *Creeds of Christendom*, vol. 3, Evangelical Protestant Creeds (Grand Rapids: Baker Book House, 1985 reprint), p. 743.

30 Schaff, *Creeds of Christendom*, vol. 3, pp. 100, 104.

31 Schaff, *Creeds of Christendom*, vol. 3, pp. 808–809.

32 Schaff, *Creeds of Christendom*, vol. 3, p. 615.

33 Schaff, *Creeds of Christendom*, vol. 3, pp. 816-817.

34 J. F. Baldwin, *The Deadliest Monster: An Introduction to Worldviews* (New Braunfels, TX: Fishermen Press, 1998), p. 20.

35 Paul Vitz, *Psychology as Religion—The Cult of Self-Worship* (Grand Rapids: Eerdmans Publishing Company, 1994), Introduction, "About This Book."

36 Ibid, pp. 4, 5.

37 Ibid, p. 46.

38 Ibid, p. 46.

39 Edward Welch, *Blame It on the Brain?—Distinguishing Chemical Imbalances, Brain Disorders and Disobedience* (Phillipsburg, NJ: P&R Publishing, 1998), chapter 10, "Alcoholism."

40 Charles Colson and Nancy Pearcey, *How Now Shall We Live* (Wheaton, IL: Tyndale House, 1999), Part 4 on Redemption. Note the chapters showing false hopes of deliverance from man's problems through Marxist liberation (chapter 24), sexual freedom (chapter 25), science (chapter 26), escape from problems (chapter 27), and New Age mysticism (chapter 28).

41 Colson, *How Now Shall We Live?*, p. 279.

MAN AS THE OBJECT OF REDEMPTION

42 J. D. Douglas, ed., "Redeemer, Redemption," *The Illustrated Bible Dictionary* (Leicester, England: InterVarsity Press, 1980), vol. 3, pp. 1321, 1323.

43 Cairns, "Justification," pp. 244-245.

44 Geisler and Saleeb, *Answering Islam*, p. 141.

45 Paul Kurtz, ed., *A Secular Humanist Declaration* (Buffalo, NY: Prometheus Books, 1980), p. 18.

46 Randy Alcorn, *Heaven* (Tyndale House and Eternal Perspective Ministries, 2004), pp. 152-153.

47 *Worship and Service Hymnal* (Carol Stream, IL: Hope Publishing Company, 1974), hymn 27.

48 William Arndt and William Gingrich, *A Greek-English Lexicon of the New Testament* (Chicago, IL: University of Chicago Press, 1957), p. 513.

49 Cairns, "Repentance," pp. 379-380.

50 Millard Erickson, *Introducing Christian Doctrine* (Grand Rapids: Baker Book House, 1992), p. 299.

51 Schaff, *Creeds of Christendom*, volume 3, p. 818, Reformed Episcopal Church Articles of Religion.

52 Kurtz, *A Secular Humanist Declaration*, pp. 18–19.

53 Jack Mendelson, *Why I Am a Unitarian-Universalist*, p. 68.

54 *The Holy Qur'an*: Arabic Text, English Translation & Commentary (Translation and commentary by Allama Abdullah Yusuf Ali; Muhammad Ashraf Publishers, Lahore, Pakistan, 1979 edition), pp. 1317, 1628.

55 Charles Russell, *Studies in the Scriptures* (Brooklyn, NY: Watchtower Bible and Tract Society, 1889), p. 106.

56 John Gerstner, *The Theology of the Major Sects* (Grand Rapids: Baker Book House, 1960), p. 46, quoting Joseph Smith.

57 William Webster, Salvation, *The Bible and Roman Catholicism* (Carlisle, PA: The Banner of Truth Trust, 1990), p. 171, quoting a modern Roman Catholic catechism.

58 Jim Berg, *Changed into His Image: God's Plan for Transforming Your Life* (Greenville, SC: Bob Jones University Press, 2000).

59 Cairns, "Sanctification," p. 397.

60 William Hendriksen, *New Testament Commentary: Galatians* (Grand Rapids: Baker Book House, 1968, p. 219.

61 Note the documentation of the harmful effects of drug abuse on the brain and body at https://drugabuse.com/drug-alcohol-effects. (Accessed 3/16/2019).

62 Kurtz, *Humanist Manifestos I and II*, pp. 13-17.

63 Vitz, p. xiii.

64 Vitz, p. 2.

65 Vitz, p. 3.

66 Vitz, pp. 3-4.

67 Vitz, p. 74.

68 Jay Adams, *The Christian Counselors Manual* (Grand Rapids, Zondervan, 1973).

69 John MacArthur, *Our Sufficiency in Christ* (Dallas, TX: Word Publishing, 1991), pp. 94, 96-97.

70 MacArthur, *Our Sufficiency in Christ*, p. 30.

71 Note "The Association of Certified Biblical Counselors" at https://biblicalcounseling.com. (Accessed 3/16/2019).

72 https://www.bju.edu/about/positions.php, "Biblical Counseling." (Accessed 3/16/2019).

73 Michael Barrett, *Complete in Him: A Guide to Understanding and Enjoying the Gospel* (Greenville, SC: Ambassador-Emerald International, 2000), appendix 3, "Union with Christ: The Ground of Sanctification."

74 Barrett, *Complete in Him*, p. 266.

CHAPTER 5

THINKING BIBLICALLY ABOUT CREATION VERSUS EVOLUTION

CREATION VERSUS EVOLUTION AS A WORLDVIEW CONFLICT

THE CHRISTIAN CREATIONIST WORLDVIEW

There is a major and foundational clash in thinking between the Christian worldview and the Humanist worldview about the matter of creation and the origins of man and the world. People often wonder about the origins of mankind, the earth, sun, and stars and ask, "Where did it all come from? Why is all of this here?" The Christian and Humanist worldviews give very different answers to these questions.

Humanists try to portray the conflict about Creation versus evolution as religion versus science. However, that is not an accurate description of the conflict. Christians who affirm the biblical account of Creation and reject evolution do believe in scientific study, and they see scientific evidences for Biblical creation. A number of Christians who believe in the biblical account of creation have earned a college degree in an area of science. Humanists have their own religious/philosophical presuppositions themselves, as philosopher Roy Clouser points out:

> "Virtually all the major disagreements between competing theories in science and in philosophy can ultimately be traced back to differences in their religious presuppositions. . . . Religious beliefs all have in common that they believe in something or other as the non-dependent divinity on which all else depends. . . . A person who believes matter/energy to be self-existent, would, indeed, be regarding it to be divine and would have a materialist religious belief."[1]

Both Humanists and Christians use science. However, neither Humanists, nor Christians, nor any other person were present to observe the origin of the universe, the earth, or life on earth. Both Humanists and Christians look at observable evidence in the present features of the material world as they answer the worldview question, "How did man and his world get here?" People who believe in evolution have presuppositions about religion and science that govern their thinking and they interpret evidence by their worldview.

Humanists who believe in evolution and Christians who believe in biblical creation interpret differently what they observe in features of the earth and life on earth in relation to origins. The Humanist worldview interprets evidence based on the finite and fallible thinking of man, totally apart from any written Divine revelation. The Christian worldview interprets evidence in light of the authority of the Bible as the Word of God. The Bible reveals God as Creator, who tells man in His written Word about the fact of Creation and how He created.

The Christian worldview has answers to basic worldview questions from the Bible as God's Word. The Christian worldview uses the Bible to answer the question, "Where did it all come from?" It began with God's creation of all things in six actual days about six-thousand years ago: "In the beginning God created the heavens and the earth" (Gen. 1:1). The Bible teaches that space and matter had a beginning, with the creative work of God. Christians look at the material universe and observe abundant evidence for creation by God.

The Christian worldview can also answer the question, "Why is all of this here?" God created everything for His glory: "The heavens declare the glory of God (Psalm 19:1). The Bible also teaches that God created things for man's benefit. God created the earth so that man could live here and serve His purposes (Gen. 1:26). God created light and light-bearers for man's benefit (Gen. 1:3, 1:14–19). And God made plants and animals for man's use (Gen. 1:20–31). Christians observe abundant evidence for purposeful design in man's world.

The Humanist worldview holds to evolution, rejecting the biblical teaching of creation of all things by God. It is a materialist worldview, which argues that matter and energy are all that exists. They appeal to logic and science. However, logic itself is not material, so the materialist worldview has no explanation for how immaterial logic exists. The atheist scientist Dr. Carl Sagan stated the materialist view in his television series, "Cosmos," claiming, "The Cosmos is all that is, or ever was, or ever will be.[2]

The Christian worldview opposes the idea that the universe of matter and energy is all that exists or ever existed. God, an infinite Spirit, precedes, is distinct from and creates matter. God is eternal—matter is not. God created everything in the universe according to His will.

> "Before . . . you had formed the earth and the world, from everlasting to everlasting you are God" (Psalm 90:2).
>
> "You created all things, and by your will they exist and were created" (Rev. 4:11).

God tells us in His Word how He created. God created matter out of nothing:

"By faith we understand that the universe was created by the word of God, so that what is seen was not made out of things that are visible" (Heb. 11:3).

The Bible also tells us that **God created by His word.** He spoke and brought the universe into existence (Heb. 11:3). "The universe was created by the Word of God" (Heb. 11:3). Scripture declares, "The earth was formed . . . by the word of God" **(2 Pet. 3:5).** Genesis 1 states that God spoke into existence light, dry land, plants, light bearers, and animals.

The fact that matter had a beginning and that God made it points to God's unique distinction from His creation. Nothing in creation can adequately represent God because God is distinct from it (Rom. 1:22–23). This truth rules out pantheistic ideas. Pantheism views God as an impersonal force identical with nature. It sees everything as "god," but "theologically, it is the denial of the personality of God."[3]

The Bible tells us that God created all the kinds of fish in the sea, all the kinds of birds, all the kinds of cattle, all the kinds of animals that creep on the ground, and all the kinds of four-footed beasts (Gen. 1:20–25). **God created each kind of animal to reproduce after its own kind (Gen. 1:21–25) and then created human life separately from the animals (Gen. 1:27–28).** We observe man and different kinds of animals reproducing after their own kind. This rules out the possibility of animals evolving into a different kind of animal or man evolving from animals.

Another truth we find in the Bible is that **God made everything good** (Gen. 1:31). God called "good" His separation of dry land and waters and His creation of plants (Gen. 1:10, 1:12), light bearers in the heavens (Gen. 1:18), and animals (Gen. 1:21, 1:25). Then after God created man, "God saw everything that He had made, and behold, it was very good" (Gen. 1:31). There was no sin or evil in God's "very good" creation. Evil and death entered the world later through man's sin (Gen. 3; Rom. 5:12).

The Bible also tells us that God created with order. Genesis 1 enumerates six consecutive days of creation, with the order in which God created everything:

- On day one, God created the heavens, the earth, and light (Gen. 1:1–4).
- On day two, God separated the waters (Gen. 1:6–8).
- On day three, God created dry land and plants (Gen. 1:9–13).
- On day four, God created sun, moon, and stars (Gen. 1:14–19).
- On day five, God created animals in the water and air (Gen. 1:20–23).
- On day six, God created land animals and man (Gen. 1:24–30).

The order that Genesis 1 describes for God's work of Creation clearly does not match the ideas of evolution about the origin and order of development of the universe and life.

Also, the timescale that Genesis 1-11 describes for Creation (six days in Gen. 1) and human history (genealogies in Gen. 5 and 11) points to a recent creation by God, approximately six thousand years ago. Taking the biblical timescale in its plain sense gives a totally opposite view of time from the view of evolution. The theory of evolution claims billions of years for the development of the universe, the earth, and life. The next section in this chapter will give a defense of recent creation.

The conflict between biblical Creation and evolution truly is a battle between worldviews. It involves conflicting interpretations of evidence, based upon different ultimate authorities and different worldview assumptions. The basic issues are:

1. Will we begin our thinking with God our Creator, or will we assume nature is all there is?
2. Will we accept the account of the Word of God about Creation, the Word of our Creator Who was there, or will we instead favor the finite and fallible thinking of men, who were not there?

People with a Christian worldview are not opposed to science. They believe that the Christian worldview gives the foundation for scientific study. There are Bible-believing Christians who are science teachers or who are involved in scientific research. People who believe in evolution and people who believe in biblical Creation look at the same evidence, but they interpret the evidence differently based on their worldview assumptions.

To have a clear understanding of this clash between the Christian worldview and the Humanist worldview about Creation versus evolution, **it is important to understand the difference between "operational science" and "origins science."** People who believe in evolution often fail to note this important distinction. The Answers in Genesis website gives a helpful explanation about this matter. See their website to read the full article about "operational science" and "origins science." Here are some key statements from that article:

> "1. Operation science uses the so-called 'scientific method' to attempt to discover truth, performing observable, repeatable experiments in a controlled environment to find patterns of recurring behavior in the present physical universe. . . . Both creationists and evolutionists use this kind of science, which has given rise to computers, space shuttles, and cures for diseases. 2. Origin science attempts to discover truth by examining reliable eyewitness testimony (if available); and circumstantial evidence, such as pottery, fossils, and canyons. Because the past cannot be observed directly, assumptions greatly affect how these scientists interpret what they see. . . . Molecules-to-man evolution is a belief about the past. It assumes, without observing it, that natural processes and lots of time are sufficient to explain the origin and diversification of life. . . . Thus, creationists and

> evolutionists develop totally different reconstructions of history. But they accept and use the same methods of research in both origin and operation science. The different conclusions about origins arise from different starting assumptions, not the research methods themselves. So the battle between the Bible and molecules-to-man evolution is not one of religion versus science. Rather, it is a conflict between worldviews—a creationist's starting assumptions (a biblical worldview) and an evolutionist's starting assumptions (an anti-biblical worldview)."[4]

People who hold to the Christian worldview definitely believe in operational science, the scientific method, scientific observation and research. Dr. Henry Morris documents that many past and present scientists have believed in God as Creator and the biblical account of Creation.[5] They effectively engaged in operational science. However, because the Christian worldview and the Humanist worldview interpret the evidence differently, based on their different worldview assumptions, there is a strong disagreement when it comes to origin science.

EVOLUTION AS A WORLDVIEW

In chapter one, we gave quotes documenting that all varieties of Humanism hold to evolution as a foundational belief. Secular Humanism, Marxist Humanism, Postmodern Humanism, New Age Humanism and Religious Humanism all are firmly committed to the idea of evolution. They all reject the biblical account of Creation.

Secular, Marxist, and Postmodern Humanists generally favor an atheistic or agnostic view of evolution. New Age Humanists tend to be pantheistic in their view of evolution. Religious Humanists would favor the idea that God started the process of evolution to bring everything into existence as it is today. But all Humanists view the process of evolution as a fact, rather than believing in the direct creation of everything by God. For example, Julian Huxley, a leading evolutionist, stated:

> "Modern science must rule out special creation. . . . The first point to make about Darwin's theory is that it is no longer a theory, but a fact."[6]

In his book, *Understanding the Times,* Dr. David Noebel documents statements from the varieties of Humanism in favor of biological evolution. He documents that Karl Marx, in a letter to his collaborator, Frederick Engels, stated that Darwin's book on evolution gave the scientific basic for Marxism.[7] He notes that Pierre Teilhard Chardin, a Roman Catholic paleontologist, tried to reconcile Christianity and evolution and ended up with pantheistic views and an approach to science that influenced Cosmic or New Age Humanism.[8] Dr. Noebel also documents various Postmodernists in favor of evolution.[9]

Religious Humanists, while believing in some form of Deity, do not hold to orthodox Biblical views of God. They reject the full inspiration and infallibility of the Bible. Liberal religious Humanists hold to theistic evolution, that God started the process of evolution and that man and the world came into being through a process of evolution.

Evolutionists see evolution as broader than biological evolution. They see evolution as a total worldview, including the evolution of matter, evolution of living things, and evolution of human culture. One evolutionist refers to it this way:

> "Although this article is concerned with biological evolution, it should be recognized that the concept of evolution is much broader. . . . There is also cosmic, or inorganic evolution, and evolution of human culture."[10]

Julian Huxley, a leading advocate of evolution, similarly stated:

> "The overall process of evolution in this comprehensive sense comprises three main phases . . . We may call these three phases the inorganic, or, if you like, cosmological; the organic or biological; and the human or psycho-social."[11]

In summary then, **evolutionists speak of three kinds of evolution:**

1. **Inorganic evolution**—the cosmic evolution of the material universe.
2. **Organic evolution**—the biological evolution of all life from a common ancestor.
3. **Societal evolution**—the social evolution of human culture.

Evolution is foundational to the worldview of all Humanists. All of the varieties of Humanism would reject the biblical account of Creation. The next sections in this chapter will set forth a defense of the biblical view of creation by God and the worldwide Flood and show fallacies in evolution. The controversy between biblical creationists and evolutionists involves a basic worldview conflict. It is not a controversy between science and religion, because Humanism has religious elements and Christians believe in using science.

A scientist who believes in evolution summarizes the evolutionary Humanist view about origins of the universe, earth and life:

> **"Man's world view today is dominated by the knowledge that the universe, the stars, the earth, and all living things have evolved through a long history that was not foreordained or programmed, a history of continual, gradual change shaped by more or less directional natural processes consistent with the laws of physics."**[12]

A Christian astronomer summarizes how scientists who believe in evolution describe the evolution of the universe:

> "Evolutionists believe that the universe is billions of years old. It originated in a "big bang"—a rapid expansion of space, time, and energy from a single infinitesimally

> small point. Energy cooled and became matter, which condensed into stars and galaxies . . . some of which condensed to become planets. Our solar system in particular was formed about 4.5 billion years ago from a collapsing gas cloud."[13]

A scientist who is an evolutionist summarizes the view of biological evolution:

> "The millions of diverse living species we find around us in the modern world are all descended from a common ancestor that lived in the remote past. The processes that have brought this diversity about are collectively called evolution."[14]

A standard dictionary defines biological evolution as:

> "A change in the gene pool of a population from generation to generation by such processes as mutation, natural selection, and genetic drift. . . . the theory that all existing organisms developed from earlier forms by natural selection."[15]

Evolution as held by all varieties of Humanism involves a total worldview that clashes with the Christian worldview. In his book, *The Lie—Evolution,* Ken Ham summarizes the worldview conflict between the Christian worldview and the evolutionist worldview:

> "There are two world views with two totally different belief systems clashing in our society. . . . It is my contention that this spiritual conflict is rooted in the issue of origins (creation/evolution). . . . Both creation and evolution are belief systems that result in different models and totally different interpretations of the evidence."[16]

Charles Darwin popularized evolution in modern times with his book, *The Origin of Species By Means of Natural Selection,* in 1859. Darwin's theory of evolution caused a tremendous change in thinking around the world. Evolutionists have recognized the tremendous worldview significance of Darwin's writings about evolution:

> "I am taking a new look at the Darwinian revolution of 1859, perhaps the most fundamental of all intellectual revolutions in the history of mankind. It . . . affected every metaphysical and ethical concept."[17]

> "Evolution . . . is a general condition to which all theories, all systems, all hypotheses must bow and which they must satisfy henceforward if they are to be thinkable and true. Evolution is a light illuminating all facts."[18]

> "Linguistics, social anthropology, and comparative law and religion, began to be studied from an evolutionary angle, until today we are enabled to see evolution as a universal and all-pervading process."[19]

Also, David Breese, a Christian worldview writer and speaker, wrote a book, *Seven Men Who Rule the World from the Grave.* In this book, he devotes the first three chapters to Charles Darwin and his theory of evolution.[20] He shows the continuing worldview significance of Darwin's view of evolution and notes the influence of evolution on the other men he writes about.

As we have previously noted, worldviews involve controlling assumptions. The theory of evolution has become a controlling assumption in the Humanist worldview. Evolution has become a controlling assumption of the majority of scientists in our modern world. Scientists do their research and study with presuppositions. They are not neutral.

Thomas Kuhn has written a book about the history of scientific theories. He notes that scientists always think within a "paradigm," that is, with certain presuppositions. In other words, all scientists have assumptions that guide their research. They have a paradigm, or worldview. No one is totally neutral. Some assumptions are necessary to think and to research information. Scientists may even change some assumptions based on further research. Kuhn makes these observations based on his research of the history of scientific study:

> "A paradigm is an accepted model or pattern. . . . Philosophers of science have repeatedly demonstrated that more than one theoretical construction can always be placed upon a given collection of data. . . . There is no such thing as research in the absence of any paradigm. . . . If, as I have already urged, there can be no scientifically or empirically neutral system of language or concepts, then the proposed construction of alternate tests and theories must proceed from within one or another paradigm-based tradition."[21]

Our culture likes to present scientists as totally neutral investigators. However, as Kuhn points out, all scientists, including those who believe in evolution, have presuppositions and a worldview. Scientists interpret evidence in light of their presuppositions, although they might adjust their "paradigm" or assumptions based on further research and evidence.

When it comes to scientific study and the subject of evolution, the worldview of evolutionists guides their interpretation of evidence. They are not unbiased or neutral. For example, consider this statement from a scientist who believes in evolution:

> "It is not that the methods and institutions of science somehow compel us to accept a material explanation of the phenomenal world. On the contrary, we are forced by our prior adherence to material causes to create an apparatus of investigation and a set of concepts that produce material explanations, no matter how counter-intuitive, no matter how mystifying to the uninitiated. Moreover, that materialism is an absolute, for we cannot allow a Divine Foot in the door."[22]

For further illustrations of bias by evolutionists, see Jonathan Sarfati, *Refuting Evolution.*[23]

The quotes above illustrate the truth of Scripture concerning the bias of fallen man in relation to the testimony of Scripture and the observable evidence about creation by God. People with a Humanist worldview are not without bias in the matter of evolution versus creation. Their worldview drives the way they look at evidence. Evolutionists hold a worldview that leads them to look for naturalistic explanations for the world and to ignore evidence for biblical Creation.

In Scripture we are told that unbelievers are prone to "suppress the truth" and "willfully forget" information when it comes to the matter of direct creation of all things by God. They are not neutral in their thinking. Look at what God's Word says about this matter:

> "For the wrath of God is revealed from heaven against all ungodliness and unrighteousness of men, who by their unrighteousness suppress the truth. For what can be known about God is plain to them, because God has shown it to them. For his invisible attributes, namely his eternal power and divine nature, have been clearly perceived, even since the creation of the world, in the things that have been made. So they are without excuse" (Rom. 1:18–20).
>
> "For they deliberately look over this fact, that the . . . earth was formed . . . by the word of God " (2 Pet. 3:5).

CREATION, EVOLUTION, AND SPLIT THINKING

The Humanist worldview has had a negative influence on religious thinking in our culture. Humanists stress thinking about history, science, education, government, money matters, family problems, etc., strictly from the viewpoint of man's wisdom. Many Humanists are tolerant of other people holding religious views as long as they keep such views to themselves and do not try to apply their "religious" views to "secular" areas of life.

As a result, many people tend to split areas of life into separate compartments that are unrelated to each other. Some Christian worldview writers have labeled this kind of thinking "the two-story worldview." Many people tend to put "spiritual" or "religious" matters into the upper story of their mind, or worldview. The upper story is higher up and close to God. Then people tend to compartmentalize the rest of life into the lower story of their mind, or worldview. The lower story is closer to life on earth and unrelated to the religious realm.

The two-story worldview involves split thinking. It fails to see the relevance of the Bible, as God's Word, to all of life. We could define the "two-story view" as the splitting of life into two unrelated realms of "spiritual" and "non-spiritual." Such a view involves a "sacred/secular" split in thinking. It also involves a "faith/fact" split in thinking. With this thinking people see some matters as secular and others as spiritual and unrelated to each other. With this thinking people tend to split religious faith from scientific and historical facts.

Nancy Pearcey is a Bible-believing Christian who has done much research in philosophy and history and has written a book that deals with the problem of the two-story view. She notes Western philosophers and scientists in history who divided thinking into two realms.

These philosophers and scientists influenced educators and ministers, who then passed on this thinking in schools and churches.

She notes how theologian Francis Schaeffer used the illustration of a two-story building to describe how people divide their thinking into upper story and lower story thinking. She emphasizes that a Christian worldview must reject this division of thinking between sacred and secular realms. See her book, *Total Truth.*[24]

The sacred/secular split is an example of two-story thinking. Some Christians tend to put things they regard as "sacred" into a separate upper story of their thinking. These would include matters such as Bible study, prayer, church services, giving to the church, and evangelism. The tendency here is to view these matters as "spiritual" and all other matters as "non-spiritual."

Some Christians then tend to put the rest of the areas of their life into the lower story of their thinking. These areas of life would include "secular" school subjects such as math, science, social studies, and language studies. Other secular areas include government, possessions, health, recreation, technology, and jobs that are not "full-time Christian service." This way of thinking fails to see the relevance of the teaching of the Bible in these "secular" areas.

As a result of the two-story view, Christians can easily get out of balance in the way they think. Some believers may so emphasize the "sacred" realm that they fail to see any biblical value or meaning in "secular" areas of life. On the other hand, a number of believers focus so much on "secular" areas that they give insufficient attention to the "sacred" areas. Both types of Christians fail to recognize that the Bible applies to every area of life.

Non-Christians adopt the sacred/secular split in their thinking. They would also put "spiritual matters" in the upper story of their worldview. Many of them would allow freedom for people to pursue spiritual areas. However, secular non-Christians do not see the value of them and tend to focus on the lower story "secular areas" instead. Religious non-Christians think about spiritual matters in unbiblical ways.

Another example of two-story thinking is the faith/fact split. "Faith" includes religious beliefs and values. "Facts" include what we observe in the world. This way of thinking puts religious beliefs and values into a separate story of thinking. In the lower story of thinking, the views of secular scientists and historians are facts and their conclusions govern public life. Upper story religious beliefs are just faith and are not necessarily based on historical facts.

For example, the hypothesis of secular scientists about evolution is accepted as fact over the clear teaching of the biblical account of Creation. Ideas of modern secular historians are accepted over the eyewitness testimony of biblical writers to ancient historical events. In other words, the opinions of finite and fallible people have become more authoritative in our culture than the testimony of God's Word.

The faith/fact split undermines biblical beliefs. If secular scientists and historians are the ultimate authorities for facts, then they can view their interpretations of evidence as superior to the Bible. Christian faith then has no firm historical basis. As a result, many Christians try to reinterpret plain statements of Scripture to fit views of secular scientists and historians. And some end up rejecting the inerrancy of Scripture all together.

For example, secular scientists have attacked the Bible with their evolutionary views. Secular historians have attacked historical assertions in Scripture. Secular scholars claim the Bible has historical and scientific errors. As a result of these attacks, many people in churches who have split thinking have ended up denying the inerrancy of Scripture.[25] They view the Bible as useful only in "spiritual matters" and accept secular scientists and historians as ultimate authorities.

The faith/fact split also undermines biblical values. Faith and values become just a matter of personal opinions and feelings. Many people have lost confidence in the reliability of Scripture when it addresses scientific and historical matters because of dogmatic statements made by secular scientists and historians. As a result, they conclude that the Bible is not an absolute authority for moral conduct either. They end up following man's thinking in surrounding culture about what is right and wrong, even if such thinking contradicts the Bible.

For instance, some professing Christians may harbor doubts about the Bible because they've heard attacks upon the Bible by evolutionary scientists or critical historians. They then find that they are reluctant to dogmatically turn to the Bible's authority when Scripture says homosexual behavior or abortion is wrong. Nancy Pearcey made these observations about the faith/fact split in thinking:

> "It's a familiar but tragic story that devout young people, raised in Christian homes, head off to college and abandon their faith . . . largely because young believers have not been taught how to develop a biblical worldview."[26]
>
> "Secularists . . . consign religion to the value sphere, which takes it out of the realm of true and false. . . . 'Religious belief' . . . is merely a matter of private feelings."[27]
>
> "The divide between fact and value was clinched by Darwinism. . . . The fact/value dichotomy has become part of the familiar landscape of the American mind. Children pick it up every day in the typical classroom. . . . Theories like Darwinian evolution are not open to question."[28]

> "In a recent Zogby poll, 75 percent of American college seniors said their professors teach that there is no such thing as right and wrong in a universal or objective sense."[29]

> "Liberalism adopts the 2-layer concept of truth. It accepts a naturalistic account of science and history in the lower story, while relegating theology to the upper story where it is reduced to personal experience."[30]

Two-story thinking goes against the Christian worldview. The Bible does not split the sacred and the secular into two realms of thinking. Scripture does not split facts and faith into two different realms of truth. The Bible is authoritative when it speaks about every area, including matters of science and history.

According to 1 Corinthians 10:31, Christians are to do everything to God's glory. That includes even "secular" matters such as eating and drinking. In fact, it includes all matters of life. Believers should seek to glorify God in every area of study, work, and even recreation—not just while they're in church on Sunday.

And 2 Corinthians 10:5 teaches that believers are to bring all of their thinking into submission to Christ. God commands us to love Him with our entire mind (Matt. 22:37-38). God's Word calls believers to transformation by the renewing of our mind (Rom. 12:2). Therefore, Christians should govern their thinking in every area of life by the written Word of God. Where Scripture teaches in matters describing the created world and human history, it is true and authoritative.

Also consider the teaching of Colossians chapter two. In verses three and four, note that it is Christ who has "all wisdom and knowledge." And verse eight warns believers to be aware of the danger of worldly philosophy: "See to it that no one takes you captive by philosophy and empty deceit." Christians should reject the philosophy and thinking of finite, fallible man when it is contrary to the teaching of the Bible, God's Word.

Believers can observe many examples of unbiblical thinking based on worldly philosophy in the areas of science (evolution), history (denial of biblical miracles), literature (pornography), the media (opposition to Christians), government (pro-abortion), etc. God's Word says: "Blessed is the man who walks not in the counsel of the wicked. . . . but his delight is in the law of the Lord and on his law meditate day and night (Psalm 1:1–2).

Believers must think about and apply God's Word to life every day of the week, not just on Sunday at church. And Christians need to recognize that the Bible gives God's instruction for all areas of life, including family, government, work, money, and education. Scripture warns us about the mind of the unbeliever: "The mind that is set on the flesh is hostile to God; for it does not submit God's law" (Rom. 8:7). The unbeliever seeks to suppress the truth about God (Rom. 1:18) and willingly ignores evidence for God as Creator (2 Pet. 3:5).

Humanist scientists and historians are neither neutral nor infallible. Modern scientists and historians were not eyewitnesses to the origin of the world or to the events of ancient history. They do not know everything. Christians must not give more weight to their interpretations of man's past than the testimony of the Bible as God's Word.

The Bible gives God's authoritative revelation of the origins of man and his world (Gen. 1–11). And Scripture gives God's authoritative Word regarding human history. The Bible is filled with eyewitness testimony (Luke 1:1–4, 24:48; 2 Pet. 1:16). The Bible bases Christian faith on historical facts (John 20:30–31; 1 Cor. 15:1–8). Christians must avoid the faith/fact split in their thinking.

In summary, against two-story thinking, Christians must:

1. Live every area of life to God's glory (1 Cor. 10:31).
2. Submit every area of thinking to Christ and His Word (2 Cor. 10:5).
3. Reject worldly philosophy (Col. 2:8).
4. Replace worldly thinking with daily meditation on God's Word (Psalm 1:1–3).
5. Recognize that the thinking of secular scientists, historians, and professors is neither neutral nor infallible (Rom. 1:18; 8:7).

THE CASE FOR RECENT CREATION

Creation by God involves real history that is recorded in the Bible. Scripture sets forth a unified story of God's creation of man, man's fall into sin, and God's redemption of sinful man through Christ. Ken Ham gives a helpful way to remember the basic history of the Bible with 7 Cs: **Creation** (the beginning of all things), **Corruption** (the Fall), **Catastrophe** (the Flood), **Confusion** (of languages at Babel), **Christ** (incarnation as God in the flesh), **Cross** (Christ's death and resurrection to redeem man), and **Consummation** (Christ's second coming).[31]

God's plan of redemption is tied to biblical history. God's plan of redemption of man only makes sense in the context of the biblical historical account of God's creation of man and man's fall into sin (Gen, 1-5; Rom. 1:16-21; 5:12). God's promise of redemption of man is tied to the biblical genealogies (Gen. 5 and 11; Matt. 1; Luke 3) that show that Jesus is the promised Redeemer and King, descended from Adam and Eve (the promised seed of the woman), Abraham (the promised seed of Abraham), and David (the promised seed of David).

Jesus, the Son of God, refers to the first man and woman as real people at the beginning of creation (Matt. 19:4-5), and He refers to the Flood as a real historical event (Matt. 24:37-39).

Also, Christ's apostles in Scripture refer to Adam and Eve as real people (1 Tim. 2:13-14) and the Genesis Flood as a real event (2 Pet. 3:5-6). If the stories of Adam and Eve and of the Genesis Flood are myths, then Christ and His apostles are wrong, and if Jesus is wrong, He could not truly be God in the flesh as the Bible teaches.

The Bible connects salvation to believing what the Scripture says about key historical events—the incarnation of Jesus as God in the flesh (John 1:1-4; 20:26-31) and Christ's atoning death and bodily resurrection (1 Cor. 15:1-4). The Bible claims that all Scripture is inspired by God (2 Tim. 3:16), which would include the Genesis account of historical Creation, Fall and Flood, and the Messianic genealogies (Gen. 1-11; Luke 3). If Genesis 1-11 is myth and not real history, how can we be sure that Scripture about Christ is real history?

Dr. Al Mohler is a respected Biblical theologian. He gave a helpful presentation, recorded on DVD, "Right from the Start: Creation and the Gospel in One Storyline."[32] In this presentation, he rejects theistic evolution and defends the Scripture as the inspired Word of God and as real history. He shows how the Bible message of Creation-Fall-Redemption and Christ's return to restore all things are tied together in one grand historical narrative of Scripture. He warns us about people who are denying a real Adam and Eve and original sin.

Genesis 1-11 is written as straightforward historical narrative. As historical narrative, we should approach the text as literal history and not as an allegory. If we take Genesis 1 in its plain sense, we would understand the Bible to teach creation in six consecutive, literal, 24-hour days, including the creation of man on Day six. The genealogy of Jesus in Luke 3 traces Jesus' human ancestry generation by generation, all the way back to the first man, Adam, in Genesis.

Then, if we take Genesis 5 and 11 in its plain sense, as real consecutive history, we would understand the Biblical genealogies to set forth only a few thousand years of human history. From the first man, the genealogies in Genesis 5 and 11 give the age of the father at the time of the birth of his son in each succeeding generation. There is no room for gaps in generations when we take a plain reading of these chapters.

Thus, Genesis 1-11 teaches that all people descend from a literal Adam and Eve, who were created on day six of Creation week, which included six literal days of creation of all things. Then Genesis 5 and 11 give ages generation by generation, which enable us to calculate time for human history. A literal reading of Genesis 1-11 would indicate that the world was created about six thousand years ago.

In his commentary on Genesis, Dr. Henry Morris gives a table with the biblical timeline based on genealogies in Genesis 5 and 11. He states:

> "There are no reasons to think there are any gaps in this record or that the years are anything other than normal years. . . . There was a total of 1656 years from the Creation to the Flood."[33]

From the Flood to the first coming of Christ would be about four-thousand years of human history. Then two-thousand years from the first coming of Christ to our present time would give us a total of approximately six-thousand years of human history since the creation of the earth. Thus a literal reading of Genesis 1-11 indicates a recent creation.

Many fine Christian people—from recent generations and the present generation—who believe in the full inspiration and inerrancy of Scripture and believe in God as Creator, have believed that the earth is billions of years old. However, Christians before the time of Charles Darwin and his theory of evolution and his claims of billions of years for the age of the earth did not understand the Bible to teach such an old age for the earth. The idea of billions of years for the age of the earth does not match the normal sense of the language in Genesis.

To correctly interpret what the Bible says in Genesis that relates to the age of the earth, we need to use sound principles of what theologians call hermeneutics, which is the science of the interpretation of Scripture. In chapter two, in the section on the inspiration of Scripture, we covered basic principles of sound interpretation of Scripture. We will briefly paraphrase here what we communicated there from a textbook on the interpretation of Scripture:

1. As a foundational principle, we must approach the Bible as the inspired Word of God.[34]
2. As God's Word, Scripture is totally true and does not contradict itself. Therefore, we must interpret specific passages in light of other clear passages of Scripture and in a way that does not contradict the overall teaching of Scripture.[35]
3. We should interpret words in their normal sense and in light of their grammatical usage.[36]
4. We should interpret Scripture in light of its surrounding context and its historical background.[37]

The Bible does include examples of symbolic prophetic visions, such as in the book of Revelation. Christians differ in their interpretation of the book of Revelation, but they generally agree that, for example, the "beast" in Revelation 13 is symbolic and does not require a literal animal to fulfill it. The Bible does include figures of speech in conversation. For example, Christ refers to Himself as the Vine, but not in a literal sense (John 15). The Bible contains figurative poetical expressions, such as describing rivers clapping hands (Psalm 98:8).

However, in Genesis 1-11, we need to realize that we are dealing with a context of narrative history. We have seen that Christ and His apostles refer to people and events in Genesis 1-11 as real history (Matt. 19:4-6; Matt. 24:38-39; Rom. 5:12-14; 2 Pet. 3:4-7). We should interpret historical narrative literally. Genesis 1, read in a straightforward way, clearly states that God created in six, 24-hour, consecutive days.

Genesis, like most of the Old Testament, was written in Hebrew. The account of creation in Genesis 1 does not contain obvious figures of speech or poetry or symbolic prophetic visions. Hebrew scholars point out that Hebrew poetry differs in form from Hebrew narrative in its pattern of verb use and use of parallel lines. Hebrew scholar Dr. E. J. Young said, "Hebrew poetry had certain characteristics, and they are not found in the first chapter of Genesis."[38]

Dr. Stephen Boyd, another Hebrew scholar, studied Hebrew verbs in poetic and narrative sections of the Old Testament. He found that the verb pattern in Genesis 1 clearly matched Hebrew narrative, and he did not find poetic patterns. He concluded:

> "It is not statistically defensible to interpret Genesis 1:1–2:3 as poetry or metaphor. . . . When Genesis 1:1–2:3 is read as narrative, there is only one tenable view. God created everything during six literal days."[39]

Genesis 1 plainly teaches that God created in six actual days. The phrase "evening and morning" is used with each of the six days of Creation (verses 5, 8, 13, 19, 23, and 31). This expression is a clear reference to a normal-length day of approximately twenty-four hours. When the phrase "evening and morning" is used elsewhere in the Old Testament, it refers to a normal-length day. See examples in Leviticus 24:3, 1 Samuel 17:16, and 1 Chronicles 16:40.

The word translated "day" in Genesis 1 is the Hebrew word *yom*. In Genesis 1 a number is used with the word *yom* (verses 5, 8, 13, 19, 23, and 31). Elsewhere in the Old Testament, when a number is used with *yom* (day), it refers to a 24-hour day. Look at the examples in Joshua 6:4 and Exodus 12:6. **God states that He created everything in six consecutive, normal-length days** and His six-day creation forms the pattern for our seven-day week:

> "For in six days the Lord made the heavens and the earth, the sea, and all that is in them, and rested the seventh day" (Exo. 20:11).

Dr. James Barr is a Hebrew scholar who does not accept the inerrancy of Scripture or a recent creation. However, he believes that the clear intent of the author of Genesis 1 was to communicate that God created in six days:

> "So far as I know there is no professor of Hebrew or Old Testament at any world-class university who does not believe that the writer(s) of Genesis 1–11 intended to convey to their readers the idea that creation took place in a series of six days, which were the same as the days of 24 hours we now experience."[40]

Dr. Jonathan Sarfati, a Christian creationist and a scientist, summarized the matter well:

> "In Genesis, the word day (*yom*) has certain grammatical contexts, any of which alone point strongly to 24 hour days: (1) with a number, (2) with evening and morning, (3) when associated with night. Yet Genesis 1 has all three features, so this becomes overwhelming evidence that the days are ordinary length days. In fact, one must ask: just suppose that God really did mean to communicate creation in six ordinary days. How could He have done so more clearly?"[41]

Dr. Robert Reymond, a Bible-believing theology professor, came to this conclusion:

> "I can discern no reason, either from Scripture or from the human sciences, for departing from the view that the days of Genesis were ordinary 24 hour days. . . . The qualifying words "evening and morning" . . . occur together outside of Genesis in 37 verses. In each instance these words are employed to describe an ordinary day. In the hundreds of other cases in the Old Testament where *yom* stands in conjunction with an ordinal number . . . it never means anything other than a normal, literal day."[42]

Christians historically have believed in a six-day Creation. Dr. Jonathan Sarfati has done a study of what Christians have stated in church history about Creation. He gives historical evidence that Christian writers in past centuries commonly believed that Genesis 1 teaches a six-day Creation.[43] It is basically just in the last 150 years, since Darwin's theory of evolution became popular, that many Christians have tried to reinterpret Genesis 1 to fit the idea of billions of years for the age of the earth.

In England during the 1600s, Protestant Christian leaders put together the Westminster Confession of Faith. In the same century, Baptists and Congregationalists in England used this confession as a model for their own confessions of faith. They put together the London Baptist Confession and Savoy Confession of Faith. These confessions have influenced many churches since that time. Notice what these confessions said about creation:

> "It pleased God the Father, Son and Holy Ghost, for the manifestation of the glory of His eternal power, wisdom and goodness, in the beginning, to create or make of nothing the world and all things therein, whether visible or invisible, in the space of six days."[44]

Several Presbyterian theologians have written books that defend the six-day creation wording of the Westminster Confession of Faith and six-day creation as taught in Genesis. Dr. Joseph Pipa and Dr. David Hall edited a scholarly work that shows that six-day Creation was the historic Christian view of Genesis 1.[45] Dr. Ken Gentry composed a scholarly work that refutes the Framework Hypothesis view of Genesis 1-2 and defends six-day Creation.[46] Dr. Douglas Kelly wrote a book setting forth a biblical and scientific defense of recent creation.[47]

However, in the last 150 years, since Darwin's theory of evolution became popular, many Christians have tried to reinterpret Genesis 1. Many people assume that scientists have proved that the earth is billions of years old. So they use different theories and attach them to the Bible to allow for the idea that the earth is billions of years old.

The Gap Theory claims that there is a gap of time between the events of Genesis 1:1 and 1:2. This theory suggests that billions of years took place between "the beginning" and the rest of the events in Genesis 1. Advocates of the Gap Theory translate Genesis 1:2 as, "The earth became without form and void." However, English translations uniformly translate Genesis 1:2 as, "The earth was without form and void"—which is the plain reading.

The Day Age Theory claims that each of the days of Creation represents long periods of time. However, the repeated use of the phrase "evening and morning," as well as a number before each day, indicates that the days in Genesis 1 are literal twenty-four hour days. Exodus 20:9–11 clearly confirms that the days of creation are six consecutive, normal days.

The Framework Hypothesis claims that Genesis 1 uses a non-literal literary framework to communicate that God created everything and that the text does not really teach how long God took to create. However, as we discussed earlier, Hebrew scholars point out that Genesis 1 is narrative literature, not poetry. The days in Genesis 1 and the genealogies in Genesis 5 and 11 clearly give a time frame of only a few thousand years of earth history.

Any view that inserts billions of years into the book of Genesis also puts the fossil record in the time of Genesis 1. But the fossil record speaks of death. And evolutionists interpret the fossil record in terms of billions of years. **So trying to fit the fossil record into Genesis 1 puts billions of years of death before Adam entered the world and, thus, before he sinned.**

But the Bible teaches that death is the punishment for sin (Gen. 2:17; Rom. 6:23). Adam's sin brought death into the world (Rom. 5:12). God concluded His creative acts in Genesis 1 by pronouncing everything "very good" (Gen. 1:31). But death is not "very good"—it is an enemy (1 Cor. 15:26).

Some people, with their commitment to evolution and billions of years for the earth, have given up previously held beliefs in the historicity of Adam and Eve in Genesis 1. But that undermines the biblical message of Creation, Fall, and Redemption. For a good biblical and scientific defense of the historicity of Adam in Scripture, see the book edited by Terry Mortenson, *Searching for Adam*.[48] There are answers to the claims of billions of years.

Distant starlight is a common argument evolutionists use for the idea of billions of years for the age of the universe and the earth. Scientists estimate from their current understanding of the way light travels that stars most distant from the earth may be as much as billions of light years away. Therefore, many conclude that the stars and the earth must be billions of years old.

However, God's Word reveals that God created light on Day One (Genesis 1:3–5) and the sun, moon, and stars on Day Four (Genesis 1:14–18). Genesis reveals that a number of stars, closer to earth and visible to the eye, must have been visible to man from the beginning:

> "And God said, 'Let there be lights in the expanse of the heavens to separate the day from the night; and let them be for signs and seasons, and for days and years; and let them . . . give light upon the earth,' and it was so" (Gen. 1:14–15).

We know that God has finished His original creation (Gen. 2:1–3). And no man was present to observe the physical processes associated with distant starlight that went on during Creation week. However, the Bible does describe God stretching out the heavens and the stars:

> "He is wise . . . who alone spreads out the heavens" (Job 9:4, 8).
>
> "Bless the Lord . . . stretching out the heavens like a tent" (Psalm 104:1, 2).
>
> "The Lord your Maker, who stretched out the heavens" (Isa. 51:13).

Bible-believing scientists who believe in a young earth take into account God's creation of stars for earth's benefit in Genesis 1 and the biblical descriptions of God stretching out the heavens. They recognize that light from some stars must have been visible on earth from the beginning (Gen. 1:14–17) and they accept the common scientific understanding of the speed of light. They have offered explanations for distant starlight that are consistent with the Bible and with observable facts of science.

One explanation is that possibly God put in place certain physical forces during Creation week that, consistent with present laws of relativity and gravity, distorted time. Physicists point out that very intense gravitational pull can distort time. What if God initially created matter close together in a great mass with intense gravitational pull and then stretched out the heavens (Psalm 104:2)? Light might travel billions of light years in a few days of earth time. Dr. Sarfati notes,

> "*Starlight and Time* by physicist Dr. Russell Humphreys points out that under general relativity, gravity distorts time. Professor John Hartnett . . . in his new book *Starlight, Time, and the New Physics*, applies this successful physics to a universe centered on our galaxy. . . . Hartnett shows that the light from distant stars could have traveled to Earth in the biblical timescale, as measured by Earth clocks."[49]

Another possibility is that we need to adjust our conception about the one-way speed of light. Consistent with Einstein's theories of physics, some argue that light travels instantly one way across great distances. The round trip of light is still 186,000 miles per second as observed. This explanation is not contrary to observational science. Dr. Jason Lisle, an astronomer, says:

> "Contrary to popular belief, it is possible for light to move instantaneously, even today. So, the amount of time it takes for light to travel from the most distant stars to earth is actually zero, not only during Day Four of Creation, but today as well. . . . A less well known aspect of Einstein's physics is that the speed of light in one direction is not objectively measured and so it must be stipulated (agreed upon by convention). . . . We may choose to regard the speed of light as being instantaneous when travelling toward us, providing the round trip speed is always 186,000 miles per second. . . . Genesis 1:15 teaches that God made the lights in the heavens to give light upon the earth . . . . Genesis 1:15 also says "and it was so," which implies that the stars instantly began fulfilling their God-ordained role."[50]

Dr. Danny Faulkner, an astronomer with Answers in Genesis, offers another view. He believes that after the week of Creation the speed of light has continually been the same as what we measure today. However, he suggests that God caused light from stars visible to man's eye to more rapidly travel at first to reach the earth by Day Four or Day Six of Creation week:

> "Any realistic solution to the light travel time problem must explain how Adam could have seen any stars on the evening following Day Six. . . . On Day Three, plants did not instantly appear. . . . Rather it was an abnormally very rapid growth and development of plants. . . . The plants (including trees with fruit) had to have mature fruit by Days Five and Six, for animals and people made then required them for food, which God ordained for them (vv. 29–30). . . . The Day Three parallel can be very useful in solving the light travel time problem. . . . In a similar manner, the stars could not fulfill their functions of marking seasons and days and years (v. 14) unless they were visible by Day Six. . . . I propose that the light had to abnormally "grow" or "shoot" its way to the earth to fulfill this function . . . . Rather than light moving very quickly, I suggest that it was space itself that did the moving, carrying light along with it. This understanding is consistent with the concept of the spreading out of the heavens found in the Old Testament (for example, Job 9:8; Psalm 104:2; Isaiah 40:22, 42:5, 44:24, 45:12, 51:13). . . . This new proposal relies upon God's miraculous intervention. . . . I do not require a physical mechanism for this proposal. . . . Creation by its very nature was a miraculous event/process."[51]

Evolutionists have their own light travel problem. The big bang model has a problem explaining the uniform temperature in the universe with cosmic microwave background and how light could travel from one end of the universe to the other even within several billion light years. Dr. Jason Lisle, a Christian astronomer, explains the issue in an article at the Creation Ministries International website:

> "Cosmic Microwave Background (CMB) comes from all directions in space. . . . The temperature of the CMB is essentially the same everywhere—in all directions. . . . However (according to big bang theorists), in the early universe, the temperature of the CMB would have been very different at different places in space due to the random nature of the initial conditions. . . . More distant regions would come to equilibrium by exchanging radiation (i.e. light). The radiation would carry energy from warmer regions to cooler ones until they had the same temperature. The problem is this: even assuming the big bang timescale, there has not been enough time for light to travel between widely separated regions of space. So, how can the different regions of the current CMB have such precisely uniform temperatures if they have never communicated with each other? This is a light-travel–time problem. . . . At the time the light was emitted . . . space already had a uniform temperature over a range at least ten times larger than the distance that light could have travelled. . . . So, how can these regions . . . have the same temperature? . . . This is called the 'horizon problem.' Secular astronomers have proposed many possible solutions to it, but no satisfactory one has emerged to date. . . . So big-bangers should not criticize creationists for hypothesizing potential solutions, since they do the same thing with their own model. . . . "[52]

Dr. Lisle goes on to explain in this article that proponents of the Big Bang, in order to deal with this problem, conjecture that there was a rapid expansion of space ("inflation") faster than the speed of light. However, he notes that there are conflicting models for inflation and many problems with inflation models. Of interest to creationists, he notes that even some secular astronomers suggest that the speed of light must have been much faster in the distant past.

The other main argument evolutionists use to claim billions of years for the earth's age is radiometric dating of rocks. Some rocks contain radioactive elements that certain instruments can detect. Scientists have observed decay of these elements over time from a "parent" element into a "daughter" element. They measure current rates of decay and extrapolate back to come up with billions of years. Evolutionists make assumptions about radiometric dating that are impossible to prove. Concerning these assumptions, Dr. Henry Morris noted,

1. "The process must always have operated at the same rate at which it functions today.
2. The system in which the process operates must always have functioned as a closed system.
3. The initial condition of the various components of the system must be known."[53]

In other words, **one must assume a constant rate of decay, a closed system with no washing out of elements, and a condition of no presence of the daughter element at the beginning.** Recorded human history is only a few thousand years. So how could anyone know that nothing altered the rate of decay, or that nothing washed out any elements, or that no daughter element was already present in the beginning over an alleged millions of years?

God's Word testifies that God caused water to powerfully act upon the earth during Creation week (Gen. 1:1–10; 2 Pet. 3:5) and the worldwide Flood (Gen. 7:17–24). The rate of decay of elements found in rocks would not be constant because of these two events. The powerful effects of water over the whole earth during Creation week and the worldwide Flood likely washed out certain elements within the rocks.

Creation scientists published a study that refutes evolutionary geological assumptions and shows the effects of the Genesis Flood.[54] This book, *Thousands, Not Billions,* concludes:

> "The concept of accelerated decay arises many times in the RATE work. . . . The episodes of increased nuclear activity appears to have occurred during the creation week and also during the Flood of Noah's day. . . . Accelerated nuclear decay involves millions or billions of years worth of decay occurring in just days or months."[55]

The various chapters in the book give scientific evidence for their conclusions.

Evolutionists use potassium-argon and uranium-lead dating. Carbon-14 should decay out of such rocks in thousands of years. Creation scientists have found traces of carbon-14 in rocks allegedly billions of years in age. They have found newly formed rocks dated at millions of years. And sometimes different dating methods used on the same rock varied by millions of years. In *Thousands, Not Billions,* creation scientists note these findings:

> "The presence of C-14 in "very old" fossils, rocks, coal, and diamond samples is clearly in major conflict with the long-age time scale. . . . Discordance exists among the various radioisotope dating methods. . . . RATE radioisotope studies reveal large-scale errors for volcanic rocks known to be less than a century old. . . . There is abundant evidence for a significant episode of accelerated decay during the Genesis flood event. . . . The rocks resulting from this catastrophic event give clear evidence of nuclear decay with resulting daughter products."[56]

There are other scientific evidences refuting billions of years and supporting recent creation. In 1980 the volcanic eruption of Mount Saint Helens sent out massive mudflows that carved out deep canyons in a short amount of time. Dr. Steve Austin, a Christian geologist, has done valuable research on Mount Saint Helens.[57] He notes that what happened at Mount Saint Helens illustrates how events associated with the biblical Flood would have carved out the Grand Canyon in a short time, showing that millions of years are not necessary to form canyons or rock layers.

Answers in Genesis has published an article on evidences for a young earth in their Answers magazine.[58] Dr. Danny Faulkner is a Christian astronomer. He notes the observation of comets losing size and that they could not be billions of years old. He also points out evidence of the sun's core temperature increasing over time, which means billions of years ago the sun would not have put out sufficient heat to warm the earth adequately.[59]

Dr. Georgia Purdom, a Christian biologist, points out DNA breaks down quickly. However, in the year 2000, scientists examined bacteria from salt crystals dated by evolutionists as 250 million years old and were surprised to find the DNA still intact. Because the DNA was intact, the time frame for the depositing of the salt beds fits the time of Noah's Flood.[60]

Dr. David Menton, another Bible-believing scientist, notes that a scientist has recently found soft tissue in fossilized dinosaur remains.[61] Evolutionists say dinosaurs died out on earth millions of years ago. But soft tissue could not be in a fossil if it was really that age. However, soft tissue in a dinosaur fossil fits well with the time of the Flood a few thousand years ago.

Dr. Andrew Snelling is a Christian geologist. He observes that scientists have confirmed a steady decay over time in the earth's magnetic field.[62] At the current rate of decay, the field and thus the earth must be less than twenty-thousand years old. He also notes,

> "In many mountainous areas, rock layers thousands of feet thick have been bent and folded without fracturing. How can that happen if they were laid down separately over hundreds of millions of years and already hardened?"[63]

Dr. Snelling also points out if the earth's seas were billions of years old, sediments that have been accumulating on ocean floors should be many miles deep. We should see about 250 times more sediment than we observe. He also notes observation of a steady flow of salt into the oceans, which means there should be much more salt in the oceans if the earth was actually several billion years old.[64]

He mentions, too, that carbon-14 should decay out of fossils and diamonds after a few thousand years. However, scientists have found carbon-14 in fossils and diamonds that evolutionists have dated as hundreds of millions of years old.[65] He also says that helium in radioactive rocks should decay out in less than 100,000 years. However, scientists have found rocks full of helium that evolutionists have dated to be many millions of years in age.[66]

Also, some people argue that tree rings on some trees apparently indicate ages for these trees numbering several thousand years older than the biblical time scale for Creation and the Flood. These people assume that the trees consistently add just one tree ring per year. However, a creation science article about tree rings observes:

> "Experiments show trees can grow more than one ring in unusual seasons. Some experiments have even suggested that many periods of time could have been characterized by the growth of one extra ring every one to four years, with

> evidence in controlled laboratory situations showing extra ring growth tied to short drought periods.[67]

Also, evolutionists claim that ice cores in Greenland show over 100,000 years of ice buildup. However, those claims are based on uniformitarian assumptions that claim the ice has slowly built up steadily in layers year by year. However, Roger Patterson of Answers in Genesis notes:

> "From the biblical creationist perspective, the Greenland . . . ice sheets are remnants of the Ice Age that followed the Genesis Flood, which ended about 3,500 years ago, and then slowed as the oceans continued to cool. As evidence of the possibility of rapid growth of the sheets, eight World War II planes were abandoned in Greenland in 1942 and were found in 260 feet of ice in the late 1980s."[68]

THE CASE FOR THE WORLDWIDE FLOOD

The Christian worldview, based upon the Bible, views the earth in light of the biblical account of Creation by God and the Bible's account of God's judgment on the world with a worldwide Flood. Biblical Creation and the worldwide Flood are keys to understanding the features we see in the world. People who hold to the Humanist worldview reject what the Bible says about Creation and the Flood and interpret what they observe about the earth in light of the hypothesis of evolution.

Secular scientists look at the earth today and try to interpret what they observe apart from the revelation of God's Word. They assume gradual processes over hundreds of millions of years have produced the features we now see on the earth. However, if we accept the Bible's testimony in Genesis 6–8 about the Flood, we would understand that it was a catastrophic judgment that produced—and explains—many features we see on the earth today, including fossils.

People who do not believe this testimony of the Bible about the Flood adopt a belief called "uniformitarianism."[69] They think that present processes have always happened the same way and at the same rate in the past and that present processes of water, wind, and volcanic activities explain all of the earth's features. They hold to a closed system that does not allow for God's direct intervention in judgment on the world. However, Scripture warns about false teachers arising who hold this kind of a philosophy. The apostle Peter says:

> "Scoffers will come in the last days with scoffing, following their own sinful desires. They will say, 'Where is the promise of His coming? For ever since the fathers fell asleep all things are continuing as they were from the beginning of creation.' For they deliberately overlook this fact, that the heavens existed long ago, and the earth was formed out of water and through water by the word of God, and that by means of these the world that then existed was deluged with water and perished. But by the

same word the heavens and earth that now exist are stored up for fire, being kept until the day of judgment and destruction of the ungodly" (2 Pet. 3:3–7).

The Bible teaches a general uniformity of physical processes based on God's preservation of His creation (Gen. 8:22; Neh. 9:6). Such general uniformity makes scientific study possible. However, the Bible does not teach an absolute uniformitarianism. Scripture clearly teaches that God has directly and supernaturally intervened in physical processes on earth at times in the past, such as in the worldwide Flood (2 Pet. 3:3-7; Gen. 6-8).

Look at what the Bible says about a worldwide Flood in the book of Genesis. After man's fall into sin (Gen. 3), man multiplied on the earth and became totally rebellious against God:

> "The Lord saw that the wickedness of man was great in the earth and that every intention of the thoughts of his heart was only evil continually. . . . The earth was filled with violence. . . . All flesh had corrupted their way on the earth" (Gen. 6:5, 11-12).

God was longsuffering and gave mankind many years to repent (1 Pet. 3:20; Gen. 6:3), but the people of the world did not repent. Because of this worldwide corruption and rebellion, God determined to destroy man and his world with a great Flood:

> "I will destroy them with the earth. . . . I will bring a flood of waters upon the earth, to destroy all flesh in which is the breath of life under heaven. Everything that is on the earth shall die" (Gen. 6:13, 17).

This was a righteous judgment by God because all mankind was totally rebellious and refused to repent after many years of warning.

However, God's grace preserved Noah and enabled him to live a righteous life in an unrighteous world: "But Noah found favor in the eyes of the Lord. . . . Noah was a righteous man. . . . Noah walked with God" (Gen. 6:8–9). God empowered Noah to be a preacher of righteousness (2 Pet. 2:5) to his generation.

God instructed Noah to prepare a great Ark in order to preserve his family and the animals so they could begin life again in the post-Flood world. God told Noah the dimensions and materials for building the Ark (Gen. 6:14-16). He instructed Noah to take into the ark a male and female pair of every kind of bird and land animal (Gen. 6:19-20). God also instructed Noah about storing food on the Ark (Gen. 6:21).

This Ark was a huge ship that was completely adequate to house two of every kind of land animal and bird (Gen. 6:15–16, 19–21). God brought Noah's family and the animals into the Ark before the Flood began.

> "Then the Lord said to Noah, 'Go into the ark, you and all your household . . . Of birds and of everything that creeps on the ground, two and two, male and female, went into the ark to Noah . . . as God had commanded" (Gen. 7:1, 9).

Then great volcanic explosions happened around the world (Gen. 7:11). The rain came for forty days and forty nights, and water covered the earth for 150 days (Gen. 7:12, 24).

God's Word clearly describes the Flood as worldwide, covering all mountains and killing all people:

> "The waters prevailed so mightily on the earth that all the high mountains under heaven were covered . . . All flesh died that moved on the earth, birds, livestock, beasts, all swarming creatures that swarm on the earth, and all mankind. Everything on the dry land in whose nostrils was the breath of life died. . . . Only Noah was left and those who were with him in the ark" (Gen. 7:19, 21-23).

Some people try to argue it was a local flood rather than a worldwide flood. But if the Flood was only local, then there was no need for Noah to build the Ark. He, his family, the animals, and everyone else for that matter, would have had many years to migrate a safe distance away.

It is important to note that Jesus Christ, the Son of God, described the Flood in Noah's day as a real historical event:

> "For as in those days before the Flood they were eating and drinking, marrying and giving in marriage until the day when Noah entered the ark, and they were unaware until the flood came and swept them all away, so will be the coming of the Son of Man" (Matt. 24:38-39).

Also, Christ's apostle, Peter, wrote under inspiration by God. Peter described Noah, the ark, and the Flood as real history, and he clearly states in Scripture that the Flood was worldwide:

> "God's patience waited in the days of Noah, while the ark was being prepared, in which a few, that is eight persons, were brought safely through water" (1 Pet. 3:20).

> "God did not spare . . . the ancient world, but preserved Noah, a herald of righteousness, with seven others, when he brought a flood upon the world of the ungodly" (2 Pet. 2:5).

> "The world that then existed was deluged with water and perished" (2 Pet. 3:6).

So we see that the Bible clearly describes the Flood as a real historical event and as worldwide in scope. The Bible describes the flooding as lasting forty days, the waters prevailing on the earth for 150 days and all people and animals on the earth dying in the Flood (Gen. 7:17, 21, 24). Such a massive event would surely leave evidence of itself on the earth. And there is abundant evidence of a worldwide Flood that confirms what the Bible says.

Dr. Gary Parker is a scientist and a Christian who believes in biblical Creation. He was a former atheist and evolutionist. However, he was persuaded of the truth of biblical Creation and a worldwide Flood. He aptly says about these matters, "What we see in God's world agrees with what we read in God's Word."[70] A book that greatly influenced the thinking of Dr. Parker and also Ken Ham at Answers in Genesis is *The Genesis Flood*, which Dr. Henry Morris and Dr. John Whitcomb coauthored in the 1960s.[71]

Dr. Henry Morris was a scientist with special expertise in hydrology. Dr. John Whitcomb was a well respected Bible scholar and seminary professor. Both coauthors of *The Genesis Flood* had earned doctorate degrees. Their book defends the plain meaning of the worldwide nature of the Flood as told in Genesis 6–8. And the book relays factual, **observable evidence of the effects of the Flood such as the tremendous evidence around the world of sedimentary rock and fossils.** They state:

> "The entire account plainly yields the inference that tremendous quantities of earth and rock must have been excavated by the waters of the Flood. . . . Never since the world was formed could there ever have been such extensive erosion of soil and rock beds on a global scale as during the Genesis Flood. And the materials that were eroded must eventually have been redeposited somewhere and necessarily in stratified layers, such as we find everywhere around the world today in the great sedimentary rock systems. . . . There must have been uncounted multitudes of living creatures, as well as plants, trapped and eventually buried in the moving masses of sediments and of course under conditions eminently conducive to fossilization. Never before or since could there have been such favorable conditions for the formation of fossiliferous strata."[72]

Sedimentary rocks, by definition, are rocks laid down by water.[73] Secular scientists have found and observed sedimentary rock deposits all over the earth. Dr. Henry Morris notes secular scientists that observe this fact and that this fact supports a worldwide Flood. He writes,

> "About 3/4, perhaps more, of the land area of the earth, 55 million square miles, has sedimentary rock as the bedrock. . . . The thickness of the stratified rock ranges from a few feet to 40,000 or more at any one place. . . . This is exactly to be expected if the waters of a universal Flood ever covered the earth."[74]

Also, there are millions of plant and animal fossils all over the world. In a book defending the worldwide Flood, Ken Ham, observes, "The conditions during the Flood were ideal for fossil formation. . . . Noah's Flood would easily account for the majority of the fossils."[75] Dr. Henry Morris states:

> "Under ordinary processes of nature as now occurring, fossils are very rarely formed. The only way they can be preserved long enough from the usual processes of decay, scavenging and disintegration is by means of quick burial in aqueous sediments. William Miller, Emeritus Professor of Geology at UCLA

points this out: 'Comparatively few remains of organisms now inhabiting the earth are being deposited under conditions favorable for their preservation as fossils. . . . It is nevertheless remarkable that so vast a number of fossils are embedded in the rocks."[76]

Scientists have also found marine fossils on high mountains. Massive water action had to produce and deposit those fossils, which means water had to cover the mountains at some point. Genesis 7:19–20 says the Flood covered all of the mountains on earth. Henry Morris points out,

"Nearly all of the great mountain areas of the world have been found to have fossils . . . near their summits. . . . Surely this fact accords well with the Biblical statements."[77]

Another testimony to the reality of the biblical account of the Flood is through oral tradition about the Flood found in people groups around the world. Since these stories are not inspired, they sometimes conflict with each other or Scripture at points. However, the traditions have the same story of one family preserved in a great boat during a worldwide Flood. How did these diverse people groups come up with the same general story? Dr. Morris explains:

"Sir James George Frazier, Folk-Lore in the Old Testament . . . describes over 100 flood traditions from Europe, Asia, Australia, the East Indies, Melanesia, Micronesia, Polynesia, South America, Central America, North America, and East Africa. . . . An interesting chart representing the principal ideas of the Biblical account of the Deluge in non-Biblical traditions may be found in Byron Nelson, *The Deluge Story in Stone.*"[78]

Skeptics also attack the credibility of the account of Noah's ark. Answers in Genesis has sponsored the construction of a full-size replica of the ark, called "The Ark Encounter." They provide detailed explanations of how Noah could have had two of every kind of bird and land animal on the ark and cared for them. See the Ark Encounter website for details.[79]

Also, a recent book, *Inside Noah's Ark: Why It Worked,* explains how all the animals could have fit on the ark and how Noah's family could have cared for them.[80] And Dr. Nathaniel Jeanson has written a helpful recent article at the AIG website explaining what kinds of animals would have been on the ark.[81] Also, Answers in Genesis has a recent article that answers skeptics about how all of the animals could have fit on the ark:[82]

"The Ark Encounter calculated the size of the ark based on a 20.4-inch (52 cm) cubit. The result is a vessel 510 feet (155 m) long, 85 feet (26 m) wide, and 51 feet (16 m) high.

. . . The Bible informs us that the ark housed representatives of every land-dependent, air-breathing animal. . . . Skeptics often assert that there are millions of species in the world—far more than the number that could fit on the ark. . . . Noah was only sent select representatives from relevant kinds. . . . Species have developed since the time of the flood. Therefore, species are simply varying expressions of a particular kind. . . . Noah's ark was much larger than it is usually depicted, and many of the animals were probably smaller than shown in popular pictures. . . . The Ark Encounter team estimates that there were around 1,400 animal kinds on the ark. . . . The Ark Encounter team projects that there were fewer than 7,000 animals on board the ark."

And AIG has an article that explains how Noah's family could have cared for all the animals:[83]

> "If containers were stacked efficiently, the Ark could easily store food and water for thousands of animals. Larger animals could live in central pens, while reptiles, birds, and smaller mammals could be stacked in cages on the sides and bottom deck. . . . Noah could easily have installed efficient ways to gather fresh rainwater into cisterns below the roof and then distributed the water through bamboo pipes and simple valves to containers in each pen. . . . To simplify urine removal, it could easily have drained down sloping floors into a system of bamboo pipes. Animal-powered pulleys could then dump liquid and solid waste into an empty cavity inside the ship that opened into the ocean (called a moon pool inside modern vessels)."

Another issue concerning the biblical account of the Flood is the matter of dinosaurs and the ark. The Bible teaches that two of every kind of land animal went onto the Ark (Gen. 7:8–9). That would have included dinosaurs. The rest of the dinosaurs outside of the Ark died in the Flood (Gen. 7:20-24), which produced dinosaur fossils. After the Flood, dinosaur pairs left the Ark and started reproducing in the post-Flood world, like the dinosaur-type creatures mentioned in Job 40:15–41:34. Skeptics claim that dinosaurs were too large to fit onto the ark.

Answers in Genesis has a helpful book, *Dinosaurs: Is There a Biblical Explanation?*[84]

According to this book, most dinosaurs in the fossil record were closer to the size of sheep and only a few kinds were extremely large. Also, Noah would have taken younger dinosaurs that were not fully grown to fit onto the ark and to reproduce after the Flood. Noah needed only a small number of dinosaur pairs that represented the basic kinds of dinosaurs.

Dinosaurs that came off the Ark and reproduced evidently found it more difficult than other animals to survive in the harsh conditions after the Flood. Probably a combination of their inability to thrive in the cold climate, limited food supply, disease, and hunting by man (Gen. 9:2–3; 10:9) led to their eventual extinction. However, there are some testimonies in human history of humans encountering creatures called "dragons," which could have been dinosaurs.

Another issue that evolutionists raise is the matter of evidence for past ice ages on the earth. Evolutionists claim that there were multiple ice ages in the earth's past over millions of years of time. However, the after effects of the biblical Flood give a sound explanation for a single great ice age occurring just a few thousand years ago. Answers in Genesis has an informative article on the Ice Age by Roger Patterson, where he gives the following scientific explanation of the Ice Age relating to the Flood:

> "Creation scientists and uniformitarian scientists agree that there is strong evidence for a period of extreme glaciation—an ice age—in the recent past. . . . What could have triggered and then ended these events is a mystery to scientists who insist on examining the past based on the processes seen operating in the present. In order to produce an ice age, two ingredients are required: an increase in evaporation causing more precipitation and cold continents on which the snow can accumulate over time. . . . The Flood likely involved much tectonic activity. This activity provides a mechanism that explains both of the requirements for an Ice Age. As the 'fountains of the great deep' broke open, they released heated water and magma. This would have created jets of steam and the rain that accompanied the Flood. The temperature of the oceans would have increased, providing the energy to cause increased evaporation. The increase in evaporation would naturally lead to more precipitation over the continents. The cooler climate can be explained by an increase in volcanic activity. The volcanism associated with the shifting crust would have released dust and aerosols into the atmosphere. These particles would stay suspended for many years and block the incoming sunlight. The reduced sunlight would cause cooler temperatures over the continents where the increased precipitation would fall as snow and accumulate to form ice sheets. Ice cores reveal volcanic activity extending through the last Ice Age. With this model, there is a built-in off switch as well. Once the tectonic activity slows to approach the rates we see today, the debris settles out of the air, allowing the continents to gradually warm. The warm oceans continue to lose energy by evaporation until precipitation approaches current rates. This point marks the peak of the Ice Age. . . . As the water evaporated out of the warm oceans and became trapped on the continents as ice sheets, sea level dropped. This created land bridges in the Bering Strait, as well as other places around the globe, allowing animals and people to populate North America during the Ice Age. As the Ice Age ended, these areas filled with water again."[85]

A couple of recent books set forth more evidences for the worldwide Genesis Flood. Dr. John Morris, the son of Dr. Henry Morris and a geologist with the Institute for Creation Research, has written a very helpful book, *The Global Flood.*[86] Dr. Andrew Snelling, a geologist with Answers in Genesis, and Dr. Stephen Boyd, a Bible scholar, have teamed up to produce a detailed biblical and scientific study, *Grappling with the Chronology of the Genesis Flood.*[87]

PROBLEMS WITH EVOLUTION

PROBLEMS WITH COSMIC EVOLUTION

We have set forth the plain teaching of the Bible about God's creation of the universe. God directly created the universe by His Word, out of nothing, a few thousand years ago.

> "In the beginning God created the heavens and the earth" (Gen. 1:1).

> "By faith we understand that the universe was created by the word of God, so that what is seen was not made out of things which are visible" (Heb. 11:3).

We pointed out that all varieties of Humanism believe in evolution and reject the account of creation in the Bible. A great worldview clash is going on in the world between Humanists who believe in evolution and Christians who hold to biblical Creation. That worldview clash involves differences about cosmic evolution—the origin and development of the heavens and earth—and biological evolution—the origin and development of life.

The Humanist worldview holds as a foundational belief that the whole universe, stars, planets, and our sun, moon, and the earth, came about by a process of evolution over billions of years. They reject the idea that God created the material universe out of nothing. The standard Humanist worldview sees the entire universe and all life as originating and developing through a process of evolution that involves gradual, naturalistic, and random processes.

A scientist who believes in evolution summarizes the evolutionary view about origins:

> "Man's world view today is dominated by the knowledge that the universe, the stars, the earth, and all living things have evolved through a long history that was not foreordained or programmed, a history of continual, gradual change shaped by more or less directional natural processes consistent with the laws of physics."[88]

And a creationist astronomer summarizes the view of cosmic evolution:

> "Evolutionists believe that the universe is billions of years old. It originated in a 'big bang'—a rapid expansion of space, time, and energy from a single infinitesimally small point. Energy cooled and became matter, which condensed into stars and galaxies . . . some of which condensed to become planets. Our solar system in particular was formed about 4.5 billion years ago from a collapsing gas cloud."[89]

There have been people in the past who held to the idea that the universe is eternal and had no beginning and continually evolved to its present form. This view is contrary to the revelation of God's Word. The Bible clearly states that God created the heavens and the earth and that time for the universe had a beginning ("In the beginning God created the Heavens and the earth," Gen. 1:1). Scientific observations also contradict the possibility of the universe being eternal.

If the universe existed from eternity past, without a beginning, the universe should not exist in its present state according to the observed scientific law, the second law of thermodynamics. The second law of thermodynamics states that the amount of available energy for use is continually decreasing. If available energy had been decreasing continually from eternity past, there should be no available heat from the sun to sustain life on earth. Also, the study of light travel and red shift in stars indicate that the universe had a beginning.

However, evolutionists now generally believe that the universe had a beginning, but most of them leave God out of the picture. Their view about the origin of the universe is popularly called "The Big Bang." They believe the universe began with an explosion and expansion of space and matter from a very small point and evolved over billions of years by natural processes to its present state. However, there are serious problems with the "Big Bang" model.

How could a big bang produce the vast numbers and order of heavenly bodies and send stars billions of light years away? This idea is contrary to all observation of explosions. We see orderly orbits of planets. We see order in galaxies. Explosions do not produce order. A scientist who is an evolutionist and who rejects the "Big Bang" view observes:

> "The big bang theory holds that the universe began with a single explosion. Yet an explosion merely throws matter apart, while the big bang has mysteriously produced the opposite effect, with matter clumping together in the form of galaxies."[90]

Besides that, where did the energy and the matter that scattered from the big bang come from? And what caused the big bang to happen in the first place? **Nothing cannot create something and something cannot create itself.** The first law of thermodynamics states that matter/energy is constant and is not being created or destroyed. In light of that, how can present scientific processes explain a chance origin of all the matter and energy in the universe?

Also, how could the "Big Bang" and random natural processes produce an earth that is so right for human life? Think of the details like the earth's liquid water, oxygen atmosphere, and perfect distance from the sun. All of that is essential for sustaining life, unique to earth and not observed on other planets. Statistical probability would say this is impossible by chance. The earth is a testimony of design by God, not chance processes (Psalm 115:16).

Spike Psarris formerly worked with the U.S. military space program. He was an atheist and an evolutionist, but after discovering scientific problems with the "Big Bang" theory and evidence for Biblical creation, he became a Christian and a biblical creationist. He produced an outstanding three-part DVD series, "What You Aren't Being Told About Astronomy."[91]

In this series, he shows evidence for a young age for the solar system. He shows how the Big Bang has scientific problems with its model and then creates more scientific problems with its conjectured rescuing devices to deal with previous problems. He gives a number of quotes from evolutionist astronomers admitting serious problems with explaining the formation of stars and galaxies and the earth through natural processes.

Dr. Jonathan Sarfati shows that either view of cosmic evolution faces scientific problems. The view that the universe is eternal, or the view that the universe had a beginning in a chance "Big Bang," conflict with the first and second laws of thermodynamics. Dr. Sarfati states:

> "The universe requires a cause because it had a beginning, as will be shown below. God, unlike the universe, had no beginning, so doesn't need a cause. In addition, Einstein's general relativity, which has much experimental support, shows that time is linked to matter and space. So time itself would have begun along with matter and space. Since God, by definition, is the creator of the whole universe, he is the creator of time. . . .
>
> There is good evidence that the universe had a beginning. This can be shown from the Laws of Thermodynamics, the most fundamental laws of the physical sciences:
>
> 1st Law: The total amount of mass-energy in the universe is constant.
>
> 2nd Law: The amount of energy available for work is running out. . . .
>
> If the total amount of mass-energy is limited, and the amount of usable energy is decreasing, then the universe cannot have existed forever, otherwise it would already have exhausted all usable energy—the 'heat death' of the universe. . . . Now, what if the questioner accepts that the universe had a beginning, but not that it needs a cause? But it is self-evident that things that begin have a cause—no one really denies it in his heart. All science and history would collapse if this law of cause and effect were denied. . . . Also, the universe cannot be self-caused—nothing can create itself, because that would mean that it existed before it came into existence, which is a logical absurdity."[92]

PROBLEMS WITH BIOLOGICAL EVOLUTION

Evolutionists believe that all life forms evolved from a simple cell millions of years ago. One scientist summarizes the evolutionary view of biology:

> "All living forms in the world have arisen from a single source that came from an inorganic beginning. So, according to the model of evolution, (a) the first living cell evolved into (b) complex multicellular forms of life; these "evolve"' into (c) animals with backbones. Fish evolved into (d) amphibian, amphibian into (e) reptiles, reptiles into (f) birds and (g) mammals, early mammals into (h) primates, and primates into (i) man."[93]

Scientists recognize, from observation, the law of biogenesis—only life begets life. They also recognize that we do not ever observe spontaneous generation. Man has never observed life developing from nonliving matter. Rather, we've always seen biogenesis—living organisms are produced by living organisms. An evolutionary scientist agrees, saying, "The Law of Biogenesis is arguably the most fundamental in biology.[94]

However, in spite of the observed law of biogenesis, evolutionists believe that a living cell arose by chance from nonliving matter. Then this simple cell eventually developed into animal life and animal life into human life. Evolutionists must assume spontaneous generation of life, contrary to scientific observation. Note this interesting admission from a scientist who is an evolutionist:

> "Most modern biologists, having reviewed with satisfaction the downfall of the spontaneous generation hypothesis, yet unwilling to accept the alternative belief in special creation, are left with nothing. I think a scientist has no choice but to approach the origin of life through a hypothesis of spontaneous generation."[95]

Evolutionists must also assume that the cell evolved gradually by chance. Charles Darwin made an interesting admission saying,

> "If it could be demonstrated that any complex organ existed which could not possibly have been formed by numerous, successive, slight modifications, my theory would absolutely break down."[96]

A cell has to have all of its various components to function at all. It could not gradually evolve. The cell is incredibly complex. The evolutionist Carl Sagan observed this fact about the cell:

> "The information content of a simple cell has been estimated as . . . comparable to about a hundred million pages of the Encyclopedia Britannica."[97]

Fred Hoyle, also an evolutionist, noted this fact about cell evolution:

> "By random processes . . . the chance of finding the whole 200,000 proteins on which life depends is 10 to the 40,000th to 1 against."[98]

Evolutionists have no explanation how the complex cell could have gradually evolved all of its functions by chance. A molecular biologist made this observation:

> "None of the papers published in *The Journal of Molecular Evolution* over the entire course of its life as a journal ever proposed a detailed model by which a complex biochemical system might have been produced in a gradual step-by-step Darwinian fashion."[99]

Dr. Jonathan Wells is a scientist and former evolutionist. In his scientific studies, he came to realize that the examples scientists commonly use to support Darwinian evolution are weak and do not really prove evolution. He examined each of the main examples used to support Darwinian evolution and documented the weaknesses of each example. He wrote a book summarizing his findings, *Icons of Evolution.*[100] Let's consider some of his findings.

For example, the Bible and all scientific observation confirm that different kinds of animals only reproduce after their kind (Gen. 1). But Darwin, in his *Origin of Species,* claimed all living things descended from a common ancestor. Dr. Wells notes from this common ancestor, Darwin constructed a "tree of life" of all living things, which included reptiles evolving into birds, apes into man, etc.[101]

To support his argument, Darwin referred to the drawings of embryos by Ernst Haeckel.[102] Haeckel's drawings purported to show great similarity between the development and appearance of human embryos and animal embryos. Darwin argued that such similarity was evidence for a common ancestor. Modern science textbooks reprint Haeckel's drawings in support of biological evolution. However, the drawings were exaggerated and fake.

In recent years some scientists have researched Haeckel's drawings and compared them to actual human embryos, concluding that Haeckel greatly exaggerated the development of human embryos in his drawings. Dr. Wells notes:

> "In 1997 British embryologist Michael Richardson published an article in the journal *Anatomy and Embryology,* comparing the textbook drawings with actual embryos. Richardson was quoted in the leading American journal Science as saying: 'It looks like it's turning out to be one of the most famous fakes in biology.' Yet even biology textbooks published after 1997 continue to carry the faked drawings."[103]

Darwin argued that a process of natural selection led to biological evolution. A standard dictionary defines natural selection as,

> "The process in nature by which, according to Darwin's theory of evolution, only the organisms best adapted to their environment tend to survive and transmit their genetic characteristics in increasing numbers to succeeding generations while those less adapted tend to be eliminated."[104]

In addition to natural selection, Darwin's followers also emphasize the idea that random mutations drive biological evolutionary change. A standard dictionary defines biological mutations as,

> "A change in the nucleotide sequence of the genome of an organism or virus, sometimes resulting in the appearance of a new character or trait not found in the parental type."[105]

Evolutionists like to use past studies of peppered moths and finches as illustrations of natural selection and evolution. In the 1800s, observers in one area of Britain noted that the population of peppered moths changed from mostly lighter colored to mostly darker colored moths.[106] However, Dr. Wells notes that "the only thing that happened was a change in the proportion of two variations of a pre-existing species of moth."[107]

During the 1800s, Darwin observed over a period of time variations in the beak sizes of finches living in the Galapagos Islands.[108] He claimed this as an illustration of evolution. However, Dr. Wells made this observation: "Selection oscillates with climatic fluctuations and does not exhibit long term evolutionary change."[109] All that happened is that a greater percentage of the finches with certain beak sizes could crack larger seeds more easily for eating, so they survived during specific climate conditions.

Evolutionists believe that the peppered moth and Galapagos finch studies provide strong evidence for evolution and natural selection. Notice, though, that the peppered moths were still peppered moths, and the finches were still finches. There was only a change in the population of moths or finches with a certain minor feature that survived. There was not an evolutionary development of new genetic information.

For one kind of animal to change into a different kind of animal would require new genetic information in the DNA. The key point is that no one has observed natural selection or mutations to produce new genetic information or a totally new kind of animal. A biologist who is also an evolutionist shared this observation:

> "The frequency with which a single non-harmful mutation is known to occur is about 1 in 1000. The probability that two favorable mutations would occur is 1 in a million. We already know that mutations in living cells appear once in ten million to once in one hundred thousand million. It is evident that the probability of five favorable mutations occurring within a single life cycle of an organism is effectively zero."[110]

Evolutionists also point to the fossil record for support of their idea about how life came about. A fossil is "preserved remains of a living organism."[111] If evolution were true, the fossil record should show many obvious transitional forms. However, even Darwin admitted fossil evidence presented a problem for his theory:

> "Why then is not every geological formation and every stratum full of such intermediate links? Geology assuredly does not reveal any such finely graduated organic chain; and this, perhaps, is the most obvious and gravest objection which can be urged against my theory."[112]

Even some paleontologists who are committed to evolution have admitted that the evidence does not show clear examples of transitional forms:

> "I fully agree with your comments about the lack of direct illustration of evolutionary transitions. If I knew of any, fossil or living, I would certainly have included them.

> . . . There is not one such fossil for which one could make a watertight argument" (Colin Patterson).[113]

> "The extreme rarity of transitional forms in the fossil record persists as the trade secret of paleontologists. . . . In any local area, a species does not arise gradually. . . . It appears all at once and fully formed" (Stephen Gould).[114]

Archaeopteryx is a fossilized bird that evolutionists often claim as a transitional form. However, Alan Feduccia, an evolutionist and an authority on birds, points out,

> "Paleontologists have tried to turn Archaeopteryx into an earth-bound, feathered dinosaur. But it's not. It is a bird, a perching bird. And no amount of "paleobabble" is going to change that."[115]

Evolutionists have also appealed to certain "ape-men" fossil finds for evidence of the evolution of man from apes. Dr. Wells notes that even many evolutionists have concluded that previous claims of "Neanderthal man" and "Java man" as ape men were wrong, and "Piltdown man" was shown to be a forgery.[116] Dr. Jonathan Sarfati found in his research of ape-men that the ape-men fossils come from scattered fragments and further study has shown that they are either man or ape, not a proven transitional form.[117]

Marvin Lubenow, a Christian and a biblical creationist, has done extensive research over many years of claims about ape-man fossils. He has written a book summarizing his findings, *Bones of Contention.*[118] He demonstrates in this book the weaknesses of the claims about ape-men fossils as transitional forms and the problems with claims of evolution based on the fossil record. His book is highly recommended.

Along with ape fossils, there are millions of animal fossils all over the world. They were not formed by a process of evolution. The Genesis Flood best explains the presence of most of the fossil record. Henry Morris gives a good treatment of this in his book, *The Genesis Flood.*[119]

With the lack of proven transitional forms in the fossil record, some evolutionary scientists have turned to a theory of "punctuated equilibrium," in which life forms evolve into different kinds of life in sudden short bursts.[120] Thus, they claim, no evolutionary evidence is left in the fossil record. However, they have no scientific proof for their theory. And it is genetically impossible for a pair of the same kind, like a reptile, to produce a different kind such as a bird.

With these problems, some evolutionary scientists have resorted to a theory that life must have developed elsewhere in the universe and then was transported somehow to Earth.[121] But this still leaves unanswered the question of how life first originated. Frances Crick, an evolutionist and scientist who studied DNA, conceded that:

> "An honest man, armed with all the knowledge available to us now, could only state that in some sense, the origin of life appears at the moment to be almost a miracle, so many are the conditions which would have had to have been satisfied to get it going."[122]

In recent years the genome project, which has studied ape and human genomes, has drawn attention. A standard dictionary defines a "genome" as "a full set of chromosomes with all its genes; the total genetic constitution of a cell or organism."[123] Genome studies have compared the genomes of chimpanzees and humans through the analysis of DNA sequence. Evolutionists claim these studies support ape to human evolution. Answers in Genesis has a helpful article by Dr. Jeffrey Tomkins, a geneticist and creationist, about the genome project:

> "Evolutionary bias literally colors every aspect of the DNA analysis. . . . In 2004, the human genome was formally completed. . . . In 2005 . . . a rough draft of the chimpanzee genome was reported with the hope that its availability would vindicate the claims of biologists who had been promoting high similarity (95% or greater) . . . associated with an ape to human evolutionary transition. . . . Perhaps the most startling human-chimpanzee genome data of recent times are the results from comparing DNA sequence from human and chimpanzee Y-chromosomes (Hughes et al. 2010). . . . What made this study unique was that the MSY region in the chimpanzee was largely assembled and constructed based on a clone-based physical map for chimpanzee, not the human physical frame-work. This allowed for a relatively reasonable comparison of the MSY sequence between human and chimp, the first time such an apparently unbiased large-scale comparison had actually been done. The results were completely unexpected and radically contradicted the standard evolutionary dogma which pervades the scientific community. The research paper title was well chosen and a very accurate one-sentence summary of the project: "Chimpanzee and human chromosomes are remarkably divergent in structure and gene content." Perhaps the most interesting highlight of the study was the difference in gene content. . . . The human MSY contained 78 genes while the chimpanzee only contained 37, a 48% difference in total gene content alone. . . . Major differences between the structure of the human and a chimpanzee genomes are now being documented as the genomic resources improve."[124]

Dr. Nathaniel Jeanson has a Ph.D. from Harvard University in cell and developmental biology and works with Answers in Genesis. He has written a new book, *Replacing Darwin*.[125] He notes Darwin formulated his view of biological evolution without knowledge of DNA.

In his book, Dr. Jeanson defends the biblical Creation model, showing fixity of kinds and recent creation and evidence for Divine design in DNA, while recognizing diversity within a species. He shows that the evolution timescale greatly overestimates mitochondrial DNA differences among humans. He shows that the biblical Creation time scale of six thousand years matches the data about differences in human mitochondrial DNA.

OTHER PROBLEMS WITH EVOLUTION

A foundational problem that evolution has is that it cannot logically provide the conditions for human knowledge. The Christian worldview can logically provide the conditions for human knowledge. Worldviews must account with their assumptions for how people come to know things. Worldviews need to explain logic, science, and morality, where they come from and how they relate to knowledge.

Dr. Jason Lisle, a scientist and defender of biblical Creation, has written a book on Christian apologetics, *The Ultimate Proof of Creation,* a book that Christians should get and study. In his book, he emphasizes that the Christian worldview, with its presuppositions of God and His Word, gives the foundation for knowledge, for logic, science, and morality. However, without God and the Bible, you do not have a sound basis for logic, science and morality. Consider some of Dr. Lisle's observations and see his book for a further detailed explanation:

> "Only the God described in the Bible can provide the foundation for the things we take for granted. Without God's Word, we would not have good reason to believe in the preconditions of intelligibility: the basic reliability of memory and senses, laws of logic, uniformity in nature, morality. . . . In order for us to reason logically, there must be laws of logic. In order for us to study nature, the universe must have an underlying orderliness. . . . Morality is required if we are to argue that people ought to have a rational basis for their worldview. . . . God has the right to make the rules. So an absolute moral code makes sense in a biblical creation worldview. . . . Rational reasoning involves using the laws of logic . . . God has made us in His image (Gen. 1:26) . . . The laws of logic are a reflection of the way God thinks and thus the way He expects us to think . . . Laws of logic make sense in a Christian worldview. . . . The Christian's presuppositions form a rational consistent worldview in which knowledge is possible.[126]

> "In the evolution worldview, right and wrong can be nothing more than electro-chemical reactions in the brain. . . . Without the biblical God, right and wrong are reduced to mere personal preferences. . . . If human beings are chemical accidents, why should we be concerned about what they do? . . . Laws of logic pose a very serious problem for the evolutionist. . . . A materialist atheist does not believe in anything beyond the physical universe. . . . Laws of logic are not matter; they are not part of the physical universe. Therefore, laws of logic cannot exist if materialism is true. . . . If evolution were true, then all the evolutionist's thoughts are merely the necessary result of chemistry acting over time."[127]

In summary, if the evolutionary Humanist worldview is true, how are logic and scientific study possible? If there is no God as Creator, and material things are the only reality, how can you have immaterial laws of logic? If there is no God as Sustainer, and the world is constantly, randomly evolving, how can you have the regularity in the world necessary for scientific study and conclusions? The Christian worldview, rooted in God and His Word, provides the basis for logic and scientific study (Gen. 1:26-27; 8:22; Neh. 9:6; Heb. 1:2-3).

Finally, if the evolutionary Humanist worldview is true, how can you have universal absolute standards of right and wrong? If there is no God as Law-giver, what right does anyone have to tell another person what is right and wrong? Who can even be sure what is right and wrong? Right and wrong would be just a matter of personal preference and chemical reactions in the brain. The Christian worldview provides a basis for absolute morality (Exo. 20:3-17; Rom. 2:14-16). The Humanist worldview does not provide the conditions for true knowledge.

Also, there are some people who reject the Bible as God's infallible Word and reject Jesus as God in the flesh, but they believe in some kind of God and mix that belief with evolution and Humanist philosophy. They adopt the idea of theistic evolution, that God used the process of evolution to bring the world and man into existence. However, there are serious problems with theistic evolution. Evolution cannot be harmonized with Genesis.

The order proposed by evolution does not fit the order of Creation in Genesis 1. Genesis puts the creation of light before the light-bearers (sun, moon, stars) and birds before land animals, ruling out birds coming from reptiles. Genesis 1 clearly teaches that animals reproduce after their own kind and that God directly created man separately from animals.

Theistic evolution leads to the belief that man evolved from animals and the denial of a literal Adam and Eve. This undermines the clear teaching of the Bible and the Gospel message of salvation. Also, evolution is foundational to atheistic Humanism and logically leads to atheism or agnosticism, because with the idea of evolution, God is unnecessary.

The atheistic evolutionist, Richard Bozarth, points out that to view man as evolved from animals involves a rejection of a literal Adam and Eve as described in the Bible and, consequently, the historical account of their fall. He also points out that this view undermines the biblical Gospel message and gives support to the atheistic view. In his book on evolution, Ken Ham quotes Bozarth:

> "Christianity is—must be—totally committed to the special creation as described in Genesis and Christianity must fight with all its full might, fair or foul, against the theory of evolution. . . . It becomes clear now that the whole justification of Jesus' life and death is predicated on the existence of Adam and the forbidden

> fruit he and Eve ate. Without the original sin, who needs to be redeemed? Without Adam's fall into a life of constant sin, terminated by death, what purpose is there to Christianity? None."[128]

Theistic evolution logically leads to an unbiblical distortion of a person's view of God. Evolution undermines God's goodness by making God the direct Creator of a long process of death and suffering apart from man's sin. But God's Word presents God as originally creating everything as very good (Gen. 1:31), and God's Word presents man's sin as the cause of death (Rom. 5:12).

Theistic evolution has also led many people to unbiblical views of God such as Deism, Pantheism, and Process Theology. Dr. Cairns, in his theological dictionary, notes how these false beliefs are connected to evolution. Deism sees God as starting the process of evolution and as not directly involved in the world.[129] Pantheism sees nature as evolving and identifies God with nature.[130] Process Theology sees God as evolving and changing along with the world.[131]

Theistic evolution commonly leads people to reject the Bible as the fully inspired and inerrant Word of God. They commonly say the Bible's account of Creation is wrong. Harold Lindsell has written a book on attacks on the inerrancy of the Bible. He notes the influence of Renaissance thinking on the development of Humanism and liberal religious views:

> "The Renaissance taught man an opposite view of the world. . . . Science was substituted in place of the moral and the religious. . . . One could not start with the presupposition that there is any God. . . . The ideas that undergirded the Renaissance penetrated . . . religious scholarship. . . . Historical-critical methodology . . . starts with a negative assumption . . . that nothing can be accepted as the Word of God unless it can be proven to be so. . . . There is no way the evolutionary hypothesis can be developed from the phenomena of Scripture without doing violence to the data. . . . Almost without exception, those who employ the historical-critical methodology are evolutionists."[132]

CHAPTER 5 STUDY GUIDE
THINKING BIBLICALLY ABOUT CREATION VERSUS EVOLUTION

KEY SCRIPTURES TO READ:

Genesis 1:1-31; Genesis 6:17-21 and 7:17-24; Exodus 20:9, 11; Nehemiah 9:6; Job 38:1, 4; Psalm 19:1-3; Psalm 139:13-16; Luke 3:23-38; Romans 1:18-21; Romans 5:12; 2 Corinthians 10:4-5; Hebrews 1:2-3 and 11:3; 1 Peter 3:20; 2 Peter 2:5; 2 Peter 3:3-7

KEY POINTS TO NOTE (NOTE BOLD TYPE IN CHAPTER):

What does Genesis 1:21-25 say about animal reproduction?

____

____

What does Genesis 1:31 about the condition of everything after God finished creating?

____

____

What does Hebrews 11:3 and 2 Peter 3:5 say about how God created?

____

____

What two areas of science are important to distinguish?

____

____

What are the seven C's of Biblical history according to Ken Ham?

____

____

What three kinds of evolution do evolutionists speak about?

____

____

What Scripture reference confirms that God created everything in six literal days in Genesis 1?

____

What unprovable assumptions must evolutionists make about radiometric dating?

____

____

____

What theological problem is created if one puts the fossil record and billions of years in Genesis 1 and what Scripture verse shows this problem?

____

____

What are two observable evidences for the worldwide Flood?

____

____

What is the problem for conjecturing the origin of the universe in the Big Bang without God?

____

____

What have some paleontologists admitted about transitional forms in the fossil record?

____

____

CRITICAL THINKING:

What did Darwin admit would pose problems for this theory and what we do know now that shows these truly are problems for Darwinian evolution?

Briefly summarize explanations for distant starlight consistent with recent creation.

Briefly summarize the case for recent creation as opposed to billions of years.

What does holding theistic evolution lead to concerning one's view of God?

CHAPTER 5 ENDNOTES

CREATION VERSUS EVOLUTION AS A WORLDVIEW CONFLICT

1 Roy Clouser, *The Myth of Religious Neutrality* (South Bend, IN: Notre Dame University Press, 1991), pp. 3, 19-20.

2 John MacArthur, *The Battle for the Beginning* (W Publishing Group, 2001), pp. 12–13.

3 Alan Cairns, "Pantheism," *A Dictionary of Theological Terms,* (Greenville, SC: Ambassador International, 2002), p. 321.

4 Ken Ham and Terry Mortenson, "Science or the Bible?" (Answers in Genesis, June 14, 2007). (https://answersingenesis.org/what-is-science/science-or-the-bible). (Accessed 3/16/2019).

5 Dr. Henry Morris, *The Biblical Basis for Modern Science* (Grand Rapids: Baker Book House, 1984), pp. 17-18, 30, 463-465.

6 David Noebel, *Understanding the Times,* revised 2nd edition (Manitou Springs, CO: Summit Press, 2006), pp. 180-181.

7 Ibid, p.187.

8 Ibid, p. 197.

9 Ibid, pp. 204-205.

10 Wendell Bird, *The Origin of Species Revisited: The Theories of Evolution and of Abrupt Appearance* (Nashville, TN: Thomas Nelson, Inc., 1991), volume 1, p. 17, quoting T. Dobzhansky.

11 Ibid, p. 32, quoting Julian Huxley.

12 Ibid, pp. 16-17, quoting Ernst Mayer.

13 Jason Lisle, *The Ultimate Proof of Creation* (Green Forest, AR: Master Books, 2009), pp. 33-34.

14 Bird, p. 18, quoting evolutionists F. Ayala & J. Valentine.

15 *Webster's College Dictionary* (New York: Random House, 1992), p. 464.

16 Ken Ham, *The Lie—Evolution* (Green Forest, AR: Master Books, 1987), pp. 21, 28, 44.

17 Henry Morris, *The Long War Against God* (Green Forest, AR: Master Book, 2000), p. 20, quoting Ernst Mayer.

18 Pierre Teilhard de Chardin, *The Phenomenon of Man* (New York: Harper & Row, 1965), p. 219.

19 Morris, *The Long War Against God,* p. 19, quoting Julian Huxley.

20 Dave Breese, *Seven Men Who Rule the World from the Grave* (Chicago: Moody Press, 1990), chapters 1-3 on Charles Darwin.

21 Thomas Kuhn, *The Structure of Scientific Revolutions,* 2nd edition (Chicago: University of Chicago Press, 1970), pp. 23, 76, 79, 146.

22 Jonathan Sarfati, *Refuting Evolution* (Brisbane, Australia: Creation Ministries International, 2007), p. 18, quoting Richard Lewontin.

23 Sarfati, *Refuting Evolution,* pp. 18-19.

24 Nancy Pearcey, *Total Truth* (Wheaton, IL: Crossway Books, 2004), pp. 2, 21.

25 Harold Lindsell, *The Battle for the Bible* (Grand Rapids: Zondervan, 1976).

26 Pearcey, p. 19.

27 Pearcey, pp. 21-22.

28 Pearcey, pp. 106-107.

29 Pearcey, p. 113.

30 Pearcey, p. 115.

THE CASE FOR RECENT CREATION

31 Ken Ham, "Seven C's of History" (Answers in Genesis, May 20, 2004; https://answersingenesis.org/bible-history/seven-cs-of-history). (Accessed 3/16/2019).

32 Al Mohler, "Right from the Start: Creation and the Gospel in One Storyline" (Answers in Genesis, 2011, DVD).

33 Henry Morris, *The Genesis Record* (Grand Rapids: Baker Book House, 1976), p. 154.

34 Bernard Ramm, *Protestant Biblical Interpretation,* 3rd revised edition (Grand Rapids, MI: Baker Book House, 1970), p. 93.

35 Ibid, p. 107.

36 Ibid, p. 125.

37 Ibid, p. 138.

38 Douglas Kelly, *Creation and Change* (Great Britain: Mentor, 1997), p. 42.

39 Don DeYoung, ed., *Thousands, Not Billions* (Green Forest, AR: Master Books, 2005), p. 169, "A Proper Reading of Genesis 1:1–2:3" by Stephen Boyd.

40 Kelly, pp. 50–51, quoting James Barr.

41 Jonathan Sarfati, *Refuting Compromise* (Green Forest, AR: Master Books, 2004), p. 105.

42 Robert Reymond, *A New Systematic Theology of the Christian Faith* (Nashville, TN: Thomas Nelson, 1998), pp. 392-393.

43 Sarfati, chapter 3, "The History of Interpretation of Genesis 1–11," in Refuting Compromise."

44 Philip Schaff, *Creeds of Christendom,* vol. 3, Evangelical Protestant Creeds (Grand Rapids, MI: Baker Book House, 1985 reprint), p. 611.

45 Joseph Pipa and David Hall, eds., *Did God Create in 6 Days?* (White Hall, WV: Tolle Lege Press, 2005).

46 Ken Gentry, *As It Is Written: Dismantling the Framework Hypothesis* (Green Forest, AR: Master Books, 2016).

47 Douglas Kelly, *Creation and Change,* cited earlier on endnote 38.

48 Terry Mortenson, ed., *Searching for Adam: Genesis and the Truth about Man's Origin* (Green Forest, AR: Master Books, 2016).

49 Jonathan Sarfati, *Refuting Evolution,* p. 95.

50 Jason Lisle, "Distant Starlight—The Anisotropic Synchrony Convention" (May 25, 2011) (https://answersingenesis.org/astronomy/starlight/distant-starlight-thesis). (Accessed 3/16/2019).

51 Danny Faulkner, "A Proposal for a New Solution to the Light Travel Time Problem" (July 24, 2013; https://answersingenesis.org/astronomy/starlight/a-proposal-for-a-new-solution-to-the-light-travel-time-problem). (Accessed 3/16/2019).

52 See Dr. Jason Lisle, "Light-Travel Time: A Problem for the Big Bang" (*Creation,* September 2003; https://creation.com/light-travel-time-a-problem-for-the-big-bang). (Accessed 3/16/2019).

53 Henry Morris, *The Biblical Basis for Modern Science* (Grand Rapids, MI: Baker Book House, 1984), p. 261.

54 Don DeYoung, ed., *Thousands, Not Billions,* (Green Forest, AR: Master Books, 2005).

55 Ibid, pp. 178-179.

56 Ibid, pp. 56, 110, 133, 151.

57 Steve Austin, "Mount St. Helens: Modern Day Evidence for the Worldwide Flood" (Compel Media, 2012, DVD).

58 "10 Best Evidences from Science that Confirm a Young Earth," *Answers Magazine* (Hebron, KY: Answers in Genesis, Oct.-Dec. 2012), pp. 46–58.

59 Ibid, pp. 51, 55–56.

60 Ibid, p. 57.

61 Ibid, pp. 50-51.

62 Ibid, pp. 52–53.

63 Ibid, p. 48.

64 Ibid, pp. 47–48, 56.

65 Ibid, pp. 54–55.

66 Ibid, pp. 53–54.

67 Lorey, F. 1994. Tree Rings and Biblical Chronology. Acts and Facts. 23: (6). Institute for Creation Research (http://www.icr.org/article/tree-rings-biblical-chronology). (Accessed 3/16/2019).

68 Roger Patterson, "Do Ice Cores Show Many Thousands of Years?" (Answers in Genesis, February 17, 2011; http://www.answersingenesis.org/articles/ee2/ice-age). (Accessed 3/16/2019).

THE CASE FOR THE WORLDWIDE FLOOD

69 Ken Ham, *The Lie: Evolution/Millions of Years*, revised edition (Green Forest, AR: Master Books, 2012), pp. 185-191.

70 Gary Parker, "From Evolution to Creation: Testimony of a Former Evolutionist" (Answers in Genesis, 2001, DVD).

71 John Whitcomb and Henry Morris, *The Genesis Flood: The Biblical Record and Its Scientific Implications* (Philadelphia, PA: Presbyterian and Reformed Publishing Company, 1961).

72 Ibid, p. 123.

73 *Webster's College Dictionary* (New York: Random House, 1992), p. 1213.

74 Whitcomb and Morris, p. 270, quoting Von Engeln and Caster.

75 Ken Ham and Bodie Hodge, *A Flood of Evidence* (Green Forest, AR: Master Books, 2016), pp. 140, 145.

76 Whitcomb and Morris, pp. 128–129.

77 Whitcomb and Morris, p. 128.

78 Whitcomb and Morris, pp. 48–49.

79 "The Ark Encounter" (https://arkencounter.com).

80 *Inside Noah's Ark: Why It Worked*, ed. Laura Welch (Green Forest, AR: Master Books, 2016).

81 Nathaniel Jeanson, "Which Animals Were on the Ark with Noah?" (Answers in Genesis, May 28, 2016). (https://answersingenesis.org/creation-science/baraminology/which-animals-were-on-the-ark-with-noah). (Accessed May 2019).

82 Michael Belknap and Tim Chaffey, "How Could All the Animals Fit on the Ark?" (Answers in Genesis, April 2, 2019). (https://answersingenesis.org/noahs-ark/how-could-all-animals-fit-ark). (Accessed May 2019).

83 Michael Belknap, "Fantastic Voyage: How Could Noah Care for the Animals?" (Answers in Genesis, November 19, 2017). (https://answersingenesis.org/noahs-ark/fantastic-voyage-how-could-noah-care-animals). (Accessed May 2019).

84 Ken Ham and others, *Dinosaurs: Is There a Biblical Explanation?* (Hebron, KY: Answers in Genesis, 2010).

85 Roger Patterson, "The Ice Age" (Answers in Genesis, February 17, 2011), https://answersingenesis.org/environmental-science/ice-age/the-ice-age-cause. (Accessed 3/16/2019).

86 John Morris, *The Global Flood: Unlocking Earth's Geologic History* (Institute for Creation Research, 2012).

87 Stephen Boyd and Andrew Snelling, *Grappling with the Chronology of the Genesis Flood: Navigating the Flow of Time in Biblical Narrative* (Master Books, 2014).

PROBLEMS WITH EVOLUTION

88 Bird, p. 17, quoting Dr. Mayer, evolutionary biologist at Harvard.

89 Lisle, *The Ultimate Proof of Creation*, pp. 33–34.

90 Bird, p. 462, quoting Fred Hoyle.

91 Spike Psarris, "What You Aren't Being Told About Astronomy," 3 volume DVD series (2009-2013, Creation Astronomy Media, www.creationastronomy.com). Volume 1: "Our Created Solar System"; Volume 2: "Our Created Stars and Galaxies"; Volume 3: "Our Created Universe."

92 Jonathan Sarfati, "If God Created the Universe, Then Who Created God?—Answering the Critics" (April 1998), https://creation.com/if-god-created-the-universe-then-who-created-god). (Accessed 3/16/2019).

93 Bird, p. 209, quoting a biologist, Thompson, of the University of Missouri.

94 Bird, p. 312, quoting P. Medawar and J. Medawar.

95 Bird, p. 374, quoting George Wald.

96 Charles Darwin, *Origin of Species*, 6th ed., 1988, New York University Press, New York, p. 154.

97 Bird, p. 298, quoting Carl Sagan.

98 Bird, pp. 118–119.

99 Behe, Darwin's Black Box, p. 176.

100 Jonathan Wells, *Icons of Evolution: Why Much of What We Teach about Evolution is Wrong* (Washington, D.C.: Regnery Publishing, 2000).

101 Ibid, chapter 3, "Darwin's Tree of Life."

102 Ibid, chapter 5, "Haeckel's Embryos."

103 Ibid, preface.

104 *The Free Dictionary*, "natural selection" (https://www.thefreedictionary.com/natural+selection) (Accessed 3/16/2019).

105 The Free Dictionary, "mutations" (https://www.thefreedictionary.com/mutations). (Accessed 3/16/2019).

106 Wells, chapter 7.

107 Wells, pp. 143-144.

108 Wells, chapter 8.

109 Wells, p. 173.

110 Bird, p. 88, quoting E. Ambrose.

111 *Webster's College Dictionary* (New York: Random House, 1990), p. 525.

112 Sarfati, *Refuting Evolution*, p. 47, quoting Darwin in Origin of Species.

113 Luther Sunderland, *Darwin's Enigma* (Green Forest, AR: Master Books, 4th ed. 1988), p. 89, quoting Colin Patterson.

114 Morris, *The Biblical Basis for Modern Science*, pp. 341, 343, quoting Stephen Jay Gould.

115 Sarfati, *Refuting Evolution*, p. 58, quoting V. Morell on archaeopteryx.

116 Wells, chapter 11, "From Ape to Human."

117 Sarfati, *Refuting Evolution*, pp. 80–82.

118 Marvin Lubenow, *Bones of Contention: A Creationist Assessment of Human Fossils* (Grand Rapids, MI: Baker Books, 2004 revised edition; 2011 e-book edition).

119 Whitcomb and Morris, *The Genesis Flood*, pp. 154-211, 270-287.

120 Morris, *The Biblical Basis for Modern Science*, pp. 343, 375.

121 Morris, *The Biblical Basis for Modern Science*, p. 235.

122 Jonathan Sarfati, *By Design—Evidence for Nature's Intelligent Designer—The God of the Bible* (Australia: Creation Book Publishers, 2008), p. 150.

123 *Webster's College Dictionary* (New York: Random House, 1992), p. 557.

124 Jeffrey P. Tomkins, "How Genomes are Sequenced and Why it Matters: Implications for Studies in Comparative Genomics of Humans and Chimpanzees" (June 22, 2011, https://answersingenesis.org/genetics/dna-similarities/how-genomes-are-sequenced-and-why-it-matters). (Accessed 3/16/2019).

125 Nathaniel Jeanson, *Replacing Darwin: The New Origin of Species* (Green Forest, AR: Master Books, 2017).

126 Lisle, *The Ultimate Proof of Creation*, pp. 40, 41, 47, 48, 52, 69.

127 Lisle, pp. 48, 49, 50, 55, 62.

128 Ken Ham, *The Lie—Evolution*, revised edition (Green Forest, AR: Master Books, 2012), pp. 118–119, quoting Richard Bozarth.

129 Cairns, "Deism," p. 128.

130 Cairns, "Panentheism" and "Pantheism," p. 321.

131 Cairns, "Process Theology," pp. 345, 346.

132 Harold Lindsell, chapter 7, "The Historical Critical Method—The Bible's Deadly Enemy," in *The Bible in the Balance* (Grand Rapids: Zondervan, 1979), pp. 277, 279, 283, 285-286.

CHAPTER 6

THINKING BIBLICALLY ABOUT THE CHURCH AND THE STATE

GOD-GIVEN INSTITUTIONS AND AUTHORITY

The Bible teaches that God has established certain societal institutions with authority over man's life in the world: "The authorities that exist are appointed by God" (Rom. 13:1b). God's Word gives instructions for how these societal institutions should function. **The three basic societal institutions that God has established on earth are the family, the civil government, and the church.**

People with an evolutionary Humanist worldview recognize that such institutions exist in the world, but they do not see these institutions as established by God. Evolutionists have stated belief in three forms of evolution—cosmic evolution (inorganic), biological evolution (organic), and societal evolution (cultural). From an evolutionary Humanist perspective, family, civil government, church, and other social institutions are the result of a process of societal evolution and are changeable. Julian Huxley, a leading advocate of evolution, stated:

> "The overall process of evolution in this comprehensive sense comprises three main phases . . . We may call these three phases the inorganic, or, if you like, cosmological; the organic or biological; and the human or psycho-social."[1]

The Islamic worldview sees the family and civil government as established by God. However, Islam does not see the Christian church as a true God-given institution. Also, Islam governs how it views the family and civil government by the Qur'an, not the Bible.

The Christian worldview sees family, civil government, and the Christian church as established by God, not evolved or merely human creations. The Bible as God's Word directly addresses how family, civil government, and the Christian church should function in life in this world. Therefore, a consistent Christian worldview will not see the basic function of these three institutions as changeable. Christians must not adapt their views of family, government, and church to changing human culture that departs from God's Word.

The Bible clearly teaches that God established the societal institutions of the family, civil government, and the Christian church. God established the institution of marriage and the family in the beginning (Gen. 1–2). About the origin of marriage and family, God's Word states:

> "Male and female He created them. Then God blessed them and God said to them, 'Be fruitful and multiply; fill the earth and subdue it; have dominion . . . over every living thing that moves on the earth.' . . . Therefore a man shall leave his father and mother and be joined to his wife, and they shall become one flesh" (Gen. 1:27, 28, 2:24).

Scripture gives instructions regarding family relationships between a husband and wife and between parents and children (Eph. 5:22–6:4).

God also designed the family to be a working unit (Gen. 1:26-28; 2:15). For instance, a man is to work and provide for his family (1 Tim. 5:8). Scripture sets forth principles for relationships with authorities in the workplace (Eph. 6:5–9; Col. 3:22-4:1).

God established the institution of civil government. God's Word defines the role of civil government (Rom. 13:3–4; 1 Pet. 2:13–14) and gives instruction for the relationship between civil government and citizens (Rom. 13:1–7). God establishes civil authorities and has authorized man to use force to deal with violence (Gen. 9:6).

God established the institution of the church. During His earthly ministry, Jesus declared that He would build His Church (Matt. 16:18). On the Day of Pentecost, the first local church was established in Jerusalem (Acts 2:41). And from there, the church continued to grow as the Lord added people to the church daily through salvation (Acts 2:47). Scripture gives instructions for how the local church should operate (Eph. 4:1–16; 1 Tim. 3). And the church teaches God's Word about how to live in relation to family, work, and civil government.

It is interesting that in his original 1828 American dictionary, Noah Webster defined government to include self-government and family government.[2] Also, church leaders have a governing role in the church (Heb. 13:7, 13:17) and employers govern within the workplace (Col. 3:22–4:1). Each of these societal institutions has a governing role and a God-given sphere of authority.

God's design for these societal institutions reflects His nature and His triune relationships. The one true God exists in three Persons—Father, Son, and Holy Spirit (Matt. 28:19). The three Persons of the Trinity have a relationship that involves unity, authority, submission, and delegation. And God's design in His Word for societal institutions involves unity, authority, submission, and delegation. See "The Truth Project" DVD series with Dr. Del Tackett for further discussion about God's triune nature and societal institutions.[3]

God designed the basic institutions of family, civil government, and church with a special relationship to Jesus Christ. The institution of marriage pictures Christ's relationship to His people (Eph. 5:22–32). In relation to the institution of civil government, Christ is exalted over all earthly civil powers and calls civil rulers to submit to His authority (Eph. 1:20–21;

Psalm 2:10–12). And in relation to the institution of the church, Jesus is the head of the church (Eph. 1:22, 5:23). This relationship involves the exercise of authority.

Christ is the ultimate authority over these basic societal institutions. But Christ delegates a measure of authority to human leaders in these institutions. Scripture declares that God establishes human authorities in societal institutions and calls for submission to those authorities:

> "For there is no authority except from God and the authorities that exist are appointed by God. Therefore whoever resists the authority resists the ordinance of God" (Rom. 13:1-2).

> "Therefore, submit yourself to every ordinance of man for the Lord's sake" (1 Pet. 2:13).

The Bible uses the word "submit" in relation to authorities within the family (Eph. 5:22), the church (Heb. 13:17), civil government (1 Pet. 2:13), and the workplace (Eph. 6:5). A Bible commentator gives this helpful explanation:

> "The verb 'to submit' (hupotasso) occurs 23 times in Paul's writings and denotes subordination. . . . Christians are to submit to civil authorities, to church leaders, to parents, and to masters. The whole structure of society as ordered by God depends on the readiness of its members to recognize these sanctions. Without them anarchy prevails."[4]

God has established civil government and has given authority to governing officials. All people must submit to the civil authorities in their nation in matters of civil government:

> "Let every soul be subject to the governing authorities" (Rom. 13:1a).

> "Remind them to be subject to rulers and authorities" (Tit. 3:1a).

God's Word also establishes order in the workplace. Scripture calls for employees to submit to decisions of their employers while on the job: "Be obedient to those who are your masters" (Eph. 6:5). Although this context refers to the master/servant relationship in that time, the principle would still apply to submission to our authorities in our work relationships now.

Also, Christ has given pastors to minister in local churches (Eph. 4:11–16). Pastoral ministry involves a leadership role in the church. Scripture exhorts Christians to submit to the leadership of pastors in the church:

> "Remember those who rule over you, who have spoken the word of God to you. . . . Obey those who rule over you, and be submissive, for they watch out for your souls" (Heb. 13:7, 17).

Submission in the family includes the marriage relationship (Eph. 5:22-33; Col. 3:18-19; Tit. 2:5; 1 Pet. 3:1). A husband must lovingly and sacrificially submit to providing for the needs of his wife and seeking her wellbeing. At the same time, a wife has a biblical responsibility to submit to the leadership of her husband:

> "Husbands, love your wives just as Christ also loved the church and gave Himself for her" (Eph. 5:25).

> "Wives, submit to your own husbands, as to the Lord" (Eph. 5:22).

The Christian worldview position of loving leadership in marriage contrasts with the Humanist and Islamic worldviews. Humanism, influenced by feminism, reacts against the idea of a woman submitting to the leadership of her husband. Contrary to the Biblical teaching of a husband loving his wife like Christ loved the church, Islam allows a husband to beat his wife.

God's Word also calls for submission in the family in the parent and child relationship:

> "Children, obey your parents in the Lord, for this is right. Honor your father and mother. . . . And you, fathers, do not provoke your children to wrath, but bring them up in the training and admonition of the Lord" (Eph. 6:1, 2, 4).

> "Let the word of Christ dwell in you richly in all wisdom, teaching and admonishing one another. . . . Children, obey your parents in all things, for this is well pleasing to the Lord" (Col. 3:16, 20).

Children have a biblical responsibility to submit to the authority of their parents. Parents have a biblical responsibility to submit to God's instructions to properly train their children.

Christian parents have a God-given responsibility to train their children for the Lord:

> "Train up a child in the way he should go and when he is old he will not depart from it" (Prov. 22:6).

> "The rod and rebuke give wisdom, but a child left to himself brings shame to his mother" (Prov. 29:15).

> "But did He not make them one? . . . And why one? He seeks godly offspring" (Mal. 2:15).

"From childhood you have known the Holy Scriptures, which are able to make you wise for salvation through faith which is in Christ Jesus" (2 Tim. 3:15).

God-given authorities do not have license from God to govern in any way they choose. They have a responsibility to submit to the teaching of God's Word as it pertains to the function of family, government, church, or workplace. God has superior authority to any human authority and must be obeyed supremely (Eph. 1:20–21). **If submission to authority involves disobedience to God's Word, then we must obey God's Word rather than that human authority (Acts 5:29).**

For example, if a human authority forbids a believer to practice what God's Word commands, then a believer must obey God rather than that human authority. In God's Word, the apostles teach that "we ought to obey God rather than men" (Acts 5:29). The apostles made this statement while resisting human authorities who commanded them not to spread the Gospel. Also, Daniel resisted the command of a civil authority that forbade prayer to God (Dan. 6).

Also, if a human authority commands a believer to do something that God's Word forbids, the believer must resist that command. For example, Shadrach, Meshach, and Abednego disobeyed the king's command to bow down in worship before his golden image (Dan. 3). God honored these men and delivered them from the king's wrath.

So, if a husband, parent, civil ruler, church leader, or employer asks a believer to do something sinful in violation of the teaching of God's Word, the believer should not obey that request. A believer may suffer negative consequences for not obeying the person in authority in that situation, but a Christian must obey God rather than submit to a request to sin. A Christian worldview writer makes this observation, based upon biblical principles, about resistance to the unbiblical exercise of human authority:

> "The civil government, as all of life, stands under the Law of God. In this fallen world, God has given us certain offices to protect us from the chaos which is the natural result of that fallenness. But when any office commands that which is contrary to the Word of God, those who hold that office abrogate their authority and they are not to be obeyed."[5]

One more area to note in the area of societal institutions is the matter of education. God's Word gives to the Christian church an educational responsibility to teach its members the Word of God (Matt. 28:19, Eph. 4:11-16; Col. 3:16-17; 2 Tim. 3:13-4:2). God's Word gives parents the responsibility to treasure God's Word in their heart themselves and to train their children to know and follow the Lord (Deut. 6:6, 7; Psalm 78:5-7; Eph. 6:4).

The Bible describes a person upon whom God pours out His blessing. God's Word calls on people to turn away from unbiblical counsel and instruction. In place of unbiblical instruction, the Bible calls on people to daily meditate on and submit to the instruction of God's Word:

> "Blessed is the man who walks not in the counsel of the ungodly, nor stands in the path of sinners, nor sits in the seat of the scornful, but his delight is in the law of the Lord and in His law he meditates day and night. He shall be like a tree planted by the rivers of water, that brings forth its fruit in its season, whose leaf also shall not wither; and whatever he does shall prosper" (Psalm 1:1-3).

Scripture recognizes the possibility of parents using the assistance of tutors or guardians in the upbringing of their children (Gal. 4:1-2). The God-given institutions of the family and the Christian Church can cooperate together to fulfill their Biblical mandate to train the next generation in the ways of the Lord. As result, Christian schools have formed in past history and in our present time.

It was common in America from the 1600s through the 1800s for churches and families in Christian majority local communities to cooperate in the formation and support of schools. Such schools reflected the Christian views of the community, taught Biblical Christianity to students and had prayer, along with instruction in other subjects. They taught history and science from a Christian perspective. And some Christian parents taught their children at home.

In the twentieth century, a secular and Humanist philosophy started to dominate the public education system in America. In the 1960s the United States Supreme Court ruled that local public schools could not have prayer and Bible reading in school. Public school textbooks began teaching evolution as fact and excluded the teaching of biblical Creation. Public school sex education courses began teaching an amoral view of sex. In response many Bible-believing churches and many Christian parents cooperated to start new Christian schools.

In our time, Christian schools exist that provide an alternative to secular education. Many Christian parents use these schools as a help in training their children. Parents voluntarily place their children in these institutions and these Christian schools are an extension of the ministry and authority of parents. As such, children should submit to school teachers and administrators, unless their instruction violates the Word of God.

All four varieties of Humanism are active in influencing public education. Humanist writers note the dominance of Secular Humanism in public education.

> "Public education is the parochial education for scientific humanism."[6]

> "The battle for humankind's future must be waged and won in the public school classrooms by teachers who correctly perceive their role as proselytizers of a new faith—a religion of humanity."[7]

New Age writer Marilyn Ferguson notes New Age Humanism coming into public education:

> "Of the Aquarian Conspirators surveyed, more were involved in education than in any other single category of work. . . . Altered states of consciousness are taken seriously—'centering' exercises, meditation, relaxation, and fantasy."[8]

Marxist and Postmodern varieties of Humanism are especially prominent in American colleges. The U.S. News and World Report estimated that there are 10,000 Marxist professors in American colleges.[9] And a number of Postmodernists are on faculties of American colleges, too.[10] This trend is not surprising since government-controlled, secular education was one of the planks of the *Communist Manifesto* of Karl Marx.[11]

Research shows that evolution dominates the curriculum of public schools in America and most other nations, where public schools teach evolution as a fact.[12] Studies show that the teaching of evolution as fact has contributed to many teens from Christian homes coming to doubt the Bible and to leave the church.[13] And research also shows that Humanist sex education and immoral school peers have contributed to widespread sexual promiscuity.[14]

Humanism has influenced many leaders of public education. John Dewey is recognized as the father of modern American education philosophy. He was an evolutionist, a signer of the first *Humanist Manifesto,* and a believer in education as a secular religion.[15] Francis Parker, who influenced Dewey, held to an evolutionary view of public education: "True education is the presentation of the conditions necessary for the evolution of the personality into freedom."[16]

John Stormer is a best-selling Christian author and has been active in Christian education. He wrote a book about the problems in public education, calling Christians away from Humanism and making an appeal for Christian education. He gives this observation:

> "A Bible-based education is mandatory. . . . It is impossible to teach true science or true history or true government—or even give a true understanding of mathematics—without recognizing the place of Jesus Christ. . . . Even if a secular school offers good academics in a disciplined orderly setting, the courts make it impossible for the Lord Jesus to have first place—His deserved preeminence there. . . . Psalm 1:1–3 . . . God's Word says that to be blessed . . . children cannot be under the counsel or teaching of the ungodly. . . . There are many fine Christians teaching in government schools. However, their schools are controlled by a humanistic philosophy and court decisions which are hostile to God. Therefore they cannot legally challenge students to fulfill the second condition Psalm 1 sets forth for being happy and prospering in all things. Only in a Christian school or home school can children be challenged to "meditate in the law of the Lord day and night."[17]

THINKING BIBLICALLY ABOUT THE CHURCH

THE DISTINCTIVENESS OF THE BIBLE-BELIEVING CHURCH

In the preceding section, we showed from the Bible that God established the basic societal institutions of the family, civil government, and the Christian church. God's Word also teaches that the family is a working unit and that the workplace has developed as a social institution, with biblical instruction for its relationships. The local church brings together believers who have relationships with each of these societal institutions. The church has a responsibility to minister the instruction of God's Word about each of these institutions.

The Islamic and Humanist worldviews have their own substitute for the Bible-believing church. Followers of Islam have built structures, which they call mosques, to house their religious meetings for prayer, worship, and exhortation.[18] People with a Humanist worldview have formed organizations and group meetings. Some atheists have started groups that meet weekly like churches and include singing, instruction, and mutual encouragement.[19] Secular Humanists recognize "religious Humanists" such as the Unitarian-Universalist church.[20]

The Christian church is distinct from such groups, though. It is a God-given institution with distinctive beliefs and practices based on God's Word. The word church is translated from the Greek word *ecclesia*. A Greek lexicon says the basic meaning of this term is "assembly."[21] A Baptist theologian helpfully explains the word church in the New Testament:

> "In the New Testament, the word "church" has two senses. On the one hand, it denotes all believers in Christ at all times and places. This universal sense is found in Matthew 16:18; Ephesians 1:22–23, 4:4, 5:23. More frequently, however, "church" refers to a group of believers in a given geographical locality."[22]

The Bible-believing Christian church is distinctive in its origin, operations, and organization.

The Christian church has a distinctive origin. It is not the product of societal evolution. It was not formed through human scheming. The New Testament Scriptures describe the origin of the Christian church as an institution. God supernaturally established the Christian church. Jesus Christ declared that He would build His Church (Matt. 16:18). After His ascension, Jesus poured out the Holy Spirit and brought three-thousand people to salvation in Jerusalem and formed them into a church:

> "Then those who gladly received his word were baptized, and that day about three thousand souls were added to them. And they continued steadfastly in the apostles' doctrine and fellowship, in the breaking of bread and in prayers. . . . And the Lord added to the church daily those who were being saved" (Acts 2:41–42, 47).

Jesus founded the Christian church through the preaching and teaching of the apostles, with Himself as its Head (Eph. 1:22–23, 2:19–21, 4:11–13). And He gave His written Word as the authority to govern the church (2 Tim. 3:15–17). Christ's apostles won converts to Christ and formed them into local churches in nations around the world. The book of Acts relates the beginning of local churches (Acts 2:41–47; 9:31; 11:26; 14:23, 27). The New Testament epistles address Christians in local churches.

Jesus Christ declared that the gates of Hell would not prevail against His church (Matt. 16:18). Satan attacked the Christian church in its beginning with persecution and false religious teachers and tried to destroy it (Acts 8:1, 20:28–30; Rev. 2–3). However, Jesus Christ preserved His church through persecution and the onslaught of false teachers. Bible-believing Christian churches continue to exist.

The Christian church as described in the New Testament spread through peaceful persuasion, despite opposition against it. Church historians document that the early church continued to spread by peaceful means in the Roman empire after the time of the apostles, in spite of wide-spread persecution.[23] The way the Christian church began and continued despite persecution is a testimony to the fact that God supernaturally instituted the church.

In contrast, Marxist Humanists came to power in various nations through violent revolution.[24] Similarly, Islam began and grew in the world through violent conquest. Robert Spencer, who has done detailed historical research on Islam, observes:

> "The early spread of Islam and that of Christianity sharply contrast in that Islam spread by force and Christianity didn't."[25]

The Bible-believing church is distinctive in its operations from man-made societal institutions. One theologian summarizes biblical church functions as worship, evangelism, edification, and social concern.[26] **In relation to God, the church has a function of worship. In relation to its members, the church has a function of spiritual edification and charitable help. In relation to the outside world, the church has a function of evangelism.**

God is seeking a people to worship Him (John 4:23–24). And the Christian church, in its biblical function of worship, worships God as Creator (Rev. 4:11) and Redeemer (Rev. 5:13-14). That distinguishes the Christian church from Humanist groups that meet weekly for church-like services. Also, unlike Islam, the Christian church is distinct in worshipping the Triune God revealed in the Bible (Matt. 28:19). Scripture emphasizes God's people assembling together in worship:

> "Oh that men would give thanks to the Lord for His goodness and for His wonderful works to the children of men! Let them exalt Him also in the assembly of His people" (Psalm 107:31–32).

The church has a biblical function of edification in relation to its members. To edify is to spiritually build up a believer. Christ has given gifted pastors/teachers to the church to edify believers and help them know God's Word and become more like Christ:

> "He Himself gave some to be . . . pastors and teachers, for the quipping of the saints for the work of ministry, for the edifying of the body of Christ, till we all come to the unity of the faith and of the knowledge of the Son of God, to a perfect man, to the measure of the stature of the fullness of Christ" (Eph. 4:11–13).

Church ministers and members edify each other in love, encouraging and helping each other as they grow together to be more like Jesus Christ (Gal. 6:10; Eph. 4:15–16; 1 Tim. 5:3–16; 1 John 3:17–18).

In relation to the world, the church has a biblical function of evangelism. In distinction from other organizations, the church has a biblical task to spread the Gospel message of redemption from sin through Christ. God's Word praises local churches that spread the Word of God in their areas (1 Thess. 1). Jesus gives the Christian church the responsibility to proclaim the Gospel message and make disciples of all nations:

> "Repentance and remission of sins should be preached in His name to all nations" (Luke 24:47).
>
> "Go therefore and make disciples of all the nations, baptizing them in the name of the Father and of the Son and of the Holy Spirit, teaching them to observe all that I have commanded you" (Matt. 28:19–20).

Also, the Bible-believing Christian church is distinct in its organization from other societal institutions and from other religions. Its organization consists of a unique membership with an organized and well-defined leadership. And its practices and beliefs are specifically based upon the teaching of God's Word, the Bible.

The local church has a distinctive membership. The apostles in the New Testament address the people in the church as "saints," people who are set apart to Christ (1 Cor. 1:2; Rom. 1:7; Eph. 1:1). The church is to consist exclusively of people redeemed by Christ (also known as saints). However, the Christian church is to include any redeemed person regardless of ethnicity, economic status, or gender (Gal. 3:28).

The local church has distinctive officers. The New Testament does not describe ministers in churches as priests. Instead, it uses the terms "pastors," "elders," and "overseers" interchangeably to describe the same office of a minister (Acts 20:17, 28; 1 Tim. 3:1–7; 1 Pet. 5:1–4).[27] These ministers lead and teach God's Word to the church (Heb. 13:17; 1 Tim. 3:2; Tit. 1:9). Scripture also limits this office to men, since it forbids women to teach the Bible to men or to exercise authority over men in the church according to 1 Timothy 2:12.[28]

The Bible also refers to "deacons" who serve in the church (1 Tim. 3:13; Phili. 1:1). This office was established to help with material needs of people within the church (Acts 6:1–7). As deacons watch over material and financial matters, they free up pastors to focus on the ministry of the Word and prayer (Acts 6:3–4). Scripture lists the spiritual qualifications for both those serving in the ministerial office and deacons in 1 Timothy 3:1–13.

The local church has distinctive biblical ordinances to observe in obedience to Christ, its head. Jesus instituted the ordinances of baptism and the Lord's Supper, or Communion, for the local church to observe as reminders of Christ's redemptive work. Christians do not merit eternal life by practicing these ordinances, but they are important for the spiritual life of the church.

Jesus commands His church to practice water baptism to identify His people as His followers (Matt. 28:19). And as the apostle Paul explains, Jesus instituted the Lord's Supper for His followers to observe and remember His work of redemption on the Cross saying, "Do this in remembrance of Me." . . . "For as often as you eat this bread and drink this cup, you proclaim the Lord's death" (1 Cor. 11:24b, 26).

The Bible-believing local church has distinctive beliefs about the Bible, God, Christ, salvation, marriage, and sexual morality. Jesus Christ founded His church and He wants it to be united upon the teaching and the faith He revealed through the apostles in the Scriptures (Acts 2:41–42; Eph. 2:19–21, 4:4–6, 4:11–14). Local churches have a responsibility to govern what they believe and how they function by the written Word of God.

God's Word also exhorts believers not to receive false teachers in the church who contradict the Christian faith (Matt. 7:15–20; Jude 1:3–4). Ministers must preach God's Word and oppose false teachers who contradict God's Word. The apostle Paul instructs us:

> "Note those who cause divisions and offenses contrary to the doctrine which you have learned and avoid them" (Rom. 16:17).
>
> "Imposters will grow worse and worse, deceiving and being deceived. But you must continue in the things which you have learned. . . . Preach the word!" (2 Tim. 3:13-14; 4:2).

THE NEED FOR THE BIBLE-BELIEVING CHURCH

With the wide-spread secularizing influence of Humanism in our culture, the majority of people do not attend Christian churches. Many religious people who believe in God think they do not need a church at all. Some people think if they do need a church, they can be part of any kind of church. Neither way of thinking is consistent with a Christian worldview. We need to understand the importance of the Bible-believing local church.

A number of religious people who believe in God think that they can just worship God by themselves out in nature or in their home. Many who profess to be Christians do not regularly attend church, thinking they can just occasionally read the Bible or a religious book at home and pray in private when the need arises. However, in order to fully live the Christian life the way God intends, every Christian does need the Bible-believing local church—and the local church needs them.

Recent surveys have shown that many young adults who were raised in church no longer attend. Christian writer Josh McDowell noted a survey that found that only one-third of young people raised in church said that they will continue in church when they get out on their own.[29]

Surveys have also shown that young adults who no longer attend church stray from biblical thinking in other areas of their lives.[30] They need the teaching of a Bible-believing church to help them have a comprehensive Christian worldview based on God's Word.

Professing Christians who think they do not need the church are not thinking consistently with the Christian worldview. The Bible gives good reasons why believers actually need the local church—and why the local church needs believers to actively participate. The church is a God-given institution with God-given purposes for His people. Consider the following reasons from God's Word why every believer needs the local church.

Believers need the church to be obedient to Scripture. Christians are called to love one another, biblically exhort one another, and encourage each other to do good works, and they need to assemble together in their local churches to do that. Refusing to meet together with believers is disobedience to God. God's Word commands church attendance:

> "And let us consider one another in order to stir up love and good works, not forsaking the assembling of ourselves together, as is the manner of some, but exhorting one another" **(Heb. 10:24–25).**

Christians need to gather together around God's Word in order to function together as the body of Christ. Just as we need the various parts of our physical body, not just one part, the local church needs its members to function together:

> "God composed the body . . . that the members should have the same care for one another" (1 Cor. 12:24-25).

Believers need the church for group fellowship and prayer. In the Bible, people in the church gathered for fellowship. They ate and talked and prayed together:

> "Then those who gladly received his word . . . continued steadfastly in the apostles' doctrine and fellowship, in the breaking of bread, and in prayers" **(Acts 2:41-42)**.

True fellowship involves believers taking time to be together to study the Bible and talk about their spiritual concerns and needs. Christians need that spiritual fellowship with people of similar beliefs and values for encouragement in their lives. The Christians in the early church regularly prayed together. Scripture calls on believers to "pray for one another"

(James 5:16) and "bear one another's burdens" (Gal. 6:2). Christians need to be together to know one another's spiritual concerns and intercede in prayer for each other.

Believers need the church for group worship in song and for biblically exhorting one another. Scripture exhorts Christians: "Let the Word of Christ dwell in you richly in all wisdom, teaching and admonishing one another in psalms and hymns and spiritual songs, singing with grace in your hearts to the Lord" (Col. 3:16–17). God desires group worship from His people:

"Sing to the Lord a new song and His praise in the assembly of saints" (Psalm 149:1).

Believers need the church for assistance when they have an unmet basic material need. The Bible exhorts believers to show their love for one another by helping believers who need basic food and clothing **(1 John 3:17).** Scripture speaks of collecting offerings for the saints (1 Cor. 16:1). As part of a church, believers can pool offerings together and help meet even more needs than if they were trying to help people just on their own.

But what if you stayed away from the local church and then had an unexpected material need? How would others know to help you? Believers who are faithful in church and develop loving relationships with fellow believers are in a better position to make their needs known. Also, as local churches meet the needs of their members, they give a testimony of Christ's love to a watching world (John 13:34–35).

Believers need the church to help spread the Gospel. Christ calls all of His followers to have a part in the Great Commission to make disciples of people in all nations (Matt. 28:19). Believers can help spread the gospel by working together in the church to financially support and pray for missionaries and ministers of the gospel (1 Cor. 9:13–14; Eph. 6:18–20). The apostle Paul urged believers to work together in the local church to advance the gospel (Phili. 1:27).

Believers need the church for gifted teaching of God's Word. The church began with believers learning together under biblical teaching (Acts 2:41–42). And even today, Jesus gives pastors and teachers to the church to minister God's Word and help believers serve Christ, learn the doctrinal truths of the Christian faith, and continue to grow spiritually **(Eph. 4:11–16)**.

Believers need to feed on God's Word ministered by a skilled pastor or teacher (1 Pet. 5:2–3).

Believers particularly need a Bible-believing local church. Scripture repeatedly warns believers about false teachers within churches who contradict essential doctrines of the Christian faith (Matt. 7:15–20; Acts 20:28–30; 2 Pet. 2:1; Jude 4). And the Bible also tells believers to avoid them (Rom. 16:17; 2 John 7–11).

Christians should look for a church that has a Bible-believing statement of faith. Note the Christian statements of faith in chapter one. You can use these statements of faith as a guide and look for a church that confesses belief in these basic Bible doctrines. Avoid churches that contradict or refuse to confess basic biblical doctrines in their beliefs and teaching.

For Bible-believing local churches to thrive, they need the commitment of Christian people. Local churches need the attendance of Christian people at services in order to have corporate worship and group instruction from the Bible. They need the giving of Christian people to support the ministry of pastors and missionaries. And believers need to join together to pray for one another and help each other.

Believers need the local church and the local church needs believers. There are helpful sources for Christians to gain a deeper biblical understanding about the local church.[31] For further study about the importance of the church, see the book by Joshua Harris, *Why Church Matters?*[32]

THINKING BIBLICALLY ABOUT CIVIL GOVERNMENT

THE BIBLICAL ROLE OF CIVIL GOVERNMENT

People have differing controlling assumptions about the role of civil government. Concerning civil government, the Islamic worldview looks to Mohammad and the Qur'an for guidance and the Humanist worldview looks to man's thinking and experience for guidance. In contrast, the Christian worldview appeals to the teaching of the Bible concerning the role of civil government.

The Humanist worldview sees civil government as a product of human societal evolution. The Islamic worldview sees civil government as instituted by God to advance and preserve Islam. The Christian worldview sees civil government as instituted by God, not as a product of societal evolution, and as designed by God to accomplish purposes revealed in the Bible. The Bible reveals that God established civil government in the world.

Fallen man is prone to commit evil against his fellow man. Before the Flood, the world was filled with violence (Gen. 6:11–12). After the Flood, God told Noah and all mankind to fill the earth and govern the animals (Gen. 9:1–3). Then God authorized man to exercise a governing function in the world to deal with recurring violence, when He commanded, "Whoever sheds man's blood, by man his blood shall be shed" (Gen. 9:6).

Ever since that beginning of human government in Genesis, God has providentially established human governing authorities in the world. The apostle Paul declares, "For there is no authority except from God and the authorities that exist are appointed by God" (Rom.

13:1b). God's Word reveals that God is in control of human rulers to accomplish His purposes in the world (Prov. 21:1).

So God's Word establishes that God has established human government. But what is the role for civil government? Two key passages in Scripture state God's purpose for civil government:

> "Therefore, submit yourselves to every ordinance of man for the Lord's sake . . . to governors as to those who are sent by him for the punishment of evildoers and for the praise of those who do good. For this is the will of God, that by doing good you may put to silence the ignorance of foolish men. . . . But let none of you suffer as a murderer, a thief, an evildoer" (1 Pet. 2:13-15; 4:15).

> "For rulers are not a terror to good works, but to evil. . . . Do what is good and you will have praise from the same. For he is God's minister to you for good. But if you do evil, be afraid, for he does not bear the sword in vain. For he is God's minister, an avenger to execute wrath on him who practices evil" (Rom. 13:3-4).

According to these two key Scripture passages, God has given civil government a limited two-fold task—civil authorities should punish people who do evil and praise people who do good. God's Word teaches that God uses civil government to execute His justice against evil and to restrain fallen man. Civil authorities carry out God's wrath on people who do evil against other people (Rom. 13:4). King Solomon stated in Scripture:

> "Because the sentence against an evil work is not executed speedily, therefore the heart of the sons of men is fully set in them to do evil" (Eccl. 8:11).

One God-given role of civil authorities is to "praise" or "approve" people who do good. (1 Pet. 2:14). A civil ruler can encourage good conduct by giving public praise to people who do good things for others (Rom. 13:3). A Bible commentator observes,

> "Paul may be thinking specifically of the practice of Roman authorities of publishing on inscriptions the names of benefactors of society."[33]

Rulers should also "praise" people who do good by condoning them, or approving them and not harming them:

> "For rulers are not a terror to good works, but to evil. Do you want to be unafraid of authority? Do what is good and you will have praise from the same" (Rom. 13:3).

People who are "in authority" should let people who gather to worship God and who try to live out their faith in the home and community, "lead a quiet and peaceable life" (1 Tim. 2:1–2).

Civil rulers are also responsible to punish people who do evil (1 Pet. 2:14). Scripture says a civil ruler is to execute God's wrath on evil doers (Rom. 13:4). To do that, civil rulers "bear the sword" (Rom. 13:4), which means God authorizes civil authorities to use armed force to deal with evildoers.

In the verses preceding the discussion about civil authorities in Romans 13, the apostle Paul teaches believers not to seek personal revenge (Rom. 12:19). They should trust God to work through rulers to take care of personal injuries involving evil conduct that violates God's laws of loving one's neighbor (Rom. 13:4, 13:9–10). Theologian Vern Poythress observes that "the State deals with injuries against other human beings."[34]

In the context of Romans 13, doing evil would refer to violating God's moral law. Right after discussing the role of civil government to punish evil doers in Romans 13:1–7, the apostle Paul brings up God's moral law in the Ten Commandments and the law to love one's neighbor. He mentions God's laws against adultery, murder, stealing, bearing false witness, and coveting (Rom. 13:8-9). Then he concludes that "love does no harm to a neighbor" (Rom. 13:10a).

God has put His moral law on the conscience of all people, even those who are not familiar with God's written Word. Therefore, even unsaved civil authorities have a basic awareness of justice. Scripture says that even people who do not know God's Word have God's moral law written on their conscience, so they have a basic knowledge of right and wrong (Rom. 2:14, 15).

However, rulers must exercise their authority in a righteous manner. Scripture says that civil rulers bring a blessing to people they govern when they govern justly and with the fear of God (2 Sam. 23:3-4). Proverbs, God's inspired book of wisdom, declares that civil authorities set forth just laws and act with justice when they govern by God's wisdom revealed in Scripture (Prov. 8:12, 15).

One way civil government "bears the sword" and punishes evildoers is by engaging in just warfare. God judges nations for aggressive, unjust wars (Amos 1; Ezek. 38). However, Scripture gives examples of just warfare, such as using armed force to rescue captured people (Gen. 14:20) and driving out foreign nations who invade and oppress one's nation (Judges 2:16-18). God's Word describes justly defending one's homeland against attack. When pagan people threatened to attack Jerusalem, God led their leader, Nehemiah, to tell His people:

> "Remember the Lord, great and awesome, and fight for your brethren, your sons, your daughters, your wives, and your houses" (Neh. 4:14).

The Bible even describes soldiers coming to salvation. God's Word did not require them to leave the military but to change how they treated others—not to intimidate innocent people or falsely accuse them (Luke 3:14). Believers who are in the military or law enforcement should avoid assaulting innocent people. Most conservative Protestant Christians would agree with the statement in the Lutheran Confession concerning Christians in the military or law enforcement:

> "Christians may lawfully . . . appoint just punishments, engage in just war."[35]

However, Christians should also respect the beliefs of those who think it is always wrong, even in just warfare, to kill people. Amish and Mennonite groups sincerely believe Christians should never kill anyone, even in defense in war and other Christians should respect and protect their liberty of conscience in the matter (Acts 24:16).[36]

God also authorizes civil authorities to use "the sword," or armed force, against criminals (Rom. 13:4; 1 Pet. 2:13-14; 1 Pet. 4:15). Civil authorities can organize police and militia forces in local areas to keep the peace and deter violent mobs. Scripture describes civil government using an armed force to stop a violent mob and to intervene to protect innocent citizens (Acts 21:33–35).

Punishing those who commit crimes is also part of "bearing the sword." One of the most serious crimes is murder. Biblically, this is so serious because man is made in God's image. **God Himself has said that the death penalty is the just punishment for murder:**

> "Whoever sheds man's blood, by man his blood shall be shed, for in the image of God He made man" (Gen. 9:6).

Therefore, Christians should not advocate the elimination of the death penalty for murder.[37]

In a book about the Bible and civil government, Robert Culver notes,

> "The formal establishment of human government under divine auspices took place in the form of a covenant of God with the survivors of the Flood (Gen. 9:4–6). . . . Because man bears the divine image, and because of the biblical implication drawn thereby (Gen. 9:6; Ro. 13:4), believers will hardly be numerous among those advocating less than capital punishment for capital crimes."[38]

Biblical theological writer Vern Poythress similarly states,

> "The mention of the sword in Romans 13:4 indicates the legitimacy of the continuation of the death penalty. . . . Principles of general equity, as well as the specific content of Genesis 9:6, clearly enjoin the death penalty as a universal penalty for murder."[39]

Civil authorities can also use "the sword" or armed force to compel citizens to appear in court and deal with charges associated with property crimes and to arrest criminals. God has moral laws that protect private property. God's commandments cover how we should treat our neighbor, including forbidding theft and financial fraud:

> "You shall not steal . . . You shall not covet . . . anything that is your neighbor's" (Exo. 20:15, 17). "You shall not cheat your neighbor or rob him. . . . You shall do no injustice in judgment, in measurements of length, weight or volume. You shall have honest scales, honest weights" (Lev. 19:13, 35-36).

Proverbs, which gives God's wisdom for people in all nations, affirms the principle of restitution (Prov. 7:30-31). Jesus affirms the principle of restitution (Luke 19:8–10). God's Law called for restitution from the guilty party to the victims of property crimes (Exo. 22:9). An article in *The International Standard Bible Encyclopedia* states:

> "Offenses against property were punished by exacting more than the value of the things taken (Luke 19:8), the excess going to the injured party, thus differing from a fine, which goes to the treasury of the community."[40]

The Bible teaches man to show respect for people who serve in civil government when it says, "Honor the king" (1 Pet. 2:17b). Christians should be in favor of civil government having enough power to fulfill its God-given purpose to praise those who do good and to punish those who do evil (Rom. 13:1–7). In order for the government to fulfill its God-given purpose, all citizens, including Christians, should pay taxes to the civil government:

> "For because of this you also pay taxes, for they are God's ministers, attending continually to this very thing" (Rom. 13:6).

Jesus told His followers to give Caesar the things that are Caesar's (taxes; Matt. 22:21). However, Jesus also taught His followers to give God the things that are His (Matt. 22:21). God calls on His people to support the God-given institutions of the family (1 Tim. 5:8) and the church (1 Cor. 16:1–2), so believers need the financial freedom to do that. Christ is the Head of the church and is greater than earthly rulers (Eph. 1:19–23, 5:23), so civil authorities should not interfere with the liberty of churches to follow Christ's authority.

God's Word does not give unlimited power to civil government. Believers must "obey God rather than men" (Acts 5:29), if rulers require disobedience to the Word of God. Believers have the right as priests of God to study the Bible and determine what they should believe and how they should practice their religious faith (1 Pet. 2:9; Acts 17:11). Scripture does not give civil rulers authority over the beliefs and practice of the church.

The apostle Paul set an example for believers of persuading civil authorities about preserving our religious liberty (Acts chapters 16, 22, 25, and 26). Believers should respectfully persuade rulers about their religious liberty. Scripture says: "By long forbearance a ruler is persuaded and a gentle tongue breaks a bone" (Prov. 25:15). Believers should appeal to whatever laws exist that call for religious liberty.

Civil authorities should protect believers from harm by others, not do harm to them (Rom. 13:3–4). God's revealed will is that believers have the civil liberty to practice their faith freely and to proclaim the Word of God freely. Scripture exhorts believers to pray that God would move in the hearts of civil authorities to protect their religious liberty:

> "Therefore, I exhort first of all that prayers . . . be made for . . . kings and all who are in authority, that we may lead a quiet and peaceable life in all godliness and reverence" (1 Tim. 2:1–2).

The Bible teaches that no one is naturally righteous (Rom. 3:10). That includes civil authorities. With a fallen nature, civil authorities are prone to abuse their power if there are not checks on their power. If believers have the opportunity to influence civil authorities by voting or persuasion, they need to beware of advocating for too much government power.

It is right for civil government to have laws and regulations to protect people from physical harm or financial harm. However, God's Word condemns civil rulers for assuming too much power. Throughout history many civil rulers have abused their power by overtaxing their people and wrongly killing or unjustly imprisoning many people. But civil authorities will each have to face God's judgment and give account of their actions to God (Rom. 14:12).

God's Word warns about unrighteous rulers, saying that such rulers oppress their people (Prov. 29:2). Scripture condemns "the throne of iniquity, which devises evil by law" (Psalm 94:20). God destroyed King Ahab and his wife, Jezebel, in Israel for unjustly executing a citizen and wrongly stealing his land (1 Kings 21:17–25). Jesus also warned His followers about oppressive worldly rulers: "Rulers over the Gentiles lord it over them. . . . Yet it shall not be so among you" (Mark 10:42-43).

In the Bible, God judged rulers for claiming Divine-like power. For example, Nebuchadnezzar in pride had an image made of himself and commanded that the people bow to it in worship (Dan. 3). God later took away his power for a time in judgment (Dan. 4). God also brought death to the wicked King Herod, who in pride accepted praise of the people as a god (Acts 12:20–23).

Herbert Schlossberg has written a discerning book about how fallen man idolizes the State. He notes a startling quote from the European philosopher, **George Hegel, who inspired Karl Marx and other Marxist thinkers. Hegel deified civil government.** He said:

> **"The State is the Divine Idea as it exists on earth. . . . We must therefore worship the State as the manifestation of the Divine on earth."**[41]

God's Word warns that fallen man might wrongly desire a powerful national leader and transfer trust to that leader over God. Israel did this when they demanded that they be given a king like all the other nations (1 Sam. 8:5). God warned that such a civil ruler would oppress the people and as a result, the nation would cry out under the burden (1 Sam. 8:11–18). God, not the State, is man's ultimate Ruler and the true Savior from man's problems. "For the Lord is our Judge, the Lord is our Lawgiver, the Lord is our King; He will save us" (Isa. 33:22). "It is better to trust in the Lord than to put confidence in princes" (Psalm 118:9). R. J. Rushdoony has given helpful observations about how fallen man deifies the State and views it as a savior. He notes,

> "For Hellenic (Greek) thought, and for all those in the classical tradition, man is a creature of the state. . . . This ancient, classical view of man, still very much with us and greatly developed by the Enlightenment and evolutionary philosophies, is a fertile ground for a radical statism and . . . offers us a savior state as man's hope."[42]

ONE WORLD GOVERNMENT AND CLIMATE CHANGE

Scripture takes a negative view of a one-world government in this present age. After the Flood, when all people stayed in one place under the leadership of one evil man named Nimrod, God divided man's languages and scattered all people into separate nations (Gen. 10–11). God has divided fallen mankind into separate nations, instead of being under a world government, to encourage man to seek God instead of idolizing powerful rulers (Acts 17:26–27).

In light of man's fallen nature, giving power to a single person or a few people in a one-world government is dangerous. In Daniel 7, God's Word describes a succession of world empires as like wild beasts that are dangerous to man. Scripture condemns the world empire and its ruler in Revelation 13 as evil, blasphemous and economically oppressive.

Humanism, however, promotes global government, criticizes the division of mankind into separate nations, and manifests pride in human government and technology to save man from his problems. *The Humanist Manifesto* states:

> "We deplore the division of humankind on nationalistic grounds. . . . We look to the development of a system of world law and world order based upon transnational federal government. . . . Using technology wisely, we can control our environment . . . alter the course of human evolution. . . . Only a shared world and global measures will suffice. . . . No deity will save us; we must save ourselves."[43]

Speaking for New Age Humanists, Donald Keys looks forward to one world government:

"Humanity," says Donald Keys, "is on the verge of . . . a further evolutionary step unlike any other: the emergence of the first global civilization." . . . Keys calls the United Nations, "the nexus of emerging planetary values."[44]

The issue of one-world government comes up with the controversy about climate change. A number of scientists have come to believe that there is a dangerous global warming trend based on a slight rise in average temperatures over the past century, the use of fossil fuels, increased carbon dioxide in the atmosphere and projections of computer models about future warming. The United Nations and its Intergovernmental Panel on Climate Change (IPCC) have influenced many reporters, politicians, and educators to put out alarming reports about global warming and to call for global governmental action. They claim the science is settled.

Driven by fear about the future of the Earth, many people with a Humanist environmentalist worldview are pushing for strong global measures to deal with human technology and climate change. Some church groups, under pressure from the culture of the world to do something, are joining the call for global action to deal with climate change. However, such global action would lead to a one-world government.

Former Vice-President Al Gore, a leader in the movement expressing fear about global warming, says that his proposed carbon taxes would lead to "global governance."[45] Lord Monckton, former science advisor to the British government, has read the proposed treaty for nations to sign for a climate control agreement (the Kyoto treaty) and warns that it calls for a one-world government.[46] *The Humanist Manifesto* declared:

> "We can control our environment. . . . Only a shared world and global measures will suffice. . . . Ecological damage, resource depletion, and excessive population growth must be checked by international conduct."[47]

A one-world government would be dangerous. Considering previous United Nations proposals concerning children's rights versus parents[48] and concerning hate speech,[49] a one-world government would likely restrict the rights of Christian parents concerning Christian education and training of their children and the rights of churches to say homosexuality is a sin or that Islam is a false religion. The Bible has a negative view of a one-world government as rebellious toward God and oppressive to people (Gen. 11:1-9; Acts 17:26-27; Dan. 7; Rev. 13).

People with a Humanist view of man's physical environment believe the Earth and everything in it came about by evolution. They do not believe in the preservation of the Earth by an all powerful, all-wise, personal God. This affects the way they think about the environment, the earth's climate and civil government policy.

We need to think biblically about the Earth. The Bible teaches that God directly made the world out of nothing by His word (Heb. 11:3; also 2 Pet. 3:3-6). God uniquely knows the Earth's future (Isa. 46:9-11). God preserves His Creation (Neh. 9:6).

Psalm 104 describes God governing the sun, the Earth, the waters, plant life, animals, and food. Scripture says God controls the weather, not man (Job 37:3-13; Psalm 147:8-18; Amos 4:7).[50] For example, God's Word says:

> "When He utters His voice, there is a multitude of waters in the heavens; and He causes the vapors to ascend from the ends of the earth. He makes lightning for the rain; He brings the wind out of His treasuries" (Jer. 10:13).

Over the past century, environmentalists have feared global cooling and a coming ice age and then more recently switched to expressing alarm about dangerous global warming.[51] They fear that man's technology is causing a climate change that will devastate life on earth. However, believers should not fear a dangerous, extreme worldwide cooling or warming, because God promises to preserve the earth's climate: "While the earth remains, seedtime and harvest, cold and heat, winter and summer, and day and night shall not cease" (Gen. 8:22).

Some environmentalists believe global warming will cause polar ice caps and glaciers to melt and cause a massive rise in ocean levels and worldwide flooding. For example, a 2008 Science magazine article reported one environmentalist warning that most of the world would be covered by flooding from effects of global warming.[52] However, the Bible clearly states that God will preserve the Earth from a worldwide flood happening again:

> "It shall be when I bring a cloud over the earth that the rainbow shall be seen in the cloud, and I will remember My covenant which is between Me and you and every living creature of all flesh. The waters shall never again become a flood to destroy all flesh" (Gen. 9:14-15).

Christians should recognize that the science is not settled, as claimed, about global warming. Many scientists disagree with the United Nations Intergovernmental Panel on Climate Change. They do not believe that global warming has been or will be extreme or dangerous. People should consider their findings as they think about government policy.

Michael Oard is a Christian with a masters in atmospheric science. He points out that global average temperature has increased over the past century by only one degree.[53] He notes scientific evidence that there is a strong correlation between variation in sunspot activity and cooling and warming on Earth.[54] He notes that moderate warming would be beneficial by reducing deaths due to cold weather and by lengthening the growing season for food.[55]

He is one of over 31,000 scientists as of 2015 who have signed the following statement:

> "There is no convincing scientific evidence that human release of carbon dioxide, methane, or other greenhouse gasses is causing or will, in the foreseeable future, cause catastrophic heating of the Earth's atmosphere and disruption of the Earth's climate. Moreover, there is substantial scientific evidence that increases in atmospheric carbon dioxide produce many beneficial effects upon the natural plant and animal environments of the Earth."[56]

Dr. Alan White is a scientist and a Christian who has extensively studied the climate change issue. He notes problems in accuracy of temperature measurements from land-based weather stations. He also documents the fact that water vapor and clouds are responsible for most of the greenhouse effect and that man-made CO_2 contributes only a small percentage of the greenhouse effect. He notes that belief in evolution leads to lack of faith in God's preservation of His Creation.[57]

Dr. Roy Spencer has a Ph.D. in meteorology, formerly worked with NASA, and now is a research scientist. He wrote a book showing problems with global warming alarmism. He wrote his book to show that climate can change naturally and that overregulation and limitation of carbon-based fuels can deprive the poor of needed energy.[58]

Dr. Spencer also notes a survey in 2007 of over five-hundred climate scientists. Only half of the climate scientists believed that man was the primary cause of climate change. Only one-third believed climate models could accurately predict future climate conditions.[59]

Dr. Richard Lindzen, a climatology professor at MIT, was also a consultant for the Intergovernmental Panel on Climate Change (IPCC). He wrote an endorsement for Dr. Roy Spencer's book about global warming alarmism, noted above. He signed a letter to Congress, along with other scientists, pointing out that there was no warming in the previous decade.[60]

Dr. Fred Singer has a Ph.D. in physics and has written extensively showing scientific problems with global warming alarmism. See his work with The Nongovernmental International Panel on Climate Change (NIPCC) that refutes the claims of the IPCC.[61]

Brian Sussman is a meteorologist who has extensively studied the global warming issue. He documents the 2009 scandal of leaked emails from climate researchers that show manipulation of data concerning global warming:

> "The Climate Research Unit . . . emails reveal that the world's leading climate scientists were working together to block Freedom of Information requests to review their data, marginalize dissenting scientists, manipulate the peer-review process, and obscure, massage, or delete inconvenient temperature readings."[62]

Sussman documents moderate climate change, apart from human technology, in recent centuries that preceded the modern growth of industry in the twentieth century.[63] He points out evidence for a "Medieval Warm Period" from approximately 900 to 1300 AD and a "Little Ice Age" from approximately 1350 to 1800 AD, followed by another warming trend.[64]

He points out that global temperatures increased about one degree after the Little Ice Age, from 1850 to 1940.[65] He notes that the 1930s were warmer than the 1980s to 1990s.[66] Then a slight cooling trend from 1940 to 1970, as measured by NASA, sparked a 1974 *Time* magazine article expressing concern about another ice age.[67] Then the 1980s and 1990s brought the recent global warming scare based on a slight increase in temperature and computer model projections.

Consider the testimony of Dr. Robert Balling. Dr. Balling was a veteran climatologist at Arizona State University. He gave these observations:

> "Three underlying and fundamental messages are heard regularly:
>
> 1. The continued buildup of greenhouse gases will produce substantial warming, thereby generating a variety of undesirable outcomes.
>
> 2. Realistic options are available that can reduce or even eliminate the greenhouse threat.
>
> 3. We must act now. . . .The professional literature in climatology is full of articles that demonstrate the weaknesses in these three statements and yet this literature often is overlooked in presenting the greenhouse catastrophe to the public and policymakers. . . . Major weaknesses remain in the models; in particular, the role of the ocean in absorbing CO2 and storing and transporting heat is not adequately included. . . . Clouds play a critical role in maintaining the energy balance of the earth and cloud representations are particularly questionable in the models. . . . We have so far totally neglected the fact that other non-greenhouse gases are being added to the atmosphere that can have strong local and regional cooling effects. . . . Researchers have found that the length of the solar sunspot cycle is related strongly to the fluctuations in temperatures on the earth. . . .
>
> Government groups have expanded in recent years and their very fate is tied to the perception that global warming represents a significant threat to the planet."[68]

Christopher Horner has carefully studied the economic impact of the international Kyoto Treaty to deal with the matter of global warming. He shares information from a 2002 *Science* magazine article. The article documents testimony from scientists and economists that it is not possible to radically limit greenhouse gas emissions without severe impact to the economy, that implementing the Kyoto Treaty would reduce global warming by only 0.08 degrees by the year 2100 and that in doing nothing, global warming would increase only two degrees by 2100.[69]

If global action forces immediate and drastic carbon-based energy reduction, it could lead to a great decline in usable energy for heat and air in buildings, lights, refrigeration, and transportation. Rather than turning to a one-world government and economically harmful international treaties, individual nations who want alternatives to fossil fuels can encourage making technology longer-lasting and more affordable for alternative energy such as solar-powered homes and buildings and electric-powered cars.

GOVERNMENT AND PROBLEMS WITH SOCIALISM

One form of civil government that many nations have tried in modern times is socialism. Many nations have socialist political parties and these groups would try to influence Christians to vote for and support their agenda. However, there are serious problems with socialism. Socialism undermines important biblical principles such as personal and church charity, private property, the right to pass on a family inheritance, the work ethic, the key role of the father/husband in providing for the family, and trusting God's provisions. God's Word teaches:

1. God created the Earth for man, with useful but finite material resources, and God gave a mandate to man to study, govern, and use the animals and material resources of the Earth (Gen. 1:26-28).
2. Man is not basically good, but rather all people have a sinful nature and engage in sinful actions, which include sinful actions in relation to financial matters (Rom. 3:10, 20, 23; Deut. 5:19, 21; 1 Tim. 6:10).
3. As a result of man's fall into sin, God cursed the ground of the Earth, which made it more difficult for man to get to the earth's productive food resources (Gen. 3).
4. As Creator, God, not government, owns man, the Earth, and all of its resources (Psalm 24:1-2), and God gifts people with abilities to work on the Earth (Exo. 31:1-6).
5. As Sovereign Lord, God entrusts individual adults or households with property and financial assets, who serve as a steward of material possessions for God (Luke 16:1-13; Prov. 3:9-10; 27:23-27; 31:10-31).
6. God's moral law is for all people, and it protects private property and condemns theft and coveting the possessions of other people as sins (Exo. 20:15, 17; Rom. 3:19-20 and 7:7).
7. Civil rulers also have a sinful nature and they can be guilty before God for theft of the property of their citizens (1 Kings 21) or for excessive and unjust and hurtful taxation (1 Sam. 8:10-18; 1 Kings 12:1-24; Luke 19:1-10).
8. Adults should engage in honest work to provide for their personal needs (Eph. 4:28; 2 Thess. 3:10)
9. An adult man is responsible to provide for the basic needs of his wife and children, help aged parents and close relatives who are widows in need, and he has a biblical right to leave an inheritance for children (1 Tim. 5:4, 8; Matt. 15:3-6; Prov. 13:22; 19:14).
10. Individuals have a responsibility to give to help needy people as they have ability and opportunity (Prov. 3:27-28; Eph. 4:28), and churches have a responsibility to collect offerings to give to Christians in need in their churches (2 Cor. 8-9).
11. The model God gave to Israel for helping needy people in their nation was requiring people to set aside ten percent of their production in their local community to

help the needy and allow the poor to glean leftovers in the fields (Deut. 14:28-29; 24:19-21).

12. National debt and economic decline in God's nation of Israel was a sign of God's judgment on the nation for departing from God's laws (Deut. 28).

These biblical economic principles include personal responsibility, the work ethic, private property for individuals and families, family responsibility and inheritance, church giving and private charity, limits on taxation, obedience to God's moral law against theft and coveting, viewing all resources as owned by God, and viewing people as individual stewards of material possessions for God. These biblical principles led Christians to develop free enterprise, private property, private charity and limited government in America.

In contrast, the Humanist worldview rejects the Bible as revelation from God and as any kind of authority on economic matters. They appeal solely to man's thinking and experience to guide thinking about government and the economy. A Christian economist, Tom Rose, notes:

> "The most popular 'religion' of our day is Humanism (as contrasted with Christianity, which Christians regard as . . . biblical revelation from the Creator). The Humanist regards man as the apex of an evolutionary process through eons of time. . . . A Christian operates from a different set of spiritually based premises than does the world, especially when dealing with the nature of man. Let us always beware of the fact that differing premises may sometimes direct the Christian to a policy outcome entirely different from one at which his secular associate might arrive."[70]

Dr. David Noebel, in his book, *Understanding the Times,* documents that a number of Secular Humanists in the past have favored the establishment of socialistic governments and economies in nations.[71] A standard dictionary defines socialism in the full sense as, "a system of social organization in which the means of production and distribution of goods are controlled collectively by the government."[72]

Karl Marx especially influenced a movement in the world towards socialism. In his book *Seven Men Who Rule the World from the Grave,* David Breese notes the continuing influence of Karl Marx on economic thinking around the world.[73] Marx, as an atheist, wrote about economic matters from a Humanist, anti-Christian perspective. In 1848, Marx wrote *The Communist Manifesto,* in which he advocated violent revolution and establishment of socialistic governments and economies in nations around the world.[74]

The planks of *The Communist Manifesto* violate teachings of the Bible. The Bible protects private property and prohibits theft and coveting (Exo. 20:15-17). In contrast, *The Communist Manifesto* called for the abolition of private property and for the State to seize and take control of industries and the means of communication and transportation.[75] The Bible gives families the right to pass on an inheritance to children and grandchildren (Prov. 13:22; 19:14), but *The Communist Manifesto* calls for abolishing family inheritance.[76]

The Bible teaches that God gifts people with abilities and desires for specific forms of work (Exo. 31:1-6). However, Marx rejected the existence of God and called for the State to form industrial and agricultural armies, with government dictating to people what work they did and where they lived.[77] As an atheist, Marx believed that the material world is all there is and he rejected Biblical teaching about man having a soul and life after death.[78]

Marx rejected God as Creator and advocated belief in evolution and survival of the fittest. He believed in societal evolution and economic determinism, that socialism or communism was the inevitable outcome of societal evolution. He believed that man could participate in societal evolution by engaging in violent revolution to overthrow existing social order and establish socialist dictatorships in nations.[79] He believed this would improve the lives of laborers.

Marx inspired Vladimir Lenin, who led the Russian Revolution of 1917 and established Marxist socialism with dictatorial control over the Soviet Union. Communism spread in the twentieth century to nations in Eastern Europe, China, North Korea, Vietnam, Cambodia, Cuba, and some nations in Africa.[80] Communist governments killed people they believed stood in the way of their economic plans. *The Black Book of Communism* states:

> "Communism imposed wholesale repression, culminating in a state-sponsored reign of terror . . . the mass murder of human beings . . . executions by various means . . . starvation . . . deportation . . . forced labor . . . The total approaches 100 million killed."[81]

Government repression, agriculture failures, and shortage of needed items due to socialist policies in communist nations showed the failure of socialism. Many people fled communist nations, the Soviet Union, Eastern Europe, China, North Korea, Cuba, Vietnam, etc. Some were killed trying to escape. Nazi Germany in the 1930s to 1940s was another example of a violent form of socialism, which brought death and terror to millions of people.

In reaction to the violence and terror of communism, many nations in Europe and Latin America have tried more peaceful forms of socialism. And many nations are semi-socialistic. They allow privately owned businesses and individual private property. But they impose heavy regulations that hurt economic growth, high and varying tax rates, control of the economy through the State, redistribution of wealth, secular government control of education, and a nationalized welfare system that creates dependence on the State.

Even with the fall of the Soviet empire in the 1990s, there are still many Marxists and other socialists around the world. Socialists appeal to concerns about helping the poor and providing economic security for everyone and concerns about some businesses exploiting their workers. Some socialists advocate that Christian churches join the movement for socialism in order to help the poor, but in the way they think is best, which is through the central government.

The Bible does teach us to be concerned about helping the poor (Prov. 28:27; Acts 20:34-35). God's law sets forth legislation to protect people from being cheated or deceived in economic transactions (Lev. 19:13, 35-36). God's Word says God will judge wealthy employers who cheat or defraud their employees (James 5:1-6). However, a nation can have charitable institutions to help the poor and laws to regulate commerce and employer/employee relations to prevent fraud and abuse without having a socialistic government and economy.

Some people have claimed that the practice of the early church in Acts teaches socialism. Acts 2:44–45 and 4:32–34 describe Christians selling their private property and giving their possessions to help those in need and having all things in common. But what they did was voluntary, not government enforced. Church leaders, not civil government, directed distribution, specifically to needy Christians. Having all things in common was a temporary practice in a particular area to meet a crisis situation and not a permanent or universal practice of the church.

A Christian economist studied the early Christian settlers in the original American colonies, who tried common ownership of property. They found that it did not work economically. But when they turned to private property for individuals and families, family responsibility, and emphasis on the personal work ethic, they thrived economically.[82]

Economic scholars Brian Crozier and Arthur Seldon studied socialism in the twentieth century and they document the economic failure of socialism. They found in their research that when it comes to helping the poor, "The plain evidence from around the world is that the poor have a better chance of being raised out of poverty in capitalism than they have under socialism."[83] Crozier and Seldon document that socialistic and semi-socialistic policies brought about economic decline in many nations,[84] while other nations prospered through free markets.[85]

Sven Rydenfelt, an economic scholar, also studied socialistic and semi-socialistic national economies and found a decline in productive work. He concludes, "Human beings without incentives will not work. The stronger the incentives, the better the results."[86] If taxes on income from work are too high and government subsidies for not working are generous, then people will lose their incentive to work. Rydenfelt also documents economic decline in nations with a socialistic type of economy[87] and nations with free markets prospered more.[88]

A number of people with a Humanist worldview do not advocate socialism and embrace private property and free enterprise. The problem they face involves authority for their position. The Christian worldview can appeal to God's Word as authority for protecting private property and prohibiting theft. Secular Humanists can appeal only to human opinion about protecting property and prohibiting theft. However, Marxist Humanists believe stealing property is moral if it advances Marxism. Engels, the associate of Karl Marx, stated:

> "Thou shalt not steal. Does this law thereby become an eternal moral law? By no means. . . . Our morality is wholly subordinate to the interest of the class-struggle of the proletariat."[89]

Marxists and other socialists criticize free markets because they say private businesses have abused workers and defrauded customers in free markets. However, civil governments that allow free markets can prosecute fraud, theft, and extortion by dishonest business men without the government taking over businesses and without oppressive tax rates. With a free market, honest business men who better serve customers can take the place of dishonest business men.

Leaders in socialist governments have the same fallen nature that dishonest business men have. If all power is concentrated in the hands of a few in a socialist government and they commit fraud, there is no one else to hold them accountable. If a socialist government takes over all businesses and they are dishonest or fail, there is no competition to replace the failed businesses.

Socialists want government-forced redistribution of wealth through high taxes. But that is a form of theft. Socialist governments must resort to high taxes, heavy borrowing, and inflation to finance all of their promises to pay for education, health care, welfare, retirement, and housing. Many socialist and semi-socialist nations are facing declining economies, a major government debt crisis and uncertainty about funding future benefits as a result.

Socialism emphasizes economic equality and removing the gap between rich and poor. However, socialistic nations have created their own wealthy class of government leaders and socialist party leaders, and their policies have often led to economic decline for the rest of the people in the nation. Michael Voslensky wrote *Nomenklatura: The Soviet Ruling Class.* His research found that the rulers in the former Soviet Union gained great wealth and power and the rest of the people lost rights and wealth and experienced oppression by their rulers.[90]

The Bible does not advocate that everyone have the same amount of money and possessions. In the parable of the talents (Matt. 25) and the parable of the pounds (Luke 19), Jesus describes the Lord giving differing amounts of possessions over which to be stewards and individuals increasing their wealth by differing amounts. The Bible describes God giving varying degrees of rewards to His people based on the quality and faithfulness of their service.

People are motivated to improve their condition by reward for their work. People who provide greater quality and quantity of goods and services to meet the needs and desires of other people rightly gain more. "The soul of a lazy man desires and has nothing, but the soul of the diligent shall be made rich" (Prov. 13:4).

God warned His people of Israel about turning away from Him and giving their trust and allegiance to powerful human rulers like idolatrous nations had (1 Samuel 8). God warned the people that such powerful rulers would take the best of their lands for their use and take ten percent of their production on top of the religious tithes and charitable tithes (twenty percent total) they already had to pay under the Mosaic law (1 Sam. 8:10-17). God said they would cry out in anguish under the burden of the rule of those kings (1 Sam. 8:18).

Socialism advocates helping workers and needy people through centralized government planning, high taxes and forced redistribution of wealth, and a national welfare system. The Bible differs from socialism in how to help people in need. God's Word teaches us to love our neighbor (Matt. 22:39–40), and Scripture teaches us how to do that.

(1) Individuals should willingly help people in need, according to their ability:

> "Do not withhold good from those to whom it is due, when it is in the power of your hand to do so" (Prov. 3:27).
>
> "Therefore, as we have opportunity, let us do good to all, especially to those who are of the household of faith" (Gal. 6:10).

(2) Families should care for the needs of each member of the household:

> "But if anyone does not provide for . . . those of his household, he has denied the faith" (1 Tim. 5:8).

The apostle Paul applied the general principle of 1 Timothy 5:8 in the immediate context to helping widowed relatives in need (1 Tim. 5:4, 16). However, the principle would also apply to providing for one's wife and children, as they are members of one's "household." Scripture teaches a husband to care for his wife (Eph. 5:25-29), parents to provide for children (2 Cor. 12:14), and adults to help aged parents who are in need (Matt. 15:3–6).

(3) Churches should help care for church members with material needs:

"Now concerning the collection for the saints, as I have given orders to the churches . . . so you must do also" (1 Cor. 16:1).

Also note 2 Corinthians 8-9 on giving to believers in need. Churches should help Christian widows who do not have family to support them (1 Tim. 5:3, 5:16). Christians should give offerings to support the Lord's work on earth (Prov. 3:9), and support ministers of the Word by their giving (1 Cor. 9:4-14; 1 Tim. 5:17–18).

(4) God's plan for the nation of Israel was to help the needy in local communities through tithes (a tenth of income) and to let people in need glean leftovers in fields.

"You shall bring out the tithe of your produce of that year and store it up within your gates. And the Levite . . . the stranger and the fatherless and the widow who are within your gates may come and eat and be satisfied" (Deut. 14:28–29).

"When you reap your harvest in your field and forget a sheaf in the field, you shall not go back to get it. . . . When you gather the grapes of your vineyard, you shall not glean it afterward. It shall be for the stranger, the fatherless and the widow" (Deut. 24:19, 21).

If people applied the wisdom of this plan in their local communities today, rather than national government welfare, they could more efficiently help the needy and have lower taxes.

We are told in God's Word that charitable giving should come from love in the heart:

"Now concerning the ministry to the saints . . . let each one give as he purposes in his heart, not grudgingly or of necessity, for God loves a cheerful giver" (2 Cor. 9:1, 7).

"And though I bestow all my goods to feed the poor . . . but have not love, it profits me nothing" (1 Cor. 13:3).

In contrast, government welfare comes from forced taxes, with high varying rates far above ten percent. The high taxes to fund the welfare state decrease voluntary giving, make it difficult for families to care for themselves and hard for private charities to operate. R. J. Rushdoony observes:

"The modern state sees itself in messianic terms and as man's savior. . . . Welfare programs have worked to displace Christian charity."[91]

When considering charitable giving, Christians should be discerning about the reasons people are in poverty. People can be poor due to circumstances beyond their control such as a job layoff, a genuine physical disability and inability to work, devastating medical bills, or losing their home to a natural disaster. Such people truly need charitable help.

But God's Word teaches that some people become poor by their refusal to work:

> "I went by the field of a lazy man. . . . And there it was all overgrown. . . . So shall your poverty come like a prowler" (Prov. 24:30-31, 34).

God's Word also teaches that people can become poor through sinful choices. Scripture mentions drunkenness, gluttony, and sexual immorality as causes of poverty:

> "An immoral woman . . . remove your way far from her . . . lest you give . . . your years to the cruel one; lest aliens be filled with your wealth . . . and you mourn at last" (Prov. 5:3, 8-11). "For the drunkard and the glutton will come to poverty" (Prov. 23:21).

Individuals, families, churches, and charitable institutions should have the legal freedom to require behavior changes in people they serve in order for them to receive assistance.

America has a free enterprise system and is not a socialist nation. However, it has instituted a national government welfare program similar to socialist nations. Charles Murray researched American federal welfare programs. He found:

> "What emerged in the 1960s was an almost unbroken intellectual consensus that . . . poverty was not a consequence of indolence or vice. . . . Poverty was not the fault of the individual but of the system."[92]

Murray also notes the observation of a family court judge: "Every day, sitting in court, I amass new evidence that the relief setup is sapping [the recipient's] will to work."[93] Murray found that aid to single pregnant mothers led to increased pregnancies outside of marriage.[94] And federal welfare programs led to no decrease in poverty levels over time.[95] A ten-year federal study concluded that federal welfare programs decreased work incentives.[96]

Marvin Olasky has written about Christian charity in early America. He found that Christians distinguished reasons for poverty and called for behavior changes in the poor whose sinful choices led to their poverty.[97] He found that churches formed societies to help the poor gain self-supporting employment, and churches started charity schools to teach children from poor households about the Lord and train them to become productive workers.[98]

In modern America, Star Parker is an African American woman who became involved in drug abuse, pregnancies outside of marriage, and dependence on government welfare. She said things started to change through a "pastor challenging my economic worldview. . . .'God is your source, not the government,'" and then she escaped dependence on welfare through faith in Christ as Lord and Savior and by "changing my worldview."[99] She forsook her immoral lifestyle and became productive in work and private charity. She studied government welfare and found this:

> "Robert Rector points out in multiple studies for the Heritage Foundation that means-tested welfare spending in America exceeds $400 billion annually. That

> is a whopping 14 percent of the federal budget. . . . Rector's data shows that less than twenty cents of each dollar actually gets into the hands of the people society is trying to help. Eighty percent is the bureaucracy. . . . Up until 1965, Census Bureau statistics show that 78 percent of black households were comprised of intact families with a husband, wife and children. But by 1995, after the political manipulations of the welfare state, black marriage rates had dramatically declined and 69 percent of its children were being birthed outside of wedlock."[100]

Dr. Walter Williams, an African American with a Ph.D. in economics, has written about the welfare state as immoral.[101] He appeals to man's conscience concerning theft and argues that we would not think it right to steal from a neighbor to help someone we saw in need. It should be voluntary charitable giving. Likewise, he argues, we should not use government to forcefully tax our neighbors to give to another favored individual who did not earn it.

Karl Marx, in his plan for socialism and welfare, advocated high taxes through the central government, with varying rates and redistribution of wealth from people who earned it to people who did not earn it.[102] In contrast, when God set forth a plan for helping people in need in a nation, He established a flat rate of ten percent for people to pay and a plan to collect it and apply it at the local level (Deut. 14:19-21). God's law also condemned coveting the assets that belong to other people (Deut. 5:21). Herbert Schlossberg observed about Marxism:

> "Marx called religion the opium of the people. He rightly saw that Christian faith is antithetical to the envy, the grasping for more, on which his revolution depends."[103]

National government welfare programs have assisted many needy people. And a Christian might seek government assistance due to the laws in one's nation, the severity of one's personal situation and lack of help from private sources. In many places Christians have to live under a socialist government. However, national government welfare has serious problems.

Christians should support private sector alternatives to helping people. Christians in America can become part of a Christian health care sharing organization such as Samaritan Ministries (www.samaritanministries.org), Medi-Share (www.mychristiancare.org), or Christian Health Care ministries (www.chministries.org). Christians should support their churches in giving to members who have legitimate needs. Believers can give to Christian homes for troubled teens, city rescue missions, crisis pregnancy centers, and Christian school scholarships.

Christian author George Grant has written a helpful study of the problems with national government welfare and biblical teachings about helping the needy. He emphasized helping the poor through sharing the Gospel with them, teaching them Scripture about work, and poverty-causing sinful choices and helping them find work. In his book, *Bringing in the Sheaves: Replacing Government Welfare with Biblical Charity,* he gives these observations:

> "This is the essence of Biblical charity: helping the poor to help themselves. . . . First, the poor, like all others, must be instructed in the life-transforming tenets of the Gospel of grace. . . . Biblical charity is not rooted in the Social Gospel. It is rooted in the Gospel. . . . Never be deterred from the evangelistic opportunities that Biblical charity presents. . . . We've been most charitable when we've taught others how to avoid needing charity. . . . Biblical charity is . . . doing anything and everything necessary to enable the poor to stand on their own, to provide for their families and to prepare for the future. . . . Charity to the sluggardly, on the other hand, involves admonition . . . of immorality (Proverbs 5:10), of sloth (Proverbs 6:11) . . . of drunkenness (Proverbs 21:17) . . . of thievery (Proverbs 28:22). . . . Because of the debilitating effects of the federal welfare system, which indisputably encourages indolence and sloth, many of the chronically unemployed poor will need . . . comprehensive reeducation. So in order to free them from the trap of dependency, our charity outreaches will have to teach them basic principles of regeneration, finances, providence, health and hygiene and industry. . . . To help the poor help themselves, biblical charity will need to find them jobs, train them for jobs. . . . Biblical charity . . . is designed to provide the poor with a hand, not a handout."[104]

CHAPTER 6 STUDY GUIDE THINKING BIBLICALLY ABOUT THE CHURCH AND THE STATE

KEY SCRIPTURES TO READ:

Genesis 8:22; Genesis 9:6-7; Genesis 9:14-15; Exodus 20:12-17; Psalm 1:1-3; Matthew 28:18-20; Acts 2:41-47; Romans 13:1-7; 1 Corinthians 9:13-14 and 16:1-2; Ephesians 4:11-16; Ephesians 5:18-6:4; Colossians 3:16-22; 1 Timothy 2:1-7; 1 Timothy 3:1-13; Titus 2:4-10; Titus 3:1-2; Hebrews 10:24-25; Hebrews 13:7 and 17; 1 Peter 2:13-18; 1 Peter 3:1-7; Jude 1:3-4; 1 John 3:14, 17; 2 John 1:7-11

KEY POINTS TO NOTE (NOTE BOLD TYPE IN CHAPTER):

What are the 3 basic societal institutions in the Bible that God has established on earth for man?

____

____

God designed these 3 basic societal institutions with a special relationship to ____________.

What word does the Bible especially use in relation to authorities in these basic God-given institutions?

____

____

If submission to authority involves disobedience to God's Word, then we must (Acts 5:29):

____

____

What Biblical function does the church have in relation to:

God? ____

Its Members? ____

The World?____

What are six key reasons that the believer needs the local church? (Heb. 10:24-25, Acts 2:41-42, Col. 3:16-17, 1 John 3:17, 1 Cor. 9:13-14, Eph. 4:11-16)

____

____

What is the basic God-given responsibility of civil government (Rom. 13:3-4; 1 Pet. 2:14)?

How did George Hegel, who influenced Karl Marx, view the state, or civil government?

What do Genesis 8:22 and Genesis 9:14-15 say about climate change and the earth?

CRITICAL THINKING:

How do the Christian and Humanist worldviews differently explain the origin of man's basic societal institutions?

Based on the teaching of God's Word, what are some specific situations that would require a Christian to not obey someone in authority?

What kind of influence does Humanism have on public education in Western nations?

What is the attitude of Scripture toward world empires and how does Humanism view one world government? What are potential dangers with a one-world government?

Compare and contrast the views of Karl Marx and the Bible on private property, family inheritance, theft and private charity.

CHAPTER 6 ENDNOTES

1 W. R. Bird, *The Origin of Species Revisited,* volume 1 (Nashville, TN: Thomas Nelson, 1991), p. 32, quoting Julian Huxley.

2 Gary DeMar, *God and Government: A Biblical, Historical and Constitutional Perspective* (Powder Springs, GA: American Vision, 2011), pp. 6, 7.

3 Del Tackett, *The Truth Project* (Focus on the Family, 2006, DVD), "Sociology: The Divine Imprint."

4 Skevington Wood, *Expositor's Bible Commentary: Ephesians,* vol. 11, Frank Gabelein, ed. (Grand Rapids, MI: Zondervan Publishing House, 1978), p. 75.

5 DeMar, *God and Government,* p. 112, quoting Francis Schaeffer.

6 Bruce Short, *The Harsh Truth about Public Schools* (Vallecito, CA: The Chalcedon Foundation, 2004), p. 17.

7 Ibid, p. 40.

8 Ibid, p. 40.

9 David Noebel, *Understanding the Times,* 2nd edition (Manitou Springs, CO: Summit Press, 2006), p. 23.

10 Ibid, p. 119.

11 R. J. Rushdoony, *The Messianic Character of American Education* (Nutley, NJ: The Craig Press, 1968), p. 35.

12 Jonathan Sarfati, *Refuting Evolution* (Brisbane, Australia: Creation Ministries International, 2007), pp. 13-14.

13 Ken Ham, *Already Gone* (Green Forest, AR: Master Books, 2009), pp. 32, 57, 60, 78.

14 Short, pp. 69-91.

15 Paul Kurtz, ed., *Humanist Manifestos 1 and 2* (Buffalo, NY: Prometheus Books, 1973), pp. 7-11.

16 Rushdoony, *The Messianic Character of American Education,* p. 101.

17 John Stormer, *None Dare Call it Education* (Florissant, MO: Liberty Bell Press, 1998), pp. 183-185.

18 "Mosque: Place to Worship," Britannica.com, http://www.britannica.com/EBchecked/topic/393679/mosque. (Accessed 3/16/2019).

19 Mandalit del Barco, "Sunday Assembly: A Church for the Godless Picks Up Steam," NPR.org, http://www.npr.org/2014/01/07/260184473/sunday-assembly-a-church-for-the-godless-picks up steam. (Accessed 3/16/2019).

20 Kurtz, pp. 7-11, 15.

21 William Arndt and F. Wilbur Gingrich, *A Greek-English Lexicon of the New Testamen*t (Chicago: University of Chicago Press, 1957), p. 240.

22 Millard Erickson, *Introducing Christian Doctrine* (Grand Rapids, MI: Baker Book House, 1992), p. 330.

23 Philip Schaff, *History of the Christian Church,* volume II (Grand Rapids, Eerdmans Publishing Company, 1973 reprint), chapters 1, 2, 3 on "The Spread of Christianity," "The Persecution of Christianity" and "The Literary Contest of Christianity."

24 Cleon Skousen, *The Naked Communist* (Ensign Publishing Company, 1961), chapters 5 and 9-11.

25 Robert Spencer, *The Politically Incorrect Guide to Islam* (Washington, D. C.: Regnery Publishing, 2005), p. 107.

26 Erickson, pp. 336–339.

27 Homer Kent, *The Pastoral Epistles* (Chicago: Moody Press, 1958), p. 121.

28 John Piper and Wayne Grudem, *Recovering Biblical Manhood and Womanhood: A Response to Evangelical Feminism* (Wheaton, IL: Crossway Books, 1991), pp. 60, 61.

29 Josh McDowell, *The Last Christian Generation* (Holiday, FL: Green Key Books, 2006), p. 13, referring to a George Barna survey.

30 Ibid, pp. 14–18.

31 Thabiti Anyabwile, *What is a Healthy Church Member?* (Wheaton, IL: Crossway Books, 2008).

32 Curtis Thomas, *Life in the Body of Christ: Privileges and Responsibilities in the Local Church* (Cape Coral, FL: Founders Press, 2006).

33 Douglas Moo, *The Epistle to the Romans* (Grand Rapids: Eerdmans Publishing Company, 1996), p. 800.

34 Vern Poythress, *The Shadow of Christ in the Law of Moses* (Phillipsburg, NJ: P&R Press, 1991), p. 159.

35 Philip Schaff, *Creeds of Christendom,* vol. 3 (Grand Rapids: Baker Book House, 1985 reprint), pp. 16-17, The Lutheran Augsburg Confession, Civil Affairs.

36 "A Statement on Peace, War and Military Service, 1937" (Mennonite Church, http://home.mennonitechurch.ca/1937-statementonwar). (Accessed 3/16/2019).

37 Ron Gleason, *The Death Penalty on Trial: Taking a Life for a Life Taken* (Ventura, CA: Nordskog Publishing, 2008).

38 Robert Culver, *Toward a Biblical View of Civil Government* (Chicago: Moody Press, 1974), pp. 72, 275.

39 Poythress, pp. 171, 173.

40 James Orr, general editor, "Punishments," in *The International Standard Bible Encyclopedia,* vol. IV (Grand Rapids: Eerdmans Publishing Company, 1957 reprint), p. 2504.

41 Herbert Schlossberg, *Idols for Destruction* (Wheaton, IL: Crossway Books, 1990), p. 178.

42 R. J. Rushdoony, *Christianity and the State* (Vallecito, CA: Ross House Books, 1986), pp. 15, 17.

43 Kurtz, pp. 21, 14, 16.

44 Douglas Groothuis, *Unmasking the New Age* (Downers Grove, IL: Intervarsity Press, 1986), p. 118.

45 Bob Unruh, "Gore Boasts Global Governance Coming with Carbon Tax," World Net Daily, July 10, 2009 (https://www.wnd.com/2009/07/103634). (Accessed 3/16/2019).

46 Jerome R. Corsi, "Copenhagen Goal is 1-World Government," World Net Daily, October 17, 2009 (https://www.wnd.com/2009/10/113219). (Accessed 3/16/2019).

47 Kurtz, pp. 14, 21.

48 "United Nations' Threat: No More Parental Rights," WorldNetDaily, February 5, 2009 (https://www.wnd.com/2009/02/87929). (Accessed 3/16/2019).

49 Bob Unruh, "U.S. Sponsors Plan to Restrict Free Speech: Joins Egyptians in Proposal to United Nations Human Rights Council," WorldNetDaily, October 19, 2009 (https://www.wnd.com/2009/10/112886). (Accessed 3/16/2019).

50 Jerry Bridges, chapter 6: "God's Power Over Nature," in *Trusting God* (NavPress, 2008), pp. 98-101.

51 Christopher Horner, *The Politically Incorrect Guide to Global Warming and Environmentalism* (Washington, D.C.: Regnery Publishing, 2007), chapter 8, "Media Mania."

52 *A Pocket Guide to Global Warming—A Scientific and Biblical Expose of Climate Change* (Petersburg, KY: Answers in Genesis, 2008), pp. 45, 50.

53 Ibid, p. 32.

54 Ibid, chapter by Michael Oard, "How Much Global Warming is Natural?"

55 Ibid, p. 39.

56 Ibid, pp. 27-28, and updated petition and signature count at http://www.oism.org/pproject. (Accessed 3/16/2019).

57 Alan White, *Answers Book 4,* chapter 16, "Should We Be Concerned About Climate Change?" (Petersburg, KY: Master Books), shared online at Answers in Genesis (www.answersingenesis.org), August 22, 2014.

58 Roy Spencer, *Climate Confusion: How Global Warming Hysteria Leads to Bad Science, Pandering Politicians and Misguided Policies that Hurt the Poor* (New York: Encounter Books, 2008), pp. IX, X, 6, 7.

59 Ibid, p. 85.

60 Bob Unruh, "Scientists to Congress—The Sky is Not Falling," WorldNetDaily, July 1, 2009, (https://www.wnd.com/2009/07/102750/). (Accessed 3/16/2019).

61 Dr. Fred Singer, Nongovernmental International Panel on Climate Change, http://climatechangereconsidered.org/lead-authors. (Accessed 3/16/2019).

62 Brian Sussman, *Climategate: A Veteran Meteorologist Exposes the Global Warming Scam* (Washington, D.C.: WorldNetDaily Books, 2010), p. 16.

63 Ibid, chapter 2, "Climate Lobotomy."

64 Ibid, pp. 22-30.

65 Ibid, p. 61.

66 Ibid, p. 55.

67 Ibid, p. 56.

68 Robert Balling, chapter 3: "Global Warming," in Ronald Bailey, ed., *The True State of the Planet* (New York: The Free Press, 1995), pp. 85, 89, 95, 104.

69 Horner, pp. 246, 282.

70 Tom Rose, *Economics: Principles and Policy from a Christian Perspective,* 2nd edition (Mercer, PA: American Enterprise Publications, 1986), pp. 15, 18.

71 Noebel, pp. 369-373.

72 *Webster's College Dictionary,* p. 1270.

73 David Breese, *Seven Men Who Rule the World from the Grave* (Chicago: Moody Press, 1990), chapter 4 on Karl Marx.

74 Ibid, pp. 62-65.

75 Ibid, p. 63, planks 1, 4, 6 and 7 of the *Communist Manifesto.*

76 Ibid, p. 63, plank 3 of the *Communist Manifesto.*

77 Ibid, pp. 63-64, planks 7, 8, and 9 of the *Communist Manifesto.*

78 Ibid, pp. 68-69.

79 Ibid, pp. 70-71.

80 Stéphane Courtois and others, ed., *The Black Book of Communism: Crimes, Terror, Repression,* translated into English by Jonathan Murphy and Mark Kramer (Cambridge, MA: Harvard University Press, 1999).

81 Ibid, pp. 2, 4.

82 Dr. Gary North, "Common Ownership," chapter 1 in *Puritan Economic Experiments* (Tyler, TX: Institute for Christian Economics, 1988).

83 Brian Crozier and Arthur Seldon, *Socialism: The Grand Delusion* (New York: Universe Books, 1986), p. 38.

84 Ibid, chapters 10-15.

85 Ibid, pp. 38-39, 72.

86 Sven Rydenfelt, *A Pattern for Failure: Socialist Economies in Crisis* (New York: Harcourt, Brace, Jovanovich, 1984), p. 47.

87 Ibid, pp. 28, 30, 47, 71, 86-87, 99, 110-111, 125-127, 132.

88 Ibid, pp. 5, 10-11, 13-14, p. 85.

89 Cleon Skousen, *The Naked Communist* (Salt Lake City, UT: Ensign Publishing Company, 1961), p. 52, quoting Lenin.

90 Michael Voslensky (translated by Eric Mosbacher), Nomenklatura: *The Soviet Ruling Class* (Garden City, New York, 1984).

91 Rushdoony, Christianity and the State, p. 33.

92 Charles Murray, *Losing Ground—American Social Policy 1950-1980* (New York: Basic Books, 1984), p. 29.

93 Ibid, p. 16.

94 Ibid, pp. 125-127.

95 Ibid, pp. 63-65.

96 Ibid, pp. 149-152.

97 Marvin Olasky, *The Tragedy of American Compassion* (Wheaton, IL: Crossway Books, 1992), chapters 1, 2, 3.

98 Marvin Olasky, *Fighting for Liberty and Virtue: Political and Culture Wars in 18th Century America* (Wheaton, IL: Crossway Books, 1995), chapter 5.

99 Star Parker, *Uncle Sam's Plantation: How Big Government Enslaves America's Poor and What We Can Do about It,* revised edition (Nashville, TN: Thomas Nelson, 2010), pp. 44, 40.

100 Ibid, pp. 5, 69-70.

101 Walter Williams, "Welfare State: Immoral and Irredeemable," WorldNetDaily, June 5, 2012. (https://www.wnd.com/2012/06/the-welfare-state-immoral-and-irredeemable/). (Accessed 3/16/2019).

102 Breese, p. 63, plank 2 of *The Communist Manifesto.*

103 Schlossberg, p. 137.

104 George Grant, *Bringing in the Sheaves: Replacing Government Welfare with Biblical Charity,* 3rd Revised Edition (Franklin, TN: Ars Vitae, 1995), pp. 155, 157, 158, 159, 160, 162.

CHAPTER 7

THINKING BIBLICALLY ABOUT MARRIAGE AND SEXUAL ISSUES

THINKING BIBLICALLY ABOUT MARRIAGE

THE MARRIAGE RELATIONSHIP

Marriage is not a product of evolution. God instituted marriage when He first created man. God caused the first man to sense his loneliness as he named the animals (Gen. 2:18–20). The animals were not like him. They had mates. God said, "It is not good that man should be alone; I will make him a helper comparable to him" (Gen. 2:18).

Then God created the woman to be a close companion to the man (Gen. 2:22–23).

Scripture tells us that God made the first woman from Adam's side (Gen. 2:21–22). Adam recognized that the woman was of his flesh (Gen. 2:23). And God pronounced that man and woman shall become "one flesh" in marriage (Gen. 2:24). All people descend from the original union of Adam with his wife, Eve, who is "the mother of all living" (Gen. 3:20).

We see from the beginning that God's Word describes the marriage relationship in terms of companionship and permanence. To further emphasize the permanence of marriage, God's Word calls marriage a covenant. A covenant is a binding agreement. It has witnesses. Marriage is like this. It is a covenant union between one man and one woman who commit to one another for life.

Two passages in Scripture bring together these ideas of a covenant and companionship in the same verse describing marriage. Proverbs 2:16–17 warns of "the immoral woman . . . who forsakes the companion of her youth and forgets the covenant of her God." And **Malachi 2:14** rebukes divorce, describing a wife as "your companion and your wife by covenant." According to the Bible, God designed marriage as a binding covenant and intimate companionship.

Christian counselor and Bible scholar, Dr. Jay Adams, has written a helpful study on the nature of marriage.[1] Based on Scripture, **Dr. Adams describes marriage as a "Covenant of Companionship."** He makes these observations about the meaning of marriage:

> "God tells us that He Himself established . . . marriage at the beginning of human society (Gen. 2). . . . Gen. 2:18 . . . the reason for marriage is to solve the problem of loneliness. . . . In the Bible, marriage is described in terms of companionship . . . Proverbs 2:17 . . . Malachi 2:14. . . . Marriage, I have called (with good biblical reason) a 'Covenant of Companionship'. . . . In both passages where companionship is prominently mentioned, so is the covenantal aspect of marriage."[2]

Covenants in the Bible were binding agreements. Scripture describes marriage as a covenant relationship. **As a covenant relationship, God designed the marriage relationship to be a life-long, permanent union.** Note the emphasis in God's Word on God's design for marriage as a life-long relationship:

> God's original creation of marriage: "Therefore a man shall leave his father and his mother and be joined to his wife, and they shall become one flesh" (Gen. 2:24).
>
> The Old Testament prophets: "The Lord has been witness between you and the wife of your youth, with whom you have dealt treacherously; yet she is your companion and your wife by covenant" (Mal. 2:14).
>
> Christ's teaching: "They are no longer two, but one flesh. Therefore, what God has joined together, let not man separate" **(Matt. 19:6).**
>
> The apostles: "For the woman who has a husband is bound by law to her husband as long as he lives" **(Rom. 7:2).**

According to God's Word, the marriage covenant involves sexual intimacy. God created sex and He established the sexual relationship as exclusively for the relationship between one man and one woman in marriage. God designed sex as a good thing for one man committed to one woman in marriage. Outside of the marriage covenant between one man and one woman, all sexual activity is sin against God. Note what God's Word says about sex in marriage:

> "Marriage is honorable among all and the bed undefiled; but fornicators and adulterers God will judge" (Heb. 13:4).
>
> "Nevertheless, because of sexual immorality, let each man have his own wife and let each woman have her own husband. Let the husband render to his wife the affection due her and likewise also the wife to her husband" (1 Cor. 7:2-3).

From the beginning in Genesis, God designed the sexual union in marriage for two good purposes. One purpose for sex in marriage is to produce children. Genesis tells us that God commanded the first husband and wife: "Be fruitful and multiply; fill the earth **(Gen. 1:28)**. This command was repeated to Noah's family after the Flood (Gen. 9:1). God wants husband and wife to know and follow the Lord and raise their children to know and follow the Lord.

"She is your companion and your wife by covenant. But did He not make them one? . . . And why one? He seeks godly offspring. . . . Let none deal treacherously with the wife of his youth" (Mal. 2:14-15).

"And you, fathers, do not provoke your children to wrath, but bring them up in the training and admonition of the Lord" (Eph. 6:4).

Another purpose in God's design for sex is to express the unique one-flesh union between one man and one woman in marriage: "They shall become one flesh" **(Gen. 2:24).** God designed sex between husband and wife to be mutually pleasurable as they express their intimate oneness with each other (Note Song of Solomon). The one flesh union of husband and wife in marriage illustrates the intimate spiritual union between Christ and the church:

"For this reason a man shall . . . be joined to his wife and the two shall become one flesh. This is a great mystery, but I speak concerning Christ and the church" (Eph. 5:31-32).

A Christian writer on marriage gives this observation about sex in marriage:

"Sexual intercourse is more than a physical act. It is the symbol of a spiritual relationship and the expression of the complete oneness of two persons in married love."[3]

This one-flesh union of marriage also includes a spiritual union as husband and wife become as one person. God's Word gives instructions to believers on how a husband and wife can live together in harmony in the marriage relationship (1 Pet. 3:1–9). Husband and wife experience a harmonious marriage relationship and show their spiritual union by fulfilling their God-given roles in marriage, which God sets forth in His Word (Eph. 5:22-34).

Of the three basic God-given societal institutions—civil government, church, and family—God established the family first and the marriage relationship first in the family (Gen. 1-2). If the marriage relationship breaks down, it harms the parent-child relationship. It hurts the testimony of Christian churches when marriage breakups happen to church members. Also, widespread broken marriages lead to a breakdown in social order.

Harmony in marriage is very important. A husband needs to apply the teaching of Scripture about how he should relate to this wife (Eph. 5:25-34; Col. 3:19; Tit. 2:6; 1 Pet. 3:7). A wife needs to apply the teaching of Scripture about how she should relate to her husband (Eph. 5:22-24; Col. 3:18; Tit. 2:4-5; 1 Pet. 3:1-6). A husband and wife need to know the Lord and apply the teaching of the Bible with the help of the Holy Spirit to have harmony in their marriage relationship.

God designed distinct roles for the husband and for the wife in the marriage covenant.

The roles of the husband and wife in the marriage relationship picture the spiritual relationship of Christ and the church. **God's Word teaches the husband to love his wife like**

Christ loves the church and the wife to submit to the leadership of her husband as she would to the Lord. Note the divinely inspired teaching of the apostle Paul:

> "Wives, submit to your own husbands, as to the Lord. . . . Husbands, love your wives just as Christ also loved the church and gave Himself for her. . . . Let each one of you in particular so love his own wife as himself and let the wife see that she respects her husband" (Eph. 5:22, 25, 33).

The teaching of the Bible about roles in the marriage relationship has led to a worldview conflict. The Humanist worldview, influenced by the feminist movement, reacts negatively to the teaching in Scripture about a wife submitting to the leadership of her husband. The Islamic worldview, based on the Qur'an, has led to harsh rule of a husband over his wife, unlike the biblical teaching of a husband loving his wife like Christ loved the church. Worldly culture can lead a man to focus on fulfilling selfish desires rather than sacrificially loving his wife.

The Christian worldview strikes a balance between the Islamic and Humanist worldviews. The teaching of the Islamic worldview has led to husbands beating their wives, based on teaching in the Qur'an.[4] The Bible does not allow such action. The Humanist worldview leads to mutually self-centered and leaderless marriages, or sometimes the woman tries to take leadership. In contrast to both, the Christian worldview, based on the Bible, teaches a husband to sacrificially love his wife and exercise a loving leadership (Eph. 5:22-34).

It is important to note that submission does not mean the wife is inferior (Gal. 3:28) Jesus, the Son of God, who is equal with the Father (John 10:30), submitted to God the Father (Heb. 10:5-7). Also, biblical submission does not mean that a wife must refrain from giving counsel to her husband (Prov. 31:26—"She opens her mouth with wisdom"). In a book they wrote on marriage, a Christian couple gives this helpful statement about the husband and wife relationship:

> "How remarkable and revealing that secular culture recognizes the wisdom of authority, leadership, and defined roles in almost every other area of life—business, sports, entertainment, government, the military and education—but balks at the notion that men and women should have different roles in marriage. In God's economy and wisdom, all of life and society includes roles of leadership and subordination. This is His blessing, because without it there would be utter chaos! . . . Man and woman are completely equal in value and importance, but they fulfill roles that gloriously complement each other."[5]

Some people argue that Paul calls for mutual submission of a husband and wife ("submitting to one another" in Eph. 5:21). However, the following verses in Ephesians 5:22-34 teach a different kind of submission for a husband and for a wife. God's Word calls a husband to submit to lovingly meeting the needs of his wife and a wife to submit to the leadership of her husband. In their study on roles of men and women, John Piper and Wayne Grudem make this important point:

> "The way Paul teaches mutual submission . . . does not mean that husbands and wives should submit to each other in the same way. . . . Are Christ and the church mutually submitted? They aren't if submission means Christ yields to the authority of the church. . . . God has called men to exercise a headship that is loving, gentle, and considerate (Eph. 5:25; 1 Peter 3:7). He has called women to submit to that headship in a willing, gentle, and respectful way (Eph. 5:24, 33; 1 Peter 3:1-2)."[6]

Even if a husband is an unbeliever or is not consistently living according to God's Word as a believer, God's Word still calls a wife to submit to her husband (1 Pet. 3:1-6). Of course, the exception would be if submission to a husband involved sinful activity. In that case, the wife should "obey God rather than men" (Acts 5:29). She should not verbally nag her husband to obey God's Word (1 Pet. 3:1) or respond in anger (Prov. 21:19). She should seek help of church ministers (1 Pet. 5:1-4). She should seek to win her husband by being a godly example:

> "Wives, likewise, be submissive to your own husbands, that even if some do not obey the Word, they, without a word, may be won by the conduct of their wives, when they observe your chaste conduct accompanied by fear . . . A gentle and quiet spirit is very precious in the sight of God" (1 Pet. 3:1, 2, 4).

However, as a Christian husband loves his wife as he should, he makes it easier for a wife to submit to the leadership of her husband. A husband should get wisdom from God's Word to learn how to be right kind of leader for his wife and family. Consider what God's Word says about how a husband should love his wife. Christ's relationship with the church models how a husband should relate to his wife:

> "Husbands, love your wives just as Christ also loved the church and gave Himself for her, that He might sanctify and cleanse her with the washing of water by the word . . . Husbands ought to love their own wives as their own bodies . . . For no one ever hated his own flesh, but nourishes and cherishes it, just as the Lord does the church" (Eph. 5:25-26, 28-29).

Christ loved His people when they were unworthy as sinners (Rom. 5:8). A husband should love his wife unconditionally, remembering his own faults. Christ initiated love for His people before they loved Him and wins their love with His love. A husband should model Christ's love and initiate love for his wife and win her heart's love with his love for her.

> "In this is love, not that we loved God, but He loved us and sent His Son to be the propitiation for our sins. . . . We love Him because He first loved us" (1 John 4:10, 19).

Christ sacrificed His life to save the church from Hell (Eph. 5:25). A husband should be willing to sacrifice his own life for his wife if necessary. Like Christ who supplies the needs of His people (Phil. 4:19), a husband should provide for his wife's physical needs (1 Tim. 5:8), and he should meet her need for physical affection ("nourishes and cherishes" in Eph. 5:29).

God expresses love for His people in His Word (2 Cor. 5:14; 1 John 4:10, 19). A husband should verbally express love to his wife. The Bible says "love suffers long and is kind" (1 Cor. 13:4). A husband should be patient and kind towards his wife. Christ brings joy to His people (John 15:11) and Scripture speaks of a husband bringing happiness to his wife (Deut. 24:5; 1 Cor. 7:33). Christ understands His people's needs (Heb. 4:15). A husband should be understanding of his wife ("dwell with [her] with understanding," 1 Pet. 3:7).

There is also a worldview clash about the nature of biblical marriage. Jesus affirmed God's foundational plan for marriage in Genesis, which is one man committed to one woman:

> "Have you not read that He who made them at the beginning 'made them male and female,' and said, 'For this reason a man shall leave his father and mother and be joined to his wife, and the two shall become one flesh"? **(Matt. 19:4–5).**

But there are two prominent views of marriage in the world that are contrary to the biblical view about the nature of marriage. **These views are polygamy and same-sex marriage. Both views violate God's plan for one man with one woman in marriage.**

Polygamy is the practice of having more than one marriage partner. The Islamic worldview specifically endorses polygamy. The Qur'an teaches the practice of polygamy saying,

> "Marry women of your choice, two, or three, or four" (Qur'an 4:3).[7] Mohammed had many wives. And in nations where Islam advances, the practice of polygamy advances with it.

Polygamy violates God's original plan for marriage. God did not bring several women to Adam to give him companions and helpers; He brought one woman (Gen. 2:18–25). Some may try to argue with the Christian view of marriage by pointing out that some people of faith in the Old Testament practiced polygamy. However, the Bible does not praise their polygamy or advocate multiple marriage partners. These people all had great troubles in their polygamous marriages, which were contrary to God's original design for marriage.

For example, Jacob did not set out to take several wives, but was tricked into the arrangement by his father-in-law and he had problems with his multiple wives (Gen. 29:23–30). Samuel's father observed one of his wives making the other one miserable (1 Sam. 1:2–7). King David had many difficulties in his polygamous household (2 Sam. 12:10–11). Solomon's multiple marriages led to his downfall (1 Kings 11:3). Polygamous kings in Israel violated God's law that forbade a king to multiply wives to himself (Deut. 17:17).

In the New Testament, Scripture requires that ministers and deacons be the husband of one wife (1 Tim. 3:2, 3:12). Ministers must be godly examples to believers (1 Pet. 5:2–3), and believers should follow their example (Heb. 13:7). Christians, therefore, should not practice polygamy. Especially important is the fact that polygamy is contrary to the teaching of Jesus about God's design for marriage as one man with one woman (Matt. 19:3-6).

Same-sex marriage is another view that violates God's plan for marriage as one man with one woman. The Humanist worldview allows for varying views of marriage and accepts sex outside of biblical marriage. It rejects biblical absolutes and promotes recognition of same-sex marriage. *The Humanist Manifesto* states, "The many varieties of sexual exploration should not in themselves be considered evil."[8] And a Humanist feminist writer declares, "We have to abolish and reform the institution of marriage."[9]

Homosexual unions are contrary to God's design for marriage, which is the union of one man with one woman: "Male and female He created them. . . . and they shall become one flesh" (Gen. 1:27; 2:24). God brought a woman, not another man, for Adam in marriage when He instituted marriage. Jesus affirmed God's original design for marriage (Matt. 19:3-6).

Scripture clearly forbids same-gender sexual activity between two women or between two men (Rom. 1:26–27). Marriage involves a sexual union (1 Cor. 7:2–5). People of the same gender who claim to be married would sin by engaging in sexual acts with their "marriage partner." It would be immoral, then, for people of the same sex to marry. God judged nations in the past for widespread, unrepentant homosexuality (Jude 7; Lev. 18:22, 24).

The very nature of the homosexual lifestyle is to be sexually promiscuous rather than committed to one marriage partner. In his book about the assault on marriage and the family, William Bennett notes that a homosexual writer says, "Homosexual marriage contracts will have to entail a greater understanding of the need for extramarital outlets."[10] In contrast, God's Word limits sex to one man with one woman in marriage (Heb. 13:4).

In addition, homosexual marriage presents a big problem regarding children. Homosexuals who want to adopt children would morally corrupt children by their lifestyle. God judges those who lead children into sin (Matt. 18:6). And God's plan is for heterosexual marriages to fill the earth with people for the future (Gen. 1:27–28; Mal. 2:14-15). Obviously, homosexual unions do not produce children.

ENTERING MARRIAGE AND SINGLENESS

God has not commanded every person to enter marriage. It is a choice. However, God has communicated certain restrictions in His Word about whom a person may marry.

1. **A believer in Jesus Christ should not marry an unbeliever.**

"Do not be unequally yoked together with unbelievers" **(2 Cor. 6:14).**

To have spiritual harmony in marriage the way God designed it, a Christian should marry only a professing believer who has received Christ as Lord and Savior (1 Cor. 7:39).

2. **A person should not marry a person of the same gender (see preceding section).**

"God gave them up to vile passions. For even their women exchanged the natural use for what is against nature. Likewise also the men, leaving the natural use of the woman, burned in their lust for one another" **(Rom. 1:26–27)**.

Sex is part of marriage and God's Word forbids sexual activity with a person of the same gender.

3. **A person should not marry more than one person (see preceding section).**

"The two shall become one flesh" **(Mark 10:8)**. "A bishop then must be blameless, the husband of one wife" (1 Tim. 3:2). "The elders . . . shepherd the flock of God . . . being examples to the flock" (1 Pet. 5:1-3).

Polygamy is contrary to God's design for marriage, one man with one woman.

4. **A person should not marry a person divorced on other than Biblical grounds, if the former spouse has not remarried, in order to give a chance for reconciliation.**

"A wife is not to depart from her husband. But even if she does depart, let her remain unmarried or be reconciled to her husband. And a husband is not to divorce his wife" **(1 Cor. 7:10–11)**.

Later in this section we will discuss divorce and remarriage and the issue of Biblical exceptions.

5. **A person should not marry a close relative.**

"None of you shall approach anyone who is near of kin to him, to uncover his nakedness" **(Lev. 18:6)**.

The phrase "uncover nakedness" is a reference to engaging in sexual activity. God forbids a sexual relationship between close relatives. First Corinthians 7:1–5 makes clear that sexual relations are supposed to be part of the marriage relationship. Logically then, a person cannot rightly marry near kin if God forbids a sexual relationship in this case.

All people are descendants of Adam and Eve and therefore are distantly related (Gen. 3:20; Acts 17:26). However, God revealed through Moses that He does not want people to marry others who are closer kin than cousins (Leviticus 18:6–16). This law is not just for the nation of Israel, as God judges Gentile nations for violating these laws (Lev. 18:24-25).

In the beginning, a man had no choice but to marry a sister. That is where Cain got his wife. Adam and Eve had many sons and daughters (Gen. 3:20, 5:4). At this early time, genetic risks in pregnancies with near kin were not an issue. By the time Moses gave God's Law in Leviticus, however, pregnancies from marriages with close kin would cause genetic problems.

Now people who are close blood relatives have a much higher chance of begetting offspring with deformities. Geneticists point out, "The closer the biological relationship is between relatives, the more likely that they will have the same faulty gene in common."[11]

Studies also show that sexual acts with close relatives are commonly associated with many emotional and relationship problems.[12]

We have been focusing on what the Bible says about marriage. What about adults who are single? How should single Christian adults think about singleness and marriage? Should a Christian adult seek a marriage relationship or should they remain single? If a Christian woman or Christian man would like to find a Christian marriage partner, how should they go about the matter? How should a Christian young adult live as a single person?

First, single adults should not think they have less value than married adults. Look at singleness, sex, and marriage through the lens of Creation, Fall, and Redemption. Single and married adults are equally created in the image of God (Gen. 1:27). Single and married adults are equally fallen in sin (Rom. 3:10, 23). Single and married adults are equally objects of Christ's redemption (1 Tim. 2:4).

Scripture teaches that one particular advantage single adults have over married couples is that they can give more time to Christian service. "I say to the unmarried and to the widows, it is good for them if they remain even as I am. . . . And this I say for your own profit, not that I may put a leash on you, but for what is proper, and that you may serve the Lord without distraction" (1 Cor. 7:8, 35). Jesus teaches that God gifts some Christian adults to be content as unmarried individuals so they can give their time totally to Christ's service (Matt. 19:10–12).

Second, single adults must think biblically about how to satisfy their sex drive. They must remember that Scripture does not allow them to satisfy sexual urges through same sex activity (Rom. 1:26–27), unmarried sexual intercourse (1 Cor. 6:15–20), or mental lust and pornography (1 Thess. 4:3–7). They must marry to have the Biblical right to sexual relations (1 Cor. 7:1–2; Heb. 13:4).

Single Christian adults should replace sexual lust with close fellowship with God and fellowship with Christians who pursue sexual purity:

> "Flee also youthful lusts, but pursue righteousness . . . with those who call on the Lord out of a pure heart" (2 Tim. 2:22).

If single Christian adults who are dating or courting each other struggle with sexual desire and resisting temptation, they should marry if they are both believers, suitable partners, and able to support themselves: "But if they cannot exercise self-control, let them marry. . . . only in the Lord" (1 Cor. 7:9, 39).

Third, single adults should think practically about seeking a mate. It would be good for single Christian teens and adults to read the chapter on "Single Persons" in Dr. Jay Adams' book, *Christian Living in the Home.*[13] He gives helpful suggestions in this chapter.

Dr. Adams shows genuine concern for single Christian adults who do not believe they have the gift for remaining single and who want to be married. He points out that marriage is God's plan for the majority of people and he advises Christians to pray that God would provide a mate and then seek a mate by spending time with other Christians.

He emphasizes preparing for marriage by studying marriage responsibilities, learning how to biblically solve relationship problems, and developing a vibrant Christian personality. His book is good for single and married Christians to study. He also urges Christian parents and other believers to help Christian adults find a Christian mate.

Also, another essential aspect of looking towards marriage is for the man to make sure he has work to provide for a wife (1 Tim. 5:8). A young man should focus on preparing for work that can support a family in the future. God's Word says, "Prepare your outside work. Make it fit for yourself in the field, and afterward build your house" (Prov. 24:27).

DIVORCE AND REMARRIAGE

There is a worldview clash about the permanence of marriage. **The Christian worldview, based on the Bible, teaches that marriage is a lifelong commitment and that divorce and remarriage on other than biblical grounds constitutes adultery.** Note the emphasis in God's Word on marriage as a life-long commitment:

> "Therefore a man shall leave his father and mother and be joined to his wife, and they shall become one flesh" (Gen. 2:24).

> "So then they are no longer two but one flesh. Therefore, what God has joined together, let not man separate" **(Matt. 19:6).**

> "Whoever divorces his wife and marries another commits adultery against her. And if a woman divorces her husband and marries another, she commits adultery" **(Mark 10:11-12).**

> "The Lord has been witness between you and the wife of your youth, with whom you have dealt treacherously. Yet she is your companion and your wife by covenant. . . . For the Lord God of Israel says that he hates divorce" (Mal. 2:14, 16).

> "For the woman who has a husband is bound by the law to her husband as long as he lives. But if the husband dies, she is released from the law of her husband. So then if while her husband lives, she marries another man, she will be called an adulteress" **(Rom. 7:2-3).**

> "A wife is not to depart from her husband. But even if she does depart, she should remain unmarried or else be reconciled to her husband. And a husband is not to divorce his wife" **(1 Cor. 7:10–11)**.

Jesus warns that divorce and remarriage on unbiblical grounds involves the sin of adultery:

- If a husband divorces his wife on unbiblical grounds and marries someone else, he commits adultery (Matt. 19:9).
- If either a husband or wife divorce their spouse and marry someone else, they commit adultery (Mark 10:11–12).
- If a person marries someone who is divorced while their former spouse has not remarried, they commit adultery (Luke 16:18).
- The person who has been divorced on unbiblical grounds commits adultery when they marry someone else (Matt. 5:32).

Jesus gives a limited allowance for divorce and remarriage in the case of "sexual immorality" (Matt. 5:32; 19:9). Bible-believing Christians differ in their understanding of what this allowance means. We will discuss their views in the following pages.

However, divorce and remarriage on unbiblical grounds is not an unforgiveable sin:

> "The blood of Jesus Christ His Son cleanses us from all sin. . . . If we confess our sins, He is faithful and just to forgive us our sins" (1 John 1:7b, 9).

If a believer has divorced and remarried on unbiblical grounds, he or she should confess their sin to God, receive God's forgiveness, and be faithful to their present husband or wife. Believers who are divorced should seek reconciliation with their spouse (1 Cor. 7:10-11), as long as the other party has not remarried (Deut. 24:1-4).

In contrast to the Christian worldview, Islam and Humanism give broad allowance for divorce for many reasons. The Qur'an does not emphasize that divorce and remarriage involve adultery like the Bible does (note Surah 2:227–232).[14] And the Humanist worldview rejects biblical restrictions on divorce saying, "Ethics is autonomous and situational, needing no theological or ideological sanction. . . . The right to . . . divorce should be recognized."[15]

A couple of worldview writers note the Humanist philosophy of feminist leaders and statements by some feminist leaders attacking the institution of marriage:

> "The feminist movement was begun and has been nourished by leading Humanist women."[16]

> "Feminist Catharine MacKinnon: 'Feminism stresses the indistinguishability of prostitution, marriage, and sexual harassment.' . . . Feminist author, Robin Morgan: 'We can't destroy the inequities between men and women until we destroy marriage.'"[17]

The feminist movement attacked traditional marriage and pushed for no-fault divorce laws, which spread to all of the states.[18] The result is a recent survey in 2008 that found one-third of American adults who had married had experienced divorce.[19] The increase in divorce has also created many personal and societal problems. Consider these observations:

> "According to the scholar Lenore Weitzman, "American divorce law, with historical roots in the English common law, was based on the underlying premise that marriage was a permanent and cherished union which the Church, and then the state, had to protect and preserve. . . . The underlying assumption that divorce . . . should be obtainable only for cause (e.g., adultery and desertion) has been essentially thrown out."[20]

> "Judith Wallerstein . . . in her landmark book, *The Unexpected Legacy of Divorce,* revealed: 'Children from divorced and remarried families . . . There is earlier sexual activity, more children born out of wedlock, less marriage, and more divorce. Numerous studies show that adult children of divorce have more psychological problems than those raised in intact marriages."[21]

> "Those who divorce are far more likely to experience stress-related physical and emotional illness, to engage in substance abuse . . . to commit suicide. . . . 86% of unhappily married people who stay together find that five years later their marriages are happier."[22]

In contrast to Humanism and Islam, the Bible teaches a strict view about divorce and remarriage. However, Scripture does give a limited allowance for divorce in the case of "sexual immorality." Jesus says:

> "Whoever divorces his wife for any reason <u>except sexual immorality</u> causes her to commit adultery: (Matt. 5:32). "Whoever divorces his wife, <u>except for sexual immorality</u>, and marries another, commits adultery" (Matt. 19:9, emphasis mine).

Christians differ in their understanding of what this allowance for divorce for sexual immorality means in Scripture.

A number of Bible-believing ministers believe that the exception in Matthew 5:32 and 19:9 does not refer to sexual sin by a lawfully married husband or wife. They believe if a man and woman are in a biblically defined marriage, the Bible does not give any grounds for divorce, even for sexual sin after marriage. They note that the exception occurs only in Matthew's Gospel and that Matthew wrote especially for a Jewish audience. For example, see articles by John Piper.[23]

These ministers emphasize Paul's statement that a married person is bound to their spouse as long as that person lives and that marriage to someone else while that spouse lives involves adultery (Rom. 7:2–3). They emphasize the statements of Jesus that divorce and remarriage involve adultery (Mark 10:11–12) and that if God has joined a man and woman together in marriage, man should not dissolve that union in divorce (Mark 10:9). However, they differ among themselves on exactly what "except for sexual immorality" means in these verses.

Some of them believe the allowance for divorce refers to dissolving an unbiblical marriage union that is immoral, such as marriage to a close relative in violation of God's Law or a same-sex marriage (Lev. 18:6; Rom. 1:26–27). But they do not see any biblical grounds for dissolving a biblical marriage union. A theology professor, Carl Laney, has written a book, *The Divorce Myth,* advancing this view.[24]

Others believe this allowance refers to putting away a betrothed spouse for sexual sin during a betrothal period, but that it does not allow divorce after the marriage is finalized.[25]

The Jews had a custom of betrothal that involved a binding contract for marriage, followed later by the final wedding ceremony and the sexual union. The Jews allowed divorce from the betrothal contract in a case of sexual sin during the betrothal period (Matt. 1:18–19).

The historic Protestant view emphasizes from Scripture that marriage is a life-long commitment and opposes the idea that a person can divorce their spouse for just any and every reason. This view would agree that Scripture allowed divorce for sexual sin during the Jewish betrothal period. It would also agree that it is biblical to dissolve an unbiblical marriage relationship such as marriage to a close relative or a same-sex marriage.

However, the historic Protestant view also believes that the exception in Matthew 5:32 and 19:9 has direct reference to sexual sin by a husband or wife as grounds for divorce and remarriage. Bible-believing theologians have written books explaining this viewpoint.[26] John MacArthur has written articles supporting this view.[27] Jay Adams' book, *Marriage, Divorce and Remarriage in the Bible,* gives a very clear presentation of the historic Protestant view.[28]

Dr. Adams gives evidence that the Greek word for sexual immorality refers to every kind of sexual sin, including sexual sin by a married person.[29] He also explains that Matthew 5:32 and Matthew 19:9 are dealing with marriage, not betrothal.[30] Thus, the historic Protestant view is that the phrase "except for sexual immorality" allows a person to divorce a spouse who engages in sex (heterosexual or homosexual) with someone other than their spouse.

However, this is permission for divorce in cases of adultery through sexual sin, but not a command. Also, an opportunity should be given for the possibility of repentance and reconciliation according to 1 Corinthians 7:10–11. Note the example of the prophet Hosea in the Old Testament restoring his unfaithful wife (Hosea 3:1-3).

Those who hold the historic Protestant view would also say that if a person has biblical grounds to divorce, then they have biblical grounds to remarry.[31] They believe the exception about divorce allows the innocent spouse to divorce the sexually sinning spouse and to marry someone else if the sinning spouse does not repent, without being guilty of adultery.

The historic Protestant view also notes the regulation about divorce and remarriage in Deuteronomy 24:1-4. This passage forbids a person who divorces and marries someone else to dissolve that second marriage and go back to the first spouse. Thus, if a divorced spouse remarries someone else, the other spouse has no further hope of reconciliation as 1 Corinthians 7:10-11 calls for and would have liberty to marry someone else, according to the historic Protestant understanding of Scripture. Dr. Adams explains this further in his book.[32]

First Corinthians 7 addresses the question of divorce and remarriage in the case of an unbeliever and a believer. The Bible tells a believer not to enter a marriage with an unbeliever (2 Corinthian 6:14). However, if a Christian is in a marriage with a non-Christian, a believer should remain married if the unbeliever wants to continue the marriage (1 Corinthians 7:12–13). The historic Protestant view is that Scripture gives a believer liberty to marry another believer if an unbelieving mate divorces or abandons them (1 Corinthians 7:15, 27–28, 39).[33]

SUMMARY OF VIEWS ABOUT MARRIAGE, DIVORCE, AND REMARRIAGE

Concerning conservative Protestant differences about divorce and remarriage, the historic Protestant view understands Scripture to allow for remarriage after a divorce if:

- A person divorces a spouse because of sexual sin.
- A divorced person's spouse remarries with someone else, which eliminates the possibility of reconciliation.
- An unbeliever divorces or abandons a believer.

Other conservative Protestant views about divorce and remarriage would:

- Agree with the historic Protestant view that a person has biblical liberty to remarry after the death of a spouse;
- Disagree with the historic Protestant view about other allowances for remarriage after a divorce, believing that the Bible does not give any grounds for divorce and remarriage if the marriage is a biblical marriage union.

Although Bible-believing Christians differ in their understanding of the exception for divorce and allowance for remarriage, they agree on the biblical view of marriage as one man committed to one woman for life and would agree in opposing the broad allowance for divorce and remarriage that is found in other worldviews. It would be helpful to ask your pastor what his understanding is of the exception concerning divorce in Matthew 5:31-32 and Matthew 19:9 and the reasons for his view.

In any case, a believer must keep a clear conscience before God concerning divorce and remarriage (Acts 24:16). Believers should get biblical counsel from Christian parents and Christian pastors about a potential marriage to be sure they do not marry someone outside what the Lord through the Bible would allow (Prov. 11:14; Matt. 19:3-9). If a believer personally is not confident about whether entering a new marriage is biblically right in their situation, they should not enter the marriage, because "whatever is not from faith is sin" (Rom. 14:23).

CONCERNING WORLDVIEW DIFFERENCES ABOUT MARRIAGE

THE PERMANENCE OF MARRIAGE

- The Islamic worldview gives a broad allowance for divorce and remarriage.
- The Humanist worldview gives a broad allowance for divorce and remarriage.
- The Christian worldview views divorce and remarriage as involving adultery (except for grounds of sexual immorality) and views marriage as a life-long commitment.

THE RELATIONSHIP IN MARRIAGE

- The Islamic worldview allows a man to beat his wife.
- The Humanist worldview allows sexual activity outside of marriage and rejects the idea of a wife submitting to the leadership of her husband.
- The Christian worldview teaches that marriage is a covenant companionship that brings one man and one woman into a loving, intimate one-flesh union, with the husband as a loving leader and with no allowance for wife-beating, and that sexual activity is exclusively for one man with one woman in marriage.

TYPES OF MARRIAGE

- The Islamic worldview allows polygamy, for a man to have multiple wives.
- The Humanist worldview accepts same-gender marriage as legitimate.
- The Christian worldview teaches on the authority of the Bible, the Word of God, that the only legitimate marriage union is one man committed to one woman for life.

THE DANVERS STATEMENT ON BIBLICAL MANHOOD AND WOMANHOOD

(https://cbmw.org/about/danvers-statement)

The Danvers Statement summarizes the need for the Council on Biblical Manhood and Womanhood (CBMW) and serves as an overview of our core beliefs. This statement was prepared by several evangelical leaders at a CBMW meeting in Danvers, Massachusetts, in December of 1987. It was first published in final form by the CBMW in Wheaton, Illinois, in November of 1988.

RATIONALE

We have been moved in our purpose by the following contemporary developments which we observe with deep concern:

1. The widespread uncertainty and confusion in our culture regarding the complementary differences between masculinity and femininity;

2. the tragic effects of this confusion in unraveling the fabric of marriage woven by God out of the beautiful and diverse strands of manhood and womanhood;

3. the increasing promotion given to feminist egalitarianism with accompanying distortions or neglect of the glad harmony portrayed in Scripture between the loving, humble leadership of redeemed husbands and the intelligent, willing support of that leadership by redeemed wives;

4. the widespread ambivalence regarding the values of motherhood, vocational homemaking, and the many ministries historically performed by women;

5. the growing claims of legitimacy for sexual relationships which have Biblically and historically been considered illicit or perverse, and the increase in pornographic portrayal of human sexuality;

6. the upsurge of physical and emotional abuse in the family;

7. the emergence of roles for men and women in church leadership that do not conform to Biblical teaching but backfire in the crippling of Biblically faithful witness;

8. the increasing prevalence and acceptance of hermeneutical oddities devised to reinterpret apparently plain meanings of Biblical texts;

9. the consequent threat to Biblical authority as the clarity of Scripture is jeopardized and the accessibility of its meaning to ordinary people is withdrawn into the restricted realm of technical ingenuity;

10.and behind all this the apparent accommodation of some within the church to the spirit of the age at the expense of winsome, radical Biblical authenticity which in the power of the Holy Spirit may reform rather than reflect our ailing culture.

AFFIRMATIONS

Based on our understanding of Biblical teachings, we affirm the following:

1. Both Adam and Eve were created in God's image, equal before God as persons and distinct in their manhood and womanhood (Gen 1:26-27, 2:18).

2. Distinctions in masculine and feminine roles are ordained by God as part of the created order, and should find an echo in every human heart (Gen 2:18, 21-24; 1 Cor. 11:7-9; 1 Tim 2:12-14).

3. Adam's headship in marriage was established by God before the Fall, and was not a result of sin (Gen 2:16-18, 21-24, 3:1-13; 1 Cor. 11:7-9).

4. The Fall introduced distortions into the relationships between men and women (Gen 3:1-7, 12, 16).

A. In the home, the husband's loving, humble headship tends to be replaced by domination or passivity; the wife's intelligent, willing submission tends to be replaced by usurpation or servility.

B. In the church, sin inclines men toward a worldly love of power or an abdication of spiritual responsibility, and inclines women to resist limitations on their roles or to neglect the use of their gifts in appropriate ministries.

5. The Old Testament, as well as the New Testament, manifests the equally high value and dignity which God attached to the roles of both men and women (Gen 1:26-27, 2:18; Gal 3:28). Both Old and New Testaments also affirm the principle of male headship in the family and in the covenant community (Gen 2:18; Eph 5:21-33; Col 3:18-19; 1 Tim 2:11-15).

6. Redemption in Christ aims at removing the distortions introduced by the curse.

A. In the family, husbands should forsake harsh or selfish leadership and grow in love and care for their wives; wives should forsake resistance to their husbands' authority and grow in willing, joyful submission to their husbands' leadership (Eph 5:21-33; Col 3:18-19; Tit 2:3-5; 1 Pet 3:1-7).

B. In the church, redemption in Christ gives men and women an equal share in the blessings of salvation; nevertheless, some governing and teaching roles within the church are restricted to men (Gal 3:28; 1 Cor. 11:2-16; 1 Tim 2:11-15).

7. In all of life Christ is the supreme authority and guide for men and women, so that no earthly submission-domestic, religious, or civil-ever implies a mandate to follow a human authority into sin (Dan 3:10-18; Acts 4:19-20, 5:27-29; 1 Pet 3:1-2).

8. In both men and women a heartfelt sense of call to ministry should never be used to set aside Biblical criteria for particular ministries (1 Tim 2:11-15, 3:1-13; Tit 1:5-9). Rather, Biblical teaching should remain the authority for testing our subjective discernment of God's will.

9. With half the world's population outside the reach of indigenous evangelism; with countless other lost people in those societies that have heard the gospel; with the stresses and miseries of sickness, malnutrition, homelessness, illiteracy, ignorance, aging, addiction, crime, incarceration, neuroses, and loneliness, no man or woman who feels a passion from God to make His grace known in word and deed need ever live without a fulfilling ministry for the glory of Christ and the good of this fallen world (1 Cor. 12:7-21).

10. We are convinced that a denial or neglect of these principles will lead to increasingly destructive consequences in our families, our churches, and the culture at large.[34]

THINKING BIBLICALLY ABOUT SEXUAL ISSUES

A WORLDVIEW CLASH ABOUT SEXUAL ACTIVITY

There is a great worldview clash between the Christian worldview, the Humanist worldview and the Islamic worldview about sex and marriage. The Humanist worldview appeals to man's reason and desires as authority for its views about sex and marriage. The Islamic worldview appeals to the Qur'an, the Hadith and the example of Mohammad as authority for its views about sex and marriage. The Christian worldview appeals to the Bible as God's Word as the ultimate authority about sex and marriage.

The Bible sets forth a positive view of sex within marriage and a negative view of sex outside of marriage. Scripture teaches that God created sex and marriage (Gen. 1:28, 2:24-25). The Bible teaches that sex within marriage is a good gift from God (Heb. 13:4; Gen. 1:28-31). The book of Song of Solomon shows that God designed sex within marriage to be pleasurable for both husband and wife. Scripture teaches that a husband and a wife have equal rights to each other sexually within marriage (1 Cor. 7:2-5).

However, God's Word reveals that God judges sexual activity outside of marriage as a sinful perversion of His good design. God's Word declares:

> "Marriage is honorable among all, and the bed undefiled; but fornicators and adulterers God will judge" (Heb. 13:4).

The following pages will give further explanation from Scripture about sexual sin. Also, Scripture teaches that God's design for marriage is one man with one woman (Matt. 19:6; 1 Tim. 3:2, 12; Deut. 17:17). Polygamous marriages and same gender marriages are contrary to God's plan for marriage.

Similar to the Christian worldview, Islam generally teaches against sex outside of marriage. However, in contrast to the Christian worldview, the Islamic worldview appeals to the Qur'an and the practice of Mohammad to allow a man to have sexual relations with multiple wives.[35] And, different from the teaching of the Bible, the Qur'an gives Muslim men wide latitude for divorce.[36] See the preceding sections about marriage for the teaching of the Bible in relation to divorce and to polygamy.

Islamic teaching also motivates Muslim men in this life with the hope of having multiple women for themselves in heaven for being a devoted Muslim.[37] Some Muslim men have looked to the Qur'an to justify sexually possessing and violating women conquered in war.[38] However, this is rape, and God's Word condemns coercive sexual activity (Deut. 22:25-29).

Interestingly, the Islamic terrorist leader, Osama Bin Laden, condemned the United States for sexual immorality and sensuality. However, after he was killed, it was found that he had a huge amount of pornography on his computer.[39] Similar stories have surfaced about some other Islamic terrorists as well.

Humanism differs sharply with the Christian worldview about sexual activity. For centuries, fallen human culture has viewed sexual activity outside of marriage as acceptable behavior. God's Word describes the fallen culture of the world in relation to sexual sin:

> "For all that is in the world—the lusts of the flesh, the lusts of the eyes, and the pride of life—is not of the Father, but is of the world" (1 John 2:16).

People with a Humanist way of thinking have greatly influenced human culture in the world in non-Muslim nations about sex and marriage. Humanism in all its varieties rejects the teaching of the Bible that all sexual activity outside of marriage is sinful. For example:

> Secular Humanism: *The Humanist Manifesto* states, "The many varieties of sexual exploration should not in themselves be considered evil."[40]

> New Age Humanism: A New Age Humanist writer says, "An individual's sexual preference should be viewed as neither good nor evil."[41]

> Marxist Humanism: An expert writer on Marxism notes, "Some communist leaders advocated promiscuity to replace marriage and the family . . . and 'nationalized women.'"[42]

For a number of centuries, Christian morals, based on the teaching of the Bible, strongly influenced Western culture in Europe and America in relation to sex and marriage. Although people fell into sexual sin in these nations during that time, there was a prevailing cultural view that sex outside of marriage was wrong. However, a great sexual revolution took place.

In the mid-twentieth century, Dr. Alfred Kinsey wrote two books, from a Humanist perspective, about sexuality in males and females in America that led to a sexual revolution in America and other nations. In her book, *Sexual Sabotage,* Dr. Judith Reisman noted that Kinsey's samples included observations involving sexual abuse of children.[43] She notes the influence of Darwinian evolution on his worldview, as well as his lack of faith.[44] She states:

> "Kinsey published his distorted data in *Sexual Behavior in the Human Male* in 1948 and *Sexual Behavior in the Human Female* in 1953 and, as his fans say, the world was never the same. . . . While Kinsey's narrative described 'a period of sexual repression,' his statistics claimed that the generation was sexually immoral, promiscuous and deviant. Why the contradiction? As one who was there, I witnessed firsthand his sexual slander of heroic Americans. And, as one of the elders now, I have researched Alfred Kinsey for thirty-five years, finding that he and his cult libeled our World War II warrior generation in order to validate his own cowardly perversions by creating a 'sexual revolution.' . . . In promoting premarital and extramarital sex, Kinsey's reports had wide reaching effects on sexual relationships outside of marriage, as rampant promiscuity led to increases in venereal diseases, illegitimacy and prostitution."[45]

SINFUL SEXUAL ACTIVITY

In contrast to our Humanistic culture, the Bible teaches that all sexual activity outside of biblical marriage is sinful. Scripture warns Christians not to be deceived by the thinking of our fallen world (Rom. 12:2; 1 John 2:15-17). God's Word warns us against deceived thinking about a sexually immoral lifestyle. A person who does not repent and find deliverance through Jesus Christ from a sexually immoral lifestyle will not be part of Christ's eternal kingdom:

> "Do not be deceived. Neither fornicators . . . nor adulterers, nor homosexuals . . . will inherit the kingdom of God" (1 Cor. 6:9–10).

> "Put off, concerning your former conduct, the old man, which grows corrupt according to the deceitful lusts. . . . No fornicator . . . has any inheritance in the kingdom of Christ. . . . Let no one deceive you with empty words" (Eph. 4:22, 5:5-6).

> "Now the works of the flesh are evident, which are: adultery, fornication, uncleanness, lewdness. . . . Those who practice such things will not inherit the kingdom of God. . . . Do not be deceived. . . . He who sows to his own flesh will of the flesh reap corruption" (Gal, 5:19, 21; 6:7-8).

The Bible teaches that human beings have a fallen nature and are prone to sexual sins. Jesus said, "For from within, out of the heart of men, proceed evil thoughts, adulteries, fornications" (Mark 7:21). Some people try to twist the Scripture to get away from God's condemnation of various sexual sins. But God's Word warns about those who would pervert the teaching of Scripture to excuse lewd conduct (Jude 1:4; 2 Pet. 2:14–19, 3:16). We need to use Scripture to clearly identify sexual sins so that we can readily recognize and avoid them.

The statement of Jesus in Mark 7:21 mentions sexual immorality and adultery as sinful expressions of fallen human nature. First Corinthians 6:9-10 and Hebrews 13:4 also use these same terms together to describe sinful sexual activity. Respected commentaries on Scripture give good explanations of these terms. The biblical term "adultery" refers to unfaithfulness to the marriage covenant.[46] The biblical term "fornication" or "sexual immorality" refers to any kind of sexual act outside of biblical marriage.[47]

In the Ten Commandments, God says, "You shall not commit adultery" (Exo. 20:14). Adultery involves unfaithfulness to the marriage covenant, such as engaging in sexual acts with someone other than one's spouse (John 8:3–4). Even if a spouse consents to the other spouse having sex with another person, it is still adultery, because it violates God's law about marriage. Jesus teaches that adultery also involves sexually desiring someone outside of marriage (Matt. 5:27-30) and divorce and remarriage on unbiblical grounds (Matt. 5:31-32).

God's Word commands us to "flee sexual immorality" (1 Cor. 6:18). One man and one woman must be committed to each other in marriage before engaging in sex because it is a part of God's design for marriage (Heb. 13:4). The Apostle Paul summarizes God's perspective on sexual immorality:

> "For this is the will of God, your sanctification; that you should abstain from sexual immorality; that each of you should know how to possess his own vessel in sanctification and honor, not in passion of lust like the Gentiles who do not know God; that no one take advantage of and defraud his brother in this matter, because the Lord is the avenger of all such, as we also forewarned you and testified. For God did not call us to uncleanness, but in holiness" (1 Thess. 4:3–7).

This passage explains that believers must "abstain from sexual immorality" by refusing to engage in any sexual act outside of biblical marriage. Christians need to use their body honorably, instead of using it to express "passion of lust" like those who don't know God. "Passion of lust" can include touching that is sexually arousing outside of sexual intercourse.

The Bible warns us about "deceitful lusts" (Eph. 4:22). People might deceitfully rationalize that as long as they do not engage in sexual intercourse before marriage, they can do everything short of that and still be "okay." But God's Word forbids touching of another person's body in a sexually arousing way outside of marriage (note Prov. 5:15–20; Ezek. 23:18, 21).

Jesus also warned against sexual lust and sexual touching by telling us to cut off the hand to deal with sinful sexual desire (Matt. 5:27–30). Obviously, He is not calling for actual physical mutilation. By calling us to cut off the hand, Jesus teaches us to cut off, or abstain from, all sexual touching that expresses or arouses sexual desire outside of marriage. God has designed intimate sexual touching only for marriage (Song of Sol. 2:6–7; Prov. 5:18–19). The Christian authors of a book on sexual purity give a helpful definition:

> "Sexual purity is receiving no sexual gratification from anything or anyone outside of your husband or wife."[48]

Sexual immorality also includes homosexual conduct. The Bible clearly teaches that sexual activity between people of the same gender is sinful and judged by God. Humanism views homosexual conduct as acceptable. Some people, who try to mix Christian profession with a homosexual lifestyle, have attempted to reinterpret the Scripture to justify homosexual conduct. The Bible warns us about people who twist Scripture to justify sexual sin:

> "There will be false teachers among you . . . they allure through the lusts of the flesh. . . Untaught and unstable people twist to their own destruction . . . the Scriptures" (2 Pet. 2:1, 18; 3:16).

For example, some people try to get away from the Bible's judgment on homosexual conduct by claiming that God did not judge Sodom and Gomorrah for homosexual activity, but rather for pride in wealth and failure to help the poor. Ezekiel 16:49 does mention pride in wealth and failure to help the poor as part of the reason for God's judgment on these cities. However, Ezekiel 16:50 adds an "and," and it says that in addition to those sins, those cities also committed "abomination."

The same Hebrew word that is translated "abomination" in Ezekiel 16:50 is also used in Leviticus 18:22 to describe God's view of homosexual activity. The teaching of Leviticus 18 was not a law for Jews only, as some claim. Leviticus 18:24-25 states that God judged Gentile nations for engaging in homosexual sins, as well as other sexual sins:

> "None of you shall approach anyone who is near of kin to him, to uncover his nakedness. . . . You shall not lie carnally with your neighbor's wife. . . .You shall not lie with a male as with a woman; it is an abomination. Nor shall you mate with any animal. . . . By all these the nations are defiled which I am casting out before you. . . . Therefore I visit the punishment of its iniquity upon it" (Lev. 18:6, 20, 22-25).

The angels whom God sent to rescue Lot from Sodom faced homosexual advances from men from all over the city of Sodom (Gen. 19:4-7). God poured out His judgment on

Sodom and Gomorrah shortly after that (Gen. 19:15-29). The epistle of Jude makes it clear that homosexuality was a sin that led to God's judgment upon these cities:

> "Sodom and Gomorrah and the cities around them . . . having given themselves to sexual immorality and gone after strange flesh are set forth as an example, suffering the vengeance of eternal fire" (Jude 1:7).

God's moral law for all people forbids homosexual conduct. Some people claim the Bible writers did not understand homosexual orientation; however, **God's Word rejects as sinful both male and female homosexual desire and behavior:**

> "For this reason God gave them up to vile passions. For even their women exchanged the natural use for what is against nature. Likewise also the men, leaving the natural use of the woman, burned in their lust for one another, men with men committing what is shameful and receiving in themselves the penalty of their error which was due" **(Rom. 1:26–27).**

Homosexuals often argue that they were born that way and cannot change. Scripture does address orientation. The Bible views both heterosexual desire for sex outside of marriage (Matt. 5:27-30) and desire for homosexual sex (Rom. 1:26-27) as sinful. **God's Word teaches that Christ has power to deliver homosexual and heterosexual sinners from sin:**

> "Neither fornicators, nor adulterers, nor homosexuals . . . will inherit the kingdom of God. And such were some of you. But you were washed, you were sanctified . . . in the name of the Lord Jesus" **(1 Cor. 6:9–11).**

Also, a Christian book on sexual purity reports studies showing that a number of men and women have left homosexuality.[49] A former homosexual wrote a book about his salvation through Christ and leaving his homosexual lifestyle.[50] And in recent years a female lesbian professor came to salvation in Christ through the witness of a Christian church. She left her former lifestyle and is now married to a Christian pastor and wrote a book about her testimony.[51]

Christian scholars have written recent books that deal with homosexual claims in light of Scripture. Denny Burk and Heath Lambert have written a recent helpful book on the issue of homosexuality, orientation, and change from the perspective of God's Word.[52] Al Mohler has edited a helpful book that refutes homosexual misinterpretation of Scripture.[53]

Dr. Jeffrey Satinover is a researcher and psychologist who has written about homosexuality. He cites research that shows that most young boys who experiment with homosexuality give it up, and he documents that the claim that homosexuality is genetic is based on flawed research.[54] Dr. Satinover also found that the vast majority of homosexuals are very promiscuous and that homosexual sex is linked to AIDS and many diseases.[55]

The American Psychological Association on their website concedes:

> "Although much research has examined the possible genetic, hormonal, developmental, social and cultural influences on sexual orientation, no findings have emerged that permit scientists to conclude that sexual orientation is determined by any particular factor or factors."[56]

Peter Hubbard, a Christian minister who wrote about homosexuality, notes:

> "In 2010 the Swedish Twin Registry was examined to see how many identical twin pairs (where at least one of the pair described himself as 'gay') were both living a homosexual lifestyle . . . If homosexuality is primarily genetic we should assume that if one twin is homosexual, the other should be as well. However, the research showed that only seven out of 71 identical twin pairs were both gay. . . . When genes, hormones and environment are viewed as determinative rather than formative, we are tempted to treat ourselves and others as mere biological or hormonal machines. . . . But God offers a very different narrative. . . . We are relational beings who are created to worship our Maker. . . . Not every desire is helpful. . . . We need God to satisfy our heart."[57]

Also associated with the homosexual movement is the transgender movement, where people seek to change their sexual identity. However, God's Word makes clear that God created only two genders and made mankind either male or female from the beginning (Gen. 1:26-28). People should accept the biological gender with which they were born, because that is the way that God designed them. Many people who try to change their gender identity regret it later. And there are people who had struggles with gender acceptance who received counseling that helped them accept their biological gender.

Homosexual activists often accuse Christians of hate for opposing their lifestyle and calling it sinful. A few professing Christians wrongly engage in ugly name-calling, protest, and hatred for homosexuals. However, the Bible exhorts Christians to deal with wrong views and lifestyles by "speaking the truth in love" (Eph. 4:15).

However, it is not hate to call homosexual conduct sinful, just as it not hate to rebuke as sin pride, drunkenness, coveting, theft, heterosexual sin, dishonoring of parents, dirty talk, lying, etc. It is not hatred for a doctor to warn patients about choices that will harm their health. Likewise, it is an act of love for God and love for neighbor to lovingly warn people about sins that will lead to their destruction. Christians know they also are sinners who need God's grace. Homosexuals and all people are sinners who need God's redeeming grace (Rom. 3:23).

THE ISSUE OF ABORTION

Accompanying the modern sexual revolution has been an increase in pregnancies outside of marriage and the legalization of abortion on demand. The Humanist worldview is committed to legalized abortion on demand. *The Humanist Manifesto* urges that "the right to abortion . . . should be recognized."[58] Humanistic environmental groups advocate abortion to limit human population.[59] In recent years, the Marxist Humanist government in China limited families to one child and forced women to have an abortion or sterilization if they had a second pregnancy.[60]

A number of evolutionist biology textbooks have taught that the human embryo in the womb is like an animal embryo and recapitulates its evolutionary history in its development in the womb.[61] So, consistent with evolutionist thinking, if man evolved from animals and the human embryo is going through animal stages in the womb, and if we can kill unwanted or defective animals, why not allow the killing of an unwanted or defective fetus in the womb?

The Christian worldview opposes abortion and sees the **preborn child as a real person:**

> "You formed my inward parts; You covered me in my mother's womb. I will praise You, for I am fearfully and wonderfully made . . . My frame was not hidden from You, when I was made in secret" **(Psalm 139:13-15).**

The Bible describes specific individuals as real persons in the womb. In the womb, John the Baptist made conscious responses (Luke 1:41–44). God knew and called Jeremiah and the Apostle Paul while they were in their mother's wombs (Jer. 1:5; Gal. 1:15). And Jacob and Esau are described as struggling with one another in the womb (Gen. 25:22–23). God's Law punishes a person for causing the death of an infant in the womb (Exo. 21:22-23).

A Christian writer on the abortion issue, Randy Alcorn, reports quotes from scientists who testified before the U. S. senate about when life begins. These scientists testified that scientific evidence supports the assertion that human life begins at conception:

> "Dr. Alfred Bongioanni, professor of pediatrics and obstetrics at the University of Pennsylvania, stated, 'I have learned from my earliest medical education that human life begins at the time of conception.'
>
> Dr. Jerome LeJeune, professor of genetics . . . "After fertilization has taken place a new human being has come into being. . . . It is plain experimental evidence."
>
> Professor Micheline Matthew-Roth, Harvard University Medical School: "It is incorrect to say that biological data cannot be decisive. . . . It is scientifically correct to say that an individual human life begins at conception. . . . Our laws, one function of which is to help preserve the lives of our people, should be based on accurate scientific data."[62]

National Right to Life reports that there were over 60 million abortions in the United States from 1973-2014.[63] Carol Everett, a former abortion provider who left the industry, says,

"There are no words to describe how bad it really is. . . . They hurt and they are very painful to the baby, and yes, they are very, very painful to the woman. . . . I've seen six people hold a woman on the table while they did her abortion."[64]

A former abortion doctor says, "As a doctor, you are sitting there tearing . . . arms and legs off of babies and putting them in a stack on top of a table."[65]

Abortion involves taking the life of the preborn child. It is an intentional act. The Bible forbids murder (Exo. 20:13). And God values children and says, "Behold, children are a heritage from the Lord. The fruit of the womb is a reward" (Psalm 127:3). God demands that we respect even the life of those who are handicapped (Lev. 19:14). Therefore, we should respect the life of the innocent child in the womb, even if we think the child may be physically handicapped.

THINKING BIBLICALLY ABOUT SEXUAL LUST

Sexual lust is a serious and widespread issue. We know that is true from the repeated warnings in Scripture, human experience and current reports. Scripture repeatedly warns us about lust or sinful desires. We are not thinking biblically if we think the only problems with sex concern wrong activity and fail to see problems with lust or wrong desires. Jesus strongly warned us in God's Word that the sin of adultery can involve more than actions. **Jesus teaches that another way to commit adultery is through sexual lust** and that lust is a serious matter:

"You have heard that it was said to those of old, 'You shall not commit adultery.' But I say to you that whoever looks at a woman to lust for her has already committed adultery with her in his heart. If your right eye causes you to sin, pluck it out and cast it from you. For it is more profitable for you that one of your members perish than for your whole body to be cast into Hell" **(Matt. 5:27-29).**

It is good to sexually desire one's husband or wife in marriage. However, it is wrong to desire sex outside of marriage with someone or to sexually fantasize about someone to whom we are not married. Lust can involve other things in addition to sex, but it definitely includes sinful sexual desire. Note these many warnings in Scripture about lust (emphasis mine):

"You shall not covet your neighbor's wife" (Exo. 20:17).

"For the commandment is a lamp . . . to keep you from the evil woman. . . . Do not lust after her beauty in your heart" (Prov. 6:23-25).

"For out of the heart proceed evil thoughts . . . adulteries, fornications" (Matt. 15:19).

"Let us walk properly . . . not in lewdness and lust. . . . Make no provision for the flesh to fulfill its lusts" (Rom. 13:13-14).

"For the flesh lusts against the Spirit. . . . The works of the flesh are evident, which are adultery, fornication, uncleanness, lewdness" (Gal. 5:17, 19).

"Put off your former conduct, the old man which grows corrupt according to the deceitful lusts" (Eph. 4:22).

"Therefore put to death your members which are on the earth: fornication, uncleanness, passion, evil desire" (Col. 3:5).

" . . . Abstain from sexual immorality . . . not in passion of lust like the Gentiles who do not know God" (1 Thess. 4:3, 5).

"Flee also youthful lusts, but pursue righteousness" (2 Tim. 2:22).

"For the grace of God that brings salvation has appeared . . . teaching us that denying ungodliness and worldly lusts, we should live soberly, righteously" (Tit. 2:11-12).

"Therefore gird up the loins of your mind . . . not conforming yourselves to the former lusts . . . Abstain from fleshly lusts which war against the soul. . . . No longer live in the flesh for the lusts of men . . . doing the will of the Gentiles, when we walked in lewdness, lusts" (1 Pet. 1:13-14; 2:11; 4:2-3).

"Then the Lord knows how to . . . reserve the unjust under punishment for the day of judgment, especially those who walk according to the flesh in the lust of uncleanness . . . having eyes full of adultery" (2 Pet. 2:9, 10, 14).

"Do not love the world . . . For all that is in the world, the lusts of the flesh, the lusts of the eyes . . . is not of the Father but is of the world" (1 John 2:15-16).

"Mockers . . . who would walk according to their own ungodly lusts" (Jude 1:18).

Note that Scripture teaches that lust is deceitful (Eph. 4:22) and that ongoing lust leads to God's judgment if we do not receive God's forgiveness and deliverance (Matt. 5:29).

Every one of us are born with a sinful and deceitful heart (Jer. 17:9) and from that sinful heart come "evil thoughts . . . fornication" (Mark 7:21). All of us have been guilty of thinking impure lustful thoughts. However, for many people sexual lust has become a constant mind-dominating problem rather than an intermittent temptation. With the sexual revolution of the last century, our culture is presenting us with many more temptations to sexual lust. Every man and every woman, including Christians, face a battle with temptation to lustful thoughts.

Randy Alcorn, in his book on sexual purity, shared these observations from his many years of Christian ministry about the widespread struggle with lust that men and women face:

> "Every day, Christian men and women forfeit future happiness for the sake of temporary sexual stimulation. . . . Surveys indicate that the sexual morality of today's Christians has become almost indistinguishable from that of non-Christians. . . . Purity and impurity . . . slice to the living core of who you are and who you will become. . . . Christ's disciples did not live by lust, which truly set them apart from the pagan culture around them. . . . Lust is fed by whatever we've deposited in our brains. . . . What kind of person we are becoming is determined by what we are taking into our brains. . . . To protect out purity, we need to set mental boundaries."[66]

Christian books have been written that recognize the universal battle we face in this area. For example, Christian men Stephen Arterburn and Fred Stoeker wrote two books, *Every Man's Battle*[67] and *Every Young Man's Battle,*[68] to help adult men and teenage young men deal with the temptation to sexual lust they all face. Similarly, a Christian woman, Shannon Ethridge, wrote two books, *Every Woman's 69* and *Every Young Woman's Battle,*[70] to help adult women and teenage young women deal with the temptation to sexual lust they all face.

The Bible warns against sexual lust associated with touching private parts of the body for sexual arousal between people who are not married to each other (Matt. 5:27-29; Prov. 5:20; Ezek. 23:21; 1 Thess. 4:4-5). Scripture also warns us against sexually suggestive and arousing talk (Prov. 7:10-23; Eph. 5:3-4). Scripture warns us that sexual lust is especially stirred by sight (Matt. 5:27-28). Viewing nudity or sex acts, either live or in moving pictures or still photos, especially stirs lust.

God's Word addresses the issue of nakedness. Before their fall into sin, Adam and Eve went about naked in their work and in fellowship with God in the Garden. However, after their sin, Adam and Eve felt shame and felt the need for covering before God. God then instituted clothing for man (Gen. 3:21). Since then, it has been natural for people in the world to seek clothing (Matt. 6:31–32). John Murray, a Christian theologian, wrote about this beginning of clothing as a divine principle for human conduct. He observes:

> "God Himself clothed our first parents. By that action clothing is established as an institution and it has the force of a commandment. Hence we have an ordinance, adherence to which is required of man in his state of sin."[71]

Scripture describes nakedness as something that should be covered. A demon possessed man went about naked, but he was "clothed and in his right mind" after Jesus saved him (Mark 5:15). Noah's sons covered their father's nakedness (Gen. 9:23). Scripture instructs women to dress modestly (1 Tim. 2:9). Scripture describes uncovering of male or female buttocks or genitals or female breasts as shameful (1 Chron. 19:4; Isa. 20:4, 47:1-3; Ezek. 23:18, 21; Rev. 16:15). King David fell into sin after watching Bathsheba bathe (2 Sam. 11).

God's Word endorses nakedness between husband and wife in private in marriage (Song of Solomon). Also, people may need to be uncovered in a private, non-sexual setting to receive medical care. But we need to avoid sensual displays of the body that incite lust.

PORNOGRAPHY AND SEXUAL LUST

Our English word "pornography" is derived from 2 Greek words, graphe, which means writing, and *porneia*, which refers to fornication or sexual immorality.[72] A standard dictionary defines pornography as "writings, photographs, movies, etc., intended to arouse sexual excitement."[73] Our fallen world culture, built on the "lust of the flesh and the lust of the eyes" (1 John 2:16), uses pornography to express and arouse sexual lust and appeal to our fallen nature.

Pornography is communicated in our culture through multiple forms of media.

Viewing live strip shows, sensual television and movie scenes, and pornographic magazines stirs sexual lust. One study found television programs contained over 20,000 scenes of implied sexual intercourse in one year.[74] "Sexting," sending nude or nearly nude photos and lewd comments via phone texts, is also a widespread problem.[75] But the media outlet with the most temptation is the internet, where research shows that there are millions of pornographic websites and the number keeps growing.[76] Millions of people struggle with internet porn.

Pornographic viewing is spiritually and morally corrupting. Human experience shows that pornography draws a person away from God, takes away affection for one's spouse, and inspires sexual activity outside of marriage. Pornography is addicting. It even undermines the biblical work ethic by motivating regular users to view pornography on the job instead of doing their work and causing them to lose focus on their jobs.[77] An article at the Christian website, "Covenant Eyes," notes this testimony regarding pornography:

> "Physiology teacher Gary Wilson explained that when men look at porn, they experience surge after surge of dopamine in the brain. . . . . This imbalance in the brain leads to many problems: impotence with your spouse, frequent masturbation with very little satisfaction, anxiety, fatigue, lack of motivation, inability to concentrate, and escalating tastes for more bizarre or novel porn."[78]

Pornography is also a widespread problem among violent criminals. People begin with "soft core" pornography and then develop a desire for "hard core" pornography and then violent pornography. Pornography has fueled the desire of rapists, who then resort to violence to cover up their rape. In his book, *The Marketing of Evil,* David Kupelian notes the following:

> "Scientist and adjunct law professor of bioethics, Kelly Hollowell points out: 'Studies reveal that acts of sexual violence are commonly linked to pornography.' . . .

Hollowell disclosed, 'When one study group was exposed to as little as five hours of non-violent pornography, they began to think pornography was not offensive and that rapists deserved milder punishments. They also became more callous and negative toward women and developed an appetite for more deviant or violent types of pornography.' . . . Serial killer Ted Bundy was interviewed by Focus on the Family chief, Dr. James Dobson. . . . Bundy movingly revealed how pornography had fueled his inner thought world and later his murderous rampage, and he also confirmed the central role porn played in the lives of virtually all the other violent offenders with whom he was incarcerated."[79]

The pornography movie industry is destroying lives of actors and actresses who produce porn movies. A former porn actress, who left the industry and became a Christian, testifies from personal experience and research about the harm to the actors and actresses. Among porn actors and actresses, she documents that there is widespread drug and alcohol abuse, widespread sexually transmitted diseases, many with resulting physical problems and many with emotional and relational problems as a result of their work.[80]

The book, *The Drug of the New Millennium: The Science of How Internet Pornography Radically Alters the Human Brain and Body,* documents the harmful effects of pornography. This work shows how internet pornography is addicting, how it harms marriage relationships, and how it leads to decline in ability of addicts to focus on work. Note these findings:

"Based on its ability to produce self-medication, mask pain, escape reality and provide the means to achieve orgasm (one of the body's most powerful peak experiences), Internet pornography has been placed in direct competition with drugs! . . . Dr. Victor Cline states: 'In my clinical experience, the major consequence of being addicted to pornography is . . . its disturbance of the fragile bonds of intimate family and marital relationships. This is where the most grievous pain, damage, and sorrow occurs. There is repeatedly an interference with or even destruction of healthy love and sexual relationships with long term bonded partners.'. . . In her book, *An Affair of the Mind,* Laurie Hall shares the true-life story of her husband Jack. . . . She writes, 'After indulging in fantasy for more than 20 years, Jack lost his ability to think about anything else. . . . Too much time fantasizing meant that he also lost his ability to do his work well."[81]

Pornography is not just a male problem. Although more men are porn addicts, studies show that many women struggle with addiction to viewing pornography as well.[82] A female writer posted an article about the personal harm she experienced from viewing pornography. What she shared from her experience applies to both men and women:

"I wish that 10 years ago someone had educated me on pornography. What it is, what it does and what it reaches in and destroys in the hearts, minds and bodies

> of men and women. . . . I wish someone would have explained how dopamine, the chemical that is released every time you experience pleasure, drives you to return to what provided that feeling before. . . . I wish someone would have told me pornography would normalize things I wasn't emotionally or physically ready to handle in my relationships with men, making me feel like I had no options or control over my sex life, filling me with much regret and physical pain. I wish someone would have told me I would begin to objectify men, build up images in my mind and think of sex day in and day out, to the point where I couldn't remain focused on anything else. . . . I wish someone would have pointed out pornography can establish your sexuality completely apart from real-life relationships, causing huge problems in your intimacy with real significant others. . . . I wish someone would have told all the men I've dated that the porn they are watching is keeping them from being turned on by me, ultimately destroying our relationship. . . . I simply wish someone would have told me why it was so harmful. . . . Had I known how much it would have harmed me, I would have left it alone."[83]

In summary, **concerning the corrupting and harmful effects of pornography, researchers have documented that pornography has:**

- **Severely harmed many marriage relationships;**[84]
- **Caused many people to lose focus on their job and some people to lose their job;**[85]
- **Inspired many people to commit heterosexual or homosexual sinful acts;**[86]
- **Contributed to sexual abuse of children;**[87]
- **Fueled evil urges of many men who have raped women;**[88]
- **Led to sinful sexual acts, sexually transmitted diseases, and substance abuse in multitudes involved in the production of pornography.**[89]
- **Caused ministers in churches to fall morally and lose their ministry.**[90]

BIBLE PRINCIPLES FOR SEXUAL PURITY

Christians will have temptation to sexual sin as long as they live in this fallen world. However, God promises His enabling grace to His people to overcome sin and resist temptation. Note these encouraging promises in God's Word about overcoming sin by God's grace:

"Your word I have hidden in my heart that I might not sin against You" (Psalm 119:11).

> "Just as Christ was raised from the dead by the glory of the Father, even so we also should walk in newness of life. . . . Our old man was crucified with Him that the body of sin might be done away with that we should no longer be slaves of sin. . . . Reckon yourselves to be dead indeed to sin, but alive to God in Christ Jesus our Lord.

Therefore do not let sin reign in your mortal body that you should obey it in its lusts" (Rom. 6:4, 6, 11-12).

"No temptation has overtaken you except such as is common to man, but God is faithful, who will not allow you to be tempted beyond what you are able, but with the temptation will also make the way of escape, that you may be able to bear it" (1 Cor. 10:13).

"Walk in the Spirit and you shall not fulfill the lusts of the flesh. . . . The fruit of the Spirit is . . . faithfulness . . . self-control" (Gal. 5:16, 22, 23).

"Take the shield of faith, with which you will be able to quench all the fiery darts of the wicked one. And take the helmet of salvation and the sword of the Spirit, which is the Word of God, praying always . . . in the Spirit" (Eph. 6:16-18).

"Seeing then that we have a great high priest who has passed through the heavens, Jesus the Son of God, let us hold fast our confession. For we do not have a high priest who cannot sympathize with our weaknesses, but one was in all points tempted as we are, yet without sin. Let us therefore come boldly to the throne of grace, that we may obtain mercy and find grace to help in time of need" (Heb. 4:14-16).

In Romans 13 and Ephesians 4, the apostle Paul uses the imagery of putting off an old garment and putting on a new garment to teach people about the Christian life. Believers must put off sinful thoughts and practices of the old life and put on righteous thoughts and practices that are consistent with new life in Christ. Paul applies this principle to the problem of lust:

"Put on the Lord Jesus Christ and make no provision for the flesh, to fulfill its lusts" (Rom. 13:14).

"Put off your concerning former conduct the old man, which grows corrupt through deceitful lusts, and be renewed in the spirit of your mind, and put on the new man, which was created according God in true righteousness and holiness" (Eph. 4:22-24).

Ephesians 4 emphasizes the mind in connection with the put off/put on principle. Believers should not live like unsaved people "in the futility of their mind" (vs. 17), who "have given themselves over to lewdness" (vs. 19), but beware of "deceitful desires" (vs. 22) and "be renewed in the spirit of your mind" (vs. 23). If we apply the put off/put on principle to sexual lust, believers must (1) put off what arouses sexual lust and (2) put on Christ's purifying grace.

Jesus strongly exhorts us to put off whatever arouses sexual lust (Matt. 5:28-30):

"Whoever looks at a woman to lust for her has already committed adultery with her in his heart. If your right eye causes you to sin, pluck it out and cast it from you. For it is more profitable for you that one of your members perish than for your

> whole body to be cast into Hell. And if your right hand causes you to sin, cut if off and cast if from you."

Bible commentators point out that Jesus is not teaching us to literally cut off a hand or pluck out an eye.[91] Jesus teaches that, in comparison, it would be better to lose a hand or eye than to lose soul and body in hell by refusing to repent of sexual lust and not seeking grace from Christ to overcome it. Jesus teaches us to cut off sexually arousing touching outside of marriage (cut off the hand) and sexually arousing viewing of people other than one's spouse (pluck out the eye).

In close connection to His warning about sexual lust in the heart, Jesus also warns in the preceding verses about the problem of heart anger (Matt. 5:21-26). A person will not be able to successfully deal with sexual lust in the heart if he or she has a problem with heart anger that they are not willing to deal with. Unresolved anger or bitterness in the heart will quench the work of the Spirit that is needed to overcome lust in the heart. Galatians 5:16-24 describes lust and anger as works of the flesh.

It is important to put away temptation to lust through the internet. To help prevent viewing images that arouse lustful thoughts, it is important to use an internet filter for protection, such as "Covenant Eyes" (www.covenanteyes.com), "Clean Internet" (www.cleaninternet.com), or "Net Nanny" (www.netnanny.com). Christians must also avoid movies, television programs, magazines, and live entertainment that arouse sexual lust.

God's promise about deliverance from temptation is about situations where believers are "overtaken" by temptation (1 Cor. 10:13). Christians cannot claim that promise when they intentionally put themselves in a place of temptation because they are looking for sinful pleasure. Christians set themselves up for a fall when they intentionally get into a situation that arouses sinful sexual desires.

Christian authors of books about sexual purity can testify that these biblical principles about purity really do work. Shannon Ethridge, who wrote *Every Woman's Battle,* testifies that in her teen and young adult years she had major struggles with sexual purity and mental lust. However, she found self-control through her relationship with Jesus and His Word.

Stephen Arterburn and Fred Stoeker, who wrote *Every Man's Battle,* and Steve Gallagher, who wrote *At the Altar of Sexual Idolatry,* testify that they went through a phase in their life of addiction to pornography. However, they found victory through Christ's grace and God's Word. Steve Gallagher found victory over pornography and started Pure Life Ministries to help men struggling with pornography addiction (see www.purelifeministries.org).

To be motivated to put off what arouses sexual lust, one must have the mindset that viewing sensual images leads to sexual arousal and masturbation and that masturbation involves sinful lustful thoughts that draw one's heart away from God. The authors of *At the Altar of Sexual Idolatry,*[92] *Every Young Man's Battle,*[93] and *Every Young Woman's Battle*[94] all emphasize that one must recognize lust/masturbation as sin that needs to be conquered by God's grace. A believer should be motivated to put off sexual lust because it blocks fellowship with God.

Believers should be holy in their sex life like God is holy (1 Pet. 2:14-16). God loves all people, but He has an intimate spiritual relationship only with His believing people. God is faithful to His covenant relationship with His people. Likewise believers should have an intimate physical relationship only with their spouse in marriage and be faithful to their marriage covenant.

Sexual lust damages the marriage relationship. Fueling lust through media outlets keeps a person from being sexually satisfied with their spouse. Covenant Eyes has an article in which they report that in 2002 The American Academy of Matrimonial Lawyers found in their cases that the majority of divorces involved either a party meeting a new lover through the internet or a spouse heavily involved in internet pornography.[95]

In addition to putting off what arouses sexual lust, believers must put on Christ's purifying grace (Rom. 13:14). Believer's need Christ's forgiving grace. Christians need to confess sexual lust as sin when they engage in lustful thoughts, receive God's forgiveness through Christ's cleansing atonement, and restore fellowship with God (1 John 1:7-9).

Then believers need to go to Christ in prayer asking for His empowering grace to resist temptation to lustful thoughts (Heb. 4:14-16; Matt. 6:13). Believers must daily meditate on God's Word and store verses of instruction and encouragement for purity in their heart to enable them to resist temptation to sin (Psalm 119:11). The Word of God and prayer for the help of God's Spirit are our spiritual weapons against temptation (Eph. 6:17-19).

God's Word says, "Walk in the Spirit and you shall not fulfill the lust of the flesh. . . . The fruit of the Spirit is . . . self-control" (Gal. 5:16, 22-23). We must pray that Christ will fill us with His Spirit and produce His fruit of control of our sexual passions. We must fill our mind with the Word of God, which the Spirit inspired, to have the power of the Spirit against sinful thoughts and desires (Eph. 5:18; 6:17-18; Col. 3:5, 12, 16).

It is critical to replace lustful thoughts with devotion to God. We must replace greed for sexual pleasure through images of people with whom we are not married with delight in the spouse God gives us, if married, and delight in fellowship with God (Eph. 5:3-4,

18-25, 28-29). We believe a lie when we think we will find lasting satisfaction in sexual lust and that we will not find lasting satisfaction in fellowship with God and His people, through His Word and prayer and group worship and serving others for God's glory. God's Word says:

> "My people have committed two evils: They have forsaken Me, the fountain of living waters and hewn themselves cisterns—broken cisterns that can hold no water" (Jer. 2:13).

> "You will show me the path of life. In your presence is fullness of joy; at your right hand are pleasures forevermore" (Psalm 16:11).

In a chapter dealing with God's grace to overcome lust, John Piper gives an important principle for fighting against temptations of lust: "The fire of lust's pleasures must be fought with the fire of God's pleasures."[96] In his book, *The Purity Principle,* Randy Alcorn makes a similar statement:

> "When God calls on you to pursue purity . . . you are being called on to do what will bring you the greatest joy! To choose purity is to put yourself under God's blessing. . . . . Those who drink of immorality are never satisfied (John 4:13). Those who drink of Jesus are fully satisfied (John 6:35)."[97]

One of the most helpful books on dealing with lust and pornography is *Finally Free—Fighting for Purity with the Power of Grace,* by Heath Lambert, a Christian counselor who testifies he gained victory over pornography in his youth through Christ's grace.[98] Christians should read this book. He gives these great observations:

> "This book is about the amazing power of Jesus Christ to free you from pornography. . . . This book provides eight clear strategies to help you . . . experience freedom from your desire for pornography. . . . I have seen them work time and again. I pray you will see them work in your life and in the lives of those God has given you to help. . . . Sorrow, relationship with Jesus, radical measures, gratitude, confession, humility, accountability, your spouse. . . . Grace is the force that motivates and empowers every strategy in the book. . . . God's grace . . . forgives your sin and God's grace empowers you to live differently and be obedient to Him (Col. 2:13–14; Rom. 6:4, 11). . . . The way we . . . are transformed by the grace of Jesus is . . . asking for and believing in God's forgiveness and His power to change us."[99]

The Council on Biblical Manhood and Womanhood (CBMW) produced the "Nashville Statement" to articulate biblical teaching about sexuality, affirming what the Christian church has believed for centuries (https://cbmw.org/nashville-statement). Many conservative Protestant leaders have signed their support for this statement. This is a helpful summary of the teaching of Scripture.

NASHVILLE STATEMENT: A COALITION FOR BIBLICAL SEXUALITY

Article 1

WE AFFIRM that God has designed marriage to be a covenantal, sexual, procreative, lifelong union of one man and one woman, as husband and wife, and is meant to signify the covenant love between Christ and his bride the church.

WE DENY that God has designed marriage to be a homosexual, polygamous, or polyamorous relationship. We also deny that marriage is a mere human contract rather than a covenant made before God.

Article 2

WE AFFIRM that God's revealed will for all people is chastity outside of marriage and fidelity within marriage.

WE DENY that any affections, desires, or commitments ever justify sexual intercourse before or outside marriage; nor do they justify any form of sexual immorality.

Article 3

WE AFFIRM that God created Adam and Eve, the first human beings, in his own image, equal before God as persons, and distinct as male and female.

WE DENY that the divinely ordained differences between male and female render them unequal in dignity or worth.

Article 4

WE AFFIRM that divinely ordained differences between male and female reflect God's original creation design and are meant for human good and human flourishing.

WE DENY that such differences are a result of the Fall or are a tragedy to be overcome.

Article 5

WE AFFIRM that the differences between male and female reproductive structures are integral to God's design for self-conception as male or female.

WE DENY that physical anomalies or psychological conditions nullify the God-appointed link between biological sex and self-conception as male or female.

Article 6

WE AFFIRM that those born with a physical disorder of sex development are created in the image of God and have dignity and worth equal to all other image-bearers. They are acknowledged by our Lord Jesus in his words about "eunuchs who were born that way from their mother's womb." With all others they are welcome as faithful followers of Jesus Christ and should embrace their biological sex insofar as it may be known.

WE DENY that ambiguities related to a person's biological sex render one incapable of living a fruitful life in joyful obedience to Christ.

Article 7

WE AFFIRM that self-conception as male or female should be defined by God's holy purposes in creation and redemption as revealed in Scripture.

WE DENY that adopting a homosexual or transgender self-conception is consistent with God's holy purposes in creation and redemption.

Article 8

WE AFFIRM that people who experience sexual attraction for the same sex may live a rich and fruitful life pleasing to God through faith in Jesus Christ, as they, like all Christians, walk in purity of life.

WE DENY that sexual attraction for the same sex is part of the natural goodness of God's original creation, or that it puts a person outside the hope of the gospel.

Article 9

WE AFFIRM that sin distorts sexual desires by directing them away from the marriage covenant and toward sexual immorality—a distortion that includes both heterosexual and homosexual immorality.

WE DENY that an enduring pattern of desire for sexual immorality justifies sexually immoral behavior.

Article 10

WE AFFIRM that it is sinful to approve of homosexual immorality or transgenderism and that such approval constitutes an essential departure from Christian faithfulness and witness.

WE DENY that the approval of homosexual immorality or transgenderism is a matter of moral indifference about which otherwise faithful Christians should agree to disagree.

Article 11

WE AFFIRM our duty to speak the truth in love at all times, including when we speak to or about one another as male or female.

WE DENY any obligation to speak in such ways that dishonor God's design of his imagebearers as male and female.

Article 12

WE AFFIRM that the grace of God in Christ gives both merciful pardon and transforming power, and that this pardon and power enable a follower of Jesus to put to death sinful desires and to walk in a manner worthy of the Lord.

WE DENY that the grace of God in Christ is insufficient to forgive all sexual sins and to give power for holiness to every believer who feels drawn into sexual sin.

Article 13

WE AFFIRM that the grace of God in Christ enables sinners to forsake transgender selfconceptions and by divine forbearance to accept the God-ordained link between one's biological sex and one's self-conception as male or female.

WE DENY that the grace of God in Christ sanctions self-conceptions that are at odds with God's revealed will.

Article 14

WE AFFIRM that Christ Jesus has come into the world to save sinners and that through Christ's death and resurrection forgiveness of sins and eternal life are available to every person who repents of sin and trusts in Christ alone as Savior, Lord, and supreme treasure.

WE DENY that the Lord's arm is too short to save or that any sinner is beyond his reach.[100]

CHAPTER 7 STUDY GUIDE THINKING BIBLICALLY ABOUT MARRIAGE AND SEXUAL ISSUES

KEY SCRIPTURES TO READ:

Genesis 2:18-25; Genesis 3:10, 21; Exodus 20:14, 17; Leviticus 18:6, 20-25; Psalm 139:13-16; Proverbs 2:16-17, 5:15-20, 18:22; Malachi 2:14-16; Matthew 5:27-32, 19:3-9; Romans 1:24-27, 7:2-3, 13:14; 1 Corinthians 6:9-20, 7:2-5, 8-16, 39; Galatians 5:16, 19-24; Ephesians 4:17-24, 5:2-3, 5:22-33; Colossians 3:5-6, 18-19; 1 Thessalonians 4:3-7; 2 Timothy 2:22; Hebrews 4:14-16, 13:4; 1 Peter 1:14-15, 2:11, 3:1-7, 4:1-5; 2 Peter 2:14-19; Jude 1:4, 7; Revelation 2:20-23, 9:21, 21:8

KEY POINTS TO NOTE (NOTE BOLD TYPE IN CHAPTER):

How does Dr. Jay Adams describe marriage and what two key Scripture passages does he use?

____

____

What are two biblical purposes for sex within marriage (Gen. 1:28 and Gen. 2:24)?

____

____

What are five restrictions God sets forth in His Word about whom a person may marry?

____

____

____

____

____

What does the Bible teach that divorce and remarriage on other than biblical grounds constitute? (Matt. 19:3-9; Mark 10:11-12; Rom. 7:2-3; 1 Cor. 7:10-11).

____

____

Who wrote books from a Humanist perspective about sex that led to a sexual revolution?

____

What Scripture passage shows both female and male homosexual behavior and desire are sinful?

What is a key passage in Psalms that shows the preborn child is a real person?

CRITICAL THINKING:

How does the Christian worldview strike a balance between the Humanist and Islamic worldviews about roles in marriage?

What are some practical ways a husband can show love to his wife?

What does your pastor believe about the exception clause concerning divorce and remarriage in Matthew 5:31-32 and Matthew 19:3-9, and what reasons does he give for his views?

What are some documented negative effects of pornography and how should that affect our thinking about accessing pornography?

What are biblical principles for sexual purity that Heath Lambert sets forth and what are some practical ways to implement these principles?

Is homosexuality an unchangeable condition and lifestyle (1 Cor. 6:9-11)?

What biblical teaching and scientific evidence can you use to show that abortion is wrong?

CHAPTER 7 ENDNOTES

1 Jay Adams, Chapters 1-3 in *Marriage, Divorce and Remarriage in the Bible* (Grand Rapids, Zondervan, 1980).

2 Ibid, pp. 4, 8, 11, 15.

3 Dwight Hervey Small, *Design for Christian Marriage* (Westwood, NJ: Fleming Revell, 1959), p. 82.

4 *The Holy Qur'an: Arabic Text,* English Translation and Commentary (Translation and commentary by Allama Abdullah Yusuf Ali; Muhammad Ashraf Publishers, Lahore, Pakistan, 1979 edition), p. 195.

5 Gary and Betsy Ricucci, *Love That Lasts: When Marriage Meets Grace* (Wheaton, IL: Crossway, 2006), pp. 34, 57.

6 John Piper and Wayne Grudem, eds., *Recovering Biblical Manhood and Womanhood: A Response to Evangelical Feminism* (Wheaton, IL: Crossway Books, 1991), pp. 62, 63, 345.

7 The Qur'an, p. 184.

8 Paul Kurtz, ed., *Humanist Manifestos 1 and 2* (Buffalo, NY: Prometheus Books, 1973), p. 18.

9 David Kupelian, *The Marketing of Evil* (Nashville, TN: WND Books, 2005), pp. 111–112.

10 William Bennett, *The Broken Hearth: Reversing the Moral Collapse of the American Family* (New York: Doubleday, 2001), p. 116.

11 "When Parents are Related—Consanguinity," Centre for Genetics Education, 2013 (http://www.genetics.edu.au/publications-and-resources/facts-sheets/fact-sheet-18-when-parents-are-relatives-consanguinity). (Accessed 3/16/2019).

12 J. L. Hazelton, LA Times, "Incest Tied to Later Mental Illness," (http://articles.latimes.com/1992-12-13/news/mn-3971_1_sexual-abuse). (Accessed 3/16/2019).

13 Jay Adams, *Christian Living in the Home* (Phillipsburg, NJ: P&R Publishing, 1972), chapter 5, "Single Persons."

14 The Qur'an, pp. 91-95.

15 Kurtz, pp. 17-18.

16 David Noebel, *Understanding the Times,* 2nd ed. (Manitou Springs, CO: Summit Press, 2006), p. 261.

17 Kupelian, pp. 110, 112.

18 Bennett, pp. 22, 159–160.

19 "New Marriage and Divorce Statistics," Barna Group, March 31, 2008 (https://www.barna.com/research/new-marriage-and-divorce-statistics-released). (Accessed 3/16/2019).

20 Bennett, pp. 28–29.

21 Kupelian, *The Marketing of Evil*, p. 107.

22 Bennett, pp. 156, 158.

23 John Piper, Desiring God, http://www.desiringgod.org/all-resources/by-topic/divorce-remarriage. (Accessed 3/16/2019).

24 Carl Laney, *The Divorce Myth* (Minneapolis, MN: Bethany House, 1981).

25 James Montgomery Boyce, "The Biblical View of Divorce," *Eternity* (December 1970).

26 John Murray, *Divorce* (Philadelphia: Orthodox Presbyterian Church, 1953).

27 John MacArthur, Grace to You, http://www.gty.org/resources/questions/QA118/Whats-your-view-of-divorce-and-remarriage. (Accessed 3/16/2019).

28 Jay Adams, *Marriage, Divorce and Remarriage in the Bible.*

29 Ibid, pp. 53–54.

30 Ibid, pp. 55–56.

31 Ibid, chapters 10–15.

32 Ibid, chapters 11, 14, 15.

33 Ibid, chapters 9 and 14.

34 "Danvers Statement," CBMW.com, https://cbmw.org/about/danvers-statement, November 1988. (Accessed 3/16/2019).

SECTIONS 3 AND 4 ON SEXUAL MATTERS

35 Qur'an, Surah 4:3, p. 184.

36 Qur'an, Surah 2:227-241, pp. 91-98.

37 Qur'an, Surah 37:40-48, pp. 1141-1142.

38 Qur'an, Surah 4:3, 184.

39 "Osama Bin Laden Porn Stash? Pornography Discovered at Compound: Report," Huffingtonpost.com, https://www.huffingtonpost.com/2011/05/13/osama-bin-laden-porn_n_861664.html. (Accessed 3/16/2019).

40 Kurtz, p. 18.

41 Kevin Ryerson, *Spirit Communication: The Soul's Path* (New York: Bantam Books, 1989), p. 172.

42 Cleon Skousen, *The Naked Communist* (Salt Lake City, Utah: Ensign Publishing, 1961), p. 72.

43 Judith Reisman, *Sexual Sabotage* (Washington, D.C.: WorldNetDaily, 2010), pp. 24-35.

44 Ibid, pp. 39-40.

45 Ibid, pp. 4, 5, 126.

46 John Davis, *Moses and the Gods of Egypt* (Grand Rapids: Baker Book House, 1971), p. 208.

47 John MacArthur, *1 and 2 Thessalonians* (Chicago: Moody Press, 2002), p. 104, comments on 1 Thessalonians 4:3.

48 Stephen Arterburn and Fred Stoeker, *Every Young Man's Battle: Strategies for Victory in the Real World of Sexual Temptation* (Colorado Springs, CO: WaterBrook Press, 2002), p. 218.

49 Ibid, pp. 224-228.

50 Becket Cook, *A Change of Affection: A Gay Man's Incredible Story of Redemption* (Nashville, TN: Nelson Books, 2019).

51 Rosaria Champagne Butterfield, *The Secret Thoughts of an Unlikely Convert: An English Professor's Journey into Christian Faith* (Pittsburgh, PA: Crown & Covenant Publications, 2012).

52 Denny Burk and Heath Lambert, *Transforming Homosexuality: What the Bible Says about Sexual Orientation and Change* (Phillipsburg, NJ: P&R Publishing, 2015).

53 R. Albert Mohler, Jr., ed., *God and the Gay Christian?: A Response to Matthew Vines* (Louisville, KY: SBTS Press, 2014).

54 Jeffrey Satinover, *Homosexuality and the Politics of Truth* (Grand Rapids: Baker Book House, 1996), pp. 22, 75-79.

55 Ibid, pp. 14-17, 49-60.

56 Peter Hubbard, *Love into Light: The Gospel, the Homosexual and the Church* (Greenville, SC: Ambassador International, 2013), p. 32.

57 Ibid, pp. 36, 38, 39, 41.

58 Kurtz, p. 18.

59 Chris Horner, *The Politically Incorrect Guide to Global Warming and Environmentalism* (Washington, D.C.: Regnery Publishing, 2007), p. 10.

60 Michael Sanera and Jane Shaw, *Facts Not Fear* (Washington, D.C.: Regnery Publishing, 1996), pp. 65, 66.

61 Jonathan Wells, "Haeckel's Embryos," chapter 5 in *Icons of Evolution* (Washington, D.C.: Regnery Publishing, 2000).

62 Randy Alcorn, *Pro-Life Answers to Pro-Choice Arguments* (Sisters, OR: Multnomah Books, 1992), p. 41.

63 FS01, "Abortion in the US," pdf, Abortion Statistic, National Right to Life, https://www.nrlc.org/communications/abortionnumbers. (Accessed 3/16/2019).

64 Kupelian, p. 201.

65 Kupelian, p. 200.

66 Randy Alcorn, *The Purity Principle* (Colorado Springs, CO: Multnomah Books, 2003), pp. 13, 24, 26, 30, 41-42.

67 Stephen Arterburn and Fred Stoeker, *Every Man's Battle: Winning the War on Sexual Temptation* (Colorado Springs, CO: WaterBrook Press, 2000).

68 Stephen Arterburn and Fred Stoeker, *Every Young Man's Battle: Strategies for Victory in the Real World of Sexual Temptation* (Colorado Springs, CO: WaterBrook Press, 2002).

69 Shannon Ethridge, *Every Woman's Battle: Discovering God's Plan for Sexual and Emotional Fulfillment* (Colorado Springs, CO: WaterBrook Press, 2003).

70 Shannon Ethridge, *Every Young Woman's Battle: Guarding Your Mind, Heart and Body in a Sex-Saturated World* (Colorado Springs, CO: WaterBrook Press, 2004).

71 John Murray, *Principles of Conduct* (Grand Rapids: Eerdmans, 1957), p. 42.

72 William F. Arndt and F. Wilbur Gingrich, *A Greek English Lexicon of the New Testament and Other Early Christian Literature,* 4th revised edition (Chicago: The University of Chicago Press, 1957), pp. 165 and 699.

73 *Webster's College Dictionary* (New York: Random House, 1992), p. 1051.

74 Tim and Beverly LaHaye, *Against the Tide: How to Raise Sexually Pure Kids in a Sexually Impure World* (Sisters, OR: Multnomah Books, 1993), p. 16.

75 Kimberly Mitchell, David Finkelhor, Lisa M. Jones, Janis Wolak, "Prevalence and Characteristic of Youth Sexting: A National Study," published in *Pediatrics Magazine* in 2012 and online at pediatrics.aappublications.org/content/129/1/13. (Accessed 3/16/2019).

76 Kupelian, p. 129.

77 "Lifting the Lid on Workplace Porn," *The Sydney Morning Herald,* June 11, 2010, www.smh.com.au/small-business/blogs/work-in-progress/lifting-the-lid-on-workplace-porn-20100611-yosh.html. (Accessed 3/16/2019).

78 Luke Gilkerson, "Brain Chemicals and Porn Addiction: Science Shows How Porn Harms Us," *Covenant Eyes,* 2014 (http://www.covenanteyes.com/2014/02/03/brain-chemicals-and-porn-addiction). (Accessed 3/16/2019).

79 Kupelian, p. 129.

80 Shelley Luben, *Truth Behind the Fantasy of Porn* (Bakersfield, CA: Shelley Luben Communications, 2010), pp. 1-7.

81 Mark Kastleman, *The Drug of the New Millennium: The Science of How Internet Pornography Radically Alters the Human Brain and Body* (Orem, UT: Granite Publishing, 2001), pp. 7, 9, 241, 231-233.

82 Tanith Carey, "Why More and More Women Are Using Pornography," *The Guardian,* 2011 (https://www.theguardian.com/culture/2011/apr/07/women-addicted-internet-pornography). (Accessed 3/16/2019).

83 Lauren Dubinsky, "What I Wish I'd Known Before Watching Porn," *The Huffington Post,* 07/23/2012 (https://www.huffingtonpost.com/lauren-dubinsky/porn-addiction_b_1686481.html). (Accessed 3/16/2019).

84 Kastleman, p.241.

85 "Lifting the Lid on Workplace Porn," *The Sydney Morning Herald,* June 11, 2010.

86 Arterburn and Stoeker, *Every Young Man's Battle,* chapters 1-4 and 23.

87 Kupelian, pp. 131,134-135.

88 Ibid, p. 129.

89 Luben, pp. 1-7.

90 Steve Gallagher, *At the Altar of Sexual Idolatry* (Dry Ridge, KY: Pure Life Ministries, 2007), chapters 3 and 4.

91 John Broadus, *Matthew* (Valley Forge: Judson Press, 1886), pp. 108-110.

92 Gallagher, *At the Altar of Sexual Idolatry,* p. 37 and chapter 2, "Developing Convictions about Lust and Masturbation."

93 Arterburn and Stoeker, *Every Young Man's Battle,* Part 4, "Masturbation," chapters 9-13.

94 Ethridge, *Every Young Woman's Battle,* chapter 5, "Fueling Your Own Sexual Fire."

95 "Pornography Statistics 2014," Covenant Eyes, www.covenanteyes.com. (Accessed 3/16/2019).

96 John Piper, *Future Grace: The Purifying Power of the Promises of God,* revised edition (Colorado Springs, CO: Multnomah Books, 2012), p. 336.

97 Randy Alcorn, *The Purity Principle* (Colorado Springs, CO: Multnomah Books, 2003), pp. 21, 23, 39.

99 Heath Lambert, *Finally Free: Fighting for Purity with the Power of Grace* (Grand Rapids: Zondervan, 2013), pp. 156-159.

99 Ibid, pp. 12, 14, 15, 22, 25.

100 "Nashville Statement," CBMW.org, 2017, https://cbmw.org/nashville-statement. (Accessed 3/16/2019).

APPENDIX A

SUGGESTED STUDY SCHEDULES

SCHEDULE 1:WEEKLY CHURCH-SPONSORED BIBLE STUDY, SEPTEMBER-MAY

Settings: Sunday School, Sunday evening study, small group home study, college group study

Breaks: Thanksgiving, Christmas, New Year, Easter/Spring break, Summer

Lesson topics: See page two, chapter and section titles

Study leader: Give outline of material in the book section, share key Scriptures, lead discussion

WEEK:	LESSON SECTION IN THE BOOK:
1.	Introduction to Book/ Introduction to Course
2.	Introduction to the Christian Worldview
3.	Introduction to the Humanist Worldview
4.	Introduction to the Islamic Worldview
5.	The Inspiration of Scripture
6.	The Canon and Authority of Scripture
7.	Evidence for the Inspiration of Scripture
8.	The Case for God as Creator
9.	The Issue of God and Evil
10.	A Defense of the Trinity
11.	A Defense of the Deity of Christ
12.	Man as Created by God
13.	Man as Fallen in Sin
14.	Basic Bible Teaching about Redemption
15.	Redemption and the Believer's Present Life
16.	Creation versus Evolution as a Worldview Conflict
17.	The Case for Recent Creation
18.	The Case for the Worldwide Flood
19.	Problems with Evolution

20. God-Given Institutions and Authority
21. Thinking Biblically about the Church
22. Biblical Role of Civil Government
23. Government and Climate Change
24. Problems with Socialism
25. The Marriage Relationship
26. Marriage, Divorce, and Remarriage
27. Sexual Activity
28. Sexual Lust

SCHEDULE 2: CHRISTIAN COLLEGE OR SEMINARY SEMESTER CLASSROOM COURSE

(For a one-semester course that meets two or three times a week)

Class Lessons:

1. Teacher gives introduction and overview of the course
2. Introduction to the Christian Worldview
3. Introduction to the Humanist Worldview
4. Introduction to the Islamic Worldview
5. The Inspiration of Scripture
6. The Canon and Authority of Scripture
7. Evidence for the Inspiration of Scripture
8. Chicago Statements on Biblical Inerrancy and Hermeneutics
9. The Case for God as Creator
10. The Issue of God and Evil
11. A Defense of the Trinity
12. A Defense of the Deity of Christ
13. Man as Created by God
14. Man as Fallen in Sin
15. Basic Bible Teaching about Redemption
16. Redemption and the Believer's Present Life
17. Creation versus Evolution as a Worldview Conflict
18. The Case for Recent Creation
19. The Case for the Worldwide Flood
20. Problems with Evolution

21. God-Given Institutions and Authority
22. Thinking Biblically about the Church
23. Biblical Role of Civil Government
24. Government and Climate Change
25. Problems with Socialism
26. The Marriage Relationship
27. Marriage, Divorce, and Remarriage
28. Sexual Activity
29. Sexual Lust
30. Exam

If time allows and teacher and students are interested and have available resources, the teacher could assign each student one of the recommended worldview related books in Appendix B and have the student compose a report on that book.

SCHEDULE 3: SUMMER READING COURSE FOR A CHRISTIAN COLLEGE OR SEMINARY (MAY-AUGUST)

Week 1: Chapter 1—Introduction to Worldviews (including introduction to book)

Week 2: Chapter 2—God's Word: The Authority for Worldview Conclusions

Week 3: Chapter 3—God's Person: The Starting Point for Worldview Thinking

Week 4: Chapter 4—Man's Person: Created, Fallen, and Object of Redemption

Week 5: Chapter 5—Thinking Biblically about Creation versus Evolution

Week 6: Chapter 6—Thinking Biblically about the Church and the State

Week 7: Chapter 7—Thinking Biblically about Marriage and Sexual Issues

Week 8: Exam

Students email typed chapter summary and outline each week to course proctor

SCHEDULE 4: INDIVIDUAL PERSONAL STUDY (WEEKLY OVER THE COURSE OF A YEAR, WITH BREAKS)

1. Title Page, Introduction, Table of Contents, Building a Worldview Library (Appendix B)
2. Introduction to the Christian Worldview

3. Introduction to the Humanist Worldview
4. Introduction to the Islamic Worldview
5. The Inspiration of Scripture
6. The Canon and Authority of Scripture
7. Evidence for the Inspiration of Scripture
8. Chicago Statements on Biblical Inerrancy and Hermeneutics
9. The Case for God as Creator
10. The Issue of God and Evil
11. A Defense of the Trinity
12. A Defense of the Deity of Christ
13. Man as Created by God
14. Man as Fallen in Sin
15. Basic Bible Teaching about Redemption
16. Redemption and the Believer's Present Life
17. Creation versus Evolution as a Worldview Conflict
18. The Case for Recent Creation
19. The Case for the Worldwide Flood
20. Problems with Evolution
21. God-Given Institutions and Authority
22. Thinking Biblically about the Church
23. The Biblical Role of Civil Government
24. Government and Climate Change
25. The Marriage Relationship
26. Divorce and Remarriage
27. Sexual Activity
28. Sexual Lust
29. Danvers Statement, Nashville Statement

APPENDIX B

BUILDING A CHRISTIAN WORLDVIEW LIBRARY

Christians can help build a Christian worldview library for use by other Christians by helping their church or Christian college get the following recommended books into their library. Here are key books and DVDs by Christian authors to begin building a Christian worldview library. There are many other good resources noted in the bibliography and at the recommended websites, which could be added also to help Christians defend their worldview.

GENERAL WORLDVIEW BOOKS: (NOTE AMAZON.COM FOR USED OR NEW)

J. F. Baldwin, *The Deadliest Monster: An Introduction to Worldviews* (New Braunfels, TX: Worldview Academy, 1998).

Dave Breese, *Seven Men Who Rule the World from the Grave* (Chicago: Moody Press, 1990).

Alan Cairns, *Dictionary of Theological Terms,* Expanded 3rd Edition (Greenville, SC: Ambassador International, 2002).

Ken Ham and Britt Beemer, with Todd Hilliard, *Already Gone: Why Your Kids Will Quit Church and What You Can Do to Stop It* (Green Forest, AR: Master Books, 2009) (see AIG website).

John MacArthur, ed., *Thinking Biblically: Recovering a Christian Worldview* (Wheaton, IL: Crossway Books, 2003).

Henry Morris, *The Biblical Basis for Modern Science* (Grand Rapids: Baker Book House, 1984).

David Noebel, *Understanding the Times,* revised 2nd ed. (Manitou Springs, CO: Summit Press, 2006) (available at https://understandingthetimes.com).

Nancy Pearcey, *Total Truth* (Wheaton, IL: Crossway Books, 2004).

Herbert Schlossberg, *Idols for Destruction* (Wheaton, IL: Crossway Book, 1990).

Mark Ward, ed., *Biblical Worldview: Creation, Fall, Redemption* (Greenville, SC: BJU Press, 2017) (available at http://www.bjupress.com).

BIBLICAL CREATION VERSUS EVOLUTION BOOKS: (SEE WEBSITES TO ORDER)

Jason Lisle, *The Ultimate Proof of Creation* (Green Forest, AR: Master Books, 2009). (See website at https://biblicalscienceinstitute.com/dr-lisle).

Answers in Genesis (see AIG website at https://answersingenesis.org/store):

Don DeYoung, ed., *Thousands, Not Billions* (Green Forest, AR: Master Books, 2005).

Ken Ham, *The Lie: Evolution/Millions of Years,* revised edition (Master Books, 2012).

Ken Ham, *Six Days: The Age of the Earth and the Decline of the Church* (Green Forest, AR: Master Books, 2013).

Creation Ministries International (see CMI website at https://usstore.creation.com):

Jonathan Sarfati, *By Design: Evidence for Nature's Designer—the God of the Bible* (Australia: Creation Ministries International, 2008).

Jonathan Sarfati, *Refuting Evolution* (Australia: Creation Ministries International, 2007).

Jonathan Sarfati, *Refuting Compromise: A Biblical and Scientific Refutation of Progressive Creationism* (Master Books, 2004).

Institute for Creation Research (see ICR website at https://store.icr.org).

Marvin Lubenow, *Bones of Contention: A Creationist Assessment of Human Fossils* (Grand Rapids, MI: Baker Books, 2004 revised edition).

Henry Morris, *The Genesis Flood* (Philadelphia, PA: Presbyterian and Reformed Publishing Company, 1961).

Henry Morris, *The Genesis Record* (Grand Rapids: Baker Book House, 1976).

TOPICAL WORLDVIEW BOOKS: (NOTE AMAZON.COM FOR USED OR NEW)

Answers in Genesis: *Demolishing Supposed Bible Contradictions*, 2 volume set (Master Books, Volume 1: 2010; Volume 2: 2011).

Answers in Genesis: *A Pocket Guide to Global Warming: A Scientific and Biblical Expose of Climate Change* (Petersburg, KY: Answers in Genesis, 2008).

Adams, Jay. *Marriage, Divorce and Remarriage in the Bible* (Grand Rapids: Zondervan, 1980).

Alcorn, Randy. *If God is Good: Faith in the Midst of Suffering and Evil* (Colorado Springs, Colorado: Multnomah Books, 2009).

Alcorn, Randy. *Heaven* (Tyndale House and Eternal Perspective Ministries, 2004).

Alcorn, Randy. *Pro-Life Answers to Pro-Choice Arguments* (Sisters, OR: Multnomah Books, 1992).

Barrett, Michael, *Complete in Him: A Guide to Understanding and Enjoying the Gospel* (Greenville, SC: Ambassador-Emerald International, 2000).

Bridges, Jerry. *Trusting God—Even When Life Hurts* (Colorado Springs, CO: NavPress, 2008).

Burk, Denny and Heath Lambert, *Transforming Homosexuality: What the Bible Says about Sexual Orientation and Change* (Phillipsburg, NJ: P&R Publishing, 2015).

Butterfield, Rosaria Champagne. *The Secret Thoughts of an Unlikely Convert: An English Professor's Journey into Christian Faith* (Pittsburgh, PA: Crown & Covenant Publications, 2012).

Davis, John Jefferson. *Evangelical Ethics* (Phillipsburg, NJ: P&R Publishing, 1993).

DeMar, Gary ed. *Pushing the Antithesis: The Apologetic Methodology of Greg Bahnsen* (Powder Springs, GA: American Vision, 2007).

DeMar, Gary. *God and Government: A Biblical, Historical and Constitutional Perspective* (Powder Springs, GA: American Vision, 2011).

Dyer, John. *From the Garden to the City: The Redeeming and Corrupting Power of Technology* (Grand Rapids, MI: Kregel Publications, 2011).

Geisler, Norman and William Nix. *A General Introduction to the Bible,* revised and expanded edition (Chicago: Moody Press, 1986).

Geisler, Norman and Abdul Saleeb. *Answering Islam* (Grand Rapids: Baker Book House, 2002).

Grant, George. *Bringing in the Sheaves: Replacing Government Welfare with Biblical Charity,* 3rd Revised Edition (Franklin, TN: Ars Vitae, 1995).

Groothuis, Douglas. *Unmasking the New Age* (Downers Grove, IL: Intervarsity Press, 1986).

Hubbard, Peter. *Love into Light: The Gospel, the Homosexual and the Church* (Greenville, SC: Ambassador International, 2013).

Jones, J. Y. *Worship Not the Creature: Animal Rights and the Bible* (Ventura, CA: Nordskog Publishing, 2009).

Kupelian, David. *The Marketing of Evil* (Nashville, TN: Cumberland House Publishing, 2005).

Lambert, Heath. *Finally Free: Fighting for Purity with the Power of Grace* (Grand Rapids: Zondervan, 2013).

McDowell, Josh. *A Ready Defense: The Best of Josh McDowell,* compiled by Bill Wilson (Nashville, TN: Thomas Nelson, 1993).

MacArthur, John. *Our Sufficiency in Christ* (Dallas, TX: Word Publishing, 1991).

Piper, John and Wayne Grudem, *Recovering Biblical Manhood and Womanhood* (Wheaton, IL: Crossway Books, 1991.

White, James. *The Forgotten Trinity* (Minneapolis, MN: Bethany House Publishers, 1998).

HELPFUL WORLDVIEW DVDS: (SEE WEBSITES)

American Vision. DVD. "Moral Capitalism." (www.americanvision.org, 2011).

Answers in Genesis and Coral Ridge Ministries. DVD. "Global Warming" (answersingenesis.org, 2008).

Beisner, Calvin and Others. DVD set. "Resisting the Green Dragon" (exposing radical environmentalism) (CDR Communications/ www.CornwallAlliance.org; www.resistingthegreendragon.com, 2016).

Berg, Jim. DVD set. "Quieting a Noisy Soul: Overcoming Guilt, Anxiety, Anger, and Despair"

(BJU Press; www.bjup.com).

Comfort, Ray. DVD. "Evolution Versus God" (2013, LivingWaters.com).

Edwards, Brian. DVD set. How Do We Know the Bible is True?" (Answers in Genesis, 2008; answersingenesis.org).

Ham, Ken. DVD. "Already Gone: Why Your Kids Will Quit Church and What You Can Do to Stop It" (Answers in Genesis, 2009; answersingenesis.org).

Mahoney, Timothy. DVD. "Patterns of Evidence: Exodus." (Thinking Man Films, 2015; www.PatternsOfEvidence.com).

Mohler, Al. DVD. "Right from the Start--Creation and the Gospel in One Story Line" (Answers in Genesis, 2011; answersingenesis.org).

Parker, Gary. DVD. "From Evolution to Creation" (Answers in Genesis, 2001/answersingenesis.org).

Psarris, Spike. DVD set. "What You Aren't Being Told About Astronomy" (three DVD set, 2009-2013, Creation Astronomy Media, www.creationastronomy.com).

Tackett, Del. DVD set. "The Truth Project" (Focus on the Family, 2006; www.thetruthproject.org)

Tackett, Del. DVD. "Is Genesis History?" (IsGenesisHistory.com, 2017).

SUBJECT INDEX

BIBLIOGRAPHY

Adams, Jay. *The Christian Counselors Manual* (Grand Rapids, MI: Zondervan, 1973). *Christian Living in the Home* (Phillipsburg, NJ: Presbyterian and Reformed, 1972) *Marriage, Divorce and Remarriage in the Bible* (Grand Rapids, MI: Zondervan, 1980).

Alcorn, Randy. *Heaven* (Tyndale House and Eternal Perspective Ministries, 2004). *If God is Good: Faith in the Midst of Suffering and Evil* (Colorado Springs, Colorado: Multnomah Books, 2009). *Managing God's Money* (Carol Stream, IL: Tyndale House, 2011). *Pro-Life Answers to Pro-Choice Arguments* (Sisters, OR: Multnomah Books, 1992). *The Purity Principle* (Colorado Springs, CO: Multnomah Books, 2003).

Anderson, James. *What's Your Worldview?—An Interactive Approach to Life's Big Questions* (Wheaton, IL: Crossway, 2014).

Answers in Genesis. *Demolishing Supposed Bible Contradictions,* Volume 1 (Master Books, 2010)/ Volume 2 (Master Books, 2011) *A Pocket Guide to Global Warming—A Scientific and Biblical Expose of Climate Change* (Petersburg, KY: Answers in Genesis, 2008).

Anyabwile, Thabiti. *What is a Healthy Church Member?* (Wheaton, IL: Crossway Books, 2008).

Archer, Gleason. *Encyclopedia of Bible Difficulties* (Grand Rapids: Zondervan, 1982).

Arterburn, Stephen and Fred Stoeker. *Every Man's Battle: Winning the War on Sexual Temptation* (Colorado Springs, CO: WaterBrook Press, 2000). *Every Young Man's Battle: Strategies for Victory in the Real World of Sexual Temptation* (Colorado Springs, CO: WaterBrook Press, 2002).

Ashton, John and Michael Westcott, eds. *The Big Argument: Does God Exist?* (Green Forest, AR: Master Books, 2006).

Bahnsen, Greg. *Presuppositional Apologetics Stated and Defended* (Powder Springs, GA: American Vision, 2008).

Baldwin, J. F. *The Deadliest Monster: An Introduction to Worldviews* (New Braunfels, TX: Fishermen Press, 1998).

Barrett, Michael. *Complete in Him: A Guide to Understanding and Enjoying the Gospel* (Greenville, SC: Ambassador-Emerald International, 2000).

Behe, Michael. *Darwin's Black Box* (New York: The Free Press, 1996).

Beisner, Calvin. *Prospects for Growth: A Biblical View of Population, Resources and the Future* (Westchester, IL: Crossway Books, 1990).

Berg, Jim *Changed into His Image* (Greenville, SC: Bob Jones University Press, 2000). *Taking Time to Quiet Your Soul* (Greenville, SC: Bob Jones University Press, 2005).

Bird, Wendell. *The Origin of Species Revisited: The Theories of Evolution and of Abrupt Appearance* (Nashville, TN: Thomas Nelson, 1991).

Breese, David. *Seven Men Who Rule the World from the Grave* (Chicago: Moody Press, 1990).

Bridges, Jerry. *Trusting God—Even When Life Hurts* (Colorado Springs, CO: NavPress, 2008).

Burk, Denny and Heath Lambert. *Transforming Homosexuality: What the Bible Says about Sexual Orientation and Change* (Phillipsburg, NJ: P&R Publishing, 2015).

Butterfield, Rosaria Champagne. *The Secret Thoughts of an Unlikely Convert: An English Professor's Journey into Christian Faith* (Pittsburgh, PA: Crown & Covenant Publications, 2012).

Cairns, Alan. *Dictionary of Theological Terms*, Expanded 3rd Edition, (Greenville, SC: Ambassador International, 2002).

Caner, Ergun and Emir. *Unveiling Islam* (Grand Rapids: Kregel, 2009).

Carson, D.A. *The Gagging of God: Christianity Confronts Pluralism* (Grand Rapids, MI: Zondervan, 1996).

Clouser, Roy. *The Myth of Religious Neutrality* (South Bend, IN: Notre Dame University Press, 1991).

Colson, Charles and Nancy Pearcey. *How Now Shall We Live* (Wheaton, IL: Tyndale House, 1999).

Crozier, Brian and Arthur Seldon. *Socialism: The Grand Delusion* (New York: Universe Books, 1986).

Culver, Robert. *Toward a Biblical View of Civil Government* (Chicago: Moody Press, 1974).

Custer, Stewart. *Does Inspiration Demand Inerrancy?* (Nutley, NJ: Craig Press, 1968).

DeMar, Gary. *America's Christian History: The Untold Story* (Powder Springs, GA: American Vision, second edition, 1995). *God and Government: A Biblical, Historical and Constitutional Perspective* (Powder Springs, GA: American Vision, 2011). *Pushing the Antithesis—The Apologetic Methodology of Greg Bahnsen* (Powder Springs, GA: American Vision, 2007). *Thinking Straight in a Crooked World* (Powder Springs, GA: American Vision, 2001).

DeYoung, Don, ed. *Thousands, Not Billions* (Green Forest, AR: Master Books, 2005).

DiLorenzo, Thomas. *The Problem with Socialism* (Washington, D. C.: Regnery Publishing, 2016)

Dockery, David, ed. *The Challenge of Postmodernism* (Wheaton, IL: Victor Books, 1995).

Down, David. *The Archaeology Book* (Green Forest, AR: Master Books, 2010).

Dyer, John. *From the Garden to the City: The Redeeming and Corrupting Power of Technology* (Grand Rapids: Kregel Publications, 2011).

Elwell, Walter, ed. *The Evangelical Dictionary of Theology* (Grand Rapids, MI: Baker Book House, 1984).

Ethridge, Shannon. *Every Woman's Battle: Discovering God's Plan for Sexual and Emotional Fulfillment* (Colorado Springs, CO: WaterBrook Press, 2003). *Every Young Woman's Battle: Guarding Your Mind, Heart and Body in a Sex-Saturated World* (Colorado Springs, CO: WaterBrook Press, 2004).

Frame, John. *The Doctrine of the Knowledge of God* (Phillipsburg, NJ: Presbyterian and Reformed, 1987). *The Doctrine of the Christian Lif*e (Phillipsburg, NJ: Presbyterian and Reformed, 2008).

Gallagher, Steve. *At the Altar of Sexual Idolatry* (Dry Ridge, KY: Pure Life Ministries, 2007).

Geisler, Norman and Abdul Saleeb. *Answering Islam,* revised edition (Grand Rapids, MI: Baker Book House, 2002).

Geisler, Norman and William Nix, *A General Introduction to the Bible,* revised edition (Chicago: Moody Press, 1986).

Gentry, Ken. *As It Is Written: Dismantling the Framework Hypothesis* (Green Forest, AR: Master Books, 2016).

Gerstner, John. *The Theology of the Major Sects* (Grand Rapids, MI: Baker Book House, 1960).

Grant, George. *Bringing in the Sheaves: Replacing Government Welfare with Biblical Charity,* 3rd Revised Edition (Franklin, TN: Ars Vitae, 1995).

Groothuis, Douglas. *Unmasking the New Age* (Downers Grove, IL: Intervarsity Press, 1986).

Gurganus, Gene. *The Peril of Islam* (Taylors, SC: Truth Publishers, 2004).

Ham, Ken. *The Lie: Evolution/Millions of Years,* revised edition (Green Forest, AR: Master Books, 2012). *Six Days: The Age of the Earth and the Decline of the Church* (Green Forest, AR: Master Books, 2013).

Ham, Ken and Bodie Hodge. *A Flood of Evidence* (Green Forest, AR: Master Books, 2016).

Ham, Ken and Britt Beemer. *Already Gone: Why Your Kids Will Quit Church and What You Can Do to Stop It* (Green Forest, AR: Master Books, 2009).

Ham, Ken and Charles Ware. *One Race/One Blood* (Green Forest, AR: Master Books, 2010).

Ham, Ken and others. *Dinosaurs: Is There a Biblical Explanation?* (Hebron, KY: Answers in Genesis, 2010).

Harris, R. Laird. *Inspiration and Canonicity of the Scriptures* (Grand Rapids: Zondervan Publishing House, 1995).

Horner, Christopher. *The Politically Incorrect Guide to Global Warming and Environmentalism* (Washington, D.C.: Regnery Publishing, 2007).

Hubbard, Peter. *Love into Light: The Gospel, the Homosexual and the Church* (Greenville, SC: Ambassador International, 2013).

Jeanson, Nathaniel. *Replacing Darwin: The New Origin of Species* (Green Forest, AR: Master Books, 2017).

Jones, J. Y. *Worship Not the Creature: Animal Rights and the Bible* (Ventura, CA: Nordskog Publishing, 2009).

Kastleman, Mark. *The Drug of the New Millennium: The Science of How Internet Pornography Radically Alters the Human Brain and Body* (Orem, UT: Granite Publishing, 2001).

Kelly, Douglas. *Creation and Change* (Great Britain: Mentor, 1997).

Kuhn, Thomas. *The Structure of Scientific Revolutions*, 2nd edition (Chicago: University of Chicago Press, 1970).

Kupelian, David. *The Marketing of Evil* (Nashville, TN: WND Books, 2005).

LaHaye, Tim and Beverly. *Against the Tide: How to Raise Sexually Pure Kids in a Sexually Impure World* (Sisters, OR: Multnomah Books, 1993).

Lambert, Heath. *Finally Free: Fighting for Purity with the Power of Grace* (Grand Rapids: Zondervan, 2013).

Lindsell, Harold. *The Battle for the Bible* (Grand Rapids, MI: Zondervan, 1976). *The Bible in the Balance* (Grand Rapids, MI: Zondervan, 1979).

Lisle, Jason. *The Ultimate Proof of Creation* (Green Forest, AR: Master Books, 2009).

Lubenow, Marvin. *Bones of Contention: A Creationist Assessment of Human Fossils* (Grand Rapids, MI: Baker Books, 2004 revised edition).

MacArthur, John. *The Battle for the Beginning* (W Publishing Group, 2001). *Our Sufficiency in Christ* (Dallas, TX: Word Publishing, 1991). *Thinking Biblically: Recovering a Christian Worldview* (Wheaton, IL: Crossway Books, 2003).

McDowell, Josh. *More than a Carpenter* (Tyndale House Publishers, 2009). *The Last Christian Generation* (Holiday, FL: Green Key Books, 2006).

McDowell, Josh and Bill Wilson. *The Best of Josh McDowell: A Ready Defense* (Nashville, TN: Thomas Nelson Publishers, 1993)

McDowell, Josh and Don Stewart. *Handbook of Today's Religions* (Nashville: Thomas Nelson Publishers, 1983).

Mohler, Jr., R. Albert, ed., *God and the Gay Christian?: A Response to Matthew Vines* (Louisville, KY: SBTS Press, 2014).

Morey, Robert. *The Islamic Invasion* (Las Vegas, NV: Christian Scholars Press, 1992).

Morris, Henry. *The Biblical Basis for Modern Science* (Grand Rapids: Baker Book House, 1984). *The Genesis Record* (Grand Rapids: Baker Book House, 1976). *The Long War Against God* (Green Forest, AR: Master Book, 2000).

Morris, Henry and John Whitcomb. *The Genesis Flood: The Biblical Record and Its Scientific Implications* (Philadelphia, PA: Presbyterian and Reformed, 1961).

Morris, John. *The Global Flood: Unlocking Earth's Geologic History* (Institute for Creation Research, 2012).

Mortenson, Terry, ed. *Searching for Adam: Genesis and the Truth about Man's Origin* (Green Forest, AR: Master Books, 2016).

Murray, Charles. *Losing Ground—American Social Policy 1950-1980* (New York: Basic Books, 1984).

Murray, John. *Principles of Conduct* (Grand Rapids: Eerdmans, 1957). *Divorce* (Philadelphia: Orthodox Presbyterian Church, 1953).

Noebel, David. *Understanding the Times,* revised 2nd edition (Manitou Springs, CO: Summit Press, 2006).

Olasky, Marvin. *The Tragedy of American Compassion* (Wheaton, IL: Crossway Books, 1992). *Fighting for Liberty and Virtue: Political and Culture Wars in 18th Century America* (Wheaton, IL: Crossway Books, 1995).

Parker, Star. *Uncle Sam's Plantation: How Big Government Enslaves America's Poor and What We Can Do about It,* revised edition (Nashville, TN: Thomas Nelson, 2010).

Pearcey, Nancy. *Total Truth* (Wheaton, IL: Crossway Books, 2004).

Pipa, Joseph and David Hall, eds. *Did God Create in 6 Days?* (White Hall, WV: Tolle Lege Press, 2005).

Piper, John. *Future Grace: The Purifying Power of the Promises of God,* revised edition (Colorado Springs, CO: Multnomah Books, 2012).

Piper, John and Wayne Grudem, eds. *Recovering Biblical Manhood and Womanhood: A Response to Evangelical Feminism* (Wheaton, IL: Crossway Books, 1991).

Poythress, Vern. *The Shadow of Christ in the Law of Moses* (Phillipsburg, NJ: P&R Press, 1991).

Ramm, Bernard. *Protestant Biblical Interpretation,* 3rd revised edition (Grand Rapids, MI: Baker Book House, 1970).

Rose, Tom. *Economics: Principles and Policy from a Christian Perspective,* 2nd ed. (Mercer, PA: American Enterprise Publications, 1986).

Rushdoony, R. J. *Christianity and the State* (Vallecito, CA: Ross House Books, 1986). *The Messianic Character of American Education* (Nutley, NJ: The Craig Press, 1968).

Rydenfelt, Sven. *A Pattern for Failure: Socialist Economies in Crisis* (New York: Harcourt, Brace, Jovanovich, 1984).

Sanera, Michael and Jane Shaw. *Facts Not Fear* (Washington, D.C.: Regnery Publishing, 1996).

Sarfati, Jonathan. *By Design—Evidence for Nature's Intelligent Designer—The God of the Bible* (Australia: Creation Book Publishers, 2008). *Refuting Compromise* (Green Forest, AR: Master Books, 2004). *Refuting Evolution: A Response to the National Academy of Science's Teaching about Evolution and the Nature of Science* (Brisbane, Australia: Creation Ministries International, 2007).

Satinover, Jeffrey. *Homosexuality and the Politics of Truth* (Grand Rapids: Baker Book House, 1996).

Schaff, Philip. *Creeds of Christendom,* 3 volumes (Grand Rapids, MI: Baker Book House, 1985 reprint).

Schlossberg, Herbert. *Idols for Destruction* (Wheaton, IL: Crossway Books, 1990).

Short, Bruce *The Harsh Truth about Public Schools* (Vallecito, CA: The Chalcedon Foundation, 2004).

Sire, James. *The Universe Next Door: A Basic Worldview Catalog,* 3rd edition (Downers Grove, IL: InterVarsity Press, 1997).

Skousen, Cleon. *The Naked Communist* (Salt Lake City, UT: The Reviewer, 1961).

Smith, Wilbur. *Therefore Stand: Christian Apologetics* (Grand Rapids: Baker Book House, 1974 reprint).

Sowell, Thomas. *Marxism* (New York: William Morrow, 1985).

Spencer, Robert. *The Politically Incorrect Guide to Islam and the Crusades* (Washington, D.C.: Regnery Publishing, 2005).

Spencer, Roy. *Climate Confusion: How Global Warming Hysteria Leads to Bad Science, Pandering Politicians and Misguided Policies that Hurt the Poor* (New York: Encounter Books, 2008),

Stormer, John. *None Dare Call it Education* (Florissant, MO: Liberty Bell Press, 1998).

Sussman, Brian. *Climategate: A Veteran Meteorologist Exposes the Global Warming Scam* (Washington, D.C.: WorldNetDaily Books, 2010).

Thomas, Curtis. *Life in the Body of Christ: Privileges and Responsibilities in the Local Church* (Cape Coral, FL: Founders Press, 2006)

Thiele, Edwin. *The Mysterious Numbers of the Hebrew Kings,* new revised edition (Grand Rapids: Kregel Publications, 1994).

Torrey, R. A. and A. C. Dixon, ed. *The Fundamentals,* 4 volumes (Grand Rapids, MI: Baker Book House, 1980 reprint).

Vitz, Paul. *Psychology as Religion—The Cult of Self-Worship* (Grand Rapids: Eerdmans Publishing Company, 1994).

Voslensky, Michael (translated by Eric Mosbacher). *Nomenklatura: The Soviet Ruling Class* (Garden City, New York, 1984).

Ward, Mark, ed. *Biblical Worldview: Creation, Fall, Redemption* (Greenville, SC: Bob Jones University Press, 2017).

Webster, William. *Salvation, The Bible and Roman Catholicism* (Carlisle, PA: The Banner of Truth Trust, 1990).

Welch, Edward. *Blame It on the Brain?: Distinguishing Chemical Imbalances, Brain Disorders and Disobedience* (Phillipsburg, NJ: P&R Publishing, 1998).

Welch, Laura, ed. *Inside Noah's Ark: Why It Worked* (Green Forest, AR: Master Books, 2016).

Wells, Jonathan. *Icons of Evolution: Why Much of What We Teach about Evolution is Wrong* (Washington, D.C.: Regnery Publishing, 2000).

White, James. *The Forgotten Trinity* (Minneapolis, MN: Bethany House Publishers, 1998).

Wilson, Douglas. *The Deluded Atheist* (Powder Springs, GA: American Vision, 2008).

Wolters, Albert. *Creation Regained: Biblical Basis for a Reformational Worldview,* 2nd ed. (Grand Rapids: Eerdmans Publishing Company, 2005).

Woodmorappe, John. *Noah's Ark: A Feasibility Study* (Dallas, TX: Institute for Creation Research, 1996).

Young, Edward. *Thy Word is Truth* (Grand Rapids: Eerdmans Publishing Company, 1957).

ABOUT THE AUTHOR

Dr. Tom Wheeler grew up in a pastor's home and received Christ as Lord and Savior as a child. He attended a Christian college and then completed a Ph.D. in theology. He taught Bible and theology classes for a number of years in a Bible college and seminary and taught Bible classes in a Christian high school for a few years. He served several years as a pastor. He had a loving Christian marriage for thirty-three-and-a-half years to his wife, Becky, who went to be with the Lord after a several-year battle with cancer. He has three grown children and six grandchildren. He is actively involved in his church.

For more information about

Dr. Tom Wheeler
and
Transformed Thinking
please connect at:

www.facebook.com/tomwheelerapologetics
twtransformedthinking@gmail.com

For more information about
AMBASSADOR INTERNATIONAL
please connect at:

www.ambassador-international.com
@AmbassadorIntl
www.facebook.com/AmbassadorIntl

If you enjoyed this book, please consider leaving us a review on Amazon, Goodreads, or our website.

www.ingramcontent.com/pod-product-compliance
Lightning Source LLC
LaVergne TN
LVHW081257100826
845148LV00005B/900